Ontologies for Software Engineering and Software Technology

Coral Calero · Francisco Ruiz · Mario Piattini (Eds.)

Ontologies for Software Engineering and Software Technology

With 84 Figures and 46 Tables

 Springer

Editors

Coral Calero
Francisco Ruiz
Mario Piattini

E.S. Informática.
Paseo de la Universidad 4
13071 Ciudad Real, Spain

Coral.Calero@uclm.es
Francisco.RuizG@uclm.es
Mario.Piattini@uclm.es

ACM Computing Classification (1998): D.2, H.1, I.2

ISBN   978-3-642-07087-7   e-ISBN   978-3-540-34518-3

Springer is a part of Springer Science+Business Media

springer.com

© Springer-Verlag Berlin Heidelberg 2010

Preface

Overview

Two important challenges facing current communities of researchers and practitioners in the field of software engineering and technology (SET) are knowledge integration and computer-based automatic support. The first challenge implies wasting a lot of time and effort and this is due to one of the difficulties in human relationships, namely the lack of explicit knowledge shared among members of a group/project, with other groups and with other stakeholders. The second challenge arises because many projects include the design/construction of advanced tools for supporting different software engineering activities. These tools should provide as much functionality as possible with the smallest cost of development.

Both challenges can be better and more easily approached by using ontologies. In this book, we will mainly deal with two of the multiple applications of ontologies in software engineering and technology that have been identified in the literature: (1) sharing knowledge of the problem domain and using a common terminology among all the interested people (not just researchers); and (2) filtering the knowledge when defining models and metamodels.

The utility of the first application is obvious. However, it is important and convenient to pay it opportune attention. Communication is one of the main activities (regarding duration and impact) in software projects. It is proven that participants in projects have a different knowledge of the problem domain and/or use different languages. The ambiguity of the natural language implies mistakes and nonproductive efforts. Ontologies can mitigate these problems and, farther, some authors have intended to use ontologies as back-bone of software tools and environments.

The second application is focused on the filtering of knowledge of a given domain. Models and metamodels are abstract representations of reality and, by definition, they only include a part of the reality they are aimed at modeling, obviating the unwanted characteristics. In this sense, ontologies can also help us decide what must be extracted from the real systems to build models or what must be taken into account when defining meta-models.

So, this book should not be considered as a book written by ontology experts for ontology experts, but one written by people who use the ontologies mainly for the two applications mentioned above. For that reason, this book is oriented to researchers and practitioners in SET and includes the advanced trends in the use of ontologies within software projects and software engineering research. It also deals with two main challenges the SET discipline: (1) knowledge integration and (2) design of more powerful and generic tools.

Organization

The book is composed of eleven chapters structured into three parts: an introductory part; a part composed of ontologies that conceptualize a SET domain or subdomain; and a part where some proposals on the use of ontologies as software artifacts in some software processes and technologies are described.

The last introductory part comprises two chapters. The first one, written by Oscar Corcho, Mariano Fernández-López and Asunción Gómez-Pérez, will introduce the ontologies' concepts and the main aspects related to ontological engineering. The second chapter (by Francisco Ruiz and José R. Hilera) will deal with the state of the art of the use of ontologies in SET. Also, this chapter defines a taxonomy for classifying the uses of ontologies in SET, together with the result of the classification into this taxonomy of about 50 ontologies (including the proposals of this book).

The second part is made up of five chapters. Chapter 3 will present the engineering of the ontology for the Software Engineering Body of Knowledge, written by Alain Abran, Juan-José Cuadrado, Elena García-Barriocanal, Olavo Mendes, Salvador Sánchez-Alonso and Miguel-Angel Sicilia. An ontology for software development methodologies and endeavours will be presented by Cesar Gonzalez-Perez and Brian Henderson-Sellers in Chap. 4. Chapter 5 presents a software maintenance ontology developed by Nicolas Anquetil, Káthia M. de Oliveira and Márcio G.B. Dias, and an ontology for software measurement by Manuel F. Bertoa, Antonio Vallecillo and Félix García is the topic of Chap. 6. An ontological approach to the SQL:2003 developed by Coral Calero and Mario Piattini will be explained in Chap. 7, closing this second part.

The final part begins with the Object Management Group Ontology Definition Metamodel (Chap. 8), developed by Robert Colomb, Kerry Raymond, Lewis Hart, Patrick Emery, Chris Welty, Guo Tong Xie and Elisa Kendall. Chapter 9, written by Uwe Assmann, Steffen Zschaler and

Gerd Wagner, deals with ontologies, metamodels and the model-driven paradigm. Chapter 10 will presents the use of ontologies in software development environments in the work of Káthia Marçal de Oliveira, Karina Villela, Ana Regina Rocha and Guilherme Horta Travassos. Finally, the topic of the last chapter of the book (Chap. 11) is a semantic upgrade and publication of legacy data by Jesús Barrasa Rodríguez.

As a complement to this book, the Alarcos Group (the research group of the editors) have created a web site (http://alarcos.inf-cr.uclm.es/ontoset) to store and share, in an open way and by using standardized formats, examples of interesting ontologies in the SET discipline. In addition to the examples referred to in the book, other examples of ontologies elaborated by the international community will be included in this web site.

Audience

The audience for this book is software engineering researchers and practitioners (professors, PhD and postgraduate students, industrial R&D departments, etc.). The reader is assumed to have previous knowledge of software engineering.

Acknowledgements

We would like to express our gratitude to all those individuals and parties who helped us produce this volume. In the first place, we would like to thank all the contributing authors and reviewers who helped improve the final version. Special thanks to Springer-Verlag and Ralf Gerstner, for believing in our project and for giving us the opportunity to publish this book. We would also like to thank José Carlos Villar Herrera and Tomás Martínez Ruíz of UCLM for their support during the developement of this book.

Finally, we would like to acknowledge the public organizations that financed this work, under the research projects CALIPO (TIC2003-07804-C05-03) and ENIGMAS (PBI-05-058).

Coral Calero
Francisco Ruiz
Mario Piattini

July 2006

Contents

1. Ontological Engineering: Principles, Methods, Tools and Languages 1
   1.1 Introduction 1
   1.2 What Is an Ontology? Viewpoints from a Philosopher and from an Ontology Engineer 3
   1.3 What Are the Main Components of an Ontology? 5
   1.4 Ontological Engineering 6
   1.5 Principles for the Design of Ontologies 8
   1.6 Ontology Development Process and Life Cycle 9
   1.7 Methods, Methodologies, Tools and Languages 16
      1.7.1 Methods, Methodologies and Tools Used for the Whole Ontology Development Life Cycle 16
      1.7.2 Ontology Learning 22
      1.7.3 Ontology Alignment and Merging 25
      1.7.4 Ontology Evolution and Versioning 31
      1.7.5 Ontology Evaluation 32
      1.7.6 Ontology Implementation 34
   1.8 Conclusions 38
   1.9 Acknowledgements 39
   References 39

2. Using Ontologies in Software Engineering and Technology 49
   2.1 Introduction 49
   2.2 Kinds of Ontologies 50
      2.2.1 Heavyweight Versus Lightweight Ontologies 56
   2.3 A Review of the Uses in SET 57
      2.3.1 Ontology Versus Conceptual Model 63
      2.3.2 Ontology Versus Metamodel 64
      2.3.3 Ontologies in Software Engineering Environments 65
      2.3.4 Representing Ontologies Using Software Engineering Techniques 67
      2.3.5 Experiences and Lessons Learned in Software Engineering Research 69

2.4 A Proposal of Taxonomy 73
    2.4.1 Ontologies of Domain 74
    2.4.2 Ontologies as Software Artifacts 76
2.5 Review and Classification of Proposals in the Literature 79
    2.5.1 Proposals of Ontologies of Domain 79
    2.5.2 Proposals of Ontologies as Software Artifacts 86
References 95

3. Engineering the Ontology for the SWEBOK: Issues and
Techniques 103
    3.1 Introduction 103
    3.2 History and Principles of the SWEBOK Project 105
        3.2.1 Hierarchical Organization 107
        3.2.2 Reference Material and Matrix 108
        3.2.3 Depth of Treatment 108
    3.3 The Ontology of the SWEBOK from a Conceptual and Consensus-
    Reaching Perspective 109
    3.4 The Ontology of the SWEBOK as a Formal Artifact 112
    3.5 Fundamental Elements of the Ontology of the SWEBOK 114
        3.5.1 Activities, Artifacts and Agents 114
        3.5.2 Models, Specifications and Methods 116
        3.5.3 Theoretical Standpoints and Guidelines 117
    3.6 Conclusions 119
    References 120

4. An Ontology for Software Development Methodologies and
Endeavours 123
    4.1 Introduction 123
    4.2 Ontology Architecture 125
        4.2.1 The Communities Involved 125
        4.2.2 Usage and Ontology Domains 127
        4.2.3 Product and Process 131
    4.3 Endeavour-Related Concepts 133
        4.3.1 High-Level View 134
        4.3.2 The Process Side 135
        4.3.3 The Product Side 137
        4.3.4 The Producer Side 140
        4.3.5 Endeavour-Related Concepts: Conclusion 141
    4.4 Method-Related Concepts 142
        4.4.1 Templates and Resources 142
        4.4.2 Duality in the Method Domain 143
        4.4.3 Applying the Methodology 148

4.5 Conclusion 148
References..149

5. Software Maintenance Ontology...153
5.1 Introduction...153
5.2 Software Maintenance..154
5.3 An Ontology for Software Maintenance 156
   5.3.1 Overview of the Ontology...................................157
   5.3.2 The System Sub-ontology...................................158
   5.3.3 The Computer Science Skills Sub-ontology 160
   5.3.4 The Maintenance Process Sub-ontology..............162
   5.3.5 The Organizational Structure Sub-ontology 165
   5.3.6 The Application Domain Sub-ontology 166
5.4. Validating the Ontology...166
   5.4.1 Quality Validation..167
   5.4.2 Relevance Validation 168
5.5 Putting the Maintenance Ontology to Work 169
5.6 Conclusion 171
References..172

6. An Ontology for Software Measurement 175
6.1 Introduction...175
6.2 Previous Analysis...177
6.3 A Running Example..178
6.4 The Proposal of Software Measurement Ontology 179
   6.4.1 The SMO..179
6.5 Conclusions..194
References..195

7. An Ontological Approach to SQL:2003 197
7.1 Introduction...197
7.2 SQL Evolution 198
7.3 The Ontology for SQL:2003 201
   7.3.1 The Data Types Sub-ontology 202
   7.3.2 The Schema Objects Sub-ontology.......................204
7.4 Example 209
7.5 Conclusions..212
References..214

8. The Object Management Group Ontology Definition
Metamodel 217
8.1 Introduction...218

8.2 Why a MOF Ontology Metamodel? 219
  8.2.1 Why a Metamodel? 219
  8.2.2 Why MOF? 220
  8.2.3 Why Not UML? 221
8.3 The Ontology Development Metamodel 222
  8.3.1 RDF/OWL Metamodel 224
  8.3.2 Topic Maps 228
  8.3.3 Common Logic 231
  8.3.4 General Structure of Metamodels 233
8.4 Profiles and Mappings 235
  8.4.1 The Need for Translation 235
  8.4.2 UML Profiles 236
  8.4.3 Mappings 238
  8.4.4 Mapping CL 240
  8.4.5 Interaction of Profiles and Mappings 241
8.5 Extendibility 242
  8.5.1 Metaclass Taxonomy 242
  8.5.2 Semantic Domain Models 243
  8.5.3 *n*-ary associations 244
8.6 Discussion 244
8.7 Acknowledgments 245
References 246

9. Ontologies, Meta-models, and the Model-Driven Paradigm 249
9.1 Introduction 249
9.2 Models and Ontologies 253
  9.2.1 What's in a Model? 253
  9.2.2 What's in an Ontology? 255
9.3 Similarity Relations and Meta-modelling 257
  9.3.1 Meta-models 258
  9.3.2 Metameta-models 260
  9.3.3 The Meta-pyramid, the Modelling Architecture of MDE 261
9.4 MDE and Ontologies 262
  9.4.1 Domain and Upper-Level Ontologies 263
  9.4.2 Relationship of Ontologies and System Models on Different
  Meta-levels 264
  9.4.3 Employing Domain Ontologies in the MDA 265
  9.4.4 Conceptual Benefits of an Ontology-Aware Meta-pyramid .. 267
  9.4.5 Tools Based on an Ontology-Aware Meta-pyramid 268
  9.4.6 The mega-Model of Ontology-Aware MDE 269
9.5 Related Work 270
9.6 Conclusions 271

9.7 Acknowledgments..271
References..271

10. Use of Ontologies in Software Development Environments.........275
10.1 Introduction..275
10.2 From SDE to DOSDE...277
10.3 Domain-Oriented Software Development Environment...........279
   10.3.1 Domain Ontology in DOSDE 279
   10.3.2 Task Ontology in DOSDE 280
   10.3.3 Mapping Domain and Task...287
   10.3.4 Using Knowledge Throughout the Software Development.288
10.4 From DOSDE to EOSDE...292
10.5 Enterprise-Oriented Software Development Environments........294
   10.5.1 Enterprise Ontology 296
10.6 Tools in DOSDE and EOSDE..300
   10.6.1 Domain Theory Browser...301
   10.6.2 Sapiens: A Yellow Page's Software Tool.....................302
   10.6.3 RHPlan: A Software Tool for Human Resource Planning...304
10.7 Conclusion 305
References..306

11. Semantic Upgrade and Publication of Legacy Data.....................311
11.1 Introduction and Motivation 311
11.2 Global Approach to Database-to-Ontology Mapping................314
11.3 Mapping Situations between Databases and Ontologies............315
11.4. The R_2O Language...319
   11.4.1 A Mapping Description Specified in R_2O...................320
   11.4.2 Description of Database Schemas.................................321
   11.4.3 Definition of Concept Mappings...................................322
   11.4.4 Describing Conditions and Conditional Expressions..........324
   11.4.5 Describing Transformations...325
   11.4.6 Attribute and Relation Mappings.................................326
11.5 The ODEMapster Processor..330
11.6 Experimentation: The Fund Finder Application 330
   11.6.1 Ontologies in the Funding Domain...............................332
   11.6.2 The Presentation Part: Semantic Publishing and
   Navigation..334
11.7 Conclusions and Future Work...335
11.8 Acknowledgements 337
References..337

1. Ontological Engineering: Principles, Methods, Tools and Languages

Oscar Corcho

Information Management Group, University of Manchester, Kilburn Building, Oxford Road M13 9PL. Manchester, United Kingdom, Oscar.Corcho@manchester.ac.uk,

Mariano Fernández-López

Escuela Politécnica Superior, Universidad San Pablo CEU, Ctra. de Boadilla del Monte km 5.300, 28668 Boadilla del Monte, Madrid, Spain, mfernandez.eps@ceu.es,

Asunción Gómez-Pérez

Facultad de Informática, Universidad Politécnica de Madrid, Campus de Montegancedo s/n. 28660 Boadilla del Monte, Madrid, Spain, asun@fi.upm.es

1.1 Introduction

In 1991, the DARPA Knowledge Sharing Effort ([88], p. 37) envisioned a new way to build intelligent systems. It proposed the following:

> *Building knowledge-based systems today usually entails constructing new knowledge bases from scratch. It could be instead done by assembling reusable components. System developers would then only need to worry about creating the specialized knowledge and reasoners new to the specific task of their system. This new system would interoperate with existing systems, using them to perform some of its reasoning. In*

this way, declarative knowledge, problem-solving techniques and reasoning services would all be shared among systems. This approach would facilitate building bigger and better systems and cheaply.

Static knowledge is modeled by means of ontologies while problem solving methods specify generic reasoning mechanisms. Both types of components can be viewed as complementary entities that can be used to configure new knowledge-based systems from existing reusable components.

Since DARPA's idea, considerable progress has been made in developing the conceptual bases to build technology that allows reusing and sharing knowledge components. Ontologies and problem solving methods (PSMs) have been created to share and reuse knowledge and reasoning behavior across domains and tasks. In this evolution, the most important fact has been the emergence of the Semantic Web. According to [10], the Semantic Web is an extension of the current Web in which information is given well-defined meaning, better enabling computers and people to work in cooperation. This cooperation can be achieved by using shared knowledge components, and so ontologies and PSMs have become key instruments in developing the Semantic Web.

Currently, ontologies are widely used in knowledge engineering, artificial intelligence and computer science, in applications related to knowledge management, natural language processing, e-commerce, intelligent integration information, information retrieval, database design and integration, bio-informatics, education, etc.

In this chapter, we present the basics about ontologies, and show what activities should be carried out during the ontology development process, what principles should be followed in ontology design, and what methods, methodologies, software tools and languages are available to give support to each one of these activities. First, in Sect. 1.2, we define the word 'ontology' and we briefly explaining its roots in philosophy. Section 1.3 is devoted to explain which are the main components that can be used to model ontologies. In Sect. 1.4, we present the main ontology design principles. In Sect. 1.5, we describe the ontology development process in the context of the Semantic Web, where ontologies can be highly distributed and present many links among each other (hence the notion of networked ontologies). In Sect. 1.6, we describe the development of ontologies and the life cycle. In Sect. 1.7, we describe the methods, methodologies and tools commonly used for the whole ontology development process or only for specific activities. Among them we pay attention to those aimed at ontology learning, which reduce the effort needed during the knowledge acquisition process; at ontology merging, which generates a unique target ontology from several source ontologies; at ontology alignment, which establishes different types of mappings between ontologies (hence preserving the original ones); and at ontology evaluation, which evaluates ontology content. In the implementation activity description, we present ontology languages that can be used to implement ontologies. Finally, conclusions and future lines of research are presented in Sect. 1.8.[1]

1.2 What Is an Ontology? Viewpoints from a Philosopher and from an Ontology Engineer

The ancient Greeks were concerned with the question: "what is the essence of things through the changes?" Many different answers to this question were proposed by Greek philosophers, from Parmenides of Elea (fifth and fourth centuries bc), the precursor of ontology, to Aristotle, author of the *MetaPhysics* (a work that might well have been called *Ontology*).

In his study of the essence of things, Aristotle distinguished different modes of being to establish a system of categories (*substance*, *quality*, *quantity*, *relation*, *action*, *passion*, *place* and *time*) to classify anything that may be *predicated* (said) about anything in the world. For example, when we say "this computer *is* on the table" we are assuming a different mode of being to when we say "this computer *is* gray". The first statement is classified inside the category of *place*, while the second is inside the category of *quality*. The categorization proposed by Aristotle was widely accepted until the eighteenth century.

In the modern age, Emmanuel Kant (1724–1804) provoked a *Copernican turn*. The essence of things is determined not only by the things themselves, but also by the contribution of whoever perceives and understands them. According to Kant, a key question is "what structures does our mind use to capture the reality?" The answer to this question leads to Kant's categorization. Kant's framework is organized into four classes, each of which presents a triadic pattern: *quantity* (*unity*, *plurality*, *totality*), *quality* (*reality*, *negation*, *limitation*), *relation* (*inherence*, *causality*, *community*) and *modality* (*possibility*, *existence*, *necessity*). Therefore, our mind classifies the object John as unique, real, existing, etc.

---

[1] For a deep introduction to the ontological engineering field, we recommend Gómez-Pérez and colleagues' book [40].

A classification of categories, such as the ones mentioned above, is known as an ontology by philosophers [47]. Most modern examples of ontologies (in the context of philosophy) are due to Chisholm [16], Johanson [59], and Hoffman and Rosenkrantz [110], among others.

According to what we have said, it is very important to take into account that 'an ontology' is not the same as 'ontology'.An ontology is a classification of categories, whereas ontology is a branch of philosophy.

To answer our second question ("what is an ontology for an ontology engineer?"), we can assume that there is a parallelism between the reality perceived by people and by computers, and both can be structured in ontologies [44]. In accordance with this idea, if a computer is exclusively devoted to answering questions on travel, its reality could be structured by classifying travel as travel by train, travel by plane, etc. However, for this classification to be really an ontology for the computer, the computer must be able to reason with it. This leads to the first important difference between an ontology from a philosophical point of view and from a computer science point of view. According to the latter, an ontology has to be codified in a machine interpretable language [106, 39]. In other words, when an ontology engineer defines what an ontology is, (s)he changes the perspective from the person to the computer. Thus, if the computer does not 'understand' the ontology, it cannot be its ontology. Moreover, from a computer science point of view, an ontology is usually (although not necessarily) more specific than an ontology from a philosophical approach. Finally, due to the use of the term 'ontology', the features of reusability and shareability have become essential in the definition of this term for engineers. Nevertheless, such features are not essential in philosophical ontologies.

In conclusion, **for an ontology engineer** ([106], p. 185, with our own emphasis):

> ***An ontology*** *is a formal, explicit specification of a shared conceptualization. Conceptualization refers to an abstract model of some phenomenon in the world by having identified the relevant concepts of that phenomenon. Explicit means that the type of concepts used, and the constraints on their use, are explicitly defined. Formal refers to the fact that the ontology should be machine-readable. Shared reflects the notion that an ontology captures consensual knowledge, that is, it is not private of some individual, but accepted by a group.*

Neches and colleagues ([88], p. 40, our emphasis) gave another definition, focused on the form of an ontology:

An ontology defines the basic terms and relations comprising the vocabulary of a topic area as well as the rules for combining terms and relations to define extensions to the vocabulary.

1.3 What Are the Main Components of an Ontology?

Different knowledge representation formalisms (and corresponding languages) exist for the fomalization (and implementation) of ontologies. Each of them provides different components that can be used for these tasks. However, they share the following minimal set of components.[2]

Classes represent concepts, which are taken in a broad sense. For instance, in the traveling domain, concepts are: locations (cities, villages, etc.), lodgings (hotels, camping, etc.) and means of transport (planes, trains, cars, ferries, motorbikes and ships). Classes in the ontology are usually organized in taxonomies through which inheritance mechanisms can be applied. We can represent a taxonomy of entertainment places (theater, cinema, concert, etc.) or travel packages (economy travel, business travel, etc.). In the frame-based knowledge representation paradigm, metaclasses can also be defined. Metaclasses are classes whose instances are classes. They usually allow for gradations of meaning, since they establish different layers of classes in the ontology where they are defined.

Relations represent a type of association between concepts of the domain. They are formally defined as any subset of a product of *n* sets, that is: R ⊂ C1 × C2 × ... × C*n*. Ontologies usually contain binary relations. The first argument is known as the domain of the relation, and the second argument is the range. For instance, the binary relation `arrivalPlace` has the concept `Travel` as its domain and the concept `Location` as its range. Relations can be instantiated with knowledge from the domain. For example, to express that the flight AA7462-Feb-08-2002 arrives in Seattle we must write: `(arrivalPlace AA7462-Feb-08-2002 Seattle)`.

Binary relations are sometimes used to express concept attributes (aka slots). Attributes are usually distinguished from relations because their range is a datatype, such as *string, number*, etc., while the range of relations is a concept. The following code defines the attribute `flightNum-`

---

[2] Component names depend on the formalism. For example, classes are also known as concepts, entities and sets; relations are also known as roles and properties; etc.

ber, which is a *string*. We can also express relations of higher arity, such as "a road connects two different cities".

According to Gruber [44], *formal axioms* serve to model sentences that are always true. They are normally used to represent knowledge that cannot be formally defined by the other components. In addition, formal axioms are used to verify the consistency of the ontology itself or the consistency of the knowledge stored in a knowledge base. Formal axioms are very useful for infering new knowledge. An axiom in the traveling domain would be that it is not possible to travel from North America to Europe by train.

Instances are used to represent elements or individuals in an ontology. An example of an instance of the concept AA7462 is the flight AA7462 that arrives at Seattle on February 8, 2006 and costs 300 (US dollars, euros, or any other currency).

1.4 Ontological Engineering

The ontological engineering field has been subject to considerable study and research during the last decade. **Ontological engineering** refers to the set of activities that concern the ontology development process, the ontology life cycle, the principles, methods and methodologies for building ontologies, and the tool suites and languages that support them [39]. The notion of networked ontological engineering has come into play with the emergence of the Semantic Web, where one of the most relevant assumptions is that ontologies are distributed across different Web servers and ontology repositories and may have overlapping representations of the same or different domains.

With regard to **methods and methodologies**, several proposals have been reported for developing ontologies. In 1990, Lenat and Guha [72] published the general steps and some interesting points about the Cyc development. Some years later, in 1995, on the basis of the experience gained in developing the Enterprise Ontology [113] and the TOVE (TOronto Virtual Enterprise) project ontology [46] (both in the domain of enterprise modeling), the first guidelines were proposed and later refined in [111, 112]. At the 12th European Conference for Artificial Intelligence (ECAI'96), Bernaras and colleagues [9] presented a method used to build an ontology in the domain of electrical networks as part of the Esprit KACTUS [100] project. The methodology METHONTOLOGY [40] appeared at the same time and was extended in later papers [31, 32]. It was proposed for ontology construction by the Foundation for Intelligent

Physical Agents (FIPA),[3] which promotes interoperability across agent-based applications. In 1997, a new method was proposed for building ontologies based on the SENSUS ontology [109]. Some years later, the On-To-Knowledge methodology appeared as a result of the project with the same name [102]. A comparative and detailed study of these methods and methodologies can be found in [29].

All the previous methods and methodologies were proposed for building ontologies. However, many other methods have been proposed for specific tasks in the ontology development process, such as ontology re-engineering [42], ontology learning [3, 65], ontology evaluation [35, 40, 36, 38, 60, 61, 114, 50, 48], ontology evolution [67, 68, 92, 96, 97, 93, 104], ontology alignment [8, 14, 76, 95, 80, 101, 25, 26, 98], and ontology merging [103, 33, 107, 94], among others.

Ontology tools appeared later, in the mid-1990s, and can be classified in the following two groups:[4]

- Tools whose knowledge model maps directly to an ontology language, hence developed as ontology editors for that specific language. This group includes: the Ontolingua Server [27], which supports ontology construction with Ontolingua and KIF; OntoSaurus [109] with Loom; WebOnto [24] with OCML; OilEd [7] with OIL first, later with DAML+OIL, and finally with OWL; and SWOOP [62] and KAON2 [56] with OWL.
- Integrated tool suites whose main characteristic is that they have an extensible architecture, and whose knowledge model is usually independent of ontology languages. These tools provide a core set of ontology-related services and are easily extended with other modules to provide more functions. In this group we have included Protégé [91], WebODE [17, 1], OntoEdit [108], and KAON1 [77].

Ontology languages started to be created at the beginning of the 1990s, normally as the evolution of existing knowledge representation (KR) languages. Basically, the KR paradigms underlying such ontology languages were based on first order-logic (e.g., KIF [34]), on frames combined with first-order logic (e.g., Ontolingua [27, 43], OCML [87] and FLogic [66]), and on description logics (e.g., Loom [75]). In 1997, OKBC [15] was created as a unifying frame-based protocol to access ontologies implemented

---

[3] http://www.fipa.org/specs/fipa00086/ (last accessed, August 9, 2005).
[4] In each group, we have followed a chronological order of appearance in the enumeration of the tool.

in different languages (Ontolingua, Loom and CycL, among others). However, it was only used in a small number of applications.

The boom of the Internet led to the creation of ontology languages for exploiting the characteristics of the Web. Such languages are usually called *Web-based ontology languages* or *ontology markup languages*. Their syntax is based on existing markup languages such as HTML [99] and XML [12], whose purpose is not ontology development but data presentation and data exchange respectively. The most important examples of these markup languages are: SHOE [74], XOL [63], RDF [70], RDF Schema [13], OIL [54], DAML+OIL [55] and OWL [20]. From all of them, the ones that are being actively supported now are RDF, RDF Schema and OWL.

1.5 Principles for the Design of Ontologies

This section summarizes some design criteria and a set of principles that have been proven useful in the development of ontologies. According to [45], ontology design principles are objective criteria for guiding and evaluating ontology designs. He identified the following five principles:

- **Clarity** [45], which is defined in the following terms: *An ontology should communicate effectively the intended meaning of defined terms. Definitions should be objective. Definitions can be stated on formal axioms, and a complete definition (defined by necessary and sufficient conditions) is preferred over a partial definition (defined by only necessary or sufficient conditions). All definitions should be documented with natural language.*
- **Minimal encoding bias** [45], which means that: *The conceptualization should be specified at the knowledge level without depending on a particular symbol-level encoding.*
  Encoding bias should be minimized for knowledge sharing because agents that share knowledge may be implemented in different ways.
- **Extendibility** [45], which says that: *One should be able to define new terms for special uses based on the existing vocabulary, in a way that does not require the revision of the existing definitions.*
- **Coherence** [45], which is defined as follows: *An ontology should be coherent: that is, it should sanction inferences that are consistent with the definitions. [...] If a sentence that can be inferred from the axioms contradicts a definition or example given informally, then the ontology is incoherent.*

- **Minimal ontological commitments** [45], which is described in this way: *Since ontological commitment is based on the consistent use of the vocabulary, ontological commitment can be minimized by specifying the weakest theory and defining only those terms that are essential to the communication of knowledge consistent with the theory.*

According to this last principle, we should not commit to a specific format for dates, for currencies, etc., when designing our ontologies, since such details could be different in different systems.

Some other criteria have proven useful in ontology design, such as **the standardization of names** [2], which proposes to use the same of conventions to name related terms, in order to ease the understanding of the ontology.

1.6 Ontology Development Process and Life Cycle

In 1997, the ontology development process [31] was identified in the framework of the METHONTOLOGY methodology for ontology construction. Such a proposal was based on the IEEE standard for software development [57]. The ontology development process refers to the activities that have to be performed when building ontologies. They can be classified in the three categories presented in Fig. 1.1.

Ontology management activities include scheduling, control and quality assurance. The *scheduling* activity identifies the tasks to be performed, their arrangement, and the time and resources needed for their completion. This activity is essential for ontologies that use ontologies stored in ontology libraries or for ontologies that require a high level of abstraction and generality. The *control* activity guarantees that scheduled tasks are completed in the manner intended to be performed. Finally, the *quality assurance* activity assures that the quality of each and every product output (ontology, software and documentation) is satisfactory.

Ontology development-oriented activities are grouped, as presented in Fig. 1.1, into pre-development, development and post-development activities. During the pre-development, an *environment study* identifies the problem to be solved with the ontology, the applications where the ontology will be integrated, etc. Also during the pre-development, the *feasibility study* answers questions like: "is it possible to build the ontology?"; "is it suitable to build the ontology?"; etc.

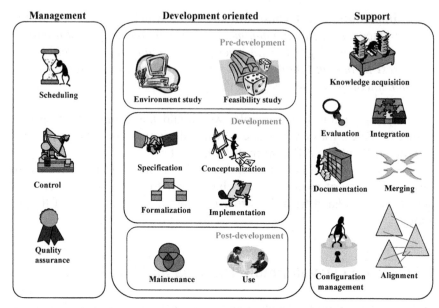

Fig. 1.1. Ontology development process (adapted from [31])

Once in development, the *specification* activity[5] states why the ontology is being built, what its intended uses are and who the end-users are. The *conceptualization* activity structures the domain knowledge as meaningful models at the knowledge level [89] either from scratch or by reusing existing models. In this last case, related activities are pruning branches of the existing taxonomies, extending the coverage of ontologies with the addition of new concepts in the higher levels of their taxonomies, or specializing branches that require more granularity. Given that the conceptualization activity is implementation-language independent, it allows modeling ontologies according to the minimal encoding bias design criterion. The *formalization* activity transforms the conceptual model into a formal or semi-computable model. The *implementation* activity builds computable models in an ontology language.

During post-development, the *maintenance* activity updates and corrects the ontology if needed. Also during post-development, the ontology

---

[5] In [28] *specification* is considered as a pre-development activity. However, following more strictly the IEEE standard for software development, the specification activity was considered part of the proper development process. In fact, the result of this activity is an ontology description (usually in natural language) that will be transformed into a conceptual model by the *conceptualization* activity.

is *(re)used* by other ontologies or applications. The evolution activity consists of managing ontology changes and their effects by creating and maintaining different variants of the ontology, taking into account that they can be used in different ontologies and applications [93].

Finally, **ontology support activities** include a series of activities that can be performed during the development-oriented activities, without which the ontology could not be built. They include knowledge acquisition, evaluation, integration, merging, alignment, documentation and configuration management. The goal of the *knowledge acquisition* activity is to acquire knowledge from experts in a given domain or through some kind of (semi-)automatic process, which is called ontology learning [65]. The *evaluation* activity [35] makes a technical judgment of the ontologies, of their associated software environments, and of the documentation. This judgment is made with respect to a frame of reference during each stage and between stages of the ontology's life cycle. The *integration* activity is required when building a new ontology by reusing other ontologies already available. Another support activity is *merging* [103, 33, 107, 94], which consists of obtaining a new ontology starting from several ontologies in the same domain. The resulting ontology is able to unify concepts, terminology, definitions, constraints, etc., from all the source ontologies. The merging of two or more ontologies can be carried out either in runtime or design time. The *alignment* activity establishes different kinds of mappings (or links) between the involved ontologies. Hence this option preserves the original ontologies and does not merge them. The *documentation* activity details, clearly and exhaustively, each and every one of the completed stages and products generated. The *configuration management* activity records all the versions of the documentation and of the ontology code to control the changes. The *multilingualism activity* consists of mapping ontologies onto formal descriptions of linguistic knowledge [22]. It has not usually been considered as an ontology support activity, but has become more relevant in the context of networked ontologies available in the Semantic Web.

As we can see, the ontology development process does not identify the order in which the activities should be performed [31] (see also [57]). This is the role of the **ontology life cycle**, which identifies *when* the activities should be carried out; that is, it identifies the *set of stages* through which the ontology moves during its lifetime, describes what activities are to be performed in each stage and how the stages are related (relation of precedence, return, etc.).

The initial version of the life cycle process model of METHONTOLOGY (see Fig. 1.2) proposes to start with a scheduling of the activities to be performed. Then, the specification activity begins, showing why the ontology will be built, what its possible uses will be, and who are its users. When the specification finishes, the conceptualization begins. The objective of the conceptualization is to organize and structure the acquired knowledge in the knowledge acquisition activity, using a set of representations easy to manipulate for the experts in the domain. Once the conceptual model has been built, METHONTOLOGY proposes to automatically implement the ontologies using translators. More details can be found in [39].

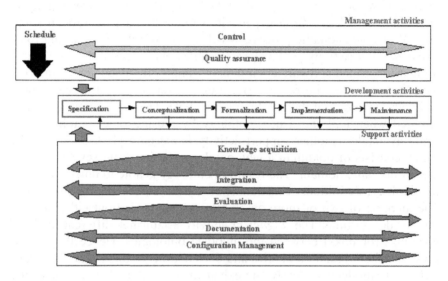

Fig. 1.2. Ontology life cycle in METHONTOLOGY

As more ontologies become available in ontology libraries or spread over the Internet, their reuse by other ontologies and applications increases. Domain ontologies can be reused to build others of more granularity and coverage, or can be merged with others to create new ones. Figure 1.3 shows different ways or possibilities of construction. Using an analogy with an underground map, it can be noted that there exists a main line (in the middle of the figure), others that start from the main line or finish in it, or lines that run parallel and fork in a point. Thus, *interdependence relationships* [42] arise between the life cycles of several ontologies, and actions of evaluation, pruning and merging can be carried out on such ontologies. That is, the life cycles of the different ontologies intersect, producing different scenarios with different technological requirements. Now we will describe some of the most common scenarios that arise during the ontology development process.

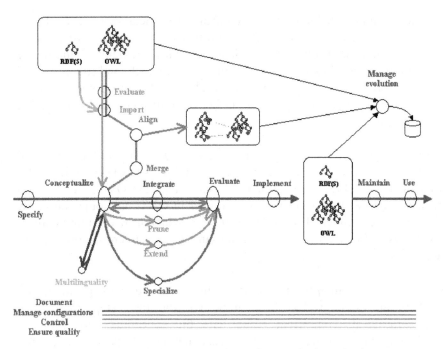

Fig. 1.3. The ontology development process of networked ontologies

- Scenario 1 **Evaluate + import**. The import of ontologies consists of incorporating an ontology available in a language or tool into another ontology tool. Often, several candidate ontologies implemented in different languages can be reused. In this case, it is necessary to inspect their content and granularity, compare them and select the best one(s). It is also necessary to analyze the expressiveness of the language in which each ontology is implemented, since important pieces of knowledge may be lost during the import if the knowledge model of the target ontology tool is less expressive than that of the language or tool where the ontology is implemented.

  Before importing an ontology, its content should be evaluated. Some ontology tools perform content evaluation before the import process, so as to avoid importing and reusing badly designed ontologies.

  Ontology import is not always successful. We can find problems due to lack of interoperability between tools, which are as follows [18]:

  - Common interchange formats normally allow representation of the same knowledge in many different ways and many of them have ex-

tensible knowledge models (by means of metaclasses). Hence, translations to and from interlinguas are usually written with regard to a specific format, making knowledge exchange difficult. Some of the interlinguas that have been used in the past are KIF and RDF.
– Interoperability with interlinguas has been only proved with the same origin and target formats, but not between different source and target formats.

However, with the standardization of the OWL language in the context of the Semantic Web the issue of importing ontologies has become less relevant in the ontology development process, since the OWL specification clearly states which primitives are allowed in OWL ontologies and how they can be combined. The use of OWL Full, which provides more expressivity possibilities, may again pose the same type of interoperability problems.

- Scenario 2. **Conceptualize + integrate + evaluate conceptualization**. Once an ontology has been imported, the next step consists of integrating its conceptual model into the conceptual model of the ontology that is being developed. Consequently, activities of integration and evaluation of the conceptualization are in the main line of the life cycle process model.
- Scenario 3. **Conceptualize + acquire knowledge**. Once the ontology has been evaluated, imported and integrated into the conceptual model of the main ontology, the activity of conceptual evaluation can reveal, both in the integrated ontologies and in the main ontology that is being developed, what parts of the ontologies are in the requirement specification document. Therefore, the options are:

  – To prune the branches of the taxonomy that are not considered necessary because they do not appear in the ontology requirement specification document.
  – To specialize those branches that require more granularity, including more specialized domain concepts and relations.
  – To extend the ontologies including (in width) new concepts and relations.
  – To search for new domain ontologies that complement the detected lacks.

If the ontology builder prunes, specializes or extends the ontologies, (s)he might need some knowledge that could be acquired using classical knowledge engineering methods and techniques, or semi-automatic methods for learning ontologies from texts or other sources.

- Scenario 4. **Semi-automatic construction of ontologies**. Despite one of the main objectives of ontologies being to decrease the knowledge acquisition bottleneck when building knowledge-intensive systems, the process of building an ontology and refining it consumes much time and resources. *Ontology learning* is the process that partially automates the construction of ontologies using some of the following methods, techniques and tools: natural language analysis, statistical methods, linguistic patterns, text mining, etc. This process uses texts, electronic dictionaries, linguistic ontologies (like WordNet), and structured and semi-structured information and data as knowledge sources.

- Scenario 5. **Evaluate and import a set of ontologies, and align them**. Quite often there are several ontologies that model the same domain. There can be situations in which we want to compare ontologies in the same domain to determine what terms of an ontology map terms of another. The correspondences between ontologies obtained by means of this procedure are called mappings. In this case, the result of this scenario is a set of mappings that establish the relationships between the two domain ontologies. There are also situations where the relationships are established between ontologies of different categories, as in the case of joining a domain ontology with an upper level ontology. Every alignment requires the evaluation and possibly the import of the ontologies in specific tools, and the generation of the result in a language where the content of the alignment can be evaluated.

- Scenario 6. **Evaluate and import a set of ontologies, and merge them**. This scenario is an extension of scenario 5. Once the mappings between the ontologies are known, the ontology engineer can merge them in a new ontology.

- Scenario 7. **Translate the ontology into another natural language (Spanish, English, French, etc.)**. Once the ontology has been conceptualized, it can require the translation of all its terms into another language using multilingual thesauri and electronic dictionaries (e.g., EuroWordNet).

- Scenario 8. **Manage the evolution of the ontology**. Given that an essential feature of ontologies is that they must be agreed, the most natural way of developing ontologies is through a collaborative construction. Ontology engineers working in parallel on the same ontology need to maintain and compare different versions, to examine the changes that others have performed, and to accept or reject the changes [93]. In a networked environment like the Semantic Web, we should keep control of the versions of each ontology and the relationships between them must be kept for several reasons. One of the reasons is that semantic markup annotations of Web resources are based on ontologies. If an ontology is changed, we should be able to deal with the effects of the change in the existing annotations. Another reason is that ontologies will be developed in different tools and languages. We must be able to keep control of their life cycle when they are exchanged back and forward between different ontology tools and when they are translated from and to different ontology languages.

- Scenario 9. **Perform support activities**. The activities of documentation, evolution management, configuration management, and quality assurance and control are carried out during the whole development process.

1.7 Methods, Methodologies, Tools and Languages

In this section, first of all we explain the methods, methodologies and tools used for the whole ontology development process. Then we focus on ontology learning, ontology merging, ontology alignment, ontology evolution and versioning, ontology evaluation and ontology implementation (in this last section we review existing ontology languages).

1.7.1 Methods, Methodologies and Tools Used for the Whole Ontology Development Life Cycle

This section presents the classical methodologies and methods used to build ontologies from scratch or by reusing other ontologies, and the new generation of ontology building platforms that support the ontology development process.

1.7.1.1 Methodologies and Methods

Concerning methods and methodologies, the approaches dealt with are the Cyc method, the Uschold and King method, the Grüninger and Fox methodology, the KACTUS approach, METHONTOLOGY, the SENSUS method, and the On-To-Knowledge methodology.

The method used to build the **Cyc** knowledge base [72] consists of three phases. The first phase consists of the manual coding of articles and pieces of knowledge, in which common sense knowledge that is implicit in different sources is extracted by hand. The second and third phases consist of acquiring new common sense knowledge using natural language or machine learning tools. The difference between them is that in the second phase this common sense knowledge acquisition is aided by tools, but mainly performed by humans, while in the third phase the acquisition is mainly performed by tools. This approach is applicable, besides the main line of the life cycle model, also to scenario 4 (semi-automatic construction of ontologies). According to the Cyc method, the resulting ontology will be divided into microtheories (or contexts), bundles of assertions in the same domain, and is implemented in the CycL language.

The **Uschold and King** method [113] proposes four phases: (1) to identify the purpose of the ontology, (2) to build it, (3) to evaluate it, and (4) to document it. During the building phase, the authors propose capturing knowledge, coding it and integrating other ontologies inside the current one. The authors also propose three strategies for identifying the main concepts in the ontology: a top-down approach, in which the most abstract concepts are identified first and then specialized into more specific concepts; a bottom-up approach, in which the most specific concepts are identified first and then generalized into more abstract concepts; and a middle-out approach, in which the most important concepts are identified first and then generalized and specialized into other concepts. This approach is applicable, besides the main line of the life cycle model, also to scenario 1 (evaluate and import).

Grüninger and Fox [46] propose a methodology that is inspired by the development of knowledge-based systems using first-order logic. They propose first to identify intuitively the main scenarios (possible applications in which the ontology will be used). Then, a set of natural language questions, called competency questions, are used to determine the scope of the ontology. These questions and their answers are used to extract the main concepts and their properties, relations and axioms of the ontology. Such ontology components are formally expressed in first-order logic. Therefore, this is a very formal methodology that takes advantage of the robustness of classical logic. It can be used as a guide to transform informal scenarios in computable models. This approach is applicable, besides the main line of the life cycle model, also to scenario 1 (evaluate + import) and scenario 2 (conceptualize + integrate + evaluate conceptualization).

In the method proposed in the **KACTUS** project [9] the ontology is built on the basis of an application knowledge base (KB), by means of a process of abstraction (i.e., following a bottom-up strategy). The more the applications are built, the more general the ontology becomes; hence, the further the ontology moves away from a KB. In other words, the authors propose to start building a KB for a specific application. Later, when a new KB in a similar domain is needed, they propose to generalize the first KB into an ontology and adapt it for both applications. Applying this method recursively, the ontology would represent the consensual knowledge needed in all the applications. A way to apply this approach is to generate an ontology by means of the generalization of several KBs that model the same domain. Therefore, the KACTUS method is applicable, besides the main line of the ontology life cycle model, also to scenario 6 (evaluate and import N ontologies (or KBs to merge them).

The method based on **Sensus** [109] is a top-down approach for deriving domain-specific ontologies from huge ontologies. The authors propose to identify a set of "seed" terms that are relevant to a particular domain. These terms are linked manually to a broad-coverage ontology (in this case, the Sensus ontology, which contains more than 50,000 concepts). Then, all the concepts in the path from the seed terms to the root of Sensus are included. If a term that could be relevant in the domain has not yet appeared, it is added manually, and the previous step is performed again, until no term is missing. Finally, for those nodes that have a large number of paths through them, the entire subtree under the node is sometimes added, based on the idea that if many of the nodes in a subtree have been found to be relevant, then the other nodes in the subtree are likely to be relevant as well. Consequently, this approach promotes the sharebility of knowledge, since the same base ontology is used to develop ontologies in particular domains. This method is especially useful in scenario 3 (conceptualize + acquire knowledge).

METHONTOLOGY [32] is a methodology, created by the Ontological Engineering Group of the Technical University of Madrid (UPM), for building ontologies either from scratch, reusing other ontologies as they are, or by a process of reengineering them. The METHONTOLOGY framework enables the construction of ontologies at the knowledge level. It includes: the identification of the ontology development process, a life cycle based on evolving prototypes (based in the one presented in Figs. 1.2 and 1.3), and particular techniques to carry out each activity. The main phase in the ontology development process using the METHONTOLOGY approach is the conceptualization phase. METHONTOLOGY considers all the scenarios presented in Sect. 1.6. In fact, such scenarios were born as a consequence of the methodological studies at UPM in the MKBEEM (IST-1999-10589) and Esperonto (IST-2001-34373) projects.

The **On-To-Knowledge** methodology [102] includes the identification of goals that should be achieved by knowledge management tools and is based on an analysis of usage scenarios. The steps proposed by the methodology are: *kick-off*, where ontology requirements are captured and specified, competency questions are identified, potentially reusable ontologies are studied and a first draft version of the ontology is built; *refinement*, where a mature and application-oriented ontology is produced; *evaluation*, where the requirements and competency questions are checked, and the ontology is tested in the application environment; and *ontology maintenance*. With regards to the scenarios to which this methodology is applicable, its authors are researching activities concerning all the scenarios; however, an ontology life cycle model that guides the order to carry out the different activities for the scenarios alternative to the main line has not been proposed. Besides, some scenarios are not integrally considered, e.g., scenario 8 (documentation + evolution management + configuration management + quality assurance and control).

If we analyze the approaches according to the part of the ontology development process that they describe, we can conclude that (see [29]):

- None of the approaches covers all the processes involved in ontology building. Most of the methods and methodologies for building ontologies are focused on the development activities, especially on ontology conceptualization and ontology implementation, and they do not pay too much attention to other important aspects related to management, learning, merging, integration, evolution and evaluation of ontologies. Therefore, such methods should be added to the methodologies for ontology construction from scratch (see an example in [30]).

- Most of the approaches are focused on development activities, especially ontology implementation, and they do not pay too much attention to other important aspects related to the management, evolution and evaluation of ontologies. This is due to the fact that the ontological engineering field is relatively new. However, a low compliance with the criteria formerly established does not mean a low quality of the methodology or method. As [53] states, a not very specified method can be very useful for an experienced group.

- Most of the approaches present some drawbacks in their use. Some of them have not been used by external groups and, in some cases, they have been used in a single domain.

- Most of the approaches do not have a specific tool that gives them technological support. Besides, none of the available tools covers all the activities necessary in ontology building.

1.7.1.2 Ontology Tools

Concerning the software platforms that give support to most of the activities of the ontology development life cycle, we will focus on the new generation of ontology engineering environments, in particular, on Protégé, WebODE, OntoEdit and KAON1.[6] They have been created to integrate ontology technology in actual information systems. As a matter of fact, they are built as robust integrated environments or suites that provide technological support to most of the ontology life cycle activities. They have extensible, component-based architectures, where new modules can easily be added to provide more functionality to the environment. Besides, the knowledge models underlying these environments are language independent.

Protégé [91] has been developed by Stanford Medical Informatics (SMI) at Stanford University. It is an open source, standalone application with an extensible architecture. The core of this environment is the ontology editor, and it holds a library of plugins that add more functionality to the environment. Currently, plugins are available for ontology language import/export (FLogic, Jess, XML, Prolog), ontology language design [69], OKBC access, constraints creation and execution (PAL), ontology merge (Prompt [94]), etc. This platform provides support for the main line of the life cycle model, for scenario 1 (evaluate and import), scenario 2 (conceptualize + integrate + evaluate conceptualization), scenario 3 (conceptualize + acquire knowledge), scenario 5 (evaluate and import N ontologies to align them), scenario 6 (evaluate and import N ontologies to merge them) and scenario 8 (manage the evolution of the ontology).

WebODE [17, 1] is the successor of ODE (Ontology Design Environment) [11], and has been developed at UPM. It is also an ontology engineering suite created with an extensible architecture. WebODE is not used as a standalone application, but as a Web server with several frontends. The core of this environment is the ontology access service, which is used by all the services and applications plugged into the server, especially by the WebODE Ontology Editor. There are several services for ontology language import/export (XML, RDF(S), OWL, CARIN, FLogic, Jess, Prolog), axiom editing, ontology documentation, ontology evaluation and ontology merging. WebODE's ontologies are stored in a relational database. Finally, WebODE covers and gives support to most of the activities involved in the ontology development process proposed by METHONTOLOGY, although this does not prevent it from being used with other methodologies or without following any methodology. This platform also provides support for the main line of the life cycle model and for scenarios 1, 2, 3, 6 and 7 (translate the ontology into another natural language).

---

[6] Other tools (Ontolingua Server, OntoSaurus, WebOnto, etc.) are described in [40].

OntoEdit [108] has been developed by AIFB at Karlsruhe University, and commercialized by Ontoprise. It is similar to the previous tools: it is an extensible and flexible environment, based on a plugin architecture, which provides functionality to browse and edit ontologies. It includes plugins that are in charge of inferring using Ontobroker, of exporting and importing ontologies in different formats (FLogic, XML, RDF(S) and OWL), etc. Two versions of OntoEdit are available: OntoEdit Free and OntoEdit Professional. This platform provides support for the main line of the life cycle model, for scenario 1 (evaluate and import) and scenario 2 (conceptualize + integrate + evaluate conceptualization).

The **KAON1** tool suite [77] is an open source extensible ontology engineering environment. The core of this tool suite is the ontology API, which defines its underlying knowledge model based on an extension of RDF(S). The OI modeler is the ontology editor of the tool suite that provides capabilities for ontology evolution, ontology mapping, ontology generation from databases, etc. This platform provides support for the main line of the life cycle model, for scenario 1 (evaluate and import), scenario 2 (conceptualize + integrate + evaluate conceptualization), scenario 3 (conceptualize + acquire knowledge), scenario 4 (semi-automatic construction of ontologies), scenario 6 (evaluate and import N ontologies to merge them) and scenario 8 (evolve the ontology).

An interesting aspect of tools is that only OntoEdit and WebODE give **support to ontology building methodologies** (On-To-Knowledge and METHONTOLOGY respectively), though this does not prevent them from being used with other methodologies or with no methodology at all.

From the **KR paradigm** point of view, KAON is based on semantic networks plus frames, and the rest of the tools allow the representation of knowledge following a hybrid approach based on frames and first-order logic. **Expressiveness of the underlying tool knowledge model** is also important. All the tools allow the representation of classes, relations, attributes and instances. Only KAON1, and Protégé provide flexible modeling components like metaclasses. Before selecting a tool for developing an ontology, it is also important to know the **inference services** attached to the tool, which include: constraint and consistency checking mechanisms, type of inheritance (single, multiple, monotonic, non-monotonic), automatic classifications, exception handling and execution of procedures. KAON1 does not have an inference engine. OntoEdit uses FLogic [66] as its inference engine, WebODE uses Ciao Prolog [52], and Protégé uses an internal PAL engine. Further, Protégé and WebODE provide ontology evaluation facilities and also include a module that performs ontology evaluation according to the OntoClean method [114, 50]. Finally, Protégé (with the OWL plugin) performs automatic classifications by means of connecting to a description logic reasoner.

Another important aspect to take into account in ontology tools is the **software architecture and tool evolution**, which considers which hardware and software platforms are necessary to use the tool, its architecture (standalone, client/server, *n*-tier application), extensibility, storage of ontologies (databases, ASCII files, etc.), failure tolerance, backup management, stability and tool versioning policies. From that perspective, all these tools are based on Java platforms and provide database storage support. Backup management functionality is just provided by WebODE, and extensibility facilities are allowed in KAON, OntoEdit, Protégé and WebODE.

Interoperability with other ontology tools, information systems and databases, as well as translations to and from some ontology languages, is another important feature in order to integrate ontologies into applications. Most of the tools export and import to ad hoc XML and other ontology markup languages. However, there is no comparative study on the quality of all these translators. Moreover, there are no empirical results about the possibility of exchanging ontologies between different tools and about the amount of knowledge that is lost in the translation processes. Some effort in this regard has been carried out in the EON 2004 workshop.[7]

Related to the **cooperative and collaborative construction of ontologies,** Protégé incorporates some synchronization functionalities. In general, more features are required in existing tools to ensure a successful collaborative building of ontologies.

1.7.2 Ontology Learning

Ontology learning is defined as the set of methods and techniques used for building an ontology from scratch, enriching or adapting an existing ontology in a semi-automatic fashion using distributed and heterogeneous knowledge and information sources, allowing a reduction in the time and effort needed in the ontology development process. Though the fully automatic acquisition of knowledge remains far off, the overall process is considered as semi-automatic, meaning that human intervention is necessary in some parts of the learning process. Several approaches have appeared during the last decade for the partial automization of the knowledge acquisition process. To carry out this automization, natural language analysis and machine learning techniques can be used. This involves the

---

[7] http://km.aifb.uni-karlsruhe.de/ws/eon2004/

inclusion of a number of complementary disciplines that feed on different types of unstructured, semi-structured and fully structured data to support semi-automatic, cooperative ontology engineering [78].

Regarding *ontology learning methods*, some of the best known ones are due to Maedche and colleagues [65], Aussenac-Gilles and colleagues [3, 4] and Khan and Luo [64]. **Maedche and colleagues' method** [65] proposes to learn the ontology using as a base a core ontology (Sensus, WordNet, etc.), which is enriched with the learned concepts. New concepts are identified using natural language analysis techniques over the resources previously identified by the user. The resulting ontology is pruned and then focused on a specific domain by means of several approaches based on statistics. Finally, relations between concepts are established applying learning methods. Such relations are added to the resulting ontology.

Aussenac-Gilles and colleagues' method [3, 4] is based on knowledge elicitation from technical documents. The method allows the creation of a domain model by analyzing a corpus with NLP tools. The method combines knowledge acquisition tools based on linguistics with modeling techniques to keep links between models and texts. After selecting a corpus, the method proposes to obtain linguistic knowledge (terms, lexical relations and groups of synonyms) at the linguistic level. This linguistic knowledge is then transformed into a semantic network. The semantic network includes concepts, relationships between concepts and attributes for the concepts.

Khan and Luo's method [64] aims to build a domain ontology from text documents using clustering techniques and WordNet [83]. The user provides a selection of documents regarding the same domain. Using these documents, a set of clusters where each cluster may contain more than one document is created, and then put into the correct place in a hierarchy. Each node in this hierarchy is a cluster of documents. For this purpose, the method proposes to use a modified algorithm, called the SOAT algorithm [115]. After building a hierarchy of clusters, a concept is assigned to each cluster in the hierarchy in a bottom-up fashion. First, concepts associated with documents are assigned to leaf nodes in the hierarchy. For each cluster of documents, these will be assigned a keyword-called topic that represents its content and uses predefined topic categories. For this purpose, a topic tracking algorithm [58] is used. Then, this topic is associated with an appropriate concept in WordNet. And finally, the interior node concepts is assigned according to the concepts in the descendant nodes and their hypernyms in WordNet. The type of relation between concepts in the hierarchy is ignored; it is only possible to know that there is a relation between them.

As we can see in this review, most of the ontology learning approaches are based on using linguistic patterns for extracting linguistic relations which would reflect ontological relations (taxonomic and non-taxonomic relations as well as possible attributes or their values, depending on the pattern's type). In the same sense, these kinds of patterns are also used for detecting attribute–value pairs. All the presented methods require the participation of an ontologist to evaluate the final ontology and the accuracy of the learning process. There are no methods or techniques for evaluating the accuracy of the learning process either.

With regard to *ontology learning tools*, we focus on Caméléon [5], LTG Text Processing Workbench [82], Prométhée [85, 86], SOAT tool [115] and Text-To-Onto [78]. **Caméléon** [5] assists in learning conceptual relations to enrich conceptual models. Caméléon relies on linguistic principles for relation identification: lexico-syntactic patterns are good indicators of semantic relations. Some patterns may be regular enough to indicate the same kind of relation from one domain to another. Other patterns are domain specific and may reveal domain-specific relations. This tool gives technological support to some steps of the Aussenac-Gilles and colleagues' method.

LTG (Language Technology Group) **Text Processing Workbench** [82] is a set of computational tools for uncovering internal structure in natural language texts written in English. The main idea behind the workbench is the independence of the text representation and text analysis. In LTG, ontology learning is performed in two sequential steps: representation and analysis. At the representation step, the text is converted from a sequence of characters to features of interest by means of annotation tools. At the analysis step, those features are used by tools of statistics gathering and inference to find significant correlations in the texts. The workbench is being used both for lexicographic purposes and for statistical language modeling.

Prométhée [85, 86] is a machine learning-based tool for extracting and refining lexical–syntactic patterns related to conceptual specific relations from technical corpora. It uses pattern bases, which are enriched with the ones extracted in the learning. To refine patterns, the authors propose the Eagle [49] learning system. This system is based on the inductive paradigm *learning from examples*, which consists of the extraction of intentional descriptions of target concepts from their extensional descriptions, and previous knowledge of the given domain. This fact specifies general information, like the object characteristics and their relations. The tool extracts *intentional* descriptions of concepts from their *extensional* descriptions. The learned definitions are later used in recognition and classification tasks.

SOAT [115] allows semi-automatic domain ontology acquisition from a domain corpus. The main objective of the tool is to extract relationships from parsed sentences based on applying phraserules to identify keywords with strong semantic links like hypernyms or synonyms. The acquisition process integrates linguistic, common sense and domain knowledge. The restrictions of SOAT mean that the quality of the corpus must be very high, in the sense that the sentences must be accurate and sufficient to include most of the important relationships to be extracted.

Text-To-Onto [78] integrates an environment for building domain ontologies from an initial core ontology. It also discovers conceptual structures from different German sources using knowledge acquisition and machine learning techniques. Text-To-Onto has implemented some techniques for ontology learning from free and semi-structured text. The result of the learning process is a domain ontology that contains domain-specific and domain-independent concepts. Domain-independent concepts are withdrawn to better adjust the vocabulary of the domain ontology. The result of this process is a domain ontology that only contains domain concepts learned from the input sources related before. The ontologist supervises the whole process. This is a cyclic process, in the sense that it is possible to refine and complete the ontology if we repeat the process.

An important conclusion that we can obtain in the revision of ontology learning tools is that there is no fully automatic tool that carries out the learning process. Some tools are focused on helping in the acquisition of lexico-semantic knowledge, others help to elicit concepts or relations from a preprocessed corpus with the help of the user, etc. A deeper description of methods and tools can be found in [41].

1.7.3 Ontology Alignment and Merging

Ontologies aim to capture the consensual knowledge of a given domain in a generic and formal way, to be reused and shared across applications and by groups of people. From this definition we could wrongly infer that there is only one ontology for modeling each domain (or even a single universal ontology). Though this can be the case in specific domains, commonly several ontologies model the same domain knowledge in different ways. For instance, in the e-commerce field there are several standards and joint initiatives for the classification of products and services (UNSPSC,[8] e-cl@ss,[9] RosettaNet,[10] NAICS,[11] SCTG,[12] etc.). This hetero-

---

[8] http://www.unspsc.org/
[9] http://www.eclass.de/

geneity of ontologies also happens in many other domains (medicine, law, art, sciences, etc.).

Noy and Musen [94] defined ontology alignment and merging as follows: (1) *ontology alignment* consists of establishing different kinds of mappings (or links) between two ontologies, hence preserving the original ontologies (see Fig. 1.4); and (2) *ontology merging* proposes to generate a unique ontology from the original ontologies. In this chapter we will assume that a *mapping* between ontologies is a set of rewriting rules that associates terms and expressions defined in a source ontology with terms and expressions of a target ontology (inspired from [84]). Table 1.1 shows the mappings that can be established between the two ontologies of Fig. 1.4. The symbol := means is transformed into, and λ is the empty word. Therefore, date := λ means that the attribute date has no correspondence with terms of the ontology 2.

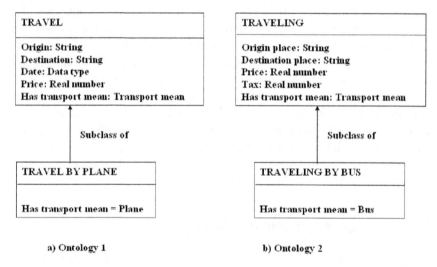

a) Ontology 1   b) Ontology 2

Fig. 1.4. Example of ontology alignment

Given that a reusable and machine interpretable database schema can be considered as an ontology (see Sect. 1.2), the galaxy of *ontology alignment methods* is huge. Some examples of these methods are: **S-Match** [101], **QOM** [25], **Pan and colleagues' proposal** [98], Artemis [8, 14], Cupid [76], AnchorPrompt [95], Similarity Flooding [80], etc. We will fo-

---

[10] http://www.rosettanet.org/
[11] http://www.naics.com/
[12] http://www.bts.gov/programs/cfs/sctg/welcome.htm

cus on the methods in bold because they show a complementary view of the problem of ontology alignment, although the three proposals share a lot of common ideas. Following Ehring and Staab's paper [25], we will present a process that subsumes most of these methods, and that allows us to comment them inside an integrated framework. The activities of this process are as follows (Ehring and Staab [25], inspired from CRISP-CM, the Cross Industry Standard Process for Data Mining)[13]:

- Activity 1. **Ontology adaptation**. The source ontologies are transformed into a format that is interpretable by the software that will carry out the process of alignment.

  QOM identifies this activity, but it does not explain how to carry it out. However, S-Match provides details on ontology adaptation. According to this method, names are morphologically analyzed in order to find all their possible basic forms (e.g., travels would be identified as a variation of travel).

  S-Match assumes that ontologies can be translated before aligning them. Further, it proposes that prepositions, conjunctions, etc., are transformed into logical connectives. For instance, `travel by plane` could be translated into "`C such as subclassOf(C, Travel) ∧ C.transporMean = Plane`".

  Concerning Pan and colleagues' proposal, their method transforms the two ontologies into a Bayesian network.
- Activity 2. Selection of the search space. If the ontologies have a large number of terms, pruning is necessary to avoid checking all the possible pairs of concepts.

  QOM gives guidelines to select the search space. Some of the identified strategies are:
  - Random. It limits the number of candidate mappings by selecting either a fixed number or a percentage from all possible mappings.
  - Label. It restricts candidate mappings to pairs of terms whose labels are near to each other in a sorted list. That is, each term could be possibly mapped with those that have a similar name.
  - Proximity. If two concepts are mapped, then it is very likely that some of their descendants or immediatelyrelated terms are also mapped.
  - Combination of different heuristics. The above-mentioned strategies can be combined to prune the candidate mappings.

  S-Match and Pan and colleagues' approach do not identify this activity.

---

[13] http://www.crisp-dm.org/

- Activity 3. **Similarity computation**. To choose the exact mappings between the possible pairs of terms, *similarity measures* are used. They associate likeness values to pairs of terms. The similarity measures compare term names, documents annotated with the terms, etc.
- Activity 4. **Similarity aggregation**. In general, there may be several similarity values for a candidate pair of terms from two ontologies, e.g., one for the similarity of their names and one for the similarity of their natural language descriptions. These different similarity values for one candidate pair must be aggregated into a single aggregated similarity value. A way to obtain the aggregated value is through the weighted means of the similarity values. This is basically QOM's approach. Neither S-Match nor Pal and colleagues' method combine similarities.
- Activity 5. **Interpretation**. Individual or aggregated similarity values are used to derive mappings between terms.

   QOM applies a threshold to discard spurious evidence of similarity, and considers as best mappings those with the highest aggregated similarity scores. Pan and colleagues follow a probabilistic and statistical analysis. Thus, if $p(C_1 \wedge C_2)$ is high, then C_1 and C_2 have a high overlap. If $p(C_1/C_2)$ is high and $p(C_2/C_1)$ is low, then it is very likely that C_1 is subclass of C_2. S-Math directly obtains the mappings trough the rules mentioned in activity 3.

- Activity 6. **Iteration**. Several methods perform an iteration over the whole process in order to take advantage of the knowledge already acquired in the first round. QOM iterates to find mappings based on lexical similarities first, and based on the structure of the ontologies later.

   S-Match proposes that the mappings generated during the first round are used as a KB to deduce other mappings. Thus, for instance, if we already know that the concept C_1 is equivalent to the concept C_2, and the concept C_2 is a subclass of the concept C_3, then we should be able to deduce that C_1 is a subclass of C_3.

   In the case of Pan and colleagues' proposal, there are mappings that can be deduced using the network obtained in the first round as a probabilistic KB.

Concerning *ontology alignment tools*, the **QOM toolset** [25] gives support to the QOM method, presented in this section. It is implemented in Java using the KAON framework (see Sect. 1.7.1.2). It has been basically used to make experiments with the method and compare it with other methods.

Table 1.1. Mappings for the two ontologies of Fig. 1.4

Description of the mapping in natural language	Rewriting rule
The concept `travel` (in ontology 1) is equivalent to the concept `traveling` (in ontology 2).	Travel := Traveling
The concept `travel by plane` (in ontology 1) is equivalent to the concept such it is a subclass of `traveling` (in ontology 2) and its transport mean is a `plane` (in ontology 2).	TravelByPlane := C such as subclassOf(C, Traveling) ∧ C.hasTransporMean = Plane
The concept such it is a subclass of `travel` (in ontology 1) and its transport mean is a `bus` (in ontology 2) is equivalent to the concept `traveling by bus` (in ontology 2).	C such as subclassOf(C, Travel) ∧ C.hasTransporMean = Bus := TravelingByBus
The attribute `origin` (in ontology 1) is equivalent to the attribute `origin place` (in ontology 2).	Origin := OriginPlace
The attribute `destination` (in ontology 1) is equivalent to the attribute `destination place` (in ontology 2).	Destination := DestinationPlace
The value `New York` of attributes `origin` and `destination` (in ontology 2) is equivalent to the value `NY` of `origin place` and `destination place` (in ontology 2).	"New York" := "NY"
The attribute `date` (in ontology 1) does not have correspondence in ontology 2.	Date := λ
The attribute `price` (in ontology 1) is equivalent to a combination of the attributes `price` and `tax` in ontology 2.	Price := Price * (1 + Tax/100)
The attribute `has transport mean` (in ontology 1) is equivalent to the attribute `has transport mean` in ontology 2.	HasTransportMean := HasTransportMean

The **S-Match** tool translates and preprocesses the input ontologies. Then, it orders the transformation of prefixes, the expansions of abbreviations, etc. Later, using resources like WordNet, it generates a first mapping base. Finally, using the SAT solvers, new mappings are generated.

Pan and colleagues [98] apply their method by combining the Google search engine and text classifiers (such as Rainbow[14] or cbacl[15]) to calculate the prior probabilities of the Bayesian network. Then, the subsequent probability is calculated using any Bayesian network tool.

OLA[16] [26] is an API for manipulating alignments between ontologies in OWL. It allows applying and combining different algorithms, and even adding newones. Currently, this API has been mainly used with mapping methods based on lexical similarity measures. OLA implements a format for expressing alignments in RDF.

With regard to *ontology merging methods and methodologies*, one of the most elaborated proposals for ontology merging is **ONIONS** [103, 33],

---

[14] http://www-2-cs-cmu.edu/~mccallum/bow/rainbow
[15] http://www.lbreyer.com/
[15] http://co4.inrialpes.fr/align

developed by the Conceptual Modeling Group of the CNR in Rome, Italy. With this method we can create a library of ontologies originating from different sources. The main underlying ideas of this method are: (1) to link the ontologies taking into account lexical relations between their terms (polysemy, synonymy, etc.); and (2) to use generic theories (part–whole or connectedness theories, for example) as common upper ontologies of the library ontologies; that is, to use generic theories as the glue to integrate the different ontologies.

FCA-Merge [107] was developed at the AIFB Institute of the University of Karlsruhe, Germany. This approach is very different from the other approaches presented in this section. FCA-Merge takes as input the two ontologies to be merged and a set of documents on the domains of the ontologies. The appearances of instances of the concepts in the different documents guides the merging of such concepts.

The **PROMPT** method [96] has been elaborated by the Stanford Medical Informatics Group at Stanford University. The main assumption of PROMPT is that the ontologies to be merged are formalized with a common knowledge model based on frames. This method proposes first to elaborate a list with the candidate operations to be performed to merge the two ontologies (e.g., merge two classes, merge two slots, etc.). Afterwards, a cyclic process starts. In each cycle the ontologist selects an operation of the list and executes it.

PromptDiff is a component of Prompt [97] that allows maintaining ontology views or mappings between ontologies. PromptDiff provides an ontologycomparison API that other applications can use to determine, for example, the mapping needs to be updated when new versions of mapped ontologies appear [93].

Concerning *merging tools*, in the mid-1990s, research groups at the Universidad del País Vasco, MCC and the University of Georgia began to develop **OBSERVER** [81]. This tool automatically merged ontologies of the same domain to access heterogeneous information sources. However, the merge process was carried out by an internal module and, therefore, it was invisible to the user. Several years later, in the late 1990s, two groups at Stanford University developed two of the most relevant ontology merge tools: Chimaera and the Prompt plugin.

Chimaera [79] was built by the Knowledge Systems Laboratory (KSL) to aid in the process of ontology merge, and the **Prompt plugin** [94], integrated in Protégé, was built by the Stanford Medical Informatics (SMI) Group. The added value of the latter was that it provided support to the ontology merge method Prompt.

Approximately at the same time, the AIFB Institute of the University of Karlsruhe developed the **FCA-Merge toolset** [107] to support the FCA-Merge method.

Finally, in 2002, **GLUE** [23] was developed at the University of Washington. GLUE is a system that semi-automatically finds mappings between concepts from two different ontologies.

The current ontology merging approaches have the following deficiencies: (1) mappings to perform the merging are usually established by hand; (2) all the tools need the participation of the user to obtain a definitive result in the merging process; and (3) no tool allows the merging of axioms and rules. The natural evolution of merging tools should lead to increased use of knowledge and to decreased participation of the people in the process. This could improve the possibilities of the merging at run-time.

In the context of the workshop on Evaluation of Ontology Tools EON2004, an experiment was performed on the quality of the mappings provided by different methods and tools. This will be continued in other efforts.

To learn more about ontology alignment and merging we recommend readers to access the Ontology Matching Web page.[17]

1.7.4 Ontology Evolution and Versioning

Ontologies are often developed by several groups of people and may evolve over time. Therefore, they cannot be understood as static entities, but rather are dynamic ones. As a consequence, ontology versioning becomes necessary and essential. This support must enable users to compare versions of ontologies and analyze differences between them [93]. Ontology engineers working in parallel on the same ontology need to maintain and compare different versions, to examine the changes that others have performed, and to accept or reject the changes. Ontology-based application developers should easily see the changes between ontology versions, determine which definitions were added or deleted, and accept or reject the changes. Let us note that, for ontologies, we must compare the semantics of the ontologies and not their serializations, since two ontologies that are exactly the same conceptually may have very different text representations when implemented in some ontology languages.

The **change management KAON plugin** allows the effects of changes through *evolution strategies* to be stablished [104]. A particular evolution strategy allows us to establish, for example, what happens with its sub-

---

[17] http://www.ontologymatching.org/

classes when a concept C is deleted: if they can also be deleted, or they can become subclasses of the superclasses of C.

The **PromptDiff algorithm** compares ontologies producing an initial set of mappings between two versions of the same ontology [93]. For instance, if a term t_1 of the version v_1 has the same type as the term t_2 of the version v_2 (both of them are concepts, both of them are properties, etc.) and t_1 has a similar name to t_2, it is assumed that the semantics of t_1 and t_2 are similar. Therefore, t_1 and t_2 are mapped as similar terms. This initial set of mappings is propagated using a fixed-point algorithm that combines the results of the previous step. Thus, for example, if all the siblings of the concept C_1 of v_1 are mapped with siblings of the concept C_2 of v_2, C_1 and C_2 are candidates to be mapped through a change operation (e.g., the addition of a new subclass). This algorithm is implemented by the **PromtDiff API** (see Sect. 1.7.3).

1.7.5 Ontology Evaluation

Work on ontology content evaluation started in 1994 [35]. In the last few years, interest in this issue has grown and extended to the evaluation of technology used to build ontologies. A survey of evaluation methods and tools can be found in [39]. These evaluation efforts can be examined under the following four perspectives.

From a *content perspective*, many libraries exist where ontologies are published and publicly available (DAML,[18] KAON,[19] Ontobroker,[20] Ontolingua,[21] Protégé,[22] SemWebCentral,[23] SHOE,[24] WebODE,[25] WebOnto,[26] etc.). No documentation is available about how ontologies available in libraries or well-known and large ontologies (e.g., Cyc [72], or Sensus [109]) were evaluated. However they have been used to build many successful applications.

From a *methodology perspective*, the main efforts to evaluate ontology content were made by Gómez-Pérez [40, 36] in the framework of

---

[18] http://www.daml.org/ontologies/
[19] http://kaon.semanticweb.org/
[20] http://ontobroker.semanticweb.org/
[21] http://www-ksl-svc.stanford.edu:5915/
[22] http://protege.stanford.edu/
[23] http://semwebcentral.org/index.jsp
[24] www.cs.umd.edu/projects/plus/SHOE/onts/index.html
[25] http://webode.dia.fi.upm.es/
[26] http://webonto.open.ac.uk/

METHONTOLOGY, and by Guarino and colleagues [114] with the Onto-Clean method.

Gómez-Pérez has identified and classified different kinds of errors in taxonomies. Such identification can be used as a checklist for taxonomy evaluation. Such a list presents a set of possible errors that can be made by ontology engineers when modeling taxonomic knowledge in an ontology under a frame-based approach. Errors are classified as: inconsistency, incompleteness and redundancy errors. The ontology engineer should not postpone the evaluation until the taxonomy is finished; the control mechanisms should be performed during construction of the taxonomy.

OntoClean is a method elaborated by the Ontology Group of the CNR in Padova (Italy). Its goal is to remove wrong *Subclass-Of* relations in taxonomies according to some philosophical notions such as *rigidity*, *identity* and *unity*. According to this method, the ontology engineer firs, assigns some meta-properties to each concept of the taxonomy (e.g., if each instance of the concept is a whole, then it applies a set of rules that establish the possible incompatibilities of values in the taxonomy). Such rules allow pruning of the wrong *subclass of* links if the values assigned to a concept are incompatible with the values assigned to its children.

From an ***implementation perspective***, we can find important connections and implications between the components we use to build ontologies (concepts, relations, properties and axioms); the KR paradigms (frames, description logics, first-order logic, and so on); and the languages we use to implement them. This is important because different KR paradigms offer different reasoning mechanisms that we can use in content evaluation (e.g., description logic classifiers, or frame-based reasoning).

From a ***technological perspective***, ontology tool developers have gained experience evaluating tools working on the OntoWeb European thematic network SIG3 (Special Interest Group on Enterprise Standard Ontology Environments). Different ontology tool developers have also conducted comparison studies of different types of ontology tools, which can be found in the OntoWeb deliverable D1.3 [37]. According to these studies, evaluation functionalities of well-known ontology development tools (Protégé, WebODE, OntoEdit, etc.) allow the checking of taxonomies. However, such evaluation functionalities are still not enough for a deep ontology evaluation.

Recently, some researchers have published a synthesis of their experience in ontology evaluation [19, 38, 48, 90]. According to their conclusions, although good ideas have been provided in this area, there are still important deficiencies. Other interesting works are those in [51] and the above-mentioned EON2004 experiment.

1.7.6 Ontology Implementation

The implementation activity (proposed by all the methods and methodologies, and supported by all the development tools) consists of building computable models in an ontology language. As stated in the introduction, two groups of languages can be identified: classical and markup. We recommend [39] for detailed descriptions of each of them, where the same ontology is implemented in each language. Now, we briefly describe the most relevant ones.

KIF [34] is a language based on first-order logic created as an interchange format for diverse KR systems. Ontolingua [43, 27], which builds on KIF, combines the KR paradigms of frames and first order predicate calculus (KIF). It is the most expressive of all the languages that have been used for representing ontologies, allowing the representation of concepts, taxonomies of concepts, n-ary relations, functions, axioms, instances and procedures. Its high expressiveness led to difficulties in building reasoning mechanisms for it.

Loom [75] was not initially meant for implementing ontologies, but for general KBs. Loom is based on description logics (DL) and production rules, and provides automatic classifications of concepts. The following ontology components can be represented with this language: concepts, concept taxonomies, n-ary relations, functions, axioms and production rules. This language has nom been superseded by Powerloom.

OCML [87] was created as a kind of operational Ontolingua. In fact, most of the definitions that can be expressed in OCML are similar to the corresponding definitions in Ontolingua, and some additional components can be defined: deductive and production rules, and operational definitions for functions. OCML was built for developing executable ontologies and models in PSM.

FLogic [66] (*Frame Logic*) combines frames and first-order logic, allowing the representation of concepts, concept taxonomies, binary relations, functions, instances, axioms and deductive rules. FLogic is the only one of the previous languages that do not have Lisp-like syntax. Any of its inference engines, OntoBroker [21] or FLORA [73], can be used for constraint checking and deducing new information.

The OKBC (*Open Knowledge Base Connectivity*) protocol [15] (which is not properly a language) allows access to KBs stored in different knowledge representation systems (KRSs). Of the systems presented above, Ontolingua and LOOM are OKBC compliant.

SHOE [74] was built first as an extension of HTML and later as a language using the XML syntax. It uses different tags from those of the HTML specification, thus it allows the insertion of ontologies in HTML documents. SHOE combines frames and rules. SHOE just allows the representation of concepts, their taxonomies, *n*-ary relations, instances and deduction rules, which are used by its inference engine to obtain new knowledge.

XOL [63] was developed as a XMLization of a small subset of primitives from the OKBC protocol, called OKBC-Lite. It is a very restricted language where only concepts, taxonomies and binary relations can be specified. No inference mechanisms are attached to it, as it was mainly designed for the exchange of ontologies in the biomedical domain.

RDF [70] was developed by the W3C (the World Wide Web Consortium) as a semantic network- based language to describe Web resources. Finally, the RDF Schema [13] language was also built by the W3C as an extension to RDF with frame-based primitives. The combination of both RDF and RDF Schema is normally known as RDF(S). RDF(S) is much less expressive than the previous languages, just allowing the representation of concepts, taxonomies of concepts and binary relations. Some inference engines have been created for this language, mainly for constraint checking.

These languages have established the foundations of the Semantic Web. In this context, three more languages have been developed as extensions to RDF(S): OIL, DAML+OIL and OWL.

OIL [54] added frame-based KR primitives to RDF(S), and its formal semantics was based on description logics. DAML+OIL [55] allows the representation concepts, taxonomies, binary relations, functions and instances. These two languages are currently no longer used.

Finally, in 2001, the W3C formed a working group called the Web-Ontology (WebOnt) Working Group.[27] The aim of this group was to devise a new ontology markup language for the Semantic Web, called **OWL** (Ontology Web Language). This language was proposed as a W3C recommendation in February 2004. Figure 1.5 shows how these languages have evolved, and it also shows the relationships of these languages with other existing KR languages and systems.

In the previous languages, only some of them are well equipped with primitives that allow exploitation of the concept of networked ontologies. These are Ontolingua, OCML, Flogic, RDF, RDF Schema and OWL (OIL and DAML+OIL also supported this notion, but they are no longer active). Based on our experience and on the case studies available from the literature, we have identified some associations between the ontology languages and the different kinds of ontology-based applications where they are applied.

---

[27] http://www.w3.org/2001/sw/WebOnt/

In e-commerce applications, ontologies are usually used for representing products and services that are offered on e-commerce platforms and are given to users in catalogues they can browse through [71]. Representational needs are not too complex: basically, we need concepts and attributes, and n-ary relations between concepts. However, reasoning needs are usually higher: if the number of products or services offered on the platform is high, automatic classifications are very useful for organizing these products or services automatically (hence, languages based on description logics are extremely helpful), and an efficient query answering is also important in this environment (this is provided by most of the studied languages).

When using PSMs and domain ontologies together two languages are strongly recommended, as they provide explicit support for this integration as well as reusable libraries: namely OCML and FLogic. In fact, both of them are operational modeling languages and solve the issue of PSM prototyping easily. A generic model of parametric design problem solving is provided in OCML [87], and KARL [28] (a customization of FLogic) has been used for PSM modeling, too.

In the context of the Semantic Web, and for exchanging ontologies between applications, languages based on XML are easily read and managed since standard libraries for the treatment of XML are available free. However, it is not difficult to adapt traditional languages to XML syntax, which could make use of the same kinds of libraries. The main advantage of RDF(S) and OWL is the strong support they receive from other communities besides the ontology community, and this means that more tools are available for editing, handling and documenting the ontologies.

The creation of upper-level ontologies requires high expressiveness and mostly there are not great needs for reasoning support. Upper-level ontologies have been generally specified in DL languages such as LOOM or CLASSIC. The Cyc KB is specified in CycL [72], which is a language based on frames and first order logic.

Some efforts are now being made now to migrate these ontologies to OWL.[28] In general, languages based on DL have been widely used in applications that needed intelligent integration of heterogeneous information sources. For instance, CLASSIC has been used in OBSERVER [81], LOOM in Ariadne [6], and OIL has been used in an urban planning process [105], among others. In addition, most of them have been used for information retrieval. For example, LOOM has been used in OntoSeek [49]. The main reason for this broad use is their inference support.

---

[28] http://www.w3.org/TR/2004/REC-owl-ref-20040210/

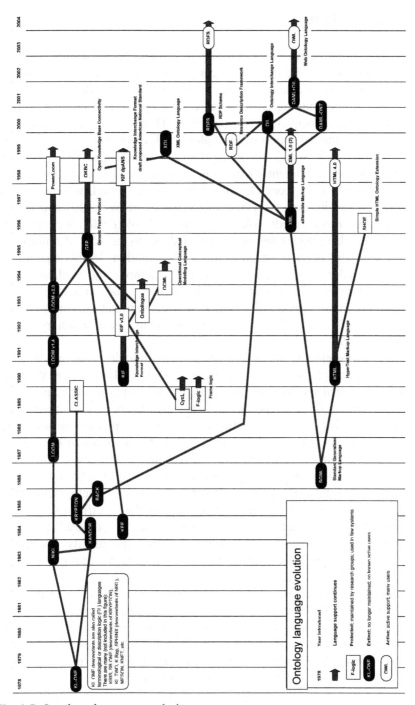

Fig. 1.5. Ontology language evolution

1.8 Conclusions

At the beginning of the 1990s ontology development was similar to an art: ontology developers did not have clear guidelines on how to build ontologies but only some design criteria to be followed. Work on principles, methods and methodologies, together with supporting technology, turned ontology development into engineering. This migration process was mainly due to the definition of the ontology development process and the ontology life cycle, which described the steps to be performed in order to build ontologies and the interdependencies among all those steps.

Though ontologies were clearly oriented to be reused, it has not been until recently, with the emergence of the Semantic Web, that appropriate support at all levels (methodologically and technologically, including implementation languages) has been provided. Many aspects of ontological engineering still need to be adapted to this situation. In this chapter we have reviewed existing ontology principles, methods and methodologies, tools, and languages, focusing especially on those that support the notion of networked ontologies, and on the new life cycle that appears as a consequence of this new framework. The following is a summary of the chaper.

Ontology engineers have available methodologies that guide them through the ontology development process. METHONTOLOGY is the methodology that provides the most detailed descriptions of the processes to be performed; On-To-Knowledge is the one that covers most activities, although with very short descriptions of processes; and the Grüninger and Fox methodology is the most formal one. All of them consider the reuse of existing ontologies during the development process, but only METHONTOLOGY has recently adapted its proposal for a life cycle to the environment of networked ontologies. In any case, the development activities are the most detailed in all of them, mainly the specification, conceptualization and implementation. There is still a lack of proposals for ontology management activities (scheduling, control and quality assurance), and for some pre-development (e.g., environment study) and post-development activities (e.g., (re)use).

Concerning support activities, some interesting contributions have been made in ontology learning, ontology merging and alignment, ontology evolution, and ontology evaluation, as described in Sect. 1.7. Nevertheless, important work has to be done in all of these activities. For example, the time when activities like ontology learning or ontology merging can be applied to heavyweight ontologies is still far away.

One of the problems that the ontology engineer can find when (s)he has to build an ontology is that (s)he has to use different methods that are not integrated. For example, ontology learning methods are not integrated in methodologies that cover the whole development process (e.g., in METHONTOLOGY or On-To-Knowledge). Some experience exists in the integration of methods in methodologies. For example, the OntoClean method has been integrated in METHONTOLOGY (see [30]).

A similar problem appears in the use of ontology tools, given that there is a lack of integrated environments for ontology development. Tools are usually created as isolated modules that solve one type of problem, but neither are fully integrated, nor do they interoperate with other tools that implement other activities of the ontology life cycle.

Finally, work on ontology languages has been constantly evolving since the first languages that were made available for ontology implementation, most of them based on existing KR languages. The existence of heterogeneous networked ontologies has been mainly considered in the recent language developments created in the context of the Semantic Web (RDF, RDF Schema and OWL), with the addition of namespaces that allow referring to ontology components that have been defined elsewhere and with the use of import primitives to include an existing model in an ontology.

1.9 Acknowledgements

This work has been partially supported by the IST project Knowledgeweb (FP6-507482) and by the Spanish project Semantic Services (TIN 2004-02660).

References

1. Arpírez JC, Corcho O, Fernández-López M, Gómez-Pérez A (2003) WebODE in a nutshell. AI Magazine 24(3): 37–38. Fall 2003
2. Arpírez JC, Gómez-Pérez A, Lozano A, Pinto HS (1998) (ONTO)^2 Agent: An ontology-based WWW broker to select ontologies. In: Gómez-Pérez A, Benjamins RV (eds) ECAI'98 Workshop on Applications of Ontologies and Problem-Solving Methods. Brighton, United Kingdom, pp. 16–24
3. Aussenac-Gilles N, Biébow B, Szulman S (2000a) Revisiting Ontology Design: A Methodology Based on Corpus Analysis. In: Dieng R, Corby O (eds) 12th International Conference on Knowledge Engineering and Knowledge Management (EKAW'00). Juan-Les-Pins, France. (Lecture Notes in

Artificial Intelligence LNAI 1937) Springer-Verlag, Berlin, Germany, pp. 172–188

4. Aussenac-Gilles N, Biébow B, Szulman S (2000b) Corpus analysis for conceptual modelling. In: Aussenac-Gilles N, Biébow B, Szulman S (eds) EKAW'00 Workshop on Ontologies and Texts. Juan-Les-Pins, France. CEUR Workshop Proceedings 51:1.1–1.8. Amsterdam, The Netherlands. http://CEUR-WS.org/Vol-51/

5. Aussenac-Gilles N, Seguela P (2000) Les relations sémantiques: du linguistique au formel. In : Condamines A (ed) Cahiers de grammaire, N° spécial sur la linguistique de corpus (Presse de l'UTM, Vol 25), Toulouse, pp. 175–198

6. Barish G, Knoblock GA, Chen Y-S, Minton S, Philpot A, Shahabi C (2000) The theaterloc virtual application. In: Engelmore R, Hirsh H (eds) 12th Annual Conference on Innovative Applications of Artificial Intelligence (IAAI'00). Austin, Texas, pp. 980–987

7. Bechhofer S, Horrocks I, Goble C, Stevens R (2001) OilEd: a reasonable ontology editor for the Semantic Web. In: Baader F, Brewka G, Eiter T (eds) Joint German/Austrian Conference on Artificial Intelligence (KI'01). Vienna, Austria. (Lecture Notes in Artificial Intelligence LNAI 2174) Springer-Verlag, Berlin, Germany, pp. 396–408

8. Beneventano D, Bergamaschi S, Castano S, Corni A, Guidetti R, Malvezzi G, Melchiori M, Vincini M (2000) Information integration: the MOMIS project demonstration. In: El Abbadi A, Brodie ML, Chakravarthy S, Dayal U, Kamel N, Schlageter G, Whang KY (eds) 26th International Conference on Very Large Data Bases, Cairo, Egypt. Morgan Kaufmann Publishers, San Francisco, California, pp. 611–614

9. Bernaras A, Laresgoiti I, Corera J (1996) Building and reusing ontologies for electrical network applications. In: Wahlster W (ed) European Conference on Artificial Intelligence (ECAI'96). Budapest, Hungary. John Wiley & Sons, Chichester, United Kingdom, pp. 298–302

10. Berners-Lee T (1999) Weaving the Web: The Original Design and Ultimate Destiny of the World Wide Web by its Inventor. HarperCollins Publishers, New York

11. Blázquez M, Fernández-López M, García-Pinar JM, Gómez-Pérez A (1998) Building Ontologies at the Knowledge Level using the Ontology Design Environment. In: Gaines BR, Musen MA (eds) 11th International Workshop on Knowledge Acquisition, Modeling and Management (KAW'98). Banff, Canada, SHARE4:1–15

12. Bray T, Paoli J, Sperberg-McQueen CM, Maler E (2000) Extensible Markup Language (XML) 1.0. W3C Recommendation. http://www.w3.org/TR/REC-xml

13. Brickley D, Guha RV (2004) RDF Vocabulary Description Language 1.0: RDF Schema. W3C Recommendation. http://www.w3.org/TR/PR-rdf-schema

14. Castano S, De AntonellisV, De Capitani diVemercati S (2001) Global viewing of heterogeneous data sources. IEEE Transactions on Knowledge and Data Engineering 13(2):277–297
15. Chaudhri VK, Farquhar A, Fikes R, Karp PD, Rice JP (1998) Open Knowledge Base Connectivity 2.0.3. Technical Report.
    http://www.ai.sri.com/~okbc/okbc-2-0-3.pdf
16. Chisholm R (1989) On Metaphysics. University of Minnesota Press, Minneapolis
17. Corcho O, Fernández-López M, Gómez-Pérez A, Vicente O (2002) WebODE: an Integrated Workbench for Ontology Representation, Reasoning and Exchange. In: Gómez-Pérez A, Benjamins VR (eds) 13th International Conference on Knowledge Engineering and Knowledge Management (EKAW'02). Sigüenza, Spain. (Lecture Notes in Artificial Intelligence LNAI 2473) Springer-Verlag, Berlin, Germany, pp. 138–153
18. Corcho O, Gómez-Pérez A (2002) Ontology Translation Approaches for Interoperability: A Case Study with Protégé-2000 and WebODE. In: Motta E, Shadbolt N, Stutt A, Gibbins N (eds) 14th International Conference on Knowledge Engineering and Knowledge Management (EKAW'02). (Lecture Notes in Artificial Intelligence LNAI 3257) Springer-Verlag, Berlin, Germany, pp. 30–46
19. Daelemans W, Reinberger ML (2004) Shallow Text Understanding for Ontology Content Evaluation. IEEE Intelligent Systems 19(4):76–78
20. Dean M, Schreiber G (2004) OWL Web Ontology Language Reference. W3C Recommendation.
    http://www.w3.org/TR/owl-ref/
21. Decker S, Erdmann M, Fensel D, Studer R (1999) Ontobroker: Ontology Based Access to Distributed and Semi-Structured Information. In: Meersman R, Tari Z, Stevens S (eds) Semantic Issues in Multimedia Systems (DS-8), Rotorua, New Zealand. Kluwer Academic Publishers, Boston, Massachusetts. pp. 351–369
22. Declerck T, Uszkoreit H (2003) State of the art on multilinguality for ontologies, annotation services and user interfaces. Esperonto deliverable D1.5.
    http://www.esperonto.net
23. Doan A, Madhavan J, Domingos P, Halevy A (2002) Learning to Map between Ontologies on the Semantic Web. In: Lassner D (ed) Proceedings of the 11th International World Wide Web Conference (WWW 2002), Honolulu, Hawaii.
    http://www2002.org/refereedtrack.html
24. Domingue J (1998) Tadzebao and WebOnto: Discussing, Browsing, and Editing Ontologies on the Web. In: Gaines BR, Musen MA (eds) 11th International Workshop on Knowledge Acquisition, Modeling and Management (KAW'98). Banff, Canada, KM4:1–20
25. Ehring M, Staab S (2004) QOM – Quick Ontology Mapping. In: McIlraith SA, Plexousakis D (eds) 3rd International Semantic Web Conference

(ISWC'04), Hiroshima, Japan. (Lecture Notes in Computer Science LNCS 3298) Springer-Verlag, Berlin, Germany, pp. 683–697

26. Euzenat J (2004) An API for Ontology Alignment. In: McIlraith SA, Plexousakis D (eds) 3rd International Semantic Web Conference (ISWC'04), Hiroshima, Japan. (Lecture Notes in Computer Science LNCS 3298) Springer-Verlag, Berlin, Germany, pp. 698–712

27. Farquhar A, Fikes R, Rice J (1997) The Ontolingua Server: A Tool for Collaborative Ontology Construction. International Journal of Human Computer Studies 46(6):707–727

28. Fensel D (1995) The Knowledge Acquisition and Representation Language KARL. Kluwer Academic Publishers, Boston, Massachusetts

29. Fernández-López M, Gómez-Pérez A (2002a) Overview and analysis of methodologies for building ontologies. The Knowledge Engineering Review 17(2):129–156

30. Fernández-López M, Gómez-Pérez A (2002b) The integration of OntoClean in WebODE. In: Angele J, Sure Y (eds) EKAW'02 Workshop on Evaluation of Ontology-based Tools (EON2002), Sigüenza, Spain. CEUR Workshop Proceedings 62:38–52. Amsterdam, The Netherlands.
http://CEUR-WS.org/Vol-62/

31. Fernández-López M, Gómez-Pérez A, Juristo N (1997) METHONTOLOGY: From Ontological Art Towards Ontological Engineering. Spring Symposium on Ontological Engineering of AAAI. Stanford University, California, pp. 33–40

32. Fernández-López M, Gómez-Pérez A, Pazos A, Pazos J (1999) Building a Chemical Ontology Using Methontology and the Ontology Design Environment. IEEE Intelligent Systems 4(1):37–46

33. Gangemi A, Pisanelli DM, Steve G (1999) An Overview of the ONIONS Project: Applying Ontologies to the Integration of Medical Terminologies. Data & Knowledge Engineering 31(2):183–220

34. Genesereth MR, Fikes RE (1992) Knowledge Interchange Format. Version 3.0. Reference Manual. Technical Report Logic-92-1. Computer Science Department, Stanford University, California.
http://meta2.stanford.edu/kif/Hypertext/kif-manual.html

35. Gómez-Pérez A (1994) Some Ideas and Examples to Evaluate Ontologies. Knowledge Systems Laboratory, Stanford University, California.
http://www-ksl.stanford.edu/KSL_Abstracts/KSL-94-65.html

36. Gómez-Pérez A (2001) Evaluation of Ontologies. International Journal of Intelligent Systems 16(3):391–409

37. Gómez-Pérez A (2002) A Survey on Ontology Tools, OntoWeb deliverable D1.3.
http://ontoweb.aifb.uni-karlsruhe.de/About/Deliverables/D13_v1-0.zip

38. Gómez Pérez A (2004) Evaluating ontology evaluation. IEEE Intelligent Systems 19(4):74–76

39. Gómez-Pérez A, Fernández-López M, Corcho O (2003) Ontological Engineering. Springer–Verlag, London, United Kingdom

40. Gómez-Pérez A, Fernández-López M, de Vicente A (1996) Towards a method to conceptualize domain ontologies. In: van der Vet P (ed) ECAI'96 Workshop on Ontological Engineering. Budapest, Hungary, pp. 41–52
41. Gómez-Pérez A, Manzano D (2003) A survey of ontology learning methods and techniques. OntoWeb deliverable D.1.5.
     http://www.ontoweb.org
42. Gómez-Pérez A, Rojas MD (1999) Ontological Reengineering and Reuse. In: Fensel D, Studer R (eds) 11th European Workshop on Knowledge Acquisition, Modeling and Management (EKAW'99). Dagstuhl Castle, Germany. (Lecture Notes in Artificial Intelligence LNAI 1621) Springer-Verlag, Berlin, Germany, pp. 139–156
43. Gruber TR (1992) Ontolingua: A Mechanism to Support Portable Ontologies. Technical report KSL-91-66, Knowledge Systems Laboratory, Stanford University, Stanford, California.
     ftp://ftp.ksl.stanford.edu/pub/KSL_Reports/KSL-91-66.ps
44. Gruber TR (1993a) A translation approach to portable ontology specification. Knowledge Acquisition 5(2):199–220
45. Gruber TR (1993b) Toward principles for the design of ontologies used for knowledge sharing. In: Guarino N, Poli R (eds) International Workshop on Formal Ontology in Conceptual Analysis and Knowledge Representation. Padova, Italy. (Formal Ontology in Conceptual Analysis and Knowledge Representation) Kluwer Academic Publishers, Deventer, The Netherlands.
     http://citeseer.nj.nec.com/gruber93toward.html
46. Grüninger M, Fox MS (1995) Methodology for the design and evaluation of ontologies. In: Skuce D (ed) IJCAI95 Workshop on Basic Ontological Issues in Knowledge Sharing, pp. 6.1–6.10
47. Guarino N (1998) Formal Ontology in Information Systems. In: Guarino N (ed) 1st International Conference on Formal Ontology in Information Systems (FOIS'98). Trento, Italy. IOS Press, Amsterdam, The Nederlands, pp. 3–15
48. Guarino N (2004) Toward Formal Evaluation of Ontology Quality. IEEE Intelligence Systems 19(4):78–79
49. Guarino N, Masolo C, Vetere G (1999) OntoSeek: Content-Based Access to the Web. IEEE Intelligent Systems 14(3):70–80
50. Guarino N, Welty C (2002) Evaluating Ontological Decisions with OntoClean. Communications of the ACM 45(2):61–65
51. Guo Y, Pan Z, Heflin J (2004) An Evaluation of Knowledge Base Systems for Large OWL Datasets. In: McIlraith SA, Plexousakis D (eds) 3rd International Semantic Web Conference (ISWC'04), Hiroshima, Japan. (Lecture Notes in Computer Science LNCS 3298) Springer-Verlag, Berlin, Germany, pp. 274–288
52. Hermenegildo M, Bueno F, Cabeza D, Carro M, García M, López P, Puebla G (2000) The Ciao Logic Programming Environment. In: Lloyd JW, Dahl V, Furbach U, Kerber M, Lau K, Palamidessi C, Pereira LM, Sagiv Y, Stuckey PJ (eds) International Conference on Computational Logic (CL'00).

London, United Kingdom. (Lecture Notes in Computer Science LNCS 1861), Springer-Verlag, Berlin, Germany

53. de Hoog R (1998) Methodologies for Building Knowledge Based Systems: Achievements and Prospects. In: Liebowitz J (ed) Handbook of Expert Systems. CRC Press, Boca Raton, Florida, Chapter 1.

54. Horrocks I, Fensel D, Harmelen F, Decker S, Erdmann M, Klein M (2000) OIL in a Nutshell. In: Dieng R, Corby O (eds.) 12th International Conference on Knowledge Engineering and Knowledge Management (EKAW'00). Juan-Les-Pins, France. (Lecture Notes in Artificial Intelligence LNAI 1937) Springer-Verlag, Berlin, Germany, pp. 1–16

55. Horrocks I, van Harmelen F (eds) (2001) Reference Description of the DAML+OIL (March 2001) Ontology Markup Language. Technical Report. http://www.daml.org/2001/03/reference.html

56. Hustadt U, Motik B, Sattler U (2004) Reducing SHIQ Description Logic to Disjunctive Datalog Programs. In: Williams MA (ed) 9th International Conference on the Principles of Knowledge Representation and Reasoning (KRR'04). Whistler, Canada, pp. 152–162

57. IEEE (1996) IEEE Standard for Developing Software Life Cycle Processes. IEEE Computer Society, New York. IEEE Std 1074-1995

58. Joachims T (1998) A probabilistic analysis of the Rocchio Algorithm with TFIDF for text categorization. In: Fisher DH (ed) 14th International Conference on Machine Learning (ICML'97). Nashville, Tennessee. Morgan Kaufmann Publishers, San Francisco, California, pp. 143–151

59. Johansson I (1989) Ontological Investigations. Routledge, New York

60. Kalfoglou Y, Robertson D (1999a) Use of Formal Ontologies to Support Error Checking in Specifications. In: Fensel D, Studer R (eds) 11th European Workshop on Knowledge Acquisition, Modelling and Management (EKAW'99), Dagsthul, Germany. (Lecture Notes in Artificial Intelligence LNAI 1621) Springer-Verlag, Berlin, Germany, pp. 207–224

61. Kalfoglou Y, Robertson D (1999b) Managing Ontological Constraints. In: Benjamins VR, Chandrasekaran A, Gómez-Pérez A, Guarino N, Uschold M (eds) IJCAI99 Workshop on Ontologies and Problem-Solving Methods (KRR-5), Stockholm, Sweden. CEUR Workshop Proceedings 18:5.1–5.13. Amsterdam, The Netherlands. http://CEUR-WS.org/Vol-18/

62. Kalyanpur A, Parsia B, Hendler J (2005) A Tool for Working with Web Ontologies. International Journal of Semantic Web and Information Systems 1(1):36–49

63. Karp PD, Chaudhri V, Thomere J (1999) XOL: An XML-Based Ontology Exchange Language. Version 0.3. Technical Report. http://www.ai.sri.com/~pkarp/xol/xol.html

64. Khan L, Luo F (2002) Ontology Construction for Information Selection. In: Ramamoorthy CV (ed.) 14th IEEE International Conference on Tools with Artificial Intelligence. Washington DC, pp. 122-127

65. Kietz JU, Maedche A, Volz R (2000) A Method for Semi-Automatic Ontology Acquisition from a Corporate Intranet. In: Aussenac-Gilles N, Biébow B, Szulman S (eds) EKAW'00 Workshop on Ontologies and Texts. Juan-Les-Pins, France. CEUR Workshop Proceedings 51:4.1–4.14. Amsterdam, The Netherlands.
http://CEUR-WS.org/Vol-51/

66. Kifer M, Lausen G, Wu J (1995) Logical Foundations of Object-Oriented and Frame-Based Languages. Journal of the ACM 42(4): 741–843

67. Klein M, Fensel D (2001) Ontology versioning on the Semantic Web. In: Cruz IF, Decker S, Euzenat J, McGuinness DL (eds) First International Semantic Web Workshop (SWWS'01). Stanford, California

68. Klein M, Fensel D, Kiryakov A, Ognyanov D (2002) Ontology versioning and change detection on the Web. In: Gómez-Pérez A, Benjamins VR (eds) 13th International Conference on Knowledge Engineering and Knowledge Management (EKAW'02). Sigüenza, Spain. (Lecture Notes in Artificial Intelligence LNAI 2473) Springer-Verlag, Berlin, Germany, pp. 197–212

69. Knublauch H, Fergerson R, Noy NF, Musen MA (2004) The Protege OWL Plugin: An Open Development Environment for Semantic Web Applications. In: McIlraith SA, Plexousakis D (eds) 3rd International Semantic Web Conference (ISWC'04), Hiroshima, Japan. (Lecture Notes in Computer Science LNCS 3298) Springer-Verlag, Berlin, Germany, pp. 229–243

70. Lassila O, Swick R (1999) Resource Description Framework (RDF) Model and Syntax Specification. W3C Recommendation.
http://www.w3.org/TR/REC-rdf-syntax/

71. Léger A, Arbant G, Barrett P, Gitton S, Gómez-Pérez A, Holm R, Lehtola A, Mougenot I, Nistal A, Varvarigou T, Vinesse J (2000) MKBEEM: Ontology domain modeling support for multilingual services in e-Commerce. In: Benjamins VR, Gómez-Pérez A, Guarino N, Uschold M (eds) ECAI'00 Workshop on Applications of Ontologies and PSMs. Berlin, Germany, pp. 19.1–19.4

72. Lenat DB, Guha RV (1990) Building Large Knowledge-based Systems: Representation and Inference in the Cyc Project. Addison-Wesley, Boston, Massachusetts

73. Ludäscher B, Yang G, Kifer M (2000) FLORA: The Secret of Object-Oriented Logic Programming.
http://www.cs.sunysb.edu/~sbprolog/flora/docs/manual.ps

74. Luke S, Heflin JD (2000) SHOE 1.01. Proposed Specification. Technical Report. Parallel Understanding Systems Group, Department of Computer Science, University of Maryland.
http://www.cs.umd.edu/projects/plus/SHOE/spec1.01.htm

75. MacGregor R (1991) Inside the LOOM classifier. SIGART Bulletin 2(3):70–76

76. Madhavan J, Bernstein PA, Rahm E (2001) Generis schema matching with Cupid. In: Apers PMG, Atzeni P, Ceri S, Paraboschi S, Ramamohanarao K, Snodgrass RT (eds) 27th International Conference on Very Large Data

Bases. Rome, Italy Morgan Kaufmann Publishers, San Francisco, California, pp. 49–58

77. Maedche A, Motik B, Stojanovic L, Studer R, Volz R (2003) Ontologies for Enterprise Knowledge Management. IEEE Intelligent Systems 18(2):26–33

78. Maedche A, Staab S (2000) Semi-automatic Engineering of Ontologies from Text. In Chang SK, Obozinski WR (eds) 12th International Conference on Software Engineering and Knowledge Engineering (SEKE'2000). Chicago, Illinois

79. McGuinness D, Fikes R, Rice J, Wilder S (2000) The Chimaera Ontology Environment. In: Rosenbloom P, Kautz HA, Porter B, Dechter R, Sutton R, Mittal V (eds) 17th National Conference on Artificial Intelligence (AAAI'00). Austin, Texas, pp. 1123–1124

80. Melnik S, García-Molina H, Rahm E (2002) Similarity Flooding: A Versatile Graph Matching Algorithm and its Application to Schema Matching. In: Georgakopoulos D (ed) 18th International Conference on Data Engineering ICDE'2002. San José, California, pp. 117–128

81. Mena E, Kashyap V, Sheth AP, Illarramendi A (1996) OBSERVER: An Approach for Query Processing in Global Information Systems based on Interoperation across Pre-existing Ontologies. In: Litwin W (ed) First IFCIS International Conference on Cooperative Information Systems (CoopIS'96). Brussels, Belgium, pp. 14–25

82. Mikheev A, Finch A (1997) A Workbench for Finding Structure in Texts. In: Grishman R (ed) 5th Applied Natural Language Processing Conference (ANLP'97). Washington, DC

83. Miller GA (1995) WordNet: a lexical database for English. Communications of the ACM 38(11):39–41

84. Mitra P, Wiederhold G, Kersten (2000) A graph-oriented model for articulation of ontology interdependencies. In: Lockemann PC (ed) 7th International Conference on Extending Database Technology, EDBT 2000. Lecture Notes in Computer Science 1777, Springer-Verlag, Berlin, Germany, pp. 86–100

85. Morin E (1998) Prométhée un outil d'aide a l'acquisition de relations semantiques entre temes. In: Zweigenbaum P (ed) 5ème National Conference on Traitement Automatique des Langues Naturelles (TALN'98). Paris, France, pp. 172–181

86. Morin E (1999) Acquisition de patrons lexico-syntaxiques caractéristiques dúne relation sémantique. TAL (Traitement Automatique des Langues) 40(1):143–166

87. Motta E (1999) Reusable Components for Knowledge Modelling: Principles and Case Studies in Parametric Design. IOS Press, Amsterdam, The Netherlands

88. Neches R, Fikes RE, Finin T, Gruber TR, Senator T, Swartout WR (1991) Enabling technology for knowledge sharing. AI Magazine 12(3):36–56

89. Newell A (1982) The Knowledge Level. Artificial Intelligence 18(1):87–127

90. Noy NF (2004) Evaluation by Ontology Consumers. IEEE Intelligent Systems 19(4):80–81

91. Noy NF, Fergerson RW, Musen MA (2000) The knowledge model of Protege-2000: Combining interoperability and flexibility. In: Dieng R, Corby O (eds) 12th International Conference on Knowledge Engineering and Knowledge Management (EKAW'00). Juan-Les-Pins, France. (Lecture Notes in Artificial Intelligence LNAI 1937) Springer-Verlag, Berlin, Germany, pp. 17–32

92. Noy NF, Klein M (2002) Ontology Evolution: Not the Same as Schema Evolution. Technical Report SMI-2002-0926, Stanford, California. http://smi-web.stanford.edu/pubs/SMI_Abstracts/SMI-2002-0926.html

93. Noy NF, Kunnatur S, Klein M, Musen MA (2004) Tracking Changes During Ontology Evolution. In: McIlraith SA, Plexousakis D (eds) 3rd International Semantic Web Conference (ISWC'04), Hiroshima, Japan. (Lecture Notes in Computer Science LNCS 3298) Springer-Verlag, Berlin, Germany, pp. 259–273

94. Noy NF, Musen MA (2000) PROMPT: Algorithm and Tool for Automated Ontology Merging and Alignment. In: Rosenbloom P, Kautz HA, Porter B, Dechter R, Sutton R, Mittal V (eds) 17th National Conference on Artificial Intelligence (AAAI'00). Austin, Texas, pp. 450–455

95. Noy NF, Musen MA (2001) Anchor-PROMPT: Using Non-Local Context for Semantic Matching. In: Gómez-Pérez A, Grüninger M, Stuckenschmidt H, Uschold M (eds) IJCAI'01 Workshop on Ontologies and Information Sharing. Seattle, Washington, pp. 63–70

96. Noy NF, Musen MA (2004a) Specifying Ontology Views by Traversal. In: McIlraith SA, Plexousakis D (eds) 3rd International Semantic Web Conference (ISWC'04), Hiroshima, Japan. (Lecture Notes in Computer Science LNCS 3298) Springer-Verlag, Berlin, Germany, pp. 713–725

97. Noy NF, Musen MA (2004b) Ontology versioning in an ontology-management framework. IEEE Intelligent Systems 19(4):6–13

98. Pan R, Ding Z, Yu Y, Peng Y (2005) A Bayesian Network Approach to Ontology Mapping. In: 4th International Semantic Web Conference (ISWC'05). Galway, Ireland. (Lecture Notes in Computer Science LNCS 3729) Springer-Verlag, Berlin, Germany, pp. 563–577

99. Raggett D, Le Hors A, Jacobs I (1999) HTML 4.01 Specification. W3C Recommendation. http://www.w3.org/TR/html401/

100. Schreiber ATh, Wielinga BJ, Jansweijer W (1995) The KACTUS View on the 'O' World. In: Skuce D (ed) IJCAI95 Workshop on Basic Ontological Issues in Knowledge Sharing, pp. 15.1–15.10

101. Shvaiko P, Giunchiglia F, Yatskevich M (2004) S-Match: an Algorithm and an Implementation of Semantic Matching. In: Fensel D, Studer R (eds) 1st European Semantic Web Symposium (ESWS'04). Heraklion, Greece. (Lecture Notes in Computer Science LNCS 3053) Springer-Verlag, Berlin, Germany, pp. 61–75

102. Staab S, Schnurr HP, Studer R, Sure Y (2001) Knowledge Processes and Ontologies. IEEE Intelligent Systems 16(1):26–34

103. Steve G, Gangemi A, Pisanelli DM (1998) Integrating Medical Terminologies with ONIONS Methodology. In: Kangassalo H, Charrel JP (eds) Information Modeling and Knowledge Bases VIII. IOS Press, Amsterdam, The Netherlands.
     http://ontology.ip.rm.cnr.it/Papers/onions97.pdf
104. Stojanovic L (2004) Methods and Tools for Ontology Evolution. PhD Thesis, FZI, Karlsrhue, Germany
105. Stuckenschmidt H (2000) Using OIL for Intelligent Information Integration. In: Benjamins VR, Gómez-Pérez A, Guarino N (eds) ECAI'00 Workshop on Applications of Ontologies and Problem Solving Methods. Berlin, Germany, pp. 9.1–9.10
106. Studer R, Benjamins VR, Fensel D (1998) Knowledge Engineering: Principles and Methods. IEEE Transactions on Knowledge and Data Engineering 25(1–2):161–197
107. Stumme G, Maedche A (2001) FCA-MERGE: Bottom-Up Merging of Ontologies. In: Bernhard Nebel (ed) Proceedings of the Seventeenth International Joint Conference on Artificial Intelligence (IJCAI 2001). Seattle, Washington. Morgan Kaufmann Publishers, San Francisco, California, pp. 225–234
108. Sure Y, Erdmann M, Angele J, Staab S, Studer R, Wenke D (2002) OntoEdit: Collaborative Ontology Engineering for the Semantic Web. In: Horrocks I, Hendler JA (eds) First International Semantic Web Conference (ISWC'02). Sardinia, Italy. (Lecture Notes in Computer Science LNCS 2342) Springer-Verlag, Berlin, Germany, pp. 221–235
109. Swartout B, Ramesh P, Knight K, Russ T (1997) Toward Distributed Use of Large-Scale Ontologies. In: Farquhar A, Gruninger M, Gómez-Pérez A, Uschold M, van der Vet P (eds) AAAI'97 Spring Symposium on Ontological Engineering. Stanford University, California, pp. 138–148
110. Thomasson AL (2004) Methods of Categorization. Invited Talk. In: Varzi AC, Vieu L (eds) Proceedings of 3rd Formal Ontoloy in Information Systems, Turin, Italy, pp. 3–16
111. Uschold M (1996) Building Ontologies: Towards A Unified Methodology. In: Watson I (ed) 16th Annual Conference of the British Computer Society Specialist Group on Expert Systems. Cambridge, United Kingdom.
     http://citeseer.nj.nec.com/uschold96building.html
112. Uschold M, Grüninger M (1996) Ontologies: Principles, Methods and Applications. Knowledge Engineering Review 11(2):93–155
113. Uschold M, King M (1995) Towards a Methodology for Building Ontologies. In: Skuce D (eds) IJCAI'95 Workshop on Basic Ontological Issues in Knowledge Sharing. Montreal, Canada, pp. 6.1–6.10
114. Welty C, Guarino N (2001) Supporting Ontological Analysis of Taxonomic Relationships. Data and Knowledge Engineering 39(1):51–74
115. Wu SH, Hsu WL (2002) SOAT: A Semi-Automatic Domain Ontology Acquisition Tool from Chinese Corpus. In: Lenders W (ed) 19th International Conference on Computational Linguistics (COLING'02), Taipei, Taiwan

2. Using Ontologies in Software Engineering and Technology

Francisco Ruiz

ALARCOS Research Group. Dept. of Information Technologies and Systems, Escuela Superior de Informática, University of Castilla-La Mancha, Spain,
francisco.ruizg@uclm.es

José R. Hilera

Computer Science Department, University of Alcalá, Spain, jose.hilera@uah.es

2.1 Introduction

In this chapter, the state of the art on the use of ontologies in software engineering and technology (SET) is presented. The chapter is organized into four parts. In the second and third sections, serving as a supplement to Chap. 1,[29] a wide review of the distinct kinds of ontologies and their proposed uses is presented respectively. In the fourth section, we offer a taxonomy for classifying ontologies in SET, in which two main categories are distinguished: (1) SET domain ontologies, created to represent and communicate agreed knowledge within some subdomain of SET, and (2) ontologies as software artifacts, with proposals in which ontologies play the role of an additional type of artifact in software processes. On the one hand, the former category is subdivided into those ontologies included in software engineering and those referring to other software technologies.

---

[29] Readers can find a more detailed study on the ontology notion in the books "Ontological Engineering" by Gómez-Pérez et al. [38] and "Ontologies: A Silver Bullet for Knowledge Management and Electronic Commerce" by Fensel [30].

On the other hand, the latter category is subdivided into development time and run time proposals according to the moment when ontologies are used. Then, in the last section, we analyze and classify (based on our taxonomy) a large number of recently published works. We also comment on and classify works which will be presented in later chapters of this book.

2.2 Kinds of Ontologies

Although the term "ontology" was introduced in the eighteenth century to refer to the general science of being ("onto" in ancient Greek), Ontology as a discipline has been practiced by philosophers since the dawn of history (previously a part of metaphysics). Etymologists may define ontology as the knowledge of beings, that is, all that relates to being. Just as we call those who study "students", we use the term "entity" to describe all things which "are". From this point of view, stones, animals or people are "entities". Mathematical objects, even those that are merely imagined, are also considered beings (be they fictitious or unreal).

All sciences and knowledges refer to or examine a type of entity: some are physical, as in the physical sciences, others abstract or mental, as in mathematics and the vast majority of the computational sciences, and still others living, as in biology.

In the scope of the computational sciences and technologies (computer science, software engineering, information systems, etc.), ontology has boomed as a field of research and application since the latter part of the twentieth century. Perhaps the principal cause of this boom has been the key role that it plays in the new generation of the advanced Web (Semantic Web).

Focusing exclusively on the scope of this publication, that is, SET, the first known proposals were presented by Gruber [40, 41], whereby ontologies are "an explicit specification of a conceptualization". Conceptualization is understood to be an abstract and simplified version of the world to be represented: a representation of knowledge based on objects, concepts and entities existing within the studied area, as well as the relationships existing among them. By "explicit" we mean that the concepts used and the restrictions applied to them are clearly defined. Later authors have considered it important to add to this definition two new requirements: that the said specification be (1) formalized and (2) shared. By "formalized" it is meant that a machine can process it. By "shared" it is understood that the knowledge acquired is the consensus of a community of experts [38]. In regards to this last requirement, common ontologies are used to describe ontological commitments for a set of agents (people or artificial systems) so that they can communicate and interact with a domain of discourse. Additionally, an agent commits to an ontology if its observable actions are consistent with the definitions of the ontology. This idea of ontological commitments was proposed by Newell [68] from a knowledge-level point of view.

Some SET researchers view ontologies as "a vocabulary" for a specific domain representing conceptual elements and the relationships existing between them. However, the ontology is not the vocabulary itself, but what the vocabulary represents, since the translation of this vocabulary into another language will not change the ontology [16].

Other researchers defend the need for ontologies to be viewed as a "theory", that is, a formal vocabulary with a set of defining axioms. These axioms express new relationships between concepts and limit the possible interpretations [75, 98]. However, many experts have concluded that ontologies of the software systems application domain, or of its design and construction processes, are of great assistance in avoiding problems and errors at all stages of the software product life cycle: from the initial requirements analysis (facilitating the analyst–client interaction), through the development and construction phase, and finaly with the maintenance stage (assuring greater understanding of the modification requests, better understanding of the maintained system, etc.).

Additionally, numerous authors have viewed ontologies from distinct vantage points. Therefore it is not surprising that in the literature we find diverse classifications of ontologies with different focuses.

According to the generality level, Guarino considers that the following ontology types exist [43]:

- *High–level ontologies*: Describe general concepts such as space, time, material, object. They are independent of a specific domain or problem. Their purpose is to unify criteria between large communities of users.
- *Domain ontologies*: Describe the vocabulary related to a generic domain (for example, information systems or medicine), by means of the specialization of the introduced concepts of high–level ontologies.
- *Task ontologies*: Describe the vocabulary related to a generic task or activity (for example, development or sales), by means of specialization of the introduced concepts of high–level ontologies.
- *Application ontologies*: Describe concepts belonging simultaneously to a domain and a task, by means of specialization of the concepts of domain ontologies and task ontologies. They generally correspond to roles played by the domain entities when executing an activity.

On the other hand, Fensel [30] established the following alternative classification:

- *Generic or common-sense ontologies*: Capture general knowledge of
  the world. They provide basic notions and concepts for space, time,
  state, events, etc, and are valid for a variety of domains.
- *Representational ontologies*: Do not belong to any particular domain.
  They offer entities without establishing what they might represent.
  Therefore, they define concepts which express knowledge in an object-
  or framework- oriented approach.
- *Domain ontologies*: Capture the knowledge valid for a particular type of
  domain (for example, electronics, medicine, etc.).
- *Method and task ontologies*: The former offer terminology specific to
  problem resolution methods, while the latter provide terms for specific
  tasks. Both offer a reasonable point of view as to the knowledge of the
  domain.

In our opinion, the two previous authors' classifications may be aligned
according to the following model as shown in Fig. 2.1.

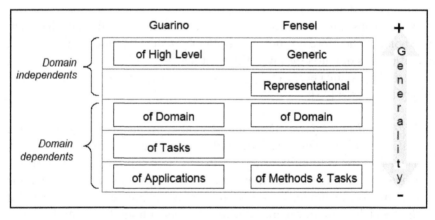

Fig. 2.1. Kinds of ontologies according to the generality level

In accordance with the <u>type of conceptualization structure</u>, Van Heijst and
colleagues established the following kinds [94]:

- *Terminological ontologies*: Specify terms to be used to represent the
  knowledge of a studied domain. Then try to obtain a unified language

related to a specified field. An example of this type would be the ULMS (Universal Medical Language System).

- *Information ontologies*: Specify the structure of database records, determining a framework for the standardized storage of information. An example is the framework for modeling medical patient clinic records.
- *Knowledge representation ontologies*: Specify knowledge conceptualizations with an internal structure that exceeds those of the previous ones. They tend to be focused on a description of a particular knowledge use.

Another possible way of classifying ontologies is according to the nature of the real-world issue that is to be modeled. In this manner, Jurisica et al. have identified the following classes [55]:

- *Static ontologies*: Describe things that exist, their attributes and the relationships existing between them. This classification assumes that the world is made up of entities which are gifted with a unique and unchangeable identity. In these, we use terms such as entity, attribute, or relationship.
- *Dynamic ontologies*: Describe the aspects of the modeled world which can change with time. To model these it may be necessary to use finite state machines, Petri nets, etc. Process, state, or state transition are examples of terminology commonly included in this category.
- *Intentional ontologies*: Describe the aspects of the world of motivations, intentions, goals, beliefs, alternatives and elections of the involved agents. Some typical terms in these types of ontologies are aspect, object, agent, or support.
- *Social ontologies*: Describe social aspects such as organizational structures, nets or interdependences. For this reason they include terms such as actor, position, role, authority, responsibility or commitment.

Some authors believe that this linear way of classifying ontologies based on only a sole criterion does not allow for adequate reflection of the problem's complexity. Along these lines, Gómez-Pérez et al. [38] suggest a bi-dimensional classification, taking into account two criteria: the richness of the internal structure, and the subject of the conceptualization. The former criterion is based on a proposal of Lassila and McGuinness [59]. The latter proposes an extension of the Van Heijst et al. [94] classification previously described.

In this bi-dimensional proposal, every ontology belongs to one of the following categories, based on the level of <u>richness of its internal structure</u>:

- *Controlled vocabularies*: Formed by a finite list of terms.
- *Glossaries*: Lists of terms with their definitions offered in natural language.
- *Thesauruses*: Differentiated from the previous categories in that they offer semantic additions to the terms, including synonyms.
- *Informal hierarchies*: Hierarchies of terms which do not correspond to a strict subclass. For example, the terms "rental vehicle" and "hotel" could be modeled informally under the hierarchy "travel" as they are considered key parts of traveling.
- *Formal hierarchies*: In this case, a strict "is-a" relationship exists between instances of a class and of its corresponding superclass. For example, a teacher "is-a" people. Its objective is to exploit the inheritance concept.
- *Frames*: Ontologies which include such classes as properties, which can be inherited by other classes in lower levels of a formal "is-a" taxonomy.
- *Ontologies with value constraints*: Include value constraints. The most typical case is that of constraints dependent on the data type of a property (for example, a day of the month must be lower than 32).
- *Ontologies with generic logical constraints*: These are the most expressive ontologies which permit specific constraints between the terms of the ontology using first-order logic.

Simultaneously, depending on the <u>subject of the conceptualization</u>, an ontology falls into one of the following types:

- *Knowledge representation ontologies*: Capture representation primitives used to formalize knowledge under a concrete paradigm of knowledge representation.
- *Common or generic ontologies*: Represent common-sense knowledge reusable in distinct domains, for example, vocabulary related to things, events, time, space, etc.
- *High-level ontologies*: Describe very general concepts and notions by which they can be related to root terms of all ontologies. An unresolved problem is that many of these high-level ontologies differ in their way of classifying general concepts. This makes it difficult to integrate and exchange ontologies.

- *Domain ontologies*: Reusable ontologies of a particular domain (for example, medicine, engineering, etc.). They offer a vocabulary for concepts related to the domain and its relationships.
- *Task ontologies*: Describe the vocabulary related to some generic activity. They provide a systematic vocabulary of terms used to solve problems that may or may not belong to the same domain.
- *Domain task ontologies*: Unlike the previous ontologies, these are reusable in a given domain, but not among different domains.
- *Method ontologies*: Provide definitions of relevant concepts and their relationships. They are applicable to a reasoning process specifically designed to carry out a particular task.
- *Application ontologies*: Are dependent on the applications. Often, they extend and specialize the vocabulary of one domain ontology or task ontology for a particular application.

In the bibliography of ontologies, the adjectives formal, informal and semi-formal are also used. In this case, the formality of the language used to represent the ontologies is being indicated. This way, the ontologies expressed using natural language are considered to be totally informal, whereas those represented using first-order logic are formal [92]. In an intermediate situation, there is the ontology represented using UML class diagrams, as UML is considered semi-formal. In this case, the level of formality may be raised using OCL to model constraints. In relation to languages and techniques used to represent ontologies, SET experts may be interested in reading "Modeling ontologies with software engineering techniques" and "Modeling ontologies with database techniques", both of which are sections included in the first chapter of the book by Gómez-Pérez et al. [38].

These numerous and varying ways of thinking about ontologies have been clarified by some researchers who have looked for an integral definition which would serve for the different fields of application (knowledge engineering, databases, software engineering, etc.), and so as to be understood by non-experts. In this manner, Uschold and Jasper elaborated the following characterization (not definition) [92]:

> *An ontology may take a variety of forms, but necessarily it will include a vocabulary of terms, and some specification of their meaning. This includes definitions and an indication of how concepts are interrelated which collectively impose a structure on the domain and constrain the possible interpretations of terms.*

With the same goal, Gómez-Pérez et al. [38] conclude that "ontologies aim to capture consensual knowledge in a generic way, and that they may be reused and shared across software applications and by groups of people".

2.2.1 Heavyweight Versus Lightweight Ontologies

In the ontological engineering community it is common to hear of light- and heavyweight ontologies. This distinction is a simplification of the classification based on the level of richness of their internal structure (as previously commented), whereby lightweight ontologies will be principally taxonomies, while heavyweight ontologies are those which model a certain knowledge "in a deeper way and provide more restrictions on domain semantics" [38]. The former include concepts, concept taxonomies, relationships between concepts, and properties that describe these concepts. The latter add axioms and constraints, in order to clarify the meaning of the terms.

In Fig. 2.2 we have represented linearly the continuum from lightweight to heavyweight ontologies. In the upper part of the line, we find the lightweight ontologies which include controlled vocabularies, glossaries, and thesauruses; while at the bottom we find the heavyweight ontologies with value constraints and general logic constraints. In between are the informal hierarchies, formal hierarchies and frames. These intermediates have some of the characteristics of the heavyweight ontologies but not all authors consider them to fall within this general category.

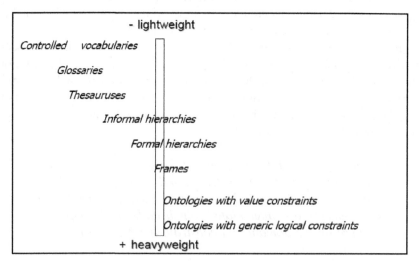

Fig. 2.2. A continuum from lightweight to heavyweight ontologies

This continuum from lightweight to heavyweight can be viewed as the two arms of a balance. The first has the advantage of being simple and the second, of being powerful. It is not possible to possess both advantages at the same time, and there is no way of determining which is better than the other, lightweight or heavyweight. It all depends on one's goals and necessities based on the particular case at hand. For example, the lightweight ontologies are more useful when the objective is, simply, to share knowledge of one domain between people. On the other hand, if it is necessary to execute some sort of logical inference or automatic calculation, it will be necessary to utilize the heavyweight ontologies. In any case, the following advice might serve the SET stakeholders: "use the lightest ontologies possible which can serve the necessities of the project at hand".

2.3 A Review of the Uses in SET

Of the utilities of ontologies in any field of human activity, we recognize the following to be principal:

- *Clarify the knowledge structure:* During the ontological analysis the domain concepts and relationships between them are defined in such a way that the adequate execution of this step eases the clear specification of the nature of the concepts and terms being used, with respect to the body of knowledge that is to be constructed [15].
- *Reduce conceptual and terminological ambiguity*: Ontological analysis provides a framework for the unification between people (and/or agents-systems) with differing necessities and/or points of view, depending on their particular context [91].
- *Allow the sharing of knowledge*: By means of an appropriate ontological analysis, it is possible to achieve a set of conceptualizations of a specific domain, and the set of terms which support it. With an adequate syntax, these conceptualizations and the relationships between them are expressed and codified in an ontology, which can be shared with any agent (person or system) having similar needs for the same domain [59].

Focusing exclusively on the scope of this book, many authors have studied and categorized the possible uses of ontologies in the software engineering and information systems disciplines. In these fields, it is possible to use ontologies of varying levels of generality. For example, the domain-level ontologies are especially useful for the development of reusable, high-quality software, as they provide a unambiguous terminology which can be shared by all the development processes. Furthermore, thanks to ontologies, the eliciting and modeling of the requirements phase can be carried out in two steps [35]: in the first, general knowledge of the domain is elicited and specified in one or more ontologies. In the second step the obtained ontologies are used as inputs to develop the specified applications. The constructed ontology also serves as the basic vocabulary to speak about the domain and is a base for the development of the specific conceptualizations for the applications that are to be constructed.

Next we will summarize the results of some of the best known surveys.

For Pisanelli et al. the most important characteristics that ontologies offer the field of software engineering are [75]:

1) an explicit semantic and taxonomy;
2) a clear link between concepts, their relationships, and generic theories;
3) lack of polysemy within a formal context;
4) context modularization;
5) minimal axiomatization to pinpoint differences between similar concepts;
6) a good politic of name choice; and
7) a rich documentation.

Uschold, Gruninger and Jasper identified the following functions [91, 92]:

Communication: Ontologies allow for the reduction of conceptual and terminological ambiguity, as they provide us with a framework for unification. They allow us to share knowledge and facilitate the communication between people and/or systems as even those having differing necessities and viewpoints, a function of their contexts and particular interests. Furthermore, in any organization, there is implicit knowledge (for example, the normative models and the network of relationships between people) that can be made explicit through ontological means. Ontologies also permit an increased consistency, eliminating ambiguity and integrating distinct user viewpoints. For person-to-person communication, an informal, unambiguous ontology may be sufficient.

Interoperability: When different users or systems need to exchange data or when different software tools are used, the concept of interoperability has some important repercussions. In this sense, the ontologies can act as an "interlingua", that is, they can be used to support the translation between different languages and representations, as it is more efficient to have a translator for each part involved (with an exchange ontology) than to design a translator for each pair of involved parts (languages or representations). A paradigm case would be the use of ontologies in the Semantic Web to look for irrelevant language factors, that is, to obtain the same results when using the term "author" or "autor" (in Spanish).

System/software engineering: The application of ontologies to support the design and development of systems, specifically software, may have the following objectives:

- Specification: The role that ontologies play in specification depends on the level of formality and automization within the methodology of the system design. From an informal perspective, ontologies assist in the requirements identification process and in the understanding of the relationships between components. This is particularly important when there are different sets of designers working in different domains. From a formal perspective, an ontology offers a declarative specification of a system, allowing designers to argue over "why" the system is being designed instead of "how" to support its functionality.
- Confidence: The informal ontologies can improve the confidence of the system by serving as a basis for the manual checking of the design, while the formal ontologies allow for the semi-automized consistency check of a software system with respect to the declarative specification that the ontology presumes.
- Reusability: To increase its usefulness, an ontology should be able to support the import and export of modules (parts of the ontology). By characterizing the domain classes and tasks within these subdomains, the ontologies can provide a framework to determine the aspects of the ontology that can be reused between different domains and tasks. The objective is, therefore, to achieve libraries of ontologies that are reusable and adaptable to different classes of problems and environments.
- Search: An ontology can be used as metadata, serving as an index for a repository of information.
- Reliability: The consistency checking may be (semi-)automatic if a formal representation of knowledge exists.
- Maintenance: One of the main efforts made during the software system's maintenance phase is the studying of the system. For this reason, using ontologies allows an improvement of the documentation and a reduction in maintenance costs. Maintenance effort is also reduced if an ontology is used as a neutral authoring language because

it only has to be maintained in one site instead of in multiple places, one for each target language.
- Knowledge acquisition: In the process of building knowledge-based systems, speed and reliability may be increased when an existing ontology is used as the starting point and guide for the knowledge acquisition.

Several years after its publication, a study was re-performed by Gruninger and Lee. Greatly abbreviating, the results were the following [42]:

- Communication:
- Between computer systems, for example, in the exchange of data between distinct software tools.
- Between humans, for example, for the acquisition of a vocabulary that unifies concepts of a specific domain.
- Between humans and computer systems, for example, an ontology may be deployed in a window so that the user can use it to better and more easily understand the vocabulary used in the application.
- Computational inference:
- For the internal representation and management of plans and planning information.
- For analysis of internal structures, algorithms, system inputs and outputs, in conceptual and theoretic terms.
- Knowledge reuse and organization:
- For the structuring and organization of libraries or repositories of plans, and planning and domain information.

In addition to these previous possible uses of ontologies, Uschold and Jasper [92] have described scenarios for applying ontologies. These scenarios are abstractions of specific applications of ontologies following the same idea of Jacobson's use cases. Each scenario includes an overview with the intended purpose of the ontology, the role of the ontology, the main actors and the supporting technologies. These authors have established four categories which include all of the identified scenarios:

- *Neutral authoring*: An information artifact is authored in a single language and is converted into a different form for use in multiple target systems. Knowledge reuse, improved maintainability and long-term knowledge retention are the main benefits of this scenario.
- *Specification*: An ontology is created and/or used as a basis for specification and possibly also for the development of some software.

Benefits of this scenario include documentation, maintenance, reliability and knowledge reuse.

- *Common access to information*: When information is required by one or more persons or systems, but is expressed using unfamiliar vocabulary or in an inaccessible format, an ontology can help to render the information intelligible by providing a shared understanding of the terms, or by mapping between sets of terms. Interoperability and more effective use and reuse of knowledge resources are the main benefits of this scenario.
- *Search*: An ontology is used for searching an information repository for desired resources (for example, documents, Web pages, names of experts). The chief benefit of this scenario is faster access to needed information resources. The technology of the Semantic Web has this same goal, using the entire Web as a repository. Because of this, ontologies play a key role in this new technology.

Other authors have studied the impact of ontologies on <u>information systems</u> (ISs). For example, Guarino identified two dimensions that should be considered [43]:

- a temporal dimension, concerning whether an ontology is used at development or at run time (that is "for" an information system or "within" an information system), and
- a structural dimension, concerning the particular way an ontology can affect the main IS components.

With respect to the <u>moment in which they are utilized</u>, the use of the ontologies can take place during the development stage or during run time. On the one hand, when the ontology is used by the IS at run time, it is referred to as an "ontology-driven information system" proper. On the other hand, when it is used during development time, it is referred to as an "ontology-driven development of the information system".

By using ontologies *at development time*, two situations might occur: (1) that we have a set of reusable ontologies organized in libraries of domain or task ontologies; or (2) that we have a generic ontology (with less detailed distinctions at a domain level between the basic entities, and meta-level distinctions as for class and relationships types), with a more limited reusability grade. In the first case, the semantic content of the ontologies can be converted into a system component, reducing the cost of analysis and assuring the ontological system correctness (given that the ontology is correct). In the second scenario, which is more realistic, the quantity of ontological knowledge available is more limited, but its quality may assist the designer in the conceptual analysis task.

When using an ontology *at run time*, one must distinguish between an "ontology-aware information system" and an "ontology-driven information system". In the first case, a system component has knowledge of the existence of a potential ontology and may make use of it with a specific proposal, while in the second case, the ontology is an additional component (generally, local to the system) which cooperates at run time in order to achieve the system's goals and functionality. One reason why ontologies are used at run time is to ease the communication between software agents, which communicate by means of messages containing expressions elaborated in accordance with the ontology.

With respect to the structural dimension, the three principal component types analyzed by Guarino for their impact are [43]:

- *Components of database*: To use an ontology at development time for the database component seems to be the most obvious use, because, in practice, an ontology has a great likeness to a database schema. In fact, some authors have created proposals whereby the ontologies play a key role during the phases of analysis and conceptual modeling [94]. The resulting conceptual model can be represented in a format understood by a computer and from there be projected to a concrete platform. During run time, there are various ways in which ontologies and databases can work together. For example, the explicit ontologies' availability as an information resource is basic in the mediation-based focus of information integration.
- *Components of user interface:* In this type, the ontologies have been used successfully in order to generate interfaces based on forms that perform data control by means of type violation constraints. Another example of use, in this case during run time, consists of deploying an ontology in a help window so that the user may use it as part of the system, for example, to understand the given vocabulary.
- *Components of application program:* The application programs tend to have much implicit knowledge about the domain, for example, in the type or class declarations, in regards to business rules or policies, etc. At development time, it is possible to generate the static part of a program with the help of an ontology. Further, ontologies which are integrated with linguistic resources may be used to assist in the development of object-oriented software, as expressed with the databases. At run time, it is possible to represent in explicit form (with an ontology) the knowledge that the program holds implicitly,

converting the program into a knowledge-based system. This could improve the maintenance, the extensibility and the flexibility of the system.

In the following sections of this chapter, we present a state of the art review in which the reader can find the most developed examples of these and other ways to use ontologies in SET.

2.3.1 Ontology Versus Conceptual Model

In the SE and IS communities, perhaps due to the historical importance of conceptual modeling, there is frequent confusion between ontology and conceptual models. In some sense, an ontology has a similar function to a database schema because the first provides meta-information that describes the semantics of the terms or data, but there are several important differences between these concepts [44, 63]:

- Languages for defining and representing ontologies (OWL, etc.) are syntactically and semantically richer than common approaches for databases (SQL, etc.).
- The knowledge that is described by an ontology consists of semi-structured information (that is, texts in natural language) as opposed to the very structured data of the database (tables, classes of objects, etc.).
- An ontology must be a shared and consensual conceptualization because it is used for information sharing and exchange. Identifiers in a database schema are used specifically for a concrete system and do not have the need to make an effort to reach the equivalent of ontological agreements.
- An ontology provides a domain theory and not the structure of a data container.

With didactic intention, Mylopoulos [67] explains with samples that an ontology is not a conceptual schema. This researcher uses the following sample situation. On one hand, there may be a university ontology defining and associating concepts such as student, course, lectures, etc. On the other hand, a conceptual schema, say, for the scholarship IS at the University of the World, may use these concepts but they are specialized in meaning. For example, the student concept may be meant to have as instances only 2005–2006 University of the World students. An ontology is meant to be reusable, whereas a conceptual schema is less so.

Spyns et al. [86] establish that the main difference between the data models and ontologies is that while the former are task specific and implementation oriented, the latter should be as much generic and task independent as possible. In this manner, to the benefits of reusability and reliability mentioned by Ushold and King [93] when ontologies are used in software and system engineering, we can also add shareability, portability and interoperability. These characteristics are identified as the common notion of "genericity".

2.3.2 Ontology Versus Metamodel

There also exists some confusion between ontologies and metamodels, which in our opinion is motivated principally because of the fact that both are frequently represented by the same languages, although their characteristics and goals are different.

Bertrand and Bezivin [7] have analyzed the relationship between low-level ontologies and metamodels, and have arrived at the conclusion that while metamodels look to improve the rigor of similar but different models, an ontology does the same but for knowledge models. Devedzic [24] noted another difference: without an ontology, different knowledge representations of the same domain can be incompatible even when using the same metamodel for their implementation.

The existing confusion is also generated due to the lack of agreement as to the definition of both terms. In the case of ontologies, we have already commented sufficiently on this fact. Similarly, for metamodels there exists no other universal consensus than the mere etymological description that a metamodel is a "model of models".

In our opinion, if one uses the definition of ontology proposed by Gruber [40] and the Object Management Group definition of metamodel, proposed in the "Model-driven Architecture" [71], the clearest distinction between them is that of intention: while an ontology is descriptive and belongs to the domain of the problem, a metamodel is prescriptive and belongs to the domain of the solution.

In Chap. 9 of this book, the reader is provided with a detailed proposal of the different roles played by ontologies and metamodels in the framework of a model-driven engineering paradigm. Also, a new idea, that of the megamodel, is introduced.

2.3.3 Ontologies in Software Engineering Environments

Other application fields for ontologies are the SEE (SEEs), which integrate diverse types of tools in order to assist the engineers in completing the software engineering processes. To begin with, in the SEE, knowledge is embedded in one or various tools or assistants but this makes it virtually impossible to be shared or reused.

The exchange of knowledge between humans is one of the major problems in software engineering projects. It has been shown that this is due in great part to the fact that the project participants have distinct domains of problem knowledge and/or use different languages, both problems which could be mitigated by using ontologies. This is why some authors have proposed the use of ontologies as the backbone of the tools and SEE [22]. For the same reason, there exist proposals of SEE architectures based on ontologies [28].

Two of these proposals will be commented on in the following subsections.

2.3.3.1 MANTIS Environment

An MANTIS is "eXtended Software Engineering Environment" for the management of software maintenance projects. By using the nomenclature "extended SEE" the intention is to emphasize the idea of integrating and widen the concepts of methodology and SEE [79]. All the MANTIS components are considered as tools of three different categories: conceptual, methodological and technical (CASE tools). A summary of the components that make up the MANTIS environment is shown in Fig. 2.3.

Conceptual tools are used in MANTIS to represent and to manage the inherent complexity of software maintenance projects. A level-based conceptual architecture is necessary to be able to work with different abstract levels. A software life cycle process framework is useful for knowing which are the other software processes related to the maintenance process. To make sure that all the concepts are correctly defined, used and represented, a set of ontologies was defined. The Maintenance Ontology represents the static aspects. They describe the concepts related to maintenance and consist of a subontology for products, another for activities, a third for processes and the fourth for describing the different agents involved in the maintenance process [79]. The intentional and social aspects are considered within the same subontology, Agents, since they are closely related. The dynamic part is represented by an ontology called Workflow Ontology, where three relevant aspects of the maintenance process are defined: decomposition of activities, temporal constraints between activities, and control of the execution of activities and projects during the process enactment. A third ontology called a Measure Ontology represents both static and dynamic aspects related to the software measurement. This ontology was included because of the importance of measurement within the software process.

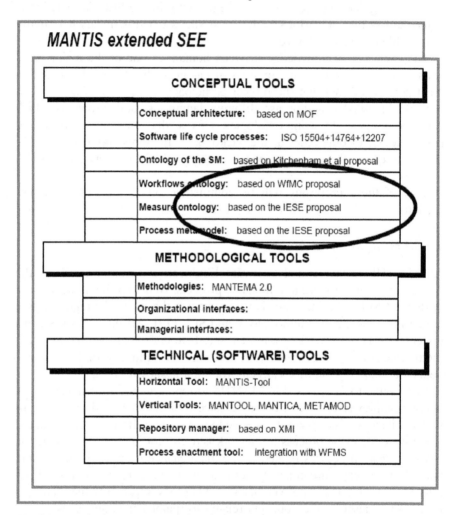

Fig. 2.3. Ontologies as conceptual tools in the MANTIS environment

The uses of the ontologies proposed in the MANTIS environment are two of the three identified by Gruninger and Lee [42]: communication (especially between humans participating in maintenance projects, and between humans and the software system of the MANTIS environment), and knowledge reuse and organization. On the other hand, the computational inference has not been included in this SEE. The importance of ontologies' use as a support for maintenance activities (particularly for the sharing and reuse of knowledge about the product and its characteristics) has been recognized by other authors as well [21].

In MANTIS the ontologies have been represented using an adaptation of the REFSENO method (see later section).

2.3.3.2 TABA Workstation

TABA Workstation is a meta-SEE, capable of generating, by means of instancing, specific SEEs adequate for the particularities of a software process, of an application domain or of a specific project [28]. Given that the meta-Environment, the created SEE instance and the tools in the TABA Workstation need to handle knowledge of the software development process, this system includes an ontology whose end is "to support the acquisition, organization, reuse, and sharing of Software Process knowledge". This software development process ontology consists of various subontologies: of activities, of procedures and of resources.

For the graphic representation of these ontologies, GLEO (Graphical Language for Expressing Ontologies) is used along with a set of axioms defined in first-order logic. Also, for each ontology, the vocabulary used is defined in a table created by two columns, one with the concept name, the other with descriptions of its function and relationship with other concepts.

2.3.4 Representing Ontologies Using Software Engineering Techniques

There are many languages, techniques and tools for the representation, design and construction of ontologies (see Chap. 1). But the great majority of these have been created for and by the knowledge engineering community. Because of this, the use of ontologies by SET professionals and researchers can be seen as an additional learning experience, and in some cases, of considerably great effort.

To avoid this problem, UML has been proposed and analyzed as a language of ontological representation in software engineering [97]. Further, the ontological fundamentals of this option have been studied by Guizzardi et al. [45]. Other potential advantages of this choice is that the extension possibilities of UML can be used: descriptive or restrictive stereotypes, and regular or restrictive extensions of the UML metamodel [82].

For more detail regarding the use of UML as a representation language of ontologies, the reader may refer to "Modelling ontologies with software engineering techniques" in Chapt. 1 of the book "Ontological Engineering" [38].

2.3.4.1 REFSENO

Some SET researchers have made an effort to approximate previous proposals in the area of artificial intelligence, to the software engineering community. A significant case of this type is that of REFSENO (Representation Formalism for Software Engineering Ontologies) [90], a proposal created by the Fraunhofer Institute for Experimental Software Engineering (IESE) in Germany, which includes a methodology in order to develop the ontologies, together with a guide for their representation, through tables and diagrams.

REFSENO provides constructs (primitives) to describe concepts where each concept represents a class of experience items. Besides concepts, its properties (named terminal attributes) and relationships (non-terminal attributes) are represented. One relevant feature of REFSENO is that it enables us to describe similarity functions, which are used for similarity-based retrieval. In this way, the implementation of retrieval components is facilitated. This similarity extends the formalism of Ostertag et al. [73] by additional integrity rules and by clearly separating the schema definition and characterization. On the other hand, REFSENO also incorporates integrity rules such as cardinalities and value ranges for attributes, assertions and preconditions.

In the hope of better adapting the characteristics and interests of software engineers, and in contrast with the usual codified knowledge in knowledge-based systems, REFSENO represents the knowledge in the form of documents having a set of templates of tables and diagrams. This election is based on the studies of Althoff et al. [1] in which an important reduction in learning effort is achieved by the storage of experiences in the form of documents.

The methodology proposed by REFSENO is an improved adaptation of METHONTOLOGY [29, 37], which imitates the software life cycle proposed by the IEEE 1074 standard. Consequentially, the main steps are:

1. Planning.
2. Specification of the ontology requirements.
3. Conceptualization. This stage is similar to the phase of design in a software system, so it is not the ontology itself.

4. Implementation. This refers to the representation and storage of the previous conceptualization through use of computer tools.

REFSENO has been used for the creation and representation of diverse ontologies. For example, in [80] an ontology for software maintenance projects management, developed by a group of software engineers and researchers, is represented using REFSENO, changing specific diagrams for UML class diagrams and with other minor adjustments. According to the authors, they chose REFSENO for the following reasons:

- It allows for the modeling of software engineering knowledge in a precise and complete manner, by using alternate representations. The ontologies specified using REFSENO are precise, since the semantic relationships are defined and are complete, in the sense that all conceptual knowledge necessary to instantiate an experience base are provided.
- It has a clear terminology, differentiating between conceptual and context-specific knowledge, thus enabling the management of knowledge from different contexts.
- It guarantees a consistent ontology since consistency criteria must be fulfilled.

2.3.5 Experiences and Lessons Learned in Software Engineering Research

In this section we present some lessons learned about the usefulness of the ontologies in software engineering research. In these, we have reflected on the experience of the Alarcos Research Group (University of Castilla-La Mancha, Spain), which has been achieved through the development of various research and development (R&D) projects. In our opinion, these conclusions and commentaries can be extended to ISs and database research, and in part to the professional work of the software engineer.

At the origin of the use of these conceptual tools were two challenges encountered in the research projects: the integration of knowledge and the automation-oriented approach by means of software tools.

The first challenge arose from the common daily difficulties in human relationships (between memberships of our group, other groups and other stakeholders), causing a waste of time and energy, due to lack of explicit or tacit shared knowledge. The second challenge arose because the great majority of projects confronted involved the design of advanced support tools for software engineering activities, which should offer the greater functionality that is possible at lower development cost.

In facing these challenges, the following two questions arose:

1. How can we achieve proposals, methods, or tools which offer more general solutions, that is, more useful for all, in research problems?
2. How can we more easily share knowledge of the different participants (researchers, groups, clients, users, managers, etc.)?

The conceptual architectures including meta-metamodels and ontologies have been the two conceptual tools best answering these questions.

The second question had the best solution when using ontologies. Of the many applications of ontologies that are identified in the bibliography [42], and that have already been commented on, for our software engineering R&D project they have been especially useful in:

1. Sharing problem domain knowledge and allowing the use of common terminology between all stakeholders (and not just the researchers).
2. The "filtering" of knowledge upon defining the models and metamodels.

This first use is evident, but its importance was considerable in the problems faced. This importance arose due to the need for communication as a main activity (in duration and importance) in R&D projects (as well as in any other type of work in software engineering or computer science) and because the ambiguity of the natural language implies errors, misunderstandings and unproductive efforts. It has been shown that this is due in great part to the project participants having differing knowledge of the domain of the problem, as well as the use of different languages, both problems which an ontology can mitigate.

The second more important use that we have found with ontologies is the filtering of knowledge (Fig. 2.4). The models and metamodels (models of models) are representations or images of reality that, by definition, only include a part of this reality. However, this is not a problem, but an assistance, as this precise factor allows for the filtering capability of undesired characteristics. In this sense, an ontology is also of assistance in deciding what should be taken out of the real systems in order to construct the model(s) of a system (correspondents at the M1 level in a conceptual architecture such as that defined in MDA-MOF [71]), or what should be taken into account in order to define metamodels (level M2 of MDA-MOF).

Although a formal and implemented ontology in a computer-adapted format may serve for knowledge inference, the characteristics of our R&D projects (with software engineering and not knowledge engineering goals) have led us to limit the use of ontologies to those of knowledge sharing and filtration. Therefore, the decision to use lightweight and non-formal (or semi-formal) ontologies has been due to the scope of projects which have been undertaken until today.

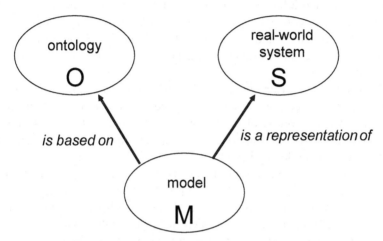

Fig. 2.4. Ontologies as filters of knowledge when defining models and metamodels

2.3.5.1 Examples

In the Alarcos Research Group we have carried out several R&D projects for software maintenance. For example, several years ago, we developed, in collaboration with the international company Atos ODS (previously Sligos), the MANTEMA methodology [76], specifically for the maintenance of software. In these projects, it was very useful to define an ontology for "managing project maintenance" [80] that solved previous misunderstanding and discussions due to, for example, not all participants (researchers, clients, maintainers) having equal understanding of the "modification request" concept.

On the other hand, in 2003, various groups from Spain and diverse countries of America held a meeting in order to define a metamodel which would permit the representation and implementation or any type of software measure. After several days of debating, it was evident to all that there did not even exist any agreement on the concepts and terms that the different researchers or groups used. Without this prior step, it was very difficult to continue advancing. For this reason, a work group was created in order to elaborate a "Software Measurement Ontology" [34]. Thanks to this ontology, the diverse groups have available a conceptual "filtering" tool to help them to create specific metamodels and models for their research. Further, it has been possible to more easily debate and truly center oneself in the reasonable differences due to distinct points of view or work philosophies. As a continuation of this work, a study was undertaken of the different standards and international norms, and it has been discovered that we are far from reaching this explicit and shared conceptualization (ontology). Even for the core concepts of "metric", "measure" and "indicator" there is no international consensus (aggravated by the inconsistencies and lack of the ISO and IEEE official standards) [33].

This absence of a prior ontology is a very common problem in software engineering and in computer science in general. Therefore, when trying to work with the new proposal of the SQL:2003 standard (14 parts and approximately 2000 pages), the Alarcos Group had major misunderstandings, because the metamodel indicated in part 11 "SQL/Schemata" [51], represented in the form of relational schemas, is illegible and has inconsistencies with other parts of the standard. These problems can be solved, or at least considerably reduced, if all the parts and thousands of pages of this standard are based on a previous ontology which makes clear the concepts and their relationships, independent of syntax and implementation aspects.

With this goal, we have begun to construct an SQL:2003 ontology, although due to this great challenge, we have opted to divide this task into various stages. Firstly, we have elaborated the ontology of the object-relational features [14] that we have represented by means of UML 2.0 class diagrams and texts organized in the form of tables. Additionally, in order to increase the level of formality, we have used OCL well-formedness rules. The ontology has been checked by mean of instantiation of an example in which most of the new object-relational features of the SQL:2003 standard are presented. It is of interest to remark that during the development process of the ontology, some inconsistencies were detected in the SQL:2003 standard.

In addition to improving didactics and easing the understanding and learning that this ontology has provided, it also has allowed us to start exploring some new research tracks the first of these being the ontology-based formalization of a set of complexity measures for object-relational schemas [5].

To conclude, in our experience with ontologies in reference to standards, we believe that ease of reading and understanding the standards would be greatly improved if the typical lists of terminology were substituted with an ontology containing the relationships between there terms (if possible, using some type of ontological diagram), its most significant properties and the main semantic constraints. Furthermore, ontology would be a tool of great use for the verification and validation of standards.

2.4 A Proposal of Taxonomy

In previous parts of this chapter, we have examined distinct types of ontologies and the possible ways of employing them. In this section, we present a taxonomy especially oriented to assist SET professionals and researchers. Although we use the previously described classification ideas, we believe that SET community viewpoints and interests require a new and specific taxonomy. Concretely, we claim, without being experts in subjects such as ontological engineering, the Semantic Web, or knowledge engineering, that this taxonomy will assist in answering the following questions:

> *What ontologies exist to better understand the knowledge of a determined SET issue or subdomain?*

> *Why and how can we use ontologies in software development or maintenance projects?*

> *What proposals of new methodologies or previous adaptations exist for the construction of ontology-driven software?*

> *What types of software artifacts can be formed by or include ontologies?*

When attempting to establish a relationship between ontologies and SET, the former are typically considered to be another technique or artifact to be applied in the software life cycle processes; however, although less typical, it is also possible to use this type of conceptual tool for the representation of SET domain knowledge. This should not be forgotten when establishing a taxonomy or classification of the possible combinations between both fields. Thus, at a basic level, we propose that the ontology taxonomy for SET be formed by the following two generic categories:

- *Ontologies of domain*: Describe knowledge of the SET domain.
- *Ontologies as software artifacts*: Used as artifacts of diverse types, in some software process.

Following a description of the fundamental characteristics of ontologies belonging to these categories, and also the subcategories that we propose in both cases, is presented.

2.4.1 Ontologies of Domain

This generic category refers to the ontologies whose main goal is to represent (at least partially) knowledge of a certain subdomain within SET matter. The existence of a universal ontology to fully conceptualize this domain of knowledge would assist in the resource annotation and localization, for example, in the Semantic Web, and would avoid the ambiguities and inconsistencies which are commonly produced when computer science academics, researchers and professionals use varying terms and concepts.

As previously indicated, there are various forms of classifying the ontologies of a domain of knowledge; however, with SET ontologies, we believe that the classification should be based on norms, recommendations and standards published by prestigious organizations and associations (such as the IEEE or ACM), having been accepted and very well known by the international community dedicated to this discipline. In order to establish the hierarchy of subcategories, we have adopted the following:

- Firstly, to distinguish software engineering from software technology, as established in the "Overview Report" of the Computing Curricula 2005 [3].
- Within software engineering, to distinguish between the generic proposals that include the complete scope of this discipline and the specifics focused on some part of it.
- For these last ontologies, to employ the classification in 10 knowledge areas defined in the 2004 version of the "Software Engineering Body of Knowledge" (SWEBOK) [49].
- Within the field of software technology, to use the extended taxonomy of the "ACM Computing Classification System" [50] to identify the subcategories with two breakdown levels.

The ACM taxonomy categories and subcategories that have been considered are those whose content refers to the field of software technology. That is to say, those identified by the letters D (software, but without software engineering because this topic corresponds to the previous category), E (data in general) and H (information technologies and systems, especially databases and Web systems).

In this chapter and book, we do not consider "Artificial Intelligence" within the umbrella of "Software Engineering and Technology". For this reason, in our proposed taxonomy, ACM category "1.2 Artificial Intelligence" (under the generic category of "I. Computing Methodologies") is not included, despite the fact that it includes such topics as "Ontology Design" and "Ontology Languages" within subcategory "1.2.12 Intelligent Web Services and Semantic Web".

Taking these factors into consideration, the taxonomy of the "ontologies of domain" is as follows:

- **Software Engineering (SE)**
  - *Generic (all-domain)*
  - *Specific (sub-domain)*
    - Software Requirements
    - Software Design
    - Software Construction
    - Software Testing
    - Software Maintenance
    - Software Configuration Management
    - Software Quality
    - Software Engineering Tools & Methods
    - Software Engineering Process
    - Software Engineering Management
- **Software Technology (ST)**
  - *Software*
    - Programming Techniques
    - Programming Languages
    - Operating Systems
  - *Data*
    - Data Structures
    - Data Storage Representations
    - Data Encryption
    - Coding and Information Theory
    - Files
  - *Information Technology and Systems*
    - Models and Principles
    - Database Management
    - Information Storage and Retrieval
    - Information Technology and Systems Applications

- Information Interfaces and Representation (HCI)

In order to simplify, in the SWEBOK-based discussion, only one level (knowledge areas) has been described, and in the ACM taxonomy section, we only detail two levels (generic categories and categories).

"*Software Engineering generic ontologies*", also denominated as "Software Engineering all-domain ontologies", has the ambitious objective of modeling the complete software engineering body of knowledge. Therefore, it can be based on three different source types: (1) glossaries (of the IEEE, for example), (2) body of knowledge guides (as SWEBOK), and (3) books of reference in the matter (Pressman [77], etc.). On the other hand, "*Software Engineering specific ontologies*" only attempts to conceptualize one part (subdomain) of this discipline, of interest for a determined goal, collective, or moment. As might be expected, there are many more proposals in this category than in the previous one.

On the other hand, some ontologies of SET subdomains are elaborated, taking into account the possibility of their integration with others, in order to extend the knowledge that is represented in a common way. This can be a good idea, as it follows the well-known strategy of synthesis to design complex systems. Taking this to the extreme, the combination of ontologies of all subdomains included in the proposed taxonomy would result in an ontology of the complete SET domain. Unfortunately, the reality is that this goal is extremely laborious, not only due to its size but also due to the numerous problems of ontology integration and merging (for example, overlapping of concepts) and, as yet, satisfactory solutions do not exist for them. Although similarities are found with the problem of database views integration, the ontology literature states that the merging ontology process is more difficult, labor intensive and error prone [87]. In the literature, we find the experiences of SET community members, not being experts in knowledge engineering–ontology, commenting on their problems in carrying out the merging of ontologies [96].

2.4.2 Ontologies as Software Artifacts

In addition to the ontologies that conceptualize the knowledge of SET (sub)domains, there are other types of proposals that use ontologies as artifacts, with varying characteristics and functionalities, during the construction or functioning of software systems. Many authors have researched the usefulness of using ontologies in this way, even basing the software development process on this technology, and giving way to what Guarino [43] has termed "*Ontology-driven Information System development*". Authors such as Pisanelli et al. [75] have assured that in the future, software will not be designed without using an ontological approach, given the shown effectiveness of this choice, particularly when adequate tools are available. And, as already presented in prior sections, there exists a great potential in the use of ontologies as knowledge's artifacts, for facilitating communication among project stakeholders and for avoiding the ambiguities of natural language, as well as for filtering knowledge when defining models and metamodels of systems to be developed [80, 96]. A pending task which may prove very interesting is the comparative study of the paradigm "Ontology-driven development" proposed by Guarino [43] and the new paradigm "Model-Driven Engineering" (MDE) [83].

Among these uses of ontologies, the World Wide Web Consortium (W3C), a main precursor in the use of ontology for the Semantic Web, also endorses the use of ontologies for software development, having recently created a work group to evaluate, among other possibilities, the potential for "Ontology Driven Software Engineering", "Ontology Driven Architectures" (ODAs) and the crossover between ontology engineering and software engineering [99].

When it comes to proposing a taxonomy or classification of the ontologies that have been used as software artifacts in recent years, it seems reasonable to do so as a function of the ontology's use as an artifact (requirements specification, system conceptual modeling, etc.). Given that the software artifacts can be employed either at development or at run time, we have opted for the first-level classification proposed by Guarino [43], where analyzing the usefulness of ontologies in the IS field distinguished between those artifacts used at system development and those used during system execution.

The first of these categories, that is, "**Ontologies as software artifacts at development time**", has been divided based on function of the software life cycle processes in which it is principally used. The process groups that we have used are defined in the ISO/IEC 15504-2 [53] and ISO/IEC 12207 [52] standards. To simplify, we have covered only two breakdown levels (process groups and process categories), without achieving a bottom level of individual processes. Basically, the distinction consists of taking into account whether the ontologies are used as artifacts in the strictly engineering processes (software development and maintenance) or in other complementary processes: support activities, project management, knowledge reuse, etc. The reference model of these standards groups the processes into three life cycle groupings which contain five categories. Table 2.1 summarizes this information.

In the case of the category referred to as "**Ontologies as software artifacts at run time**", following the same reasoning as Guarino [43], we have determined two different situations:

1. *Ontologies as architectural artifacts*: When ontologies are part of the system software architecture, as an additional component, ,cooperating with the rest of the system at run time to attain the software objective (ontology-driven software).
2. *Ontologies as (information) resources*: Are used by the software during run time for a specific purpose, as an information resource, normally remote, upon which the software operates (ontology-aware software), carrying out, for example, specific queries.

Table 2.1. Groups and categories of processes in ISO/IEC 15504-2 [53]

Group	Category	Description of included processes
Primary	Customer–Supplier	Directly impacts the customer, support development and transition of the software to the customer, and provides for the correct operation and use of the software product and/or service.
	Engineering	Directly specifies, implements, or maintains the software product, its relationship to the system and its customer documentation.
Supporting	Support	May be employed by any of the other processes (including other supporting processes) at various points in the software life cycle.
Organizational	Management	Contains practices of a generic nature which may be used by anyone who manages any type of project or process within a software life cycle.
	Organization	Establishes the business goals of the organization and development process, product, and resource assets which, when used by the projects in the organization, will help the organization achieve its business goals.

Taking into account all of the prior considerations, the taxonomy of "Ontologies as software artifacts" that we propose is the following:

- **At Development Time**
  - For Engineering Processes
    - Development process
    - Maintenance process
  - *For Other Processes*
    - Customer-Supplier processes
    - Support processes
    - Management processes
    - Organization processes
- **At Run Time**
  - *As Architectural Artifacts*

– *As (Information) Resources*

At development time and for engineering processes, the ontologies may be used as artifacts for requirements specification, conceptual modeling, programming, database design, or automatic generation of code. Use cases of ontological artifacts in other complementary processes are communication, software process management, configuration management, reuse, quality assurance, documentation, etc.

Examples of scenarios in which ontologies at run time can be used as architectural artifacts are ontology-driven software architecture, software agent architecture, Web service architecture, Web server architecture. On the other hand, ontologies as information resources at run time could be used in scenarios such as ontology-aware systems, ontology databases, software agents communication, Web services use, search engines or workflow execution.

2.5 Review and Classification of Proposals in the Literature

In this last section of the chapter, we present a summary of a large collection of SET ontology proposals. Each reference is briefly commented upon and situated within the taxonomy previously presented.

When classifying each analyzed work, its main contribution was taken into account. For instance, for the proposals using ontologies at run time of an application, it is evident that this ontology could have been created at development time. However, it has been just considered and classified in the first category, due to its great interest.

In a few cases, the proposal's characteristics have led us to make the decision to include it in more than one taxonomy category. The most typical cases of this type, although not the only ones, are proposals included both in the general category of ontologies of domain and in the ontologies as software artifacts. This happens when, for example, in Ruiz et al. [80], the same proposal includes an ontology as artifact as well as an ontology of software engineering or software technology domain, which complements the first.

2.5.1 Proposals of Ontologies of Domain

Since the late 1990s, different proposals have been published in order to elaborate ontologies of a part or of a complete knowledge domain of SET. In Tables 2.2 and 2.3 below, some of the most well known of these are presented along with their authors and taxonomy category (and subcategory) classification, according to the conceptualized knowledge domain of the ontology.

The majority of the ontologies included in this subsection have not been developed with the sole objective of representing a conceptualization of a SET domain, but, rather, they have been created by their authors to obtain or to be part of systems based on semantic technology.

2.5.1.1 Software Engineering Ontologies

Based on the SWEBOK guide, prototypes of ontologies for the representation of the complete software engineering domain have been created [49]. This includes those of Mendes and Abran [64], consisting of an almost literal transcription of the SWEBOK text, with over 4000 concepts. Another proposal included is that of Sicilia et al. [85], which established an ontology structure based on a *description part*, to characterize artifacts and activities as created and enacted by current software engineering practice, as well as a *prescriptive part*, dealing with a different aspect of reality, which comprises the approaches or rules to concrete practical activities that are "commonly accepted" as considered in the SWEBOK. In Chap. 3 of this book, the authors of both works summarize the different approaches to develop an ontology of the SWEBOK.

Another less ambitious ontology, but one that also conceptualizes the entire software engineering domain, is *OntoGLOSE*, created and based on the "Glossary of Software Engineering Terminology" published by the IEEE [48]. It basically deals with a terminological ontology including over 1500 concepts, corresponding to 1300 glossary terms with their differing meanings [47].

The remaining ontologies presented in Table 2.2 are partial representations of the software engineering domain. Falbo et al. [28] and Larburu et al.[58], for example, have proposed ontologies to model the knowledge related to the **software process**, including concepts such as *Life Cycle Model*, *Software Process*, *Activity*, *Procedure*, *Task*, *Role*, or *Artifact*, among others.

In the second case, the ontology referred to as *SPOnt* and its authors have reused concepts included in other ontologies related to decision support systems, establishing links to concepts such as *Problem* (of the *MCDA* ontology) or *Guideline* (from the *GLIF* ontology).

Table 2.2. Proposals of ontologies of domain (software engineering subdomain)

Category / subcategory	Proposal	Author(s) and reference
Generic	Issues in the development of an ontology for an emerging engineering discipline	Mendes and Abran [64]
	The evaluation of ontological representation of the SWEBOK as a revision tool	Sicilia et al. [85]
	OntoGLOSE: a light weight software engineering Ontology	Hilera et al. [47]
Specific / Software Requirements	Conceptual design model-based requirements analysis in the Win–Win framework for concurrent requirements engineering	Bose [9]
	A generic ontology for the specification of domain models	Girardi and Faria [35]
	An ontology about ontologies and models: a conceptual discussion	Sánchez et al. [81]
	OpenCyc.org: formalized common knowledge	Cyc [19]
Specific / Software Design	An ontology about ontologies and models: a conceptual discussion	Sánchez et al. [81]
	OpenCyc.org: formalized common knowledge	Cyc [19]
	XCM: a component ontology	Tansalarak and Claypool [89]
Specific / Software Maintenance	A concept-oriented approach to support software maintenance and reuse activities	Deridder [21]
	Organizing the knowledge used in software Maintenance	Dias et al. [25]
	An ontology for the management of software maintenance projects	Ruiz et al. [80]
	Merging software maintenance ontologies: our experience	Vizcaino et al. [96]
	Towards an ontology of software maintenance	Kitchenham et al. [56]
Specific / Software Quality	Identifying quality requirements conflicts	Boehm and In [8]
	An ontological approach to domain engineering	Falbo et al. [27]
Specific / SE Process	Using ontologies to improve knowledge integration in software engineering environments	Falbo et al. [28]
	Towards the implementation of a tool for supporting the software development process (in Spanish)	Larburu et al. [58]
	An ontology for software development methodologies and endeavours	González-Pérez and Henderson-Sellers [39]
	Building a knowledge base of IEEE/EAI 12207 and CMMI with ontology	Lin et al. [60]
Specific / SE Management	Towards a consistent terminology for software measurement	García et al. [33]
	REFSENO: a representation formalism for software engineering ontologies	Tautz and Greese [90]

In Chap. 4 of this book, a software development methodology ontology is described, as proposed by González-Pérez and Henderson-sellers [39], which includes a comprehensive metamodel plus a three-domain architecture that can be used to specify methodologies and then apply them to real endeavors.

Related to the knowledge domain of software process, Lin et al. [60] have realized initiatives for the creation of ontologies for the IEEE 12207 standard [76] that provides a guide for software life cycle processes, and CMMI [84] that can be applied in an organization to inspect and improve the capability of software process maturity. The goal of these authors is to combine these two ontologies in order to integrate the two knowledges (in the case of CMMI, only that relative to the maturity level 3) into a knowledge base capable of being applied by an organization in order to develop software more efficiently and correctly.

Ontologies of knowledge associated with the **software maintenance** process, having different focuses, such as the proposal by Deridder [21] or Dias et al. [25], have also been developed. In the latter case, the authors organized the ontology into five subontologies, in order to represent the knowledge related with the software systems in general, with the necessary skills required for software maintainers, with the activities of the maintenance process, with the organizational issues of the maintenance, and with the concepts and tasks that constitute any application domain. In Chap. 5 of this book there is a detailed description of the latest version of this ontology.

The ontology created by Ruiz et al. [80] is also structured in subontologies, although in this case, there are four: subontology of the products, of the activities, of the process organization, and of the agents. There is also an ontology created by Vizcaíno et al. [96] based on a combination of the previous ones. All these ontologies are based on the earlier work of Kitchenham et al. [56].

As for **software quality**, one of the first known ontologies was that used by Boehm and In [8] which included concepts related to the quality attributes of software systems, and information about the influence of software architectures and the development processes on these attributes. For example, the ontology includes relationships among the concepts of *portability, layered system architecture* and *prototyping*, in order to represent the following knowledge: "the *portability* quality attribute can be achieved when using a *layered system architecture* and a *prototyping*-based development". Falbo et al. [27] also proposed an ontology for the quality linked to concepts related to the software process, which were previously modeled in the form of a different, previously mentioned ontology [28].

Regarding the domain of **software measurement**, García et al. [33, 34] have created an ontology which attempts to establish a well-defined terminology for this field, with 21 interrelated terms that are based on four fundamental concepts: *measurement approach, measurement, measure and measurement results*. In Chap. 6, the principal characteristics and elements of this ontology are presented. Similarly, Tautz and Wangenheim [90] have developed a highly detailed ontology of the GQM paradigm *(Goal Question Metric)*, exemplifying the use of the REFSENO notation to represent SET ontologies (to model the knowledge of the software measurement planning domain). In Table 2.2, these ontologies appear classified within the subcategory of "Software Engineering Management", as the SWEBOK breakdown of this area suggests.

Related to the domain of **requirements engineering**, there have also been proposed ontologies, such as that of *Win–Win* [9], carried out by Bose in order to represent the knowledge gained from the model of the same name (established by Boehm in order to manage the necessary collaboration and negotiation produced by those involved in this software life cycle stage).

There also exist ontologies which attempt to conceptualize knowledge with respect to **system modeling**, from a software engineering point of view. Sánchez et al. [81] created an ontology to reflect upon the different meanings of the term *model*, through the incorporation of different concepts related with this term, in their ontology, such as: *model as concept* and *model as original*. In Table 2.2 this proposal is found within the subcategory of "Software Requirements", as based on the SWEBOK breakdown which includes in this knowledge area the topic "Requirements Analysis" and within this, the subtopic "Conceptual Modeling".

The subontology of UML, integrated in the upper ontology *OpenCyc* [19], is more thorough than the previous ones, as it includes over 100 concepts and their definitions, and over 50 relationships, as well as some 30 instances, in order to represent the knowledge associated with this modeling technique. Some of the concepts included in *OpenCyc* are: *UMLModelElement*, *UMLClassifier*, *UMLClass* and *UMLStateMachine*. In Table 2.2 this ontology appears classified within the subcategory "Software Requirements", for the same reason as mentioned previously. But it also falls under the subcategory of "Software Design" as the SWEBOK breakdown includes the knowledge area topic "Software Design Notations".

Another proposal related to the domain of software requirements is *ONTODM*, an ontology created by Girari and Faria [35] for the construction of domain models to be reused in the development of multi-agent applications. ONTODM represents the knowledge of techniques for the specification of the requirements of a family of multi-agent systems in an application domain. It is being used as a CASE tool to assist in the elicitation and specification of domain models.

With respect to **component-based software engineering,** there exists an ontology known as *XCM*, created by Tansalarak and Claypool [89], with its purpose being "to provide a standard for the definition of components that crosscuts the different component models and unifies the variances between the different models". This ontology includes concepts such as *Component, Method, Even, UndelayingComponent* or *Aggregation-basedComposition*. In Table 2.2, this proposal appears classified in the sub-category "Software Design" according to the SWEBOK breakdown, as this knowledge area includes the topic "Software Design Strategies and Methods" and, within this, the subtopic "Component-based Design".

2.5.1.2 Software Technology Ontologies

Among the software technologies that have been conceptualized through ontologies, we find the technologies related to the **programming languages**. For example, as part of the *SIMILE* project (Semantic Interoperability of Metadata and Information in unLike Environments) of MIT, for the creation of a collection of public ontologies [66], we find a very simplistic ontology of the Java language, which represents structural dependencies between the concepts of *Class* and *Package* of this language. Also related to Java is the proposal of Liu and Lo [61] who created an ontology based on the software architecture on which the J2EE technology is implemented.

Other interesting work linking ontologies and programming languages is that of Zimmer and Rauschmayer [101], who used a generic ontology of source code, with concepts such as *Code, Identifier* or *CodeAssociation*, in order to create programs as instances of these concepts (for example, a *Java class* would be an instance of the *Code* concept).

In the scope of **Web engineering**, very detailed ontologies have been developed for Web technologies, such as **Web services**, of which the *OWL-S* ontology stands out, being created in order to describe the properties and capabilities of Web services in an unambiguous, computer-interpretable form [62]. More recently, there is the *WSMO* ontology (Web Service Modeling Ontology), expressed in a more specialized language than the OWL, and referred to as WSML [78]. These two, previously mentioned, are characterized by their high level of detail; however, there are other ontology-oriented proposals about Web services that are more limited, such as that of Pahl [74], focused on the representation of conceptual elements necessary in order to consider Web services as a type of software component.

Also there are **software agents** technology ontologies, such as that of Brandão et al. [10], denominated as *MAS* (Multi-Agent System), that define the concepts and properties that can be used to represent dynamic models of applications based on software agents.

Other computer application types that have been the object of conceptualization are the **ubiquitous and pervasive applications**, which seamlessly integrate into the life of everyday users, providing them with services and information in an "anywhere, anytime" fashion. In this knowledge domain, Chen et al. [17] have proposed *SOUPA* (Standard Ontology for Ubiquitous and Pervasive Applications), which offers developers a shared ontology that combines many useful vocabularies from different consensus ontologies. Their objective is to assist the ubiquitous and pervasive applications developers who are inexperienced in knowledge representation, to quickly begin to building ontology-driven applications. SOUPA includes concepts such as *Agent* (to represent human users, with properties such as *Believes, Desires,* or *Intends*), *Action, Time, Device,* or *Location.*

All of the previous ontologies appear in Table 2.3 classified, according to the established taxonomy, in the category of "Software"; the first are under the subcategory "Programming Languages" and those related to Web technology and ubiquitous computing are found in the "Programming Techniques" category.

Table 2.3. Proposals of ontologies of domain (software technology subdomain)

Category / subcategory	Proposal	Author(s) and reference
Software / Programming Techniques	OWL-based Web service ontology	Martin [62]
	Web Service Modeling Ontology (WSMO)	Roman et al. [78]
	Ontology-based description and reasoning for component-based development on the Web	Pahl [74]
	Ontologies as specifications for the verification of multi-agent systems design	Brandão et al. [10]
	SOUPA: Standard Ontology for Ubiquitous and Pervasive Applications	Chen et al. [17]
Software / Programming Languages	RDF ontology collection. SIMILE project	MIT [66]
	The study on ontology integrating and applying the ontologies of IEEE/EIA 12207, CMMI, Workflow and J2EE to Web service development environment	Liu and Lo [61]
	Tuna: ontology-based source code navigation and annotation	Zimmer and Rauschmayer [101]
Data / Data Encryption	Security mechanisms ontology	Denker [20]
Information Technology and Systems / Database Management	An ontological approach to the SQL:2003	Calero and Piattini [13]
Information Technology and Systems / Information Interfaces (HCI)	An ontology based method for universal design of user interfaces	Furtado et al. [31]
	A proposal of a knowledge model aimed at the use of questionnaires in the usability evaluation (in Spanish)	García [32]

Among the proposals that are found in the "Data" category of the taxonomy are those related to the **data encryption** techniques, such as the ontology of Denker [20], whose objective is to provide notations that will allow interfacing among the various standards for security and trust. This ontology includes concepts such as *SecurityMechanism, KeyFormat, Encryption, Signature, Protocol,* or *KeyProtocol.*

In the category "Information Technology and Systems", there are, among others, the proposals of different **database** technologies, such as those presented in detail in Chap. 7 of this book, related to the object-relational features of the SQL:2003 standard [13].

Within this category, but forming part of the subcategory "Information Interfaces and Representation", are the ontology proposals about technology related to **Human Computer Interaction** (HCI) and, particularly, within the domain of user interface. The proposal of Furtado et al. [31] of an ontology-driven interface design, includes the definition of ontologies at three levels: conceptual, logical and physical. On the other hand, García [32] has developed a detailed ontology of this domain which, in addition to the representation of general concepts of user interface design, also incorporates others related to the usability of the interfaces and their evaluation.

2.5.2 Proposals of Ontologies as Software Artifacts

The proposals for ontology use as software artifacts that can be found in the literature are more abundant than those oriented towards the conceptualization of the SET knowledge domain previously described. The importance of this new approach in software development shows how, recently, special events were being established in order to present such proposals, as in the case of the *Workshop on Ontologies as Software Engineering Artifacts*, hosted in 2004 as a specific event within the *International Conference on Object-Oriented Programming, Systems, Languages, and Applications* (OOPSLA). The majority of the works presented at this event are described in this section.

In Tables 2.4 and 2.5 we present the analyzed proposals, organizeda and based on the taxonomy presented in Sect. 2.2.4, that is, as a function of ontologies as artifacts used: (1) at software development time (for the realization of the stated engineering processes or for other auxiliary processes); or (2) at software run time, as architectural artifacts (ontology-driven software) or as information resources (ontology-aware software).

Table 2.4. Proposals of ontologies as software artifacts at development time

Category / subcategory	Detail	Proposal	Author(s) and reference
Engineering / Development process	All phases	Ontology-driven software development in the context of the semantic web: an example scenario with Protegé/OWL	Knublauch [57]
	Analysis, design, coding	The role of ontologies in schema-based program synthesis.	Bures et al. [12]
	Analysis, design, coding	Building ontologies in a domain oriented software engineering environment	Mian and Falbo [65]
	Analysis, design, coding	Use of ontologies in software development environments	Oliveira et al. [72]
	Analysis, design, coding	An ontology based method for universal design of user interfaces	Furtado et al. [31]
	Analysis, design	Data modelling versus ontology engineering	Spyns et al. [86]
	Analysis, design	Ontology-based description and reasoning for component-based development on the Web	Pahl [74]
	Analysis	The use of ontologies as a backbone for use case management	Wouters et al. [100]
	Analysis	Simplifying the software development value chain through ontology-driven software artifact generation	Jenz [54]
	Analysis	Conceptual design model based requirements analysis in the Win–Win framework for concurrent requirements engineering	Bose [9]
	Analysis	Ontologies, metamodels and model-driven paradigm	Assmann et al. [2]
	Analysis	Improving analysis patterns reuse: an ontological approach	Hamza [46]
	Design, coding	Ontology-oriented programming: static typing for the inconsistent programmer	Goldman [36]
	Coding	Tuna: ontology-based source code navigation and annotation	Zimmer and Rauschmayer [101]
Engineering / Maintenance process		An ontology for the management of software maintenance projects	Ruiz et al. [80]
Non-engineering / Support processes	Quality assurance	ODE: Ontology-based software Development Environment	Falbo et al. [26]
	Verification, validation	The use of ontologies as a backbone for software engineering tools	Deridder and Wouters [22]
	Documentation	The use of an ontology to support a coupling between software models and implementation	Deridder et al. [23]

Table 2.4. *(continued)*

Category / subcategory	Detail	Proposal	Author(s) and reference
Non-engineering / Management processes		Ontology-based retrieval of software process experiences	Nour et al. [69]
		Toward the implementation of a tool for supporting the software development process (in Spanish)	Larburu et al. [58]
		ODE: Ontology-based software Development Environment	Falbo et al. [26]

2.5.2.1 Ontologies as Software Artifacts at Development Time

For Engineering Processes

Among the proposals found in this category is that of Knublauch [57], who defined a complete ontology-driven software development methodology oriented to Semantic Web applications, in which ontologies are used throughout the life cycle of an application, from development through execution.

The rest of the proposals for using ontologies at development time do not establish their use throughout the development process, but, rather, are limited to certain phases such as requirements analysis, design, or coding. The majority of the proposed works apply a domain-oriented software development to the software projects, based on the use of application domain knowledge to guide software developers across the several phases of the software process, facilitating the understanding of the problem during development. Authors such as Bures et al. [12], Mian and Falbo [65] and Oliveira et al. [72] propose to carry out the **domain analysis** through the creation of an ontology which, shortly, will be mapped in design models to be ultimately used to generate code in a determined programming language. This approach assumes the integration of ontology editors in the Domain-Oriented Software Development Environments (DOSDEs).

Bures et al. [12] proposed the automatic generation of code directly through a high-level specification, formed by models constructed from concepts of a given ontology that help to assure the consistency of the generated code.

On the other hand, Furtado et al. [31] established a design method for a user interface at three levels of abstraction, beginning with the creation of an ontology of the domain of discourse (conceptual level), and the subsequent elaboration of models (logical level) that capture instantiations of concepts identified in this ontology for producing multiple user interfaces for one design situation, and that exhibit different presentation styles, dialogues and structure. These models are subsequently transformed into code for their execution in a determined technological platform (physical level).

Spyns et al. [86] used ontologies as an alternative to traditional **data modeling** for database design, defining a method called "DOGMA ontology engineering" (and using the *DogmaModeler* tool), which adopts a classical database model-theoretic view, in which conceptual relations are separated from domain rules; but in this case, through an ontological approach, by means of an "ontology base", which contains multiple intuitive conceptualizations of a domain, and "ontological commitments", where each commitment contains a set of domain rules.

Other authors have established analysis and design methods, based on ontologies, for the development of **component**-oriented software. In this way, Pahl's proposal [74] established the convenience of using ontologies not only for modeling the domain knowledge that corresponds to the components, but also for modeling the software-related knowledge, referred to the behavior of operations or services offered by the components to be developed. In this last case, the ontological concepts would represent descriptions of service properties, while the properties or roles would be the services themselves. WSMO [78] is another ontology thought for suitable this type of development, but oriented towards components implemented in the form of Semantic Web services.

The following group of proposals shown in Table 2.4 is formed by those which refer to the use of ontologies only during **requirements analysis.** In this way, Wouters et al. [100] established a method of requirements specification based on case models represented in UML, but complemented by an annotation mechanism based on an ontology of the application domain, in order to facilitate the management of large sets of use case, improving its browseability, maintainability and scalability. Jenz [54] suggested the creation of a business process ontology with concepts such as *BusinessActivity*, *BusinessRule*, or *BusinessDocument*, having two principal goals: to allow the sharing of knowledge between domain experts and people engaged in software development, and to serve as a requirements specification from which a number of software artifacts can be automatically generated, for example, UML class diagrams.

Another proposal is that of Bose [9], using an ontology of the *Win–Win* technique domain (previously commented), and with the objective of facilitating the semi-automatic transition of the system requirements, according to the mentioned technique, to the corresponding abstract design model. The author proposes the expansion of this ontology by including the conceptualization of the elements that constitute these high-level design models, creating a mapping between these and the elements used in the *Win–Win* requirements model.

Also within this group we find the proposal of Assmann et al. [2] for using ontologies in the case of **model-driven development**, to describe the domain of a system (see Chap. 9 of this publication). And that of Hamza [46], who affirms that ontologies can assist in the reuse of high-level generic solutions in determined problems (that is, *analysis patterns*, in analogy with the known *design patterns*), that avoid facing the analysis phase of a project from scratch. The proposed method has four phases: (1) Knowledge extraction, where a collection of existing patterns of another knowledge source are analyzed. (2) Ontology development, where an ontology that captures the extracted knowledge is developed. (3) Knowledge reuse, where the knowledge included in the ontology is converted into a knowledge asset that can be reused to construct analysis models. (4) Knowledge augmentation, whose objective is to discover new knowledge, upon developing an application, in order to incorporate it into the ontology.

The rest of the proposals of ontologies as software artifacts at development time for the development process included in Table 2.4 refer to the use in activities at a lower level: **design and coding**. For instance, Goldman [36] proposes a development method called "ontology oriented programming" in which the specification of a problem's solution is expressed in the form of an ontology, with its annotations, that is compiled to produce an ontology-specific library, which is linked with other libraries and code to produce an application. Annotations allow for trade-offs between the flexibility of the generated library and its performance. This is a programming paradigm of a higher abstraction level than object-oriented programming ("concepts" versus "objects"), but which finally, through the indicated compiler, makes it possible to generate object-oriented code.

Related to programming, Zimmer and Rauschmayer [101], with the goal of enriching the source code of applications constructed by applying the well-known agile methodology "Extreme Programming" (when "the code is the model"), propose a generic ontology for the source code and a tool with which they write annotations that can be added externally without changing the source code, and that offers the possibility of making queries or navigating through the (semantic) content of the programs created.

All of these described proposals have referred to the use of ontologies in the process of software development; however, works have also been published in relation to their use in the **maintenance** process, included in the taxonomy, along with development, in the engineering processes category. In the work of Ruiz et al. [80], an ontology to assist in the management of software maintenance projects is presented. Also, it includes some elements such as *product*, *activity*, *process*, *agent*, *measure* and some dynamic aspects such as *workflow*. This ontology has been the basis of the development of an "extended software engineering environment" to manage maintenance projects (called the MANTIS environment), previously presented in this chapter, and also has been used for the construction of a knowledge management system (KM-MANTIS) for improving and supporting the management maintenance projects.

For Non-engineering Processes

There have been some proposals for the use of ontologies in other processes than pure software engineering, development and maintenance, although fewer than those previously described. These include ontologies for the processes of management, quality assurance, verification, validation or documentation.

In the case of **management processes,** Nour et al. [69] developed ontology-based techniques and tools that allow recovery of the acquired experience in previous software projects to be applied to new projects. In order to achieve this, three different ontologies for annotating knowledge stored in an "experience base" were created: (1) Skill Ontology, that describes skills and qualifications required for performing specific task types (ex. Java programming). (2) Process Ontology, that allows the definition of process structures. (3) Project Ontology, allowing the representation of information of a project context. The objective is, for a project manager, to be able to query this experience base in order to obtain the information needed to plan the current project.

On the other hand, Larburu et al. [58] created a prototype of a decision support system to assist in the deployment of software development processes, which permit the modeling and execution of software processes previously defined based on a set of four linked ontologies. This prototype has a descriptive capability sufficient for defining roles, tasks, artifacts and decision problems as class instances (concepts) defined by the mentioned ontologies. The four ontologies used are *SPont* (of the domain of software process), *GLIF* (of the Guidelines Interchange Format), *MCDA* (of the domain of multi-criteria decision analysis) and *PROAFTN* (of a fuzzy classification methodology).

The proposal by Falbo et al. [26] is related to the subcategory of management processes, but also to the quality assurance process, which belongs to the subcategory of support processes. These authors present a process-centered SET, called *ODE* (Ontology-based software Development Environment), whose goal is to facilitate the partial automation of the software process. This environment is made up of several integrated tools, oriented towards the process definition, software projects monitoring and software quality control. A main element of the environment is an ontology, resulting from the combination of others created by the same authors, related to the knowledge domains of software process, quality and software metrics [27]. The use of ODE to define processes in real-world projects assumes the instantiation of the elements previewed, including, for example: *Activity, Artifact*, or *Resource*.

In the scope of **support processes**, Deridder and Wouters [22] propose the use of ontologies to improve the creation, verification and validation of software artifacts created during the software development life cycle, through the integration of ontological engines into CASE tools. These authors classify the ontological engines into two kinds according to how they use the ontological data: (1) *"ontology-driven engines"* that retrieve data from the ontology within a given context, and use them to guide to software engineers in the performance of their tasks (for example, transforming ontological data into UML diagrams); and (2) *"ontology-based engines"* that utilize the ontology as a passive component, only needing to verify and look up data. The authors have created ontological engines of both kinds and have integrated them into the Rational Rose CASE tool.

The final work included in Table 2.4 refers to a proposal of Deridder et al. [23] for utilizing ontologies in the documentation process. It involves applying a structured approach to document a system by linking artifacts from the documentation and the implementation, using an ontology and obtaining what is referred to as "meta-documentation", which provides a coupling between the results of the analysis and design phases to the results of the implementation. The goal is to facilitate the software maintenance activities, avoiding wasted time in searching for "missing links" among artifacts it different levels of abstraction. For this, the ontology is a necessary element to establish the implicit links between related artifacts or between artifacts that represent the same concept in different languages.

2.5.2.2 Ontologies as Software Artifacts at Run Time

As Architectural Artifacts (Ontology-Driven Software)

In the proposals that were included in this taxonomy category (see Table 2.5), the software architecture is characterized by the use of one or more ontologies as central elements of the proposed system. The **knowledge-based system** (KBS) has an architecture that consists mainly of a knowledge repository that is formed by an ontology and an inference engine acting on this repository. There are numerous proposals of this type of system that could be referred to in this section. However, it is not necessary to describe all of them, as they share, in most cases, similar architecture, varying in each case just the application domain of the system. Therefore, we only refer to three proposals.

The first is that of Vieira and Casanova [95], who proposed the development of a **Workflow Management System** to integrate an ontology for representing the semantic relationships among elements such as *Workflow, Resource*, or *User*. This ontology indicates which resources and users are required to execute each workflow, and guides the discovery of possible alternatives when the execution of a workflow instance fails to proceed. This ontology is complemented by semantic rules dictating the way that alternatives can be found to allow workflow execution to continue.

Table 2.5. Proposals of ontologies as software artifacts at run time

Category	Proposal	Author(s) and reference
Architectural Artifacts (Ontology-driven software)	Flexible workflow execution through an ontology-based approach	Vieira and Casanova [95]
	An ontology-based context management and reasoning process for UbiComp applications	Chistopoulou et al. [18]
	Developing and managing software components in an ontology-based application server	Oberle et al. [70]
Information Resources (Ontology-aware software)	Swoogle: Semantic Web search	UMBC [88]
	Upgrade and publication of legacy data	Barrasa [6]
	Using ontologies as artifacts to enable databases interoperability	Brauner et al. [11]

Another example is the work of Cristopoulou et al. [18], who present an architecture for **ubiquitous computing applications**. These applications operate within an extremely dynamic and heterogeneous environment, and have to dynamically adapt to changes in their environment as a result of users' or other actors' activities. Therefore, context definition, representation, management and use are important factors affecting their operation. The authors propose the integration in the architecture of these context-aware systems, an ontology and an inference engine. The basic goal of the ontology is to support a context management process based on a set of rules which determine how a decision should be made and how it must be applied on existing knowledge represented by this ontology.

The third proposal of ontology-driven software included in Table 2.5 is that of Oberle et al. [70], who presented an ontology-based **application server**; this server, in addition to the habitual installed software components, includes an inference engine in which an ontology is loaded, with which an explicit and executable conceptual model for the administering the application server is represented. The server is implemented with J2EE technology, and the ontology conceptualizes key elements related to this technological platform, such as *Realm, User, Group* or *Roles*. It also includes concepts on security mechanisms such as *Resource, Method, ResourceGroup, Acces-Right, Invocation* or *RequestContext*; from these, the elements utilized are instantiated in order to control the server security. At run time, the server manages information in the form of semantic metadata (generated from configuration files), which are processed by the inference engine along with the content of the ontology.

The specification of the described systems and, in general, of any ontology-driven software, requires modeling techniques that can be used for the specification of the ontology integrated into the system, or for the inference engine, or for the rest of the system components. UML is an adequate notation for this purpose, having UML extension proposals such as that of Baclawski et al. [4], in order to model ontologies that can later be implemented into a language such as OWL. We must emphasize the Object Management Group (OMG) initiative to create a standard "Ontology Development Metamodel" (ODM) using the OMG's Meta Object Facility (MOF), to ease the development of ontologies with an engineering approach, more than adequate in the development of ontology-driven software. This initiative is comprehensively described in Chap. 8 of this book.

As Information Resources (Ontology-Aware Software)

Within this category are those proposals which deal with software systems that use one or more ontologies at run time in order to, for example, use their content in operations of information searching. Such is the case of **Web searchers** for the Semantic Web, such as Swoogle [88], which access over 10,000 ontologies to execute semantic searches.

Other applications framed inside this category are those that use ontologies as database substitutes, for information storage. Proposals exist to convert pre-existing databases into ontologies, assuming that the applications which previously accessed the original database now should access the ontology, constituting what has been named by us, following Guarino [43], ontology-aware software.

Among the proposals for transforming databases into ontologies is that of Barrasa [6], described in detail in Chap. 11 of this book, who has defined a language known as R_2O for mapping relational databases into ontologies, using a mapping processor called *ODEMapster*, both for generating the ontology (also called the "semantic repository of data") as well as for the execution of queries on the ontology. This facilitates the transformation of the applications that use a relational database to allow semantic access to the content available in the database.

Other work similar to that previously discussed is that of Brauner et al. [11], who have gone further, applying a mechanism of transformation to several databases, in order to create an ontology-based catalogue which serves as a mediator to federated databases, and which offers centralized access to the data.

Although no proposal of this sort has been presented in Table 2.5, to conclude we will mention the applications that are being developed for the **Semantic Web**, considered in the category of "ontology-aware software", as the use of ontologies is and will be common place in the future development of these application types. And if we have "Service-oriented Architectures" (SOAs), with the use of Semantic Web services in the form of uncoupled, self-contained, self-described and semantically annotated software components, the ontologies will be used to describe not only the domain knowledge of these services, but also the interaction process of applications with these services, in such a way that eases the discovery, composition and execution of these services, thereby offering more complex functionality. For all this, it is fundamental that ontologies are used for Web services modeling, such as WSMO [78], not only by the creators of such services, in order to semantically annotate them, but also by the consumers, for discovery and use of the services.

References

1.   Althoff, K.-D., Birk, A., Hartkopf, S., Mülle, W.: Managing Software Engineering Experience for Comprehensive Reuse. Eleventh International Conference on Software Engineering and Knowledge Engineering (SEKE), Kaiserslautern, Germany, 1999.
2.   Assmann, U., Wagner, G.: Ontologies, metamodels and model-driven paradigm. In Ontologies for Software Engineering and Technology, Springer-Verlag, Berlin, chapter 9 (2006).
3.   Association for Computing Machinery: Computing Curricula 2005 – The Overview Report. 30 September 2005. ACM, AIS, IEEE-CS. Available in: http://info.acm.org/education/curricula.html
4.   Baclawski, K., Kokar, M.K., Kogut, P.A., Hart, L., Smith, J., Holmes, W.S., Letkowski, J., Aronson, M.L., Emery, P.: Extending the Unified Modeling Language for Ontology Development. International Journal of Software and Systems Modeling (SoSyM), 1(2): 142–156, 2002.
5.   Baroni, A., Calero, C., Brito e Abreu. F. and Piattini, M. (2006) Object-Relational Database metrics formalization. Sixth International Conference on Quality Software (QSIC 2006). Beijig (China). To be published.
6.   Barrasa, J.: Semantic Upgrade and Publication of Legacy Data. In Ontologies for Software Engineering and Technology, Springer-Verlag, Berlin, chapter 11 (2006).

7.   Bertrand, T., Bézivin, J.: Ontological Support for Business Process Improvement. In D. Bustard, P. Kawalek, M.Norris (eds.), Systems Modeling for Business Process Improvement. Artech House Publishers, London, pp. 313–331 (2000).
8.   Boehm, B., In, H.: Identifying Quality Requirements Conflicts. IEEE Software, March: 25–35, 1996.
9.   Bose, P.: Conceptual design model based requirements analysis in the Win-Win framework for concurrrent requirements engineering. IEEE Workshop on Software Specification and Design (IWSSD), 1995.
10. Brandão, A.F., Torres, V., De Lucena, C.: Ontologies as Specifications for the Verification of Multi-Agent Systems Design. In Workshop on Ontologies as Software Engineering Artifacts (OOPSLA), Vancouver, Canada, 24–28 October 2004.
11. Brauner, D.F., Casanova, M.A., De Lucena, C.J.P.: Using ontologies as artifacts to enable databases interoperability. Workshop on Ontologies as Software Engineering Artifacts (OOPSLA), Vancouver, Canada, 24–28 October 2004.
12. Bures, T., Denney, E., Fischer, B., Nistor, E.C.: The role of ontologies in schema-based program synthesis. Workshop on Ontologies as Software Engineering Artifacts (OOPSLA), Vancouver, Canada, 24–28 October 2004.
13. Calero, C., Piattini, M.: An ontological approach to the SQL:2003. In Ontologies for Software Engineering and Technology, Springer-Verlag, Berlín, chapter 7 (2006).
14. Calero, C., Ruiz, F., Baroni, A.L., Brito e Abreu, F., Piattini, M.: An Ontological Approach to Describe the SQL:2003 Object-Relational Features. Computer Standards & Interfaces. Available online December 2, 2005 in: http://www.sciencedirect.com/science/journal/09205489
15. Chandrasekaran, B., Josephson, J.R., Benjamins, V.: Ontology of Tasks and Methods. In Proceedings of KAW'98, Banff, Alberta, Canada, 1998.
16. Chandrasekaran, B., Josephson, J.R., Benjamins, V.: What Are Ontologies, and Why Do We Need Them?. IEEE Intelligent Systems, 14 (1) 20–26, 1999.
17. Chen, H., Perich, F., Finin, T., Joshi, A.: SOUPA: Standard Ontology for Ubiquitous and Pervasive Applications. International Conference on Mobile and Ubiquitous Systems: Networking and Services, Boston, USAs, 22–25 August 2004, pp. 258–267.
18. Chistopoulou, E., Goumopoulos, C., Kameas, A.: An ontology-based context management and reasoning process for UbiComp applications. In Proceedings of the 2005 Joint Conference on Smart Objects and Ambient Intelligence: innovative context-aware services: usages and technologies, Grenoble, France, October 2005, pp. 265–270.
19. Cyc: OpenCyc.org: Formalized Common Knowledge. Cycorp, USA. Available in;
     http://www.opencyc.org68
20. Denker, G.: Security Mechanisms Ontology. Computer Science Laboratory, SRI International, 2002. Available in:

http://www.csl.sri.com/~denker/owl-sec/security.owl

21. Deridder, D.: A Concept-Oriented Approach to Support Software Maintenance and Reuse Activities. 5th Joint Conference on Knowledge-Based Software Engineering (JCKBSE), Maribor, Slovenia, September 2002.

22. Deridder, D., Wouters, B.: The Use of Ontologies as a Backbone for Software Engineering Tools. Fourth Australian Knowledge Acquisition Workshop (AKAW), Sydney, Australia, December 1999.

23. Deridder, D., Wouters, B., Lybaert, W.: The use of an ontology to support a coupling between software models and implementation. International Workshop on Model Engineering, 14th European Conference on Object-Oriented Programming (ECOOP), Sophia Antipolis and Cannes, France, 2000.

24. Devedzíc, V.: Understanding Ontological Engineering. Communications of the ACM, 45(4): 136–144, 2002.

25. Dias, M.G., Anquetil, N., De Oliveira, K.M.: Organizing the Knowledge Used in Software Maintenance. Journal of Universal Computer Science, 9(7): 641–658, 2003.

26. Falbo, R.A., Cruz, A.C., Mian, P.G., Bertollo, G., Borges, F.: ODE: Ontology-based software Development Environment. IX Argentine Congress on Computer Science (CACIC), La Plata, Argentina, 6–7 October 2003.

27. Falbo, R.A., Guizzardi, G., Duarte, K.C.: An Ontological Approach to Domain Engineering. In Procedings of 14th International Conference on Software Engineering and Knowledge Engineering (SEKE), Ischia, Italy, July 1992, pp. 351–358.

28. Falbo, R., Menezes, C., Rocha, A.: Using Ontologies to Improve Knowledge Integration in Software Engineering Environments. 4th International Conference on Information Systems Analysis and Synthesis (ISAS), Orlando, USA, 1998.

29. Fernández, M., Gómez-Pérez, A., Juristo, N.: METHONTOLOGY: From Ontological Art Towards Ontological Engineering. AAAI Spring Symposium, University of Stanford, Palo Alto, California (USA), pp. 33–40, 1997.

30. Fensel, D: Ontologies: A Silver Bullet for Knowledge Management and Electronic Commerce. Second Edition, Springer-Verlag, Berlin, Heidelberg (2004).

31. Furtado, E., Vasco, J., Bezerra, W., Tavares, D., Da Silva, L., Limbourg, Q., Vander-Donckt, J.: An ontology based method for universal design of user interfaces. Workshop on Multiple User Interfaces over the Internet, British Human Computer Interaction Group Conference (HCI/IHM), 2001.

32. García, E.: A proposal of a knowledge model aimed at the use of questionnaires in the usability evaluation (in Spanish). PhD Thesis, University of Alcalá, Spain, 2004.

33. García, F., Bertoa, M.F., Calero, C., Vallecillo, A., Ruíz, F., Piattini, M., Genero, M.: Towards a consistent terminology for software measurement. Information and Software Technology. Available online August 22, 2005 in: http://www.sciencedirect.com/science/journal/09505849

34. García, F., Ruiz, F., Bertoa, M.F., Calero, C., Genero, M., Olsina, L.A., Martín, M.A., Quer, C., Condori, N., Abrahao, S., Vallecillo, A., Piattini, M.: Una Ontología de la Medición del Software (in Spanish). Technical Report DIAB-04-02-2, Dept. of Computer Science, University of Castilla-La Mancha. Available in:
http://www.info-ab.uclm.es/trep.php
35. Girardi, R., Faria, C.: A Generic Ontology for the Specification of Domain Models. In Proceedings of 1st International Workshop on Component Engineering Methodology (WCEM'03) at Second International Conference on Generative Programming and Component Engineering, Erfurt, Germany, 2003.
36. Goldman, N.M.: Ontology-oriented programming: static typing for the inconsistent programmer. In International Semantic Web Conference (ISWC'2003), LNCS Vol. 2870, Sprinter-Verlag, Berlin, pp. 850–865 (2003).
37. Gómez-Pérez, A.: Knowledge sharing and reuse. In Jay Liebowitz (ed.), The Handbook of Applied Expert Systems. CRC Press, Boca Raton, Florida, 1998.
38. Gómez Pérez, A., Fernández López, M. Corcho, O.: Ontological Engineering. Springer-Verlag, London (2004).
39. González-Pérez, C., Henderson-Sellers, B.: An Ontology for Software Development Methodologies and Endeavours. In Ontologies for Software Engineering and Technology, Springer-Verlag, Berlin, chapter 4 (2006).
40. Gruber, T.R.: A translation approach to portable ontologies. Knowledge Acquisition, 5(2): 199–220, 1993.
41. Gruber, T.: Towards Principles for the Design of Ontologies used for Knowledge Sharing. International Journal of Human-Computer Studies, 43(5/6): 907–928, 1995.
42. Gruninger, M., Lee, J.: (2002): Ontology Applications and Design. Communications of the ACM, 45(2): 39–41, 2002.
43. Guarino, N.: Formal Ontology in Information Systems. In Proceedings of FOIS'98, Trento, Italy. IOS Press, Amsterdam (1998).
44. Guarino, N., Schneider, L.: Ontology-Driven Conceptual Modelling: Advanced Concepts. ER 2002. Pre-Conference Tutorials. Available in:
http://www.loa-cnr.it/odcm.html
45. Guizzardi, G., Herre, H., Wagner, G.: On the General Ontological Foundations of Conceptual Modeling. 21st International Conference on Conceptual Modeling (ER), Tampere, Finland, October 2002.
46. Hamza, H.S.: Improving Analysis Patterns Reuse: An Ontological Approach. Workshop on Ontologies as Software Engineering Artifacts (OOPSLA), Vancouver, Canada, 24–28 October 2004.
47. Hilera, J.R., Sánchez-Alonso, S., García, E., Del Molino, C.J..: OntoGLOSE: A Light-weight Software Engineering Ontology. 1st Workshop on Ontology, Conceptualizations and Epistemology for Software and Systems Engineering (ONTOSE), Alcalá de Henares, Spain, 9–10 June 2005.

48. IEEE: IEEE Std 610.12-1990(R2002): IEEE Standard Glossary of Software Engineering Terminology (Reaffirmed 2002), IEEE, New York, USA.
49. IEEE: SWEBOK - Guide to the Software Engineering Body of Knowledge 2004 version. IEEE Computer Society. Available in: http://www.swebok.org
50. IEEE: Top-Level Categories for the ACM Taxonomy (extended version of the ACM Computing Classification System 2002). Available in: www.computer.org/mc/keywords/keywords.htm
51. ISO/IEC 9075-11:2003 Information technology – Database languages – SQL – Part 11: Information and Definition Schemas (SQL/Schemata). International Organization for Standardization, Genova.
52. ISO/IEC 12207:1995. Information Technology – Software Life Cycle Processes. ISO/IEC 1995.
53. ISO/IEC 15504-2:1998. Information Technology – Software Process Assessment – Part 2: A Reference Model for Processes and Process Capability. ISO/IEC 1998.
54. Jenz, D.E.: Simplifying the software development value chain through ontology-driven software artifact generation. Jenz and Partner GmbH Strategic White Paper, 2003. Available in:
http://www.bpiresearch.com/WP_BPMOntology.pdf
55. Jurisica, I., Mylopoulos, J., Yu, E.: Using ontologies for knowledge management: an information systems perspective. In Proceedings of 62nd Annual Meeting of the American Society for Information Science (ASIS99), 1999, pp. 482–496.
56. Kitchenham, B.A., Travassos, G.H., Mayrhauser, A., Niessink, F., Schneidewind, N.F., Singer, J., Takada, S., Vehvilainen, R., Yang, H.: Towards an Ontology of Software Maintenance. Journal of Software Maintenance: Research and Practice, 11(6): 365–389, 1999.
57. Knublauch, H.: Ontology-driven software development in the context of the semantic web: an example scenario with protegé/OWL. First International Workshop on the Model-Driven Semantic Web (MDSW), 2004.
58. Larburu, I.U., Pikatza, J.M., Sobrado, F.J., García, J.J., López, D.: Hacia la implementación de una herramienta de soporte al proceso de desarrollo de software. Workshop in Artifificial Intelligence Applications to Engineering (AIAI), San Sebastián, Spain, 2003.
59. Lassila, O., McGuinness, D.: The Role of Frame-Based Representation on the Semantic Web. KSL Techical Report No. KSL-01-02, Jan-2001. Available in:
http://www.ksl.stanford.edu/people/dlm/etai/lassila-mcguinness-fbr-sw. html
60. Lin, S., Liu, F., Loe, S.: Building A Knowledge Base of IEEE/EAI 12207 and CMMI with Ontology. Sixth International Protégé Workshop, Manchester, England, 7–9 July 2003.
61. Liu, F., Lo, S.: The Study on Ontology Integrating and Applying the Ontologies of IEEE/EIA 12207, CMMI, Workflow and J2EE to Web Service Development Environment. Sixth International Protégé Workshop, Manchester, England, 7-9 July 2003.

62. Martin, D. (ed.): OWL-based Web Service Ontology. OWL-S Coalition, 2004. Available in:
    http://www.daml.org/services/owl-s
63. Meersman, R.A.: The Use of Lexicons and Other Computer-Linguistic Tools in Semantics Design and Cooperation of Database Systems. In Y. Zhang (ed.), CODAS Conference Proceedings, Springer-Verlag, Berlin (2000).
64. Mendes, O., Abran, A.: Issues in the development of an ontology for an emerging engineering discipline. First Workshop on Ontology, Conceptualizations and Epistemology for Software and Systems Engineering (ONTOSE), Alcalá de Henares, Spain, 9–10 June 2005.
65. Mian, P.G., Falbo, R.A.: Building ontologies in a domain oriented software engineering environment. IX Argentine Congress on Computer Science (CACIC), La Plata, Argentina 6–7 October 2003.
66. MIT: RDF Ontology Collection. Simile Project, Massachusetts Institute of Technology, USA, 2004. Available in:
    http://simile.mit.edu/repository/ontologies/java
67. Mylopoulos, J.: Ontologies. Visited on January 4, 2006 in:
    http://www.cs.toronto.edu/~jm/2507S/Notes04/Ontologies.pdf
68. Newell, A.: The Knowledge Level. Artificial Intelligence, 18: 87–127, 1982.
69. Nour, P., Holz, H., Maurer, F.: Ontology-based retrieval of software process experiences. ICSE Workshop on Software Engineering over the Internet, 2000.
70. Oberle, D., Eberhart, A., Staab, S., Volz, R.: Developing and Managing Software Components in an Ontology-based Application Server. 5th International Middleware Conference, Toronto, Canada, 18–22 October 2004.
71. Object Management Group: Meta Object Facility (MOF) Specification; version 1.4, April 2002.
72. Oliveira, K.M., Villela, K., Rocha, A.R., Horta, G.: Use of Ontologies in Software Development Environments. In Ontologies for Software Engineering and Technology, Springer-Verlag, Berlin, chapter 10 (2006).
73. Ostertag, E., Hendler, J., Prieto-Díaz, R., Braun, C.: Computing similarity in a reuse library system: an AI-based approach. ACM Transactions on Software Engineering and Methodology, 1(3): 205–228, 1992.
74. Pahl, C.: Ontology-based description and reasoning for component-based development on the Web. In Procedings of ESEC/FSE Workshop on Specification and Verification of Component-based Systems (SAVCBS'03), Helsinki, Finland, September 2003, pp. 84–87.
75. Pisanelli, D.M., Gangemi, A., Steve, G.: Ontologies and Information Systems: the Marriage of the Century?. In Proceedings of LYEE Workshop, Paris, 2002.
76. Polo, M., Piattini, M., Ruiz, F., Calero, C.: MANTEMA: A Software Maintenance Methodology based on the ISO/IEC 12207 Standard. 4th IEEE International Software Engineering Standards Symposium (ISESS), Curitiba, Brazil. IEEE Computer Society, pp. 76–81, 1999.

77. Pressman, R.S.: Software Engineering: A Practitioner's Approach. Sixth Edition. McGraw-Hill, New York, 2004.
78. Roman, D., Lausen, H., Keller, U. (eds.): Web Service Modeling Ontology (WSMO), SDK WSMO Working Group, 2005. Available in: http://www.wsmo.org
79. Ruiz, F., García, F., Piattini, M., Polo, M.: Environment for Managing Software Maintenance Projects. In "Advances in Software Maintenance Management: Technologies and Solutions". Idea Group Publication (USA), chapter X, pp. 255–290, 2002.
80. Ruiz, F., Vizcaíno, A., Piattini, M., García, F.: An Ontology for the Management of Software Maintenance Projects. International Journal of Software Engineering and Knowledge Engineering, 14(3): 323–349, 2004.
81. Sánchez, D.M., Cavero, J.M., Marcos, E.: An ontology about ontologies and models: a conceptual discussion. First Workshop on Ontology, Conceptualizations and Epistemology for Software and Systems Engineering (ONTOSE), Alcalá de Henares, Spain, 9–10 June 2005.
82. Schleicher, A., Westfechtel, B.: Beyond Stereotyping: Metamodeling Approaches for the UML. 34th Hawaii International Conference on System Sciences (HICSS), Maui, Hawaii (USA), January 2001.
83. Schmidt, D.C.: Model-Driven Engineering. IEEE Computer, special issue on model-driven software development, 39(2): 25–31, February 2006.
84. SEI: Capability Maturity Model Integration (CMMI), Software Engineering Institute, 2002. Available in: http://www.sei.cmu.edu/cmmi/
85. Sicilia, M.A.., Cuadrado, J.J., García, E., Rodríguez, D., Hilera, J.R..: The evaluation of ontological representation of the SWEBOK as a revision tool. In 29th Annual International Computer Software and Application Conference (COMPSAC), Edinburgh, UK, 26–28 July 2005.
86. Spyns, P., Meersman, R., Jarrar, M.: Data Modelling versus Ontology Engineering. SIGMOD Record 31(4): 12–7, 2002.
87. Stumme, G., Maedche, A.: FCA-MERGE: Bottom-Up Merging of Ontologies. Seventeenth International Joint Conference on Artificial Intelligence (IJCAI), Seattle, Washington, 2001.
88. Swoogle: Semantic Web Search. University of Maryland Baltimore County (UMBC), 2006. Available in: http://swoogle.umbc.edu
89. Tansalarak, N., Claypool, K.T.: XCM: A Component Ontology. Workshop on Ontologies as Software Engineering Artifacts (OOPSLA), Vancouver, Canada, 24–28 October 2004.
90. Tautz, C., Von Wangenheim, C.: REFSENO: A Representation Formalism for Software Engineering Ontologies. Fraunhofer IESE-Report No. 015.98/E, version 1.1, October 20, 1998.
91. Uschold, M., Gruninger, M.: Ontologies: Principles, Methods and Applications. Knowledge Engineering Review, 11(2): 93–15, 1996.

92. Uschold, M., Jasper, R.: A Framework for Understanding and Classifying Ontology Applications. In Proceedings of IJCAI Workshop on Ontologies and Problem-Solving Methods, August 1999. Visited on January 8, 2006 in: http://sunsite.informatik.rwth-aachen.de/Publications/CEUR-WS//Vol-18/

93. Uschold, M., King, M.: Towards a Methodology for Building Ontologies. In Proceedings of the Workshop on Basic Issues in Knowledge Sharing (hosts within IJCAI), 1995.

94. Van Heijst, G., Schereiber, A.T., Wielinga, B.J.: Using Explicit Ontologies in KBS Development. International Journal of Human and Computer Studies, 46(2/3), 1997, pp. 293–310.

95. Vieira, T.A., Casanova, M.A.: Flexible Workflow Execution through an Ontology-based Approach. Workshop on Ontologies as Software Engineering Artifacts (OOPSLA), Vancouver, Canada, 24–28 October 2004.

96. Vizcaíno, A., Anquetil, N., Oliveira, K., Ruiz, F., Piattini, M.: Merging Software Maintenance Ontologies: Our Experience. First Workshop on Ontology, Conceptualizations and Epistemology for Software and Systems Engineering (ONTOSE), Alcala de Henares, Spain, 9–10 June 2005.

97. Wang, X., Chan, C.W.: Ontology Modeling Using UML. 7th International Conference on Object Oriented Information Systems (OOIS), Calgary, Canada, pp. 59–68, 2001.

98. Wang, X., Chan, C., Hamilton, H.: Design of knowledge-based systems with the ontology-domain-system approach. In Proceedings of SEKE 2002, pp. 233–236.

99. World Wide Web Consortium (W3C): Ontology Driven Architectures and Potential Uses of the Semantic Web in Systems and Software Engineering. Draft 2006/02/11. Available in:
http://www.w3.org/2001/sw/BestPractices/SE/ODA/

100. Wouters, B., Deridder, D., Van Paesschen, E.: The use of ontologies as a backbone for use case management. European Conference on Object-Oriented Programming (ECOOP), 2000.

101. Zimmer, C., Rauschmayer, A.: Tuna: Ontology-Based Source Code Navigation and Annotation. Workshop on Ontologies as Software Engineering Artifacts (OOPSLA), Vancouver, Canada, 24–28 October 2004.

3. Engineering the Ontology for the SWEBOK: Issues and Techniques

Alain Abran

École de technologie supérieure, Université du Québec, 1100, rue Notre-Dame Ouest, Montréal, Québec. Canada H3C 1K3,
alain.abran@etsmtl.ca

Juan José Cuadrado, Elena García-Barriocanal

Polytechnic Building. University of Alcalá, Ctra. Barcelona km 33,600., 28871, Alcalá de Henares, Madrid (Spain)
jjcg@uah.es, elena.garciab@uah.es

Olavo Mendes

École de technologie supérieure, Université du Québec, 1100, rue Notre-Dame Ouest, Montréal, Québec. Canada H3C 1K3
olavomendes@gmail.com

Salvador Sánchez-Alonso and Miguel A. Sicilia

Polytechnic Building. University of Alcalá, Ctra. Barcelona km 33,600., 28871, Alcalá de Henares, Madrid (Spain)
salvador.sanchez@uah, esmsicilia@uah.es

3.1 Introduction

Auyang [2] described *engineering* as "the science of production". This and many other definitions of engineering put an emphasis on disciplined artifact creation as the essence of any engineering discipline. However, the material object produced by every engineering discipline is not necessarily of a similar nature. The case of software engineering is particularly relevant in the illustration of such differences, since *software* as an artifact is acknowledged as a very special piece of human work. The special nature of software was attributed by Brooks [7] to "*complexity*" as an essential characteristic. The following quote from Brook's paper illustrates the presupposed impact of complexity in the activities of engineering:

> *Many of the classic problems of developing software products derive from this essential complexity and its nonlinear increases with size. From the complexity comes the difficulty of communication among team members, which leads to product flaws, cost overruns, and schedule delays. From the complexity comes the difficulty of enumerating, much less understanding, all the possible states of the program, and from that comes the unreliability. From complexity of function comes the difficulty of invoking function, which makes programs hard to use. From complexity of structure comes the difficulty of extending programs to new functions without creating side effects. From complexity of structure come the unvisualized states that constitute security trapdoors.*

The term "essential" (as opposed to "accidental") is a well-known tool for ontology engineers [17], which helps in determining the properties of concepts that objects possess "always and in every possible world". The position of Brooks on the essentials of the object of the discipline leads to a particular conception of software engineering as a human endeavour that attempts to tackle an inherently complex problem, since it takes as a point of departure the fact that complexity is a feature that cannot be removed from the engineering process. Consequently, it is difficult to consider methods that are definitive for the production of software, and the field is expected to change as methodologies are introduced and applied in an attempt to manage, to the extent possible, the complexity of the activities. This has a consequence on research and enquiry, since the qualities of a tool or method to tackle software complexity are difficult to assess, and this in turn leads to a plurality of approaches. Such diversity leads to difficulties in contrasting the appropriateness of techniques in terms of rational enquiry methods such as those established by Popper [12] in his method for scientific discovery.

Empirical research on proposed software methods, processes, tools and techniques are of course fundamental to the discipline. In addition, ontology engineering is also important from our viewpoint for the evolution of the discipline of software engineering, at least in two dimensions. On the one hand, ontology may help in the organization and meta-analysis of empirical data and empirical approaches [6], facilitating an adequate comparison and evaluation of methods, techniques or tools. On the other hand, ontologies translated into machine-understandable representations may help in the development of computerized tools that, to some extent, take into account the purpose and consequences of the diverse software engineering activities. Even though we do not see ontologies as the "silver bullet" of every software production problem, they are promising tools to help in the work of researchers and practitioners, and they would also serve as an element of analysis and discussion for engineers and for learning about the discipline.

Consensus-reaching approaches to ontology engineering are deemed as appropriate for the crafting of representations of the concepts of some concrete domains. Nonetheless, in some domains the engineer can find pre-existing processes of consensus-reaching on conceptual frameworks. This is the case of software engineering, in which the SWEBOK project [1, 8] is the result of a considerable effort on the collaborative production of a subset of the knowledge of the discipline that is as of today subject to little controversy in the community of researchers. In addition to the collaborative effort, which will be briefly described next, the project adopts a literature-based approach [14] in selecting some relevant articles. Thus, the SWEBOK guide provides a ground of rationality and consensus that constitutes a valuable input for ontology engineering.

The chapter by Ruiz and Hilera in this volume provides an overview of current approaches to the ontology of software engineering, some of them based on the SWEBOK. This chapter now concentrates on the specifics of two approaches to SWEBOK-based ontological enquiry that are complementary in their objectives and methods.

The rest of this chapter is structured as follows. Section 3.2 provides an account of the SWEBOK as a project, its main principles and its method from creation to revision. Then, Sect. 3.3 describes some results of a process of enquiry on SWEBOK-based ontology from the viewpoint of the experimental study of the process of rational argument and consensus-reaching by software engineers. Later on, Sect. 3.4 provides the complementary view of producing ontological representations linked to common-sense knowledge bases, analysing the benefits of reuse of existing ontological engineering and of being prepared for the construction of ontology-based tools. On the basis of the experiences described in Sects. 3.3 and 3.4, Sect. 3.5 sketches the main ontological elements distilled.

3.2 History and Principles of the SWEBOK Project

The Guide to the SWEBOK should not be confused with the Body of Knowledge itself, which already exists in the published literature. The purpose of the Guide is to describe what portion of the Body of Knowledge is generally accepted, to organize that portion, and to provide a topical access to it. The Guide to the SWEBOK was established with the following five objectives:

1. To promote a consistent view of software engineering worldwide.
2. To clarify the place – and set the boundary – of software engineering with respect to other disciplines such as computer science, project management, computer engineering and mathematics.
3. To characterize the contents of the software engineering discipline.
4. To provide topical access to the software engineering Body of Knowledge.
5. To provide a foundation for curriculum development and for individual certification and licensing material.

The first of these objectives, a consistent worldwide view of software engineering, was supported by a development process which engaged approximately 500 reviewers from 42 countries in the Stoneman phase (1998–2001) leading to the Trial version, and over 120 reviewers from 21 countries in the Ironman phase (2003) leading to the 2004 version. More information regarding the development process can be found in the Preface and on the Web site (www.swebok.org). Professional and learned societies and public agencies involved in software engineering were officially contacted, made aware of this project, and invited to participate in the review process. Associate editors were recruited from North America, the Pacific Rim and Europe. Presentations on the project were made at various international venues and more are scheduled for the upcoming year.

The second of the objectives, the desire to set a boundary for software engineering, motivates the fundamental organization of the Guide. The material that is recognized as being within this discipline is organized into the first t10 Knowledge Areas (KAs) listed in Table 3.1. Each of these KAs is treated as a chapter in this Guide.

In establishing a boundary, it is also important to identify what disciplines share that boundary – and often a common intersection – with software engineering. To this end, the Guide also recognizes eight related disciplines, listed in Table 3.2. Software engineers should, of course, have knowledge of material from these fields (and the KA descriptions may make reference to them). It is not, however, an objective of the SWEBOK

Guide to characterize the knowledge of the related disciplines, but rather what knowledge is viewed as specific to software engineering.

Table 3.1. The SWEBOK Knowledge Areas (KAs)

Software requirements
Software design
Software construction
Software testing
Software maintenance
Software configuration management
Software engineering management
Software engineering process
Software engineering tools and methods
Software quality

Table 3.2. Related disciplines

◆ Computer engineering	◆ Project management
◆ Computer science	◆ Quality management
◆ Management	◆ Software ergonomics
◆ Mathematics	◆ Systems engineering

3.2.1 Hierarchical Organization

The organization of the KA descriptions or chapters supports the third of the project's objectives – a characterization of the contents of software engineering. The Guide uses a hierarchical organization to decompose each KA into a set of topics with recognizable labels. A two- or three-level breakdown provides a reasonable way to find topics of interest. The Guide treats the selected topics in a manner compatible with major schools of thought and with breakdowns generally found in industry and in the software engineering literature and standards. The breakdowns of topics do not presume particular application domains, business uses, management philosophies, development methods, and so forth. The extent of each topic's description is only that needed to understand the generally accepted nature of the topics and for the reader to successfully find reference material. After all, the Body of Knowledge is found in the reference materials themselves, and not in the Guide.

3.2.2 Reference Material and Matrix

To provide a topical access to the knowledge – the fourth of the project's objectives – the Guide identifies reference material for each KA, including book chapters, refereed papers, or other recognized sources of authoritative information. Each KA description also includes a matrix relating the reference material to the listed topics. The total volume of cited literature is intended to be suitable for mastery through the completion of an undergraduate education plus four years of experience.

In the 2004 edition of the Guide, all KAs were allocated around 500 pages of reference material, and this was the specification the associate editors were invited to apply. It may be argued that some KAs, such as software design for instance, deserve more pages of reference material than others. Such modulation may be applied in future editions of the Guide.

It should be noted that the Guide does not attempt to be comprehensive in its citations. Much material that is both suitable and excellent is not referenced. Material was selected in part because – taken as a collection – it provides coverage of the topics described.

3.2.3 Depth of Treatment

From the outset, the question arose as to the depth of treatment the Guide should provide. The project team adopted an approach which supports the fifth of the project's objectives – providing a foundation for curriculum development, certification and licensing. The editorial team (see Fig. 3.1) applied the criterion of *generally accepted* knowledge, to be distinguished from advanced and research knowledge (on the grounds of maturity) and from specialized knowledge (on the grounds of generality of application). The definition comes from the Project Management Institute: "The generally accepted knowledge applies to most projects most of the time, and widespread consensus validates its value and effectiveness."[30]

However, the term "generally accepted" does not imply that the designated knowledge should be uniformly applied to all software engineering endeavours – each project's needs determine that – but it does imply that competent, capable software engineers should be equipped with this knowledge for potential application. More precisely, generally accepted knowledge should be included in the study material for the software engi-

---

[30] *A Guide to the Project Management Body of Knowledge*, 2000 Edition, Project Management Institute, Newport Square, PA (www.pmi.org).

neering licensing examination that graduates would take after gaining four years of work experience. Although this criterion is specific to the US style of education and does not necessarily apply to other countries, it was deemed useful. However, the two definitions of generally accepted knowledge should be seen as complementary.

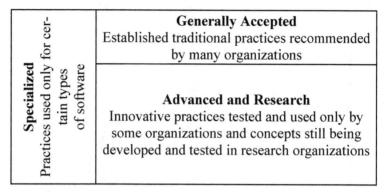

Specialized Practices used only for certain types of software	**Generally Accepted** Established traditional practices recommended by many organizations
	Advanced and Research Innovative practices tested and used only by some organizations and concepts still being developed and tested in research organizations

Fig. 3.1. Categories of knowledge

3.3 The Ontology of the SWEBOK from a Conceptual and Consensus-Reaching Perspective

This Body of Knowledge is currently organized as a taxonomy subdivided into 10 KAs designed to discriminate among the various important concepts only at the top level. Of course, the software engineering knowledge is much richer than this high-level taxonomy and currently resides in the textual descriptions of each KA. Such textual descriptions vary widely in style and content. The *conceptual* ontology approach is therefore used to analyse the richness of this body of knowledge, to improve its structuring, and to develop consensus on its detailed terminology.

The development of the software engineering domain ontology requires three phases (see Fig. 3.2): (1) Proto-ontology construction. (2) Internal validations cycle. (3) External validation (and possibly extension) cycle.

Proto-ontology construction: analysis and extraction (one SWEBOK KA at a time) of the concepts, relations between concepts and axioms (asserted necessary or necessary and sufficient conditions), terms and definitions existing in the SWEBOK Guide and related IEEE and ISO standards. Automatic term extraction tools having as input a corpus of text in natural language have been used to complete the list of concepts and relationships, identified through the analysis of the documents already mentioned.

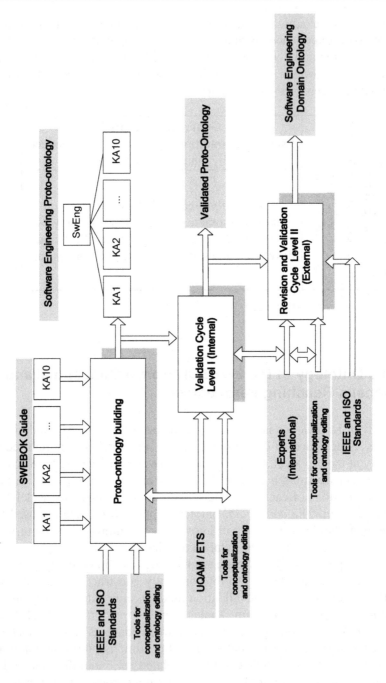

Fig. 3.2. The SWEBOK ontology project phases

Internal validation cycle: a series of validation (and possibly extension) cycles, at various instances levels (internal: ETS – UQAM – SPIN, etc.), aiming to build a progressively larger consensus, concerning the elements in the software engineering proto-ontology.

External validation cycle: a series of external validation cycles will be required, aided by internationally reputed software engineering domain experts, to build progressively a consensus concerning the concepts, attributes and relations between concepts that should be present in the final ontology.

The proto-ontology development phase has identified in the SWEBOK Guide over 4000 concepts, 400 relationships, 1200 facts as well as 15 principles. Table 3.3 presents a breakdown by KAs.

Table 3.3. Overview of quantity of elements currently in the SWEBOK proto-ontology

	Relationships	Concepts	Facts	Principles
SWEBOK main structure	4	48	55	0
Ch 01 Introduction	0*	0*	0*	0*
Ch 02 Software Requirements	24	240	72	0
Ch 03 Software Design	44	307	211	2
Ch 04 Software Construction	21	214	63	0
Ch 05 Software Testing	96	1001	165	7
Ch 06 Software Maintenance	44	706	140	0
Ch 07 Software Configuration Management	31*	85*	46*	0*
Ch 08 Software Engineering Management	33*	72*	46*	0*
Ch 09 Software Engineering Process	45	587	134	1
Ch 10 Software Engineering Tools and Methods	19	263	62	0
Ch 11Software Quality	34	447	61	5
Ch 12 Related Disciplines of Software Engineering	12	171	32	0
TOTAL	**407**	**4141**	**1087**	**15**

*: partial counting (to be finalized in the future)

The testing maintenance and process KAs include the largest number of concepts and relationships, while the testing and quality include most of the principles identified.

The major contributions expected from this approach are: (1) Identification of the main inputs, outputs and activities to be performed in order to develop the aimed ontology. (2) Identification of the main software engineering concepts, terms, definitions, relations between classes/concepts (IsA, Part–hole, and other specific relationships) and axioms describing the concepts. (3) Validation (and possibly extension) of the software engineering ontology. (4) Progressive building of a consensus concerning the concepts in the ontology aided by international software engineering domain experts.

Besides the benefits already mentioned in Sect. 3.1, the use of the "software engineering ontology" which is a result of this project may also contribute to the development of additional content validation by *automatic* cross-correlation validation (in addition to the continuous effort done by the SWEBOK review team) across the 10 KAs integrated in the SWEBOK Guide. This would ensure that all the concepts and definitions are used in a consistent manner throughout all of the SWEBOK's areas of knowledge.

3.4 The Ontology of the SWEBOK as a Formal Artifact

The SWEBOK Guide provides a foundation for the development of an ontology for software engineering, since it is the result of a process of domain expert review and validation, and provides references to other relevant sources. Nonetheless, the process of analysing the Guide to come up with a logically coherent ontology is by no means a simple process. Many of the entities described in the Guide to the SWEBOK are complex activities that produce interrelated artifacts. These entities have temporal, material and conceptual facets that should be clearly defined, and which are well known in existing upper ontologies and large commonsense bases. If the emphasis of ontology is in providing computational semantics to the representation, formal approaches are required beyond the elaboration of consensual meanings as described above. This change in focus can be considered as operational, in the sense that it is a medium towards the end of providing automation or delegating tasks to agents or software modules. This leads to a very different notion of the ontology development process in which the criterion for inclusion is usefulness for computer-based applications. Such a notion is aligned with the current view of the Semantic Web [4], which emphasizes the development of a technology based on formal description logics [3].

In practice, the formal approach entails that many of the aspects and descriptions in the SWEBOK that may be considered relevant in conceptual approaches are not appropriate for operational scenarios. For example, a statement such as the following, "Numerous models have been created to develop software, some of which emphasize construction more than others" (page 4-3 of the SWEBOK Guide), may be considered appropriate for the narrative of the Guide, but need not have a formal representation, since it is simply stating a vague narrative about a vague aspect of models. Even in the case where vagueness could be handled somewhat, it is not clear that this provides significant knowledge but instead an anecdotal statement useful for human readers only. In consequence, a formal approach for the ontology of the SWEBOK cannot be expected to cover every paragraph, but to extract only relevant, well-defined or well-definable sentences.

There exist proposals for the standardization of upper ontologies [11] that could be used as a basis for such formal semantics. In fact, the IEEE P1600.1 Standard Upper Ontology Working Group (SUO WG) is working towards that end. Given the past activity of the IEEE and other organizations in producing standards regarding the vocabulary and concepts of software engineering, there exists an opportunity to exercise and analyse the discipline from the perspective of upper ontologies as a principal case study.

A technique for validating the semantic precision of conceptual schemas is that of providing explicit links to concepts and relations that are already described in larger upper ontologies. Concretely, we make use here of the *OpenCyc* 0.9 knowledge base. This may be considered as an alternative or a complement to other analysis techniques such as the Bunge–Wand–Weber [16], whose aim is fostering the reuse of existing open knowledge engineering. In addition, the mapping to modern Web-enabled ontology languages such as OWL becomes a straightforward step.

OpenCyc is the open source version of the Cyc Knowledge Base [10], which contains over 200,000 atomic terms, and is provided with an associated efficient inference engine. Cyc attempts to provide a comprehensive upper ontology of "commonsense" knowledge, using as its underlying definition language a variant of predicate calculus called CycL. In what follows, some of the main issues in modelling the SWEBOK by linking definitions to OpenCyc are provided. The method used for such a process can be roughly described in the following steps:

1. Find one or several terms that subsume the category under consideration.
2. Check carefully that the mapping is consistent with the rest of the subsumers inside OpenCyc.

3. Provide the appropriate predicates to characterize the new category.
4. Edit it in Protégé or another editor to come up with the final formal version.

This process has the advantage of being possible for the individual work of an expert. The outcomes of the process can then be contrasted with the work of others. In any case, the process results in much more efficient and structured ontology engineering work, since the argumentation against or in favour of a given concept or predicate is put in the formal context of *OpenCyc*, which eases the process of decision making and avoids the discussion on subjective or personal opinions that are not yet put in formal terms.

3.5 Fundamental Elements of the Ontology of the SWEBOK

This section summarizes the main conceptual elements identified during the course of the research work of the authors of this chapter. The elements covered are cross-cutting many KA of the Guide and, as such, they may be considered as a "high-level" conceptual subset that gives coherence to the specifics of each KA. Here, only the more pervasive and relevant will be discussed. The exposition goes from the material elements of everyday engineering activities to the representation of prescriptive knowledge, which is by its own nature much more challenging to capture.

3.5.1 Activities, Artifacts and Agents

Engineering is basically an artifact-producing activity carried out by engineers. At this level, engineering can be seen as a flow of activities, and in an ideal world, every activity, its doer and the artifacts used, changed or created should be represented. This consideration does not care about the ways of doing the activities (the methods) but only of the representation of the activities as actually enacted. In fact, this is the recording of the actual, real empirical experience of engineering as a human activity. That objectivity makes this a somewhat easier level to be represented. First, the engineers that do the actual work can be characterized as a subset of the class `oc_IntelligentAgent`, defined in OpenCyc in the following manner: "An agent is an IntelligentAgent if and only if it is capable of knowing and acting, and capable of employing its knowledge in its actions." From an ontological viewpoint, the term `SoftwareEngineer` is not a rigid property [17], since being a software engineer is contingent to a work position, and it is not an essential property of the individuals. This leads to the first proposition for the general mapping.

Proposition #1 `SoftwareEngineers` are a class of `oc_IntelligentAgents` (excluding collectives). Software engineering activities will require individuals of this class.

It is important to separate the individual workers from collectives (e.g. organizations or teams). This entails that `SoftwareEngineer` is disjoint with `oc_MultiIndividualAgent-Intelligent`, which concretely addresses collectives with the capability of acting purposefully. Teams of software engineers might be considered relevant since productivity is connected to team dynamics as recognized in software estimation models [5]. However, individuals are the unit of responsibility and they possess specific competencies or skills that provide them with a unique meaning.

Activities are the fabric of engineering work. Activities in OpenCyc can be represented as `oc_Action` instances. These actions are defined as "The collection of `oc_Events` that are carried out by some 'doer' (see `oc_doneBy`). Instances of `oc_Action` include any event in which one or more actors effect some change in the (tangible or intangible) state of the world, typically by an expenditure of effort or energy." An `oc_Event` is in turn "a dynamic situation in which the state of the world changes; each instance is something one would say 'happens'". Going a step further, engineering activities are in fact `oc_Purposeful-Actions`, as "each instance of PurposefulAction is an action consciously, volitionally, and purposefully done by at least one actor".

Proposition #2 Actual software engineering activities, as enacted in software projects, are a specific class of `PurposefulAction` situated in the context of a project that has as its final outcome the creation or modification of a software program.

The term "software program" as a generic intellectual product can be mapped to `oc_ComputerProgram-CW` that is "distinct from computer code and from both running and installed programs." The `oc_-purposeOfEvent` predicate can be used to explicitly declare the software-creating purpose. This provides a necessary and sufficient definition to classify `SoftwareEngineeringActivity`(ies). From this definition of activities, the wide array of activities that are commonly identified in software processes can be characterized. Nevertheless, the definition of each kind of activity requires the specification of different aspects, including the kind of engineer, the outcomes, and the usual sequence with other kinds of activities. For example, according to the SWEBOK Guide "requirements elicitation" is the "first stage" and it is mainly concerned with "getting human stakeholders to articulate their requirements".

The third class of basic elements of actual engineering practice is the artifacts used, created or changed. An oc_Artifact is "an at least partially tangible thing which was intentionally created by an oc_Agent (or a group of Agents working together) to serve some purpose or perform some function".

> **Proposition #3** The elements used, created and modified in software engineering activities are specific kinds of Artifacts.

An important ontological differentiation for artifacts in software engineering is that of Documents and their "propositional" content, i.e. the information they contain. This is clear in OpenCyc with the categories of oc_InformationBearingThings and oc_Propositional-InformationThings. This allows a clarification of the difference of the propositional content and the thing that conveys it. For example, a requirements document can be broken into several documents, but the propositional content is unique irrespective of its digital or hardcopy form. When speaking about the software process, the important part is the propositional content, while the concrete things have some degree of arbitrariness in formatting, and they are only important for cataloguing processes specific to each project.

The basic definitions so far provide room for the classification of most of the elements present in the SWEBOK Guide in the form of a description of activities. However, there are specific elements that should be addressed since they have a special signification in engineering.

3.5.2 Models, Specifications and Methods

The word "model" has 297 occurrences in the SWEBOK Guide. Model-Artifact provides the appropriate semantics for the concept: "a collection of artifacts; a subset of oc_VisualInformationBearing-Thing. Each element of Model-Artifact is a tangible object designed to resemble and/or represent some other object, which may or may not exist tangibly." The ModelFn function designates all the models of a given

thing, e.g. `ModelFn(SoftwareComponent)`. This is a concrete characterization of models that seems to match all the uses of model in the
SWEBOK. As information-bearing objects, the models are information-
bearing things (`oc_IBT`) as well, so that their contents can be represented
in a propositional form, through the predicate `oc_contains-`
`InfoPropositional-IBT` (IBT PIT) that links to a propositional information thing (PIT). PITs are in themselves `microtheories`, thus allowing the definition in logical terms of the actual contents of the model.
This could be applied, for example, to develop systems that represent
UML diagrams through logics, which will enable a degree of increased
automation.

The Guide to the SWEBOK somewhat differentiates models and artifacts, as in the software design KA "The output of this process is a set of
models and artifacts that record the major decisions that have been
taken", but ontologically this distinction is irrelevant.

The word "Specification" appears 138 times in the Guide. For example,
"Requirements *specification* typically refers to the production of a document, or its electronic equivalent, that can be systematically reviewed,
evaluated, and approved." The production of a document is an
`oc_PurposefulAction`. But the `oc_Specification` itself is an
`oc_PropositionalConceptualWork`, which enables a representation
of the contents of the specification in logics (different from the "specification document" that is an `oc_InformationBearing-Thing`).

An ontologically different concept related to activities in software engineering is that of "methods" for activities, i.e. the normative specification
of "blueprints" for potential courses of activity. These specifications have
an intrinsic prescriptive character, so they should not be specified as actions, but rather as specifications.

3.5.3 Theoretical Standpoints and Guidelines

There is not currently a uniform or standard form to represent theoretical
positions or standpoints in ontological engineering. Further, the discipline
of software engineering has not produced a relevant body of theories or
laws that explain the discipline, and most of the knowledge is in the form
of guidelines or generic hypotheses. In fact, the SWEBOK Guide does not
provide a classification of theories and frameworks according to conventional scientific terms, so this is an area that is relevant for future revisions. However, some elements backed by empirical evidence are yet to be
referenced in the SWEBOK, and this calls for specific representation techniques. For example, the well-known "laws of software evolution" [9] re-

quire a careful consideration. For the sake of illustration, we will take here the following statement from these laws: "An E-type program that is used must be continually adapted else it becomes progressively less satisfactory." This requires the following elements to be addressed:

- First, a characterization of `E-TypeProgram` is required. Computer programs as conceptual works (different from their copies or physical representation) are captured by the generic `oc_ComputerProgramCW` term. Consequently, types of programs could be defined from such abstraction. E-type programs as "software that implements an application or addresses a problem in the real world" could be characterized by linking them to representations of the problem addressed.
- The representation of the evolution of the program. For this, OpenCyc provides the `oc_programCode` predicate connecting the programs as conceptual entities to `oc_ComputerCode` instances. In turn, these can be subject to a modelling of time-stamped revisions or versions that could be used to assess if a program is being subject to evolution or not. This enables the quantification of the adaptations (and even of the extent in terms of modifications) in the time scale. But the term "continually adapted" is by its nature vague, and some measure or statistical model would be required to assess it from a computational viewpoint.
- The representation of the "use" of a program. This would require a tracking of the lifecycle of the program that in some cases might be difficult, but for reasons outside the representation itself.
- A representation of what "satisfactory" means. This is probably the most controversial issue, since there is not a single universally accepted standard of "satisfactoriness". Satisfaction is usually mentioned as one of the aspects of usability [15], but other elements of the "software quality" concepts could also be considered. In addition, satisfaction is often measured through questionnaires or interviews with users, although there is not a standard measuring instrument for it.

If characterizations for the above could be clearly defined, a software agent might be in a position to examine representations of actual software projects and trigger an alert when a program is requiring an evolution. An inference rule for the state of "Software-RequiringAdaptation" could be formulated. Further, the provision of ontology-based tools to represent actual software projects could automatically find evidence against the statement.

However, as can be appreciated in the example, this requires the *operationalization* of a number of elements that are only vaguely defined in the original statement. This constitutes a research direction in itself, and is beyond the scope of a simple representation of the SWEBOK Guide. An alternative may be that of codifying such kinds of statements in a form that is useful for cataloguing a human query, but that does not entail any kind of delegation of tasks or decisions to software. This could be useful but it is not a true representation of knowledge in the area in the sense of having computational semantics. In consequence, this level of theory inside the ontology could be seen as the ultimate goal, but requiring substantial work beyond the formulation of the SWEBOK in ontology languages.

An important element introduced by the disparity of theoretical or methodological standpoints in software engineering is that of conflicting knowledge. This is prominent in the diversity of approaches to the software process, but it may also arise in more specific situations. Following the example above, it might be the case that different positions on what "continuous adaptation" is in term of frequency (or on the definition for "satisfactoriness") lead to incompatible views. This would require either the provision of separate ontologies or the use of a representational mechanism that allows such a kind of potential inconsistency or divergence. The concept of *microtheory* in *OpenCyc* provides a such representational mechanism, intended to organize assertions that depend on a "shared set of assumptions on which the truth of the assertions depends". Definitions inside the same microtheory need to be consistent, but this is not required across microtheories.

Summing up, the logical tools are prepared for the representation of theory or assumptions, but these require more elaboration. Arguably, this could be considered a future requirement for the revision and evolution of the SWEBOK.

3.6 Conclusions

The SWEBOK represents the outcome of a significant collaborative effort in shaping the scope of software engineering as a discipline. The elaboration of knowledge representations about the contents and structure of the Guide represents a further step in the clarification of such knowledge, and may also serve as a revision tool for the Guide itself [13]. Nonetheless, there are different perspectives that can be taken when developing an ontology of the SWEBOK. These range from conceptual representations that attempt to unveil some conceptual links between parts of the Guide to formal approaches oriented to develop software that automates some tasks. While the former may take the form of topic maps and can be used, for example, to provide more graphical parts of the Guide, the latter are only oriented to machine consumption. Both views and others, intermediate or similar, serve different purposes, but all of them are important tools for enquiry on the contents of the discipline.

References

1. Abran, A., Moore, J., Bourque, P., Dupuis, R., Tripp, L. (2005) Guide to the Software Engineering Body of Knowledge – SWEBOK. IEEE Computer Society Press, Computer Society Press, Los Alamitos. http://www.swebok.org
2. Auyang, S. (2004) Engineering – an endless frontier. Harvard University Press, Cambridge, MA.
3. Baader, F., Calvanese, D., McGuinness, D., Nardi, D., Patel-Schneider, P. (eds.), (2003), The Description Logic Handbook. Theory, Implementation and Applications. Cambridge University Press, Cambridge.
4. Berners-Lee, T., Hendler, J., Lassila, O. (2001). The Semantic Web. Scientific American, 284(5): 34–43.
5. Boehm, B. (1981) Software Engineering Economics. Prentice Hall, Englewodod Cliffs, NJ 1981.
6. Brooks, A. (1997) Meta analysis - a silver bullet - for meta-analysts. Journal of Empirical Software Engineering, 2: 333–338.
7. Brooks, F. (1987) No silver bullet: Essence and accidents of software engineering. IEEE Computer, 20(4): 10–19.
8. ISO/IEC TR 19759-2005 (2005) Guide to the Software Engineering Body of Knowledge (SWEBOK), International Organization for Standardization - ISO, Geneva.
9. Lehman, M. (1996) Laws of Software Evolution Revisited, pos. pap., EWSPT96, LNCS 1149. Springer-Verlag, Berlin, pp. 108–124.
10. Lenat, D.B. (1995) Cyc: A large-scale investment in knowledge infrastructure. Communications of the ACM 38(11), pp. 33–38 (17).
11. Niles, I., Pease, A. (2001). Towards a Standard Upper Ontology. In Proceedings of the 2nd International Conference on Formal Ontology in Information Systems (FOIS-2001), Chris Welty and Barry Smith (eds.), Ogunquit, Maine, October 17–19, 2001.
12. Popper. K, (1959) The Logic of Scientific Discovery. Routledge, London.
13. Sicilia, M.A., Cuadrado, J.J., García, E. Rodríguez, D., Hilera, J.R. (2005) The evaluation of ontological representation of the SWEBOK as a revision tool. In Proceedings of the First International Workshop on the Evolution of the Guide to the Software Engineering Body of Knowledge in conjunction with the 29th Annual International Computer Software and Application Conference (COMPSAC), Edinburgh, UK, 26–28 July 2005.

14. Sicilia, M.A., García-Barriocanal, E., Díaz, P., Aedo, I. (2003) A Literature-Based Approach to the Annotation and Browsing of Domain-Specific Web Resources. Information Research, 8(2).

15. Van Welie M., van der Veer G.C., Eliëns A., (1999) Breaking down usability. Procedings of Interact'99, pp. 613–620.

16. Wand, Y., Weber, R. (1995) On the deep structure of information systems. Information Systems Journal, 5: 203–223.

17. Welty, C, Guarino. N, (2001) Supporting ontological analysis of taxonomic relationships. Data and Knowledge Engineering, 39(1): 51–74.

4. An Ontology for Software Development Methodologies and Endeavours

César González-Pérez and Brian Henderson-Sellers

Department of Software Engineering, Faculty of Information Technology, University of Technology, Sydney, Australia
cesar.gonzalez@esi.es, brian@it.uts.edu.au

4.1 Introduction

Software development is a complex activity that usually involves people, organisations and technologies with very diverse characteristics. People's expectations and skills vary greatly; organisations' capability and financial constraints are diverse; and technologies keep changing and breaking through at an increasing pace. In such a context, the successful construction of a piece of software that adds value to all involved stakeholders proves difficult. As in any other complex enterprise, lack of a common vocabulary and, more generally, a common worldview, are major causes of misunderstanding and cross-talking, which, in turn, easily lead to unfulfilled expectations and stakeholder disappointment. Nowadays, software controls life-critical as well as mundane devices, from lifts to aeroplanes to telephone exchanges. In this regard, unfulfilled expectations in a piece of software usually mean faulty functionality, decreased robustness or reliability, or some other manifestation of weakened quality.

For this reason, utilising a common set of concepts, as well as a common set of terms to refer to these concepts, is crucial for the development of high-quality software. It can be argued that fewer misunderstandings and misinterpretations will arise in any communication process when the involved parties use an agreed-upon, well-defined conceptual base. For the sake of common sense, this common conceptual base, or ontology, must have the following properties:

- It must be **complete**, so that no area of software development lacks coverage.
- It must be **unambiguous**, so that misinterpretations are avoided.
- It must be taken from the appropriate domain, so that concepts are familiar and **intuitive** to their users.
- It must be as **generic** as possible, so that different usages in different contexts are possible.
- It must be **extensible**, so that new concepts can be added to it without breaking the existing ones.

Completeness can be achieved by looking at the different activities performed within software development enterprises, and by ensuring that the ontology covers all of them. Ambiguity can be avoided by providing simple and concise definitions for each concept, as well as a semi-formal model of the complete ontology. This semi-formal model is, in our case, an object-oriented class model that shows the structure of the ontology. Intuitiveness can be obtained by looking at the different communities that participate in software development enterprises and by providing a conceptual subset particularly adapted for each of them. For example, a computer programmer does not use the same concepts as a project manager. Genericity can be attained by keeping the ontology as small and as simple as possible, and by trying to *remove* from it, rather than add to it, as many concepts as possible. The aim is to achieve maximum expressiveness by being minimal. Finally, the ontology can be made extensible by providing the appropriate mechanisms and anchor points from which to add new concepts. In our case, the mechanism is strongly based in standard object-oriented mechanisms such as subtyping.

Many authors and efforts have proposed metamodels or frameworks that partially define ontologies for software development. For example, the popular UML [21, 22] defines the concepts that a software developer may use in order to describe a system (such as Class, Attribute and Operation). Standards such as ISO/IEC 12207 [14] and 15288 [15] describe the process that software developers may follow in order to design and build a system and, in doing so, make use of an implicitly defined set of concepts (such as Process and Outcome). OPEN [6] and SPEM [23] specify the relevant concepts that may be used in order to describe a process to be followed by software developers (such as Activity and Iteration). ISO/IEC 15504 [16] and CMMI [27] define the relevant concepts to perform capability or maturity assessment (such as Process and Task). Each of these approaches defines a cohesive set of concepts that, although useful in its local domain, is not complete, unambiguous, intuitive, generic and extensible enough as to qualify as an ontology for software development.

This chapter introduces an ontology for software development that exhibits all the above-mentioned properties, and which has been constructed by taking the best bits of the above-mentioned standards and organising them into a completely new architecture. This ontology contains a meta-model plus the necessary architectural infrastructure to enable method engineers and software developers to successfully interact with a common conceptual framework.

4.2 Ontology Architecture

4.2.1 The Communities Involved

The ontology presented in this chapter is intended to be understood and used by people directly involved in software development enterprises. Those people belong to two major communities:

- Software developers, who perform software development activities in order to construct software products by applying a certain methodology.
- Method engineers, who define the methodology to be used by software developers in order to develop software products.

The terms "software developer" and "method engineer" refer to roles that individuals or organisations may play. In some enterprises, the same individuals can play both, while in others different people will play different roles. Also, we need to clarify the term "method" used in "method engineer": as far as our work is concerned, "method" is a synonym of "methodology" [17, 24]. Furthermore, we must say that the usage of the term "method" or "methodology" does not imply formal, explicitly defined rules; it simply means the specification of the process followed plus the modelling approach undertaken in order to develop some software.

Given the two above-described communities, the following observations can be made. First of all, method engineers construct methodologies for software developers. Secondly, software developers use methodologies in order to construct software products. In this sense, software developers are the users of what method engineers produce, namely methodologies. This is important because, in this context, a methodology can be seen as a product developed by one community for the other, and all the usual user-oriented and quality assurance techniques that are often utilised in other engineering enterprises can also be used here. We can, therefore, assume that a methodology will have a set of requirements that method engineers will need to specify [25]; similarly, we can talk about the correctness, robustness, usability and extensibility of a methodology. Our ontology, being a framework within which methodologies will be constrained, must contemplate these quality factors appropriately.

When faced with the task of constructing a methodology, method engineers often use a given set of concepts in order to specify the process to follow and the modelling approach to be undertaken. Similarly, when software developers apply a methodology in order to construct a software product, they also employ a given set of concepts, given by the same ontology and potentially refined by the methodology being used. For example, our ontology defines the concept of Task and establishes that tasks can be performed by developers for a given purpose. This means that software developers, from the perspective of this ontology, will perform tasks. When defining a particular methodology, method engineers can refine the concept of Task into more concrete and specialized concepts, such as Capture Requirements Task or Write Source Code Task; software developers, therefore, will be able to perform tasks of either of these types. Notice how the specific task types are defined by the particular methodology being used, whereas the general concept of a Task, present at both the methodology definition and software development levels, is defined by the common ontology.

From the previous paragraphs, we can see how a concept defined by the ontology (e.g. Task) is refined by method engineers into more specific concepts and delivered as a readily usable product to software developers. The concept of Task (or, for that matter, most of the concepts in the ontology) must be understandable by both method engineers and software developers, since both communities will closely interact with it. At the same time, each of the two communities does not necessarily interact with the concept in the same fashion; for example, software developers are typically concerned with the duration of a task, while method engineers do not care about the duration of tasks, focusing instead on establishing the specific purpose of each kind of task (e.g. capturing requirements or writing code). We can say that many concepts in the ontology, such as Task, have two facets, each targeting one specific community. Although the overall concept of what a task is must be shared by both communities, the detailed location of the concept in its semantic network, as well as its particular attributes, are community-specific. Interestingly enough, some concepts in the ontology are only relevant for one of the communities. For example, the concept of a Person is only relevant for software developers, since method engineers do not consider specific, individual persons (but, rather, kinds of Roles, Teams or, more generically, Producers) when designing a methodology. Similarly, the concept of a Conglomerate (i.e. a collection of closely related method elements) is important for method engineers for organising methodology elements but not significant for software developers, who just apply the methodology.

4.2.2 Usage and Ontology Domains

The ontology presented here is an organised collection of concepts that have three major properties:

- Each *concept* is an intensional definition of a set of potential entities. For example, the Task concept stands for all possible tasks that may exist or be relevant. In this sense, a concept is very much like a type or a class [19].
- Each concept may be related to other concepts by *associations*. An association is a formalisation of potential relationships between entities of the corresponding concepts.
- Each concept is intended to be used. Since the ontology itself is just a collection of concepts, concept usage must happen through their definitions.

But, how are concepts in an ontology *used*? We can identify three major mechanisms of usage, two of which correspond to two major mechanisms in the object-oriented paradigm: subtyping and instantiation. The third mechanism is called resource usage.

Subtyping a particular concept (called the supertype) means creating a new concept (called the subtype) that intensionally specifies a subset of the entities that are specified by the supertype. For example, the concept Task can be subtyped into the concept Write Code Task. This means that the definition of Write Code Task must specify a subset of the entities specified by the definition of Task; in this example, Write Code Task specifies all those tasks that happen to focus on writing code.

Instantiating a particular concept (called the type) means creating or identifying an entity (called the instance) that conforms to the definition of the type. For example, the Write Code Task concept can be instantiated into an actual writing code task by a software developer. By actually writing some code, a software developer is creating an instance of the Write Code Task concept.

We must emphasise that a strong object-oriented approach is being taken here and, therefore, all the well-known object-oriented implications of subtyping and instantiation are relevant. For example, subtypes inherit attributes and associations from their supertypes, type conformance automatically propagates up the subtyping hierarchy and the Liskov Substitution Principle [18] applies.

The third way of using the ontology is by resource usage, i.e. by understanding and assimilating the information comprised by entities. For example, consider a Language concept, which represents any natural or formal language. This concept can be instantiated into specific languages, such as C# or Free-Form English. These instances are entities that can be used by reading the information contained in them and applying it. No further instantiation or subtyping is involved.

Given that subtyping and instantiation of the concepts in the ontology will be supposedly carried out by its users, namely method engineers and software developers, we can assume that, at any point in time during the life of this ontology, a complex network of concepts and entities will exist. For the sake of clarity, concepts and entities are partitioned into three different domains (Fig. 4.1):

- The metamodel domain, which contains a predefined, fixed collection of interrelated concepts.
- The method domain, which contains the concepts and instances derived from concepts in the ontology by method engineers.
- The endeavour domain, which contains the instances derived from concepts in the method domain by software developers.

Notice that the three domains have been defined around the communities that interact with the ontology. The metamodel domain is basically a "read-only" repository of information, which contains a predefined collection of concepts that is not intended to be changed. This collection of concepts, usually called a *metamodel*, acts as a common standard on which the other domains are based. The standardised concepts in this metamodel are fully described in following sections.

The metamodel domain is intended to be used as a starting point by method engineers so they can develop methodologies. Method engineers will typically use the concepts in the metamodel domain by subtyping and instantiation, hence creating new concepts (subtypes of existing ones) and entities (instances of concepts).

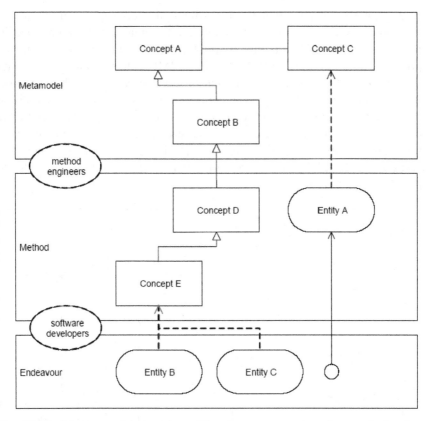

Fig. 4.1. Architecture of the ontology. The three separate domains are depicted as horizontal layers. The communities that interact with each domain are indicated by dashed ellipses. Concepts and entities are depicted, respectively, by appropriately labelled rectangles and rounded rectangles. Associations are shown as solid non-directed lines. Subtyping relationships are shown as solid arrows with a triangular arrowhead. Instantiation relationships are shown as dashed arrows with a simple arrowhead. Resource usages are shown as solid arrows with a simple arrowhead and a small circle at its origin

All these new concepts and entities created by method engineers are said to form the method domain. The method domain, in turn, is "read-only" for software developers, which may refer to it as the "method" or "methodology", since it actually defines what they are expected to do, how and why. Software developers will use it by creating instances of concepts in it and, as well, by following the guidance explained by entities. The instances thus created by software developers are said to form the endeavour domain.

We must emphasise that the placement of a concept or entity in one domain or another depends exclusively on its semantics (as defined earlier in this section), and not on any predefined structural convention. Approaches such as UML, SPEM or other OMG-centric frameworks make use of the so-called *strict metamodelling paradigm* [1], which determines in which domain (called layers) a concept belongs to based exclusively on its structural relationships to other concepts. This approach has been demonstrated to be inappropriate for the representation of complete and comprehensive methodological frameworks [8, 12]. In our ontology, concepts and entities are placed in the domain where they make most sense to the people involved (Fig. 4.2).

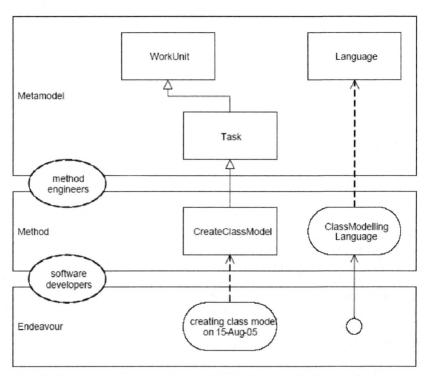

Fig. 4.2. Some sample concepts and entities in the ontology architecture. In this example, method engineers have created the Create Class Model concept as a subtype of the Task entity in the metamodel, as well as the Class Modelling Language entity as an instance of the Language entity in the metamodel. Software developers have instantiated Create Class Model into a specific instance in the endeavour domain, and are using the Class Modelling Language as a resource

For example, consider the concept of Task. Since this concept is relevant to both method engineers and software developers, and since it is deemed to be generic and common enough to be necessary in most methodologies, Task is placed in the metamodel domain. Different methodologies, perhaps pertaining to different styles to software development, may use different kinds of tasks; for example, an object-oriented methodology for information systems development may include a Create Class Model Task concept, whereas Extreme Programming [4] does not involve such a concept. Create Class Model Task is a subtype of Task, but it is not generic enough as to belong to the metamodel domain, and therefore it is placed in the method domain. When a software developer creates a class model, he/she is actually instantiating the Create Class Model Task concept and, since that particular instance is relevant only to that particular endeavour (the project he/she is working on), the instance is placed into the endeavour domain.

4.2.3 Product and Process

In previous sections we have said that a software development methodology is the specification of the process to be followed plus the modelling approach undertaken in order to develop some software. Although these two aspects are different, they are closely related and, more importantly, highly dependent on each other. A linguistic simile can be used: the specification of the process to follow consists of actions to be performed, such as create a model, verify a design or determine some requirements. Process can be therefore described in terms of verbs. These verbs denote actions that are to be performed on some objects, which are nouns. As in any natural language, the meaning of verbs cannot be specified without knowledge of the nouns to which they can be applied. For example, consider a methodology that contains a concept named Create Class Model Task. The meaning of such a concept cannot be established unless we agree on what a class model actually is. In turn, this implies agreeing on what a class is, and perhaps what attributes and associations are. When more detailed task descriptions are introduced, this need becomes even more patent; for example, the concept Add Operations to Classes Task is only meaningful in a context in which operation and class are well-known concepts and the relationship between them is agreed upon.

It is possible, however, to describe the semantics of nouns with no reference whatsoever to the verbs that may act upon them. Although a behavioural (i.e. verb-based) definition may be possible in some circumstances, a structural definition of nouns is always possible. This has been called the Principle of the Pre-existing Structure [7] and used a key foundation of the Structure–Process–Outcome model [13], in the context of which it was said that "structure must always come first" and that "without structure there can be no process" (p. 28). Although some process-centric approaches such as OPEN or Catalysis [5] try to define a set of actions without specifying the structure of concepts to which they apply, a significant number of assumptions are implicitly or explicitly made. For example, the OPEN literature explicitly says that an object-oriented approach to software development is encouraged if the process defined in the OPEN repository is to be used.

The degree to which a structure is necessary before a meaningful function can be laid on top is often underestimated. Process-centric approaches such as OPEN include product-related concepts such as Work Product or Document. These concepts are definitely useful as bridges between the process and product sides of the metamodel, but they need to be refined into more detailed concepts for the sake of referential integrity: the specification of the process makes explicit reference to countless nouns (such as class, attribute, operation and role) which are not defined at all. Without an understanding of these nouns, we cannot understand the process completely.

Despite the evidence that structure comes first, most approaches related to the description of software development concepts are either modelling-centric or process-centric, each neglecting the other side of the whole. UML is absolutely process-less, whereas SPEM and many ISO standards (12207, 15288, 15504) completely lack a modelling side. The myth that modelling and process issues can be separately determined and later plugged in together is repeated by the literature, although nobody has demonstrated that it can be successfully done, and the theoretical evidence cited earlier in this section is discouraging. Therefore, a radically new approach has been taken for the ontology presented here aimed at rectifying this dislocation, in which an integral approach has been adopted by looking at modelling and process issues simultaneously and developing them in parallel, thus guaranteeing interoperability. This does not mean that existing approaches such as UML or SPEM are automatically excluded if this ontology is adopted; they can still be used as long as they are expressed in terms of the metamodel described here. As we will see in forthcoming sections, UML is easily expressible as an instance of a small number of concepts in this new metamodel, which makes it a candidate modelling language to be used in the context of our ontology.

The following sections describe the metamodel domain of our ontology in detail, which is strongly based in the Australian Standard AS 4651 [26]. Endeavour-related concepts are described first, followed by method-related concepts. Concepts are formalised as object-oriented classes, with additional constructs such as attributes and associations that are used to convey the appropriate semantics. UML class diagrams are used as a notational means. In this regard, and given the problems inherent to UML's conception of whole/part relationships [3], white diamonds will be used in UML class diagrams to depict generic whole/part relationships, without any reference whatsoever to their secondary characteristics.

4.3 Endeavour-Related Concepts

The endeavour domain contains all the entities that are created by software developers when they apply a certain methodology. These entities are created by instantiating concepts from the method domain. In addition to creating entities in the endeavour domain, software developers often use entities in the method domain as resources. It is possible to determine the major types of concepts and entities involved in the endeavour layer, although it must be taken into account that the particular concepts and entities will depend on the actual methodology being used. For example, it can be argued that software developers *always* perform tasks in order to obtain work products, perhaps with the usage of some tools. This statement is abstract enough as to be universally valid as far as our ontology is concerned. At the same time, it shows that there exist different types of concepts in the ontology, tasks and work products being good examples. It is possible, therefore, for the metamodel domain to contain an abstract specification of the Task and Work Product concepts, for example, such that a double objective is attained:

- The specifications are generic enough as to be universal, i.e. any methodology obtained from the metamodel can be expressed in terms of them.
- The specifications are concrete enough as to be useful, i.e. their presence shapes the methodologies that can be constructed from the metamodel.

This does not mean that any methodology created from a metamodel containing the Task and Work Product concepts, for example, must use them. Method engineers are free to choose which concepts in the metamodel to use and which to discard for a given methodology.

The remainder of this section describes the concepts in the metamodel domain that represent entities in the endeavour domain. These concepts, by their very nature, are intended to be instantiated by software developers, so they must represent entities that make complete sense from a software developer's perspective.

4.3.1 High-Level View

From a high-level point of view, only five major types of entities exist in the endeavour domain (Fig. 4.3):

- Work Units, or jobs performed, or intended to be performed, within an endeavour.
- Stages, or managed time frames within an endeavour.
- Work Products, or artifacts of interest for the endeavour.
- Model Units, or atomic components of a model, which represent a cohesive fragment of information in the subject being modelled.
- Producers, or agents that have the responsibility to execute work units.

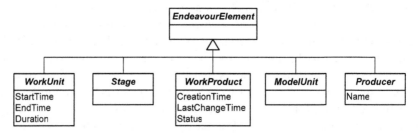

Fig. 4.3. High-level view of endeavour-related concepts in the metamodel domain

These five basic concepts can be generalised into a common, abstract concept named Endeavour Element, which represents anything in the endeavour domain. Work units are the tasks or activities that software developers perform, and have a start and end time as well as a duration. Stages are the major time frames in an endeavour, which help give work units some temporal structure. Work products, such as documents or software, are the tangible results of performing work units and have creation and last change times as well as a status. The status of a work product is always one of the enumerated list {Initial, Complete, Accepted, Approved}. Model units are the individual elements that comprise models, such as the various classes and attributes that make up a class model. Finally, producers are the people and teams that actually perform the work units in order to create work products.

Work Unit and Stage are concepts related to the process side of methodologies, while Work Product and Model Unit are concepts related to the modelling (or product) side. Producer is a people-related concept.

4.3.2 The Process Side

On the process side, there exist several subtypes of work units (Fig. 4.4):

- Tasks, which are small-grained work units that focus on what must be done in order to achieve a given purpose.
- Techniques, which are small-grained work units that focus on how the given purpose may be achieved.
- Work Flows, which are large-grained work units that operate within a given area of expertise. These can be further classified into:
  - Activities, which represent a continuous responsibility.
  - Processes, which represent a discrete piece of work.

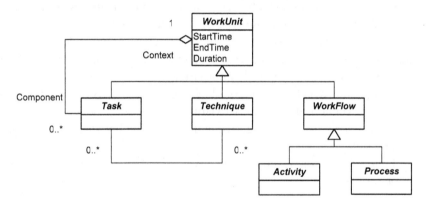

Fig. 4.4. Work unit subtypes

Tasks are simple, purpose-oriented chunks of work, usually having a name that describes the job being done, such as writing code for a class or documenting the requirements. The purpose of a task can usually be achieved in multiple ways, and techniques may be used to specify each of these. Techniques usually have a name that also describes the job being done, but suggests their "implementation" rather than the expected result, such as refactoring (one way to obtain enhanced code) or analysing text (one way to identify classes in a problem domain). Work flows, on the other hand, are large-grained chunks of work that are characterised by a given area of expertise. These, therefore, have names related to that area, such as engineering requirements or managing assets. Activities are continuous, often ongoing responsibilities, while processes are one-off jobs that can be seen as atomic from an execution perspective, i.e. they can be considered as fully done or not done at all, which is crucial for process assessment [10]. A sample activity could be managing the assets of a company (this will keep going indefinitely), and a sample process could be engineering the requirements for a given system (this will be finished at some point so that the project can proceed forward).

Sometimes, work units are too complex to be tackled directly, and for this reason they are decomposed into other, smaller work units. For example, a task breakdown structure is a good example of how larger tasks are decomposed into "smaller" tasks. Also, activities and processes tend to be implemented as a collection of tasks. This means that many work units, in fact, may be expressed as a collection of tasks, as depicted in Fig. 4.4.

Work units are often organised into stages. Different types of stages exist (Fig. 4.5):

- Instantaneous Stages, which are managed points in time within an endeavour. There is a single subtype of instantaneous stage:
  - Milestones, which mark some significant event in the endeavour.
- Stages with Duration, which are managed intervals of time within an endeavour. These can be further classified into:
  - Builds, for which the major objective is the delivery of an incremented version of an already existing set of work products.
  - Phases, for which the objective is the transition between levels of abstraction.
  - Time Cycles, for which the objective is the delivery of a final product or service.

Instantaneous stages allow the developers to manage specific points in time as especially relevant. Milestones are the best example. Stages with duration, on the other hand, are not points in time but time spans, and therefore have a duration. There are three types of them. Builds are usually small and are repeated iteratively, having the objective of incrementing an existing set of work products with some additional value. They form the basis of many incremental and iterative methodologies. Phases are usually larger than builds and not iterative in nature, focusing on the transition between abstraction levels. For example, the implementation phase in a traditional waterfall approach helps the transition from a collection of detailed designs into a working piece of software. Phases are sometimes composed of a series of builds. Finally, time cycles are again "larger" in

time than phases, and focus on the delivery of added value to some stakeholders. For example, a complete project, as well as any subprojects, can
be each modelled as a time cycle.

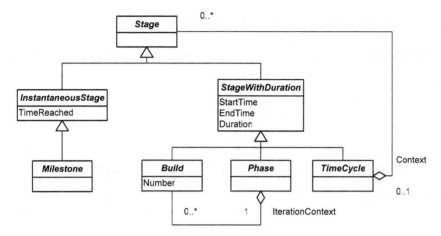

Fig. 4.5. Stage subtypes

The connection between work units and stages occurs between Work
Flow and Stage with Duration (Fig. 4.6). This means that stages with duration act as temporal "containers" for work flows.

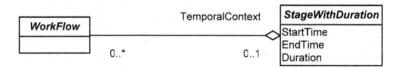

Fig. 4.6. Connection between work units and stages

4.3.3 The Product Side

On the product (or modelling) side, there are several subtypes of work
products (Fig. 4.7). Four are "simple" types:

• Software Items, which are pieces of software of interest to the endeavour.
• Hardware Items, which are pieces of hardware of interest to the endeavour.

- Models, which are formal representations of some subject that act as its surrogate for some well-defined purpose.
- Documents, which are durable depictions of a fragment of reality.

A fifth subtype allows for heterogeneous work products:

- Composite Work Products, which are composed of other work products.

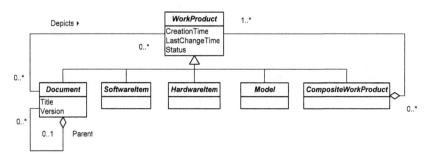

Fig. 4.7. Work product subtypes

Although the name "work product" may seem to indicate that they are always produced by the endeavour, this is not the case; actually, work products are any artifacts of interest to the endeavour, either produced by it or used for some purpose. Software items are any piece of software that is produced or used by the endeavour. Hardware items, similarly, are any piece of hardware produced or used by the endeavour. Models are formal representations of other things, and are often used as surrogates in place of the subject they represent. For example, a class model or an architectural model of a system are models. Since models are purely abstract constructs, some means of depicting them in a durable, perceivable fashion is needed; Documents are used for this purpose. Documents can also depict other things that are not models, such as policies, contracts, guidelines, etc. Documents may also be composed of subdocuments to an arbitrary depth. For example, a class diagram or a requirements specification document are documents. Notice the difference between a class diagram (a document) and the underlying model that it represents (a class model). Finally, composite work products are heterogeneous work products that may be composed of different kinds of sub-work products. For example, the final product of an endeavour is often a composite work product, since it typically contains a software item (the final software system), perhaps some hardware items, and some documents (such as the user's manual).

Although work product concepts can describe the product side of an endeavour, they are very large-grained; for example, it is possible to use our ontology to say that a software developer has created a Class Model or a Requirements Specification Document. However, in the absence of smaller grained concepts, we cannot specify what these work products contain. In consequence, tasks operating on these work products, such as Validate the Requirements or Add Operations to Classes, cannot be satisfactorily described. As we have discussed elsewhere, tasks operate at a very detailed level, which work products cannot match. Continuing with our example, and in order to fully account for the above-mentioned sample tasks, the modelling concepts of Requirement, Class and Operation need to be introduced. Of course, different methodologies will almost certainly use different modelling concepts. For example, a UML-based method would use the concepts of Class and Operation, while an agent-oriented methodology would use concepts such as Agent and Message. Therefore, the small-grained modelling concepts to be used by a method cannot be frozen in the metamodel, in the same way that specific activities and tasks to be performed cannot be frozen either.

What we can do, however, is to specify an abstract concept from which these detailed ones can be derived by subtyping by method engineers, in the same fashion that specific task concepts can be derived by subtyping from the concept Task. The concept Model Unit plays precisely this role. A model unit is an atomic component of a model, which represents a cohesive fragment of information in the subject being modelled. For example, in a method using an object-oriented approach, each class, attribute, operation and association is a model unit. In other words, model units are the basic building blocks from which models are built. This means that some kind of relationship exists between Model and Model Unit; in fact, a model can be described as a collection of model units, and any model unit can be part of multiple models (Fig. 4.8).

Fig. 4.8. Model and Model Unit

We have described work products as being either produced or used by the endeavour. This statement must be formalised in some way. In fact, work products can be seen as the "nouns" upon which "verbs" act, the "verbs" being tasks. From this, we can see work products as passive chunks of information and tasks as little processes that operate on them, reading, creating, modifying or even deleting them. Each time a task acts upon a work product in this fashion, that event is called an Action. An action, therefore, can be defined as a usage event performed by a task upon a work product. The concept Action, in fact, acts as a bridge between the process and the product side of the metamodel (Fig. 4.9).

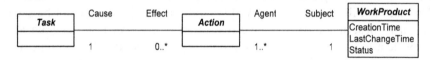

Fig. 4.9. Action connects the process (Task) and the product (Work Product) sides of the metamodel

4.3.4 The Producer Side

There is a third side to methodologies, along with process and product, which is sometimes neglected, and that is the people side. We have described how the ontology metamodel represents tasks being performed on work products, but the ultimate driving force of any endeavour is, of course, the persons that execute the tasks. Since these persons focus on producing something, they are included in what is generically referred to as Producers. There are different subtypes of producers (Fig. 4.10):

- Roles, which are collections of responsibilities that a producer can take.
- Persons, who are the individual human beings involved in an endeavour.
- Tools, which are instruments that help other producers to execute their responsibilities in an automated way.
- Teams, which are organised sets of producers that collectively focus on common work units.

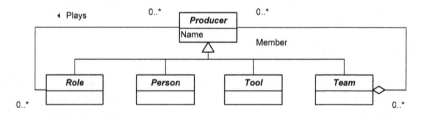

Fig. 4.10. Producer subtypes

Roles are the abstract definitions of responsibilities that form the backbone of an organisation. Some typical roles are Programmer, Software Architect and Project Manager. Each role can be played, at any time, by any producer, be it a person, a team or even a tool, allowing for maximum flexibility. Persons are the actual persons involves in the endeavour. Tools are the automated aids that producers utilise in order to make their job easier, such as compilers, integrated development environments, project tracking packages, etc. Finally, teams are groups of producers that focus on achieving the same goal, namely, performing the same work units. Notice that teams are defined as collections of any kind of producers, so it is possible to have teams within teams, and tools or roles (as well as persons) inside teams. Such a model again allows for maximum flexibility.

Since producers, by definition, perform work units, the Producer concept is connected to the process side of the metamodel (Fig. 4.11):

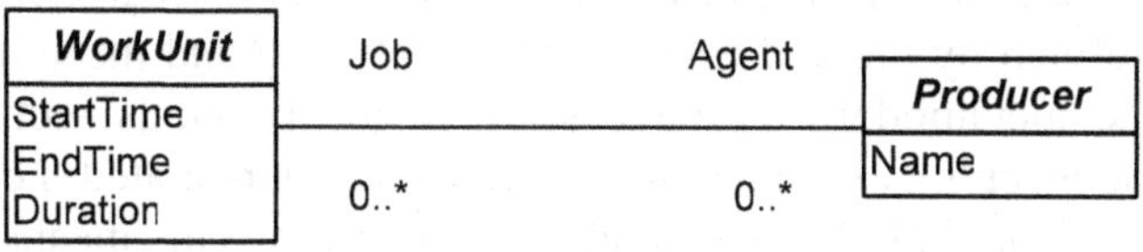

WorkUnit	Job	Agent	*Producer*
StartTime			
EndTime			Name
Duration	0..*	0..*	

Fig. 4.11. Connection between the process (Work Unit) and people (Producer) sides of the metamodel

4.3.5 Endeavour-Related Concepts: Conclusion

This section has described the concepts in the metamodel that relate directly to the endeavour domain. As we have said, the endeavour domain is not brought into being by software developers directly from the metamodel, but rather by applying a methodology, which in turn is derived from the metamodel. This means that endeavour-related concepts in the metamodel must stay simple and generic enough so that method engineers can subtype them into more detailed, method-specific concepts when creating a methodology. Because of the subtyping and instantiation semantics of the object-oriented paradigm, this allows for the metamodel to control the endeavour layer at the optimal level. For example, the metamodel dictates, as described in the previous subsections, that every document has a title and a version number. This is considered a universal property of all documents in any methodology, and therefore is frozen into the metamodel. Any document in any endeavour will, therefore, have a title and a version number. At the same time, and since any particular endeavour would be using a particular methodology, each document will be an instance of a method-specific concept subtyped from Document, rather than Document itself. These method-specific concepts can add attributes and associations to the ones predefined by the metamodel; for example, a method engineer could decide to incorporate in his/her methodology a subtype of Document called ContractualDocument, which inherits the Title and Version Number attributes from Document, and introduces a new SignedOff attribute. Using this mechanism, endeavour-related concepts in the metamodel can stay simple and generic while, at the same time, establish the overall structure and "shape" of any software development endeavour.

4.4 Method-Related Concepts

The architecture of our ontology (Fig. 4.1) establishes that methodologies are to be defined by method engineers by subtyping and instantiating concepts in the metamodel. We have seen, in the previous section, that a number of concepts in the metamodel are endeavour-related, i.e. they represent entities that belong to the endeavour domain. This means that these concepts need to be subtyped by method engineers into method-specific ones. For example, Write Code Task could be subtyped from Task in order to represent tasks that focus on writing code. Also, and as we have seen, the semantics of subtyping imply that, in doing this, method engineers can incorporate new attributes and associations to the refined concepts. Using this approach, the method domain can be populated with concepts that subtype existing concepts in the metamodel. These concepts will be instantiated by software developers when they apply the methodology.

Although this approach works, it is not enough. Two aspects of methodology development are not solved:

- Some elements in the methodology domain are intended to be used as resources rather than instantiated.
- Concepts in the methodology domain need to be described for the method engineers themselves.

The next two subsections treat these issues in full detail.

4.4.1 Templates and Resources

So far, we have described how concepts in the metamodel can be subtyped into new concepts in the method domain, which will be instantiated by software developers when they apply the methodology. However, some components of methodologies are not intended to be instantiated but to be used as information resources (see Sect. 4.2.2). For example, a methodology can contain a guideline on when to use certain techniques; this guideline is part of the methodology, and is intended to be read and understood by software developers, but it is not a class to be instantiated. Similarly, the Class Modelling Language entity in Fig. 4.2 is not a class to be instantiated. It is clear, from this situation, that a methodology must contain not only concepts that will be instantiated by software developers, but also entities that carry information to be directly used as resources. These entities can be modelled as objects in the method domain, and, therefore, they need a class in the metamodel domain from which they can be instantiated. The conclusion is that the metamodel domain contains two kinds of concepts [9]:

- Templates, which are concepts intended to be subtyped into refined concepts in the method domain, which are then instantiated into entities in the endeavour domain.
- Resources, which are concepts intended to be instantiated into entities in the method domain, which are then used as information resources from the endeavour domain.

The differentiation between templates and resources is practical and has clear semantics. However, both template and resource concepts are implemented in the metamodel equally, as regular classes. It is their usage that is different. In addition, we must emphasise that the instances of resources reside in the method domain, whereas the instances of templates reside in the endeavour domain. For this reason, we can say that resource concepts represent method entities, whereas template concepts represent endeavour entities. All the classes detailed in Sect. 4.3, therefore, correspond to template concepts. Classes that represent resource concepts in the metamodel are beyond the scope of this chapter; a full description can be found in [26].

4.4.2 Duality in the Method Domain

We can say that the discourse in the methodology domain is double: on the one hand, for example, method engineers need to specify what writing code tasks are, as opposed to requirements validation tasks; on the other hand, method engineers need to describe how the Write Code Task concept is different from the Validate Requirements Task concept. These two things may look very similar but they are not. The former refers to the entities that the Write Code Task concept stands for (i.e. the actual writing code tasks in the endeavour domain), whereas the latter describes the Write Code Task concept (in the method domain) itself. Since a concept is often used as a surrogate for the entities it represents, the difference may not be easy to grasp [12]. Table 4.1 summarises the major disparities between the two levels of discourse.

Table 4.1. Differences between the two levels of discourse in the method domain

Aspect	Solved	So Far Unsolved
Representation referent	Entities that the concept represents	Concept itself
Main audience	Software developers	Method engineers
Physical representation	Class	Object
Usage	Instantiation	Resource

The column labelled "Solved" describes the already solved part of the problem, i.e. how method-related concepts must describe what they stand for; for example, the Write Code Task concept must represent every code writing task that may exist in any conceivable endeavour domain that uses the method being defined. As we have seen, the community most interested in this are software developers ("Main audience" in the table), since they will instantiate the Write Code Task concept into actual code writing tasks. In order to achieve this, code writing tasks are represented in the method domain as a class named Write Code Task, which will be instantiated, as we have said, when the methodology is applied.

The column labelled "So Far Unsolved" describes the second level of discourse that occurs within the method domain. From this perspective, each concept in the method domain must *itself* be described; using our example from above, it is the Write Code Task concept that must be described, rather than the code writing tasks it stands for. For example, we could say that the Write Code Task concept has as a property the purpose of obtaining some code that implements a given design. This purpose is not a property of individual code writing tasks, but of the overall concept of a Write Code Task. Since this kind of information characterises concepts in the method domain themselves, which have been created (and are managed) by method engineers, the major audience of this information is, in fact, method engineers. At the same time, we must realise that each individual concept in the method domain will have its own values for a given set of individual characteristics; for example, the Write Code Task has the purpose of writing some code, while the Validate Requirements Task has the purpose of making sure that the requirements are correct and valid. Each concept has a different purpose, although both concepts have *a* purpose. This advocates the usage of objects to physically implement concepts, which will have values for their given attributes. In our example, both Write Code Task and Validate Requirements Task would be objects of some class, each one with its own value for the Purpose attribute. Finally, and since concepts are now implemented as objects (rather than classes), method engineers would use them as resources rather than by instantiation.

We have established the need to represent concepts in the method domain in two apparently contradictory ways: one asks for classes, the other for objects. Choosing one approach over the other would always detract from the ontology, and therefore we have decided to use *both* approaches simultaneously. This means that, for each concept to be introduced in the method domain, a class *and* an object are necessary. Both class and object represent the same concept, as described in Table 4.1: the class serves as a template for the entities that the concept represents and is intended to be instantiated by software developers whenever they apply the methodology, whereas the object serves as an information resource about the concept itself for method engineers. Since class and object both represent the same concept, it is convenient to formalise the conceptual link between them; the term "clabject" [2] has been introduced to describe an entity that is, simultaneously, a class and an object or, in other words, has a class facet plus an object facet. We can, therefore, think of entities in the method domain as clabjects, each composed of a class plus an object that represent the same concept.

Only one issue is still to be resolved with regard to the duality of the method domain. We know that class facets are obtained by subtyping classes from the metamodel domain. But how are object facets obtained? The usual mechanism of instantiation is valid here, if and only if appropriate classes can be determined. Following our example, and using a conventional classification technique, we can ask ourselves: what kinds of things are Write Code Task and Validate Requirements Task? Each of these describes the particularities of a whole family of tasks, namely code writing tasks and requirement validation tasks, respectively. We can say that these objects are *kinds* of tasks, or, for short, task kinds. Consider an alternative example: the metamodel concept Document can be subtyped into new concepts in the method domain: for example, Requirements Specification Document and Class Diagram. Each of these two new concepts will be represented, as we have said, by a clabject. The class facets of these clabjects will be subtypes of Document, whereas the object facets will be instances of some class that can be called Document Kind. In fact, it is correct to say that Requirements Specification Document is a kind of

Document (much like Granny Smith is a kind of Apple). The concept Document Kind, therefore, is the type for the object facets of the clabjects (Fig. 4.12).

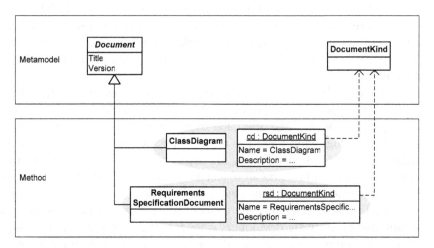

Fig. 4.12. Clabjects in the method domain. Grey ellipses are used to tie together the class/object pairs that comprise a clabject, since the UML notation does not support this concept

The situation exemplified in Fig. 4.12 can be generalised to all the classes in the metamodel that represent template concepts, since, by definition, template concepts are subtyped into new concepts in the method domain. We can now define the Rule of Duality of the method domain: for each template concept in the metamodel, a pair of classes exists, one representing the endeavour domain entities and the other representing the method domain concepts. In Fig. 4.12, Document represents endeavour domain entities (i.e. actual documents) and Document Kind represents method domain concepts (such as Class Diagram and Requirements Specification Document). Very much like each class/object pair in the method domain that is amalgamated together into a clabject, it is convenient to formalise the conceptual relationship between each class pair in the metamodel. In our example, it is evident that Document and Document Kind are closely related classes, although no conventional object-oriented relationship is suitable to appropriately capture this. A simple association could be used, but it would not offer the detailed level of description necessary for this case. A better solution is to utilise the concept of powertype [20]. A powertype has been defined as a type the instances of which are subtypes of another type, called the partitioned type (Fig. 4.13). This is so because, following the semantics of subtyping, instances of the powertype represent partitions of the set of instances of the partitioned type.

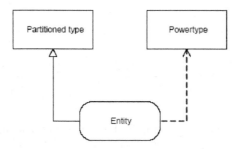

Fig. 4.13. Structure of powertypes

On the other hand, what kind of a construct is Entity in Fig. 4.13? Since it is an instance of a type, it must be an object, but since it is a subtype of another type, it must be a type as well. An answer to this question can be easily found by comparing the overall shape and structure of Fig. 4.12 and Fig. 4.13. We can tentatively say that Document Kind is a powertype of Document, and, consequently, Entity in Fig. 4.13 is a clabject. In fact, the semantic relationship between Document and Document Kind does correspond to a partitioning, and Document Kind is a powertype of Document, since its instances partition the set of instances of Document. Understanding Entity in Fig. 4.13 as a clabject also fits in the scheme, since it must be dual by definition, given that it is both a subtype and an instance. We can, therefore, adopt the usage of powertypes in the metamodel and, furthermore, define a *powertype pattern* as the combination of a powertype, its partitioned type and the relationship between both [11]. We can depict this relationship using a special notation, since it conveys very specific semantics (Fig. 4.14).

According to the Rule of Duality, a powertype class must exist in the metamodel domain for each template concept. Since we have already described in detail all the classes corresponding to template concepts (see Sect. 4.3), we will not describe their powertypes. A full description of them can be found in [26].

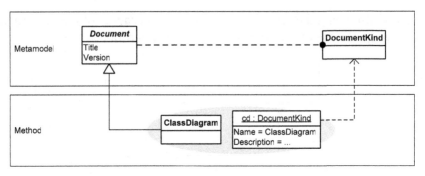

Fig. 4.14. Using powertype patterns in the metamodel domain. The dashed line with a black dot end denotes a powertype pattern relationship. The powertype is the class indicated by the black dot

4.4.3 Applying the Methodology

Previous sections have established that the method domain is composed of clabjects (for template concepts) and object entities (for resource concepts). Software developers are most concerned with applying a given methodology to particular endeavours, so the architecture of the method domain must provide a mechanism for this. In addition, the method domain must be easily accessible to method engineers themselves, who, probably assisted by automated tools, need to augment, customise and, in summary, maintain the methodology itself. From a very abstract point of view, we have seen (see Fig. 4.1 and Fig. 4.2) that software developers instantiate concepts from the method domain, as well as use entities in the method domain as resources. Instantiable concepts in the method domain, as we have seen, are always one facet of clabjects. Object entities from resources, however, are not part of clabjects (Fig. 4.15).

4.5 Conclusion

This chapter has described an ontology for software development methodologies and endeavours, including a comprehensive metamodel plus a three-domain architecture that can be used in order to specify methodologies and then apply them to real endeavours. This ontology involves both process and product aspects, being more complete than other approaches that focus only on one of these two aspects. Also, the ontology takes into account the two communities involved in software development enterprises, namely method engineers and software developers, and organises its architecture and usage mechanisms around them. Innovations such as the pervasive use of powertype patterns to model template concepts, associated with the adoption of clabjects to represent the same concept at dual levels, make this possible.

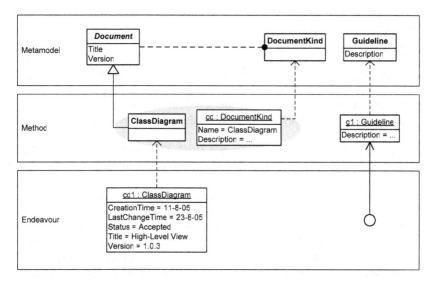

Fig. 4.15. Using elements in the method domain. Class facets from clabjects (such as Class Diagram) are instantiated into the endeavour domain, while instances of resource classes (such as Guideline) are used as information resources

References

1. Atkinson, C., 1998. Supporting and Applying the UML Conceptual Framework. In UML 1998: Beyond the Notation. LNCS 1618. Springer-Verlag: Berlin (Germany). 21–36.
2. Atkinson, C. and T. Kühne, 2000. Meta-Level Independent Modelling. In International Workshop on Model Engineering at 14th European Conference on Object-Oriented Programming. Sophia Antipolis and Cannes, France, 12–16 June 2000.
3. Barbier, F., B. Henderson-Sellers, A. Le Parc-Lacayrelle, and J.-M. Bruel, 2003. Formalization of the Whole-Part Relationship in the Unified Modeling Language. IEEE Transactions on Software Engineering. 29(5): 459–470.
4. Beck, K., 2000. Extreme Programming Explained. Upper Saddle River, NJ: Addison-Wesley.

5. D'Souza, F.D. and A.C. Wills, 1999. Objects, Components, and Frameworks with UML: The Catalysis Approach. Object Technology Series, ed. G. Booch, I. Jacobson, and J. Rumbaugh. Upper Saddle River, NJ: Addison-Wesley.
6. Firesmith, D.G. and B. Henderson-Sellers, 2002. The OPEN Process Framework. The OPEN Series. London: Addison-Wesley.
7. Gonzalez-Perez, C., 2002. Sistemas de Información para Arqueología: Teoría, Metodología y Tecnologías. BAR International Series. Vol. 1015. Oxford: Archaeopress.
8. Gonzalez-Perez, C. and B. Henderson-Sellers, 2005. A Powertype-Based Metamodelling Framework. Software and Systems Modelling. 5(1), pp.72–90.
9. Gonzalez-Perez, C. and B. Henderson-Sellers, 2005. Templates and Resources in Software Development Methodologies. Journal of Object Technology. 4(4): 173–190.
10. Gonzalez-Perez, C., T. McBride, and B. Henderson-Sellers, 2005. A Metamodel for Assessable Software Development Methodologies. Software Quality Journal. 13(2): 195–214.
11. Henderson-Sellers, B. and C. Gonzalez-Perez, 2005. Connecting Powertypes and Stereotypes. Journal of Object Technology. 4(7), pp. 83–96.
12. Henderson-Sellers, B. and C. Gonzalez-Perez, 2005. The Rationale of Powertype-Based Metamodelling. In Second Asia-Pacific Conference on Conceptual Modelling. Newcastle, NSW (Australia), 30 January–4 February 2005. Australian Computer Science Communications Vol. 7, No. 6. Australian Computer Society. 7–16.
13. Hohmann, L., 1997. Journey of the Software Professional. Upper Saddle River, NJ: Prentice–Hall.
14. ISO/IEC, 2002. Software Life Cycle Processes, Amendment 2. ISO/IEC 12207: 1995 / Amd 2: 2004. International Organization for Standardization / International Electrotechnical Commission.
15. ISO/IEC, 2002. System Life Cycle Processes. ISO/IEC 15288: 2002. International Organization for Standardization / International Electrotechnical Commission.
16. ISO/IEC, 2004. Software Process Assessment – Part 1: Concepts and Vocabulary. ISO/IEC 15504-1: 2004. International Organization for Standardization / International Electrotechnical Commission.
17. Jayaratna, N., 1994. Understanding and Evaluating Methodologies: NIMSAD, a Systematic Framework. New York: McGraw-Hill.
18. Liskov, B. and J.M. Wing, 1994. A Behavioral Notion of Subtyping. ACM Transactions on Programming Languages and Systems. 16(6): 1811–1841.
19. Martin, J. and J.J. Odell, 1995. Object-Oriented Methods: A Foundation. Englewood Cliffs, NJ: Prentice Hall.
20. Odell, J.J., 1994. Power Types. Journal of Object-Oriented Programming. 7(2): 8–12.
21. OMG, 2003. Unified Modelling Language Specification: Infrastructure, version 2. ptc/03-09-15. Object Management Group.

22. OMG, 2004. Unified Modelling Language Specification: Superstructure, version 2. ptc/04-10-02. Object Management Group.
23. OMG, 2005. Software Process Engineering Metamodel Specification, version 1.1. formal/05-01-06. Object Management Group.
24. Oxford University Press, 2005. Oxford English Dictionary (web site). Accessed on 23 August 2005. http://dictionary.oed.com/
25. Ralyté, J., 2002. Requirements Definition for the Situational Method Engineering. In Engineering Information Systems in the Internet Context. Kanazawa (Japan), 25–27 September 2002. Dordrecht: Kluwer Academic Publishers. 127–152.
26. SA, 2004. Standard Metamodel for Software Development Methodologies. AS 4651-2004. Standards Australia.
27. SEI, 2002. CMMI for Systems Engineering/Software Engineering/Integrated Product and Process Development/Supplier Sourcing, Continuous Representation, version 1.1. CMMI-SE/SW/IPPD/SS, V1.1, Continuous. Carnegie Mellon Software Engineering Institute.

5. Software Maintenance Ontology

Nicolas Anquetil and Káthia M. de Oliveira

Catholic University of Brasilia, Brasilia, DF, Brazil,
anquetil@ucb.br, kathia@ucb.br, marcio@anhanguera.edu.br,

Márcio G.B. Dias

Uni-Anhangüera University, Goiania, GO, Brazil,
marcio@anhanguera.edu.br

5.1 Introduction

One of the most practiced activities in software engineering is software maintenance (see for example [22]). After the initial development phase, software systems typically spend years in the maintenance phase where errors are corrected, functionalities are adapted to changes in the business rules, and new functionalities are added to better suit users' needs. As in many other activities in software engineering, maintenance is a knowledge-intensive activity. One needs knowledge of the application domain of the software, the problem solved, the requirements for this problem, the architecture of the system and how the different parts fit together, how the system interacts with its environment, etc. In software maintenance, the need for knowledge is all the more important because it is no longer acceptable to repeatedly ask users to explain detailed aspects of the application domain, and the documentation created during the initial development effort is lacking, outdated, incomplete or lost [23].

Tools are needed to help people communicate their understanding of an application to each other, through either documentation or direct communication. One may also think of creating categories so as to classify information gathered, evaluate knowledge needs, and decide where to find the necessary information to help maintainers perform their activity.

An important step toward this is the construction of an ontology of the knowledge useful in software maintenance. The ontology may serve different purposes:

- Organization and formalization of the knowledge needed when performing maintenance to serve as a common basis for information exchange.
- Identification of the scope of the knowledge needed to allow checking of the completeness and coverage of some information source.
- Definition of concepts that may be used as an indexing scheme to access relevant sources of information.
- Identification of the knowledge needs to ground a search for more information, to identify the most pressing needs, and to categorize possible sources of information according to the needs they may fulfill.

For example, we used an ontology in defining a knowledge elicitation method to gather, record and classify new information on a software system under maintenance. The ontology served as a guide to identify what information we should be looking for.

In this chapter, we present an ontology of the knowledge used in software maintenance. First, in Sect. 5.2, we state some basic facts about software maintenance that show the necessity of dealing better with knowledge in maintenance. We also highlight some important information needs typically encountered in maintenance projects. We present the ontology on the knowledge used in software maintenance in Sect. 5.3. We will offer an overview of the ontology and of the construction process that leads to it. The ontology is divided in five sub-ontologies that will be explained successively. In Sect. 5.4 we explain how the ontology was validated according to different criteria (quality and relevance). Then, in Sect. 5.5, we summarize an experiment in extracting knowledge from a maintained software system. This experiment gives an example of a possible use of the ontology in practice. Finally, in Sect. 5.6 we present our conclusion.

5.2 Software Maintenance

Software maintenance consists of modifying an existing system to adapt it to new needs (about 50% of maintenance projects [22]), adapt it to an ever-changing environment (about 25% of maintenance projects [22]), or to correct errors in it (20% of maintenance projects [22]). Software maintenance is not a problem in the sense that one cannot and should not try to eliminate it; it is instead the natural solution to the fact that software systems need to keep in sync with their environment and the needs of their users. Lehman [18] established in his first law of software evolution that "a program that is used, undergoes continual change or becomes progressively less useful".

Software maintenance offers significant differences over software development. For example, a software maintainer usually works in more restrictive technical conditions, and usually cannot choose his/her working environment, the programming language, the database management system, the data model, the system architecture, etc. Also, whereas development is typically driven by requirements, maintenance is driven by events [20], often external to the organization owning the software (e.g., a new law or a competitor proposing a new business model). In development, one specifies the requirements and then plans their orderly implementation. In maintenance, events require the modification of the software and there is much less opportunity for planning. Maintenance is by nature a more chaotic activity. In many cases, it can be neither avoided nor delayed by much. Organizations must keep pace with an ever-changing world, and this usually means modifying the software that supports their business activities. Software maintenance is a fact and a necessity.

These differences, in and of themselves, already turn software maintenance into an activity more difficult to perform than software development. We argue that apart from these differences, maintenance suffers from another fundamental problem: the loss (and resulting lack) of knowledge. A good part of the development activity consists of understanding the users' needs and their world (application domain, business rules) and to convert this into running code by applying a series of design decisions [27]. Whereas the knowledge needs are roughly the same in both activities, they are more difficult to fulfill during maintenance than during development. In a proper software development project, all the knowledge is available to the participating software engineers, either through some documentation (specifications, models) or through some other member of the project. In maintenance, on the contrary, much of this knowledge is, typically, either lacking, or only encountered in the source code: the business model and requirements specification may have been lost, or never properly documented; the software engineers who participated in the initial development (often years ago) are long gone; and the users already have a running system and cannot be bothered with explaining all over again how it works. Therefore, to maintain a software system, one must usually rely solely on the knowledge embodied and embedded in the source code. Business rules may be expressed in the source code or in database integrity rules. In the best cases they will also be documented in the comments. Application domain concepts may be referred to (often incidentally) in the comments, in file names, or in identifiers of variables. Design decisions will usually not be documented and may only be available through their result, i.e., how the code is organized.

As a result of this lack of knowledge, 40% to 60% of the maintenance activity involves trying to understand the system [21, p. 475], [22, p. 35]. Maintainers need knowledge of the system they work on, of its application domain, the organization using it, past and present software engineering practices, different programming languages (in their different versions), programming skills, etc. Among these different knowledge needs, knowledge about the maintained system emerges as a prominent necessity. For example, Jørgensen and Sjøberg [15] showed that sheer maintenance experience is not enough to reduce the frequency of major unexpected problems after maintenance, whereas application experience does. Other types of knowledge have also been highlighted by past research: in [2], Biggerstaff insists on the necessity of application domain knowledge; in [1], Anquetil et al. highlight the need for computer science knowledge (algorithmic, design or programming patterns, etc.); Van Mayrhauser and Vans [27], already cited, focus on the design decisions (i.e. knowledge about software development applied to the transformation of knowledge on the application domain to produce the source code).

To try to help software maintainers in their task, we started a long-term project to adapt and apply knowledge management techniques and tools to the needs of software maintenance. A central part of this approach is the definition of an ontology of the knowledge needed in software maintenance. This ontology serves as a structuring framework to our approach: it bounds the context of our research, provides a list of concepts and relations we need to consider, and serves as a classification structure.

5.3 An Ontology for Software Maintenance

From the various methodologies to design an ontology (e.g., [13]), all consider basically the following steps: definition of the ontology purpose, conceptualization, validation, and finally coding.

We defined our ontology using theses steps. The purpose is to define an ontology describing the knowledge relevant to the practice of software maintenance. The conceptualization is the longest step and requires the definition of the scope of the ontology, definition of its concepts, and a description of each one (through a glossary, specification of attributes, domain values, and constraints). It represents the knowledge modeling itself. This step was based on a study of the literature and the experience of the authors. We identified motivating scenarios and competency questions (i.e., requirements in the form of questions that the ontology must answer [13]). The result is a set of all the concepts that will be presented in this section. The validation will be discussed in Sect 5.4 and 5.5. Finally for the coding, there are various editing tools available to describe an ontology (see for example [8, 11, 24]), each one using a specific language and having particular features. We chose to focus on the identification of the knowledge itself, and did not study any of these tools. We opted for a manual representation of the ontology with a formalization using first-order logic.

5.3.1 Overview of the Ontology

We started the ontology construction by looking for motivating scenarios where the knowledge captured would be useful. Some of those scenarios are: deciding who is the best maintainer to allocate to a modification request, based on his/her experience of the technology and the system considered; learning about a system the maintainer will modify (what its documents and components are and where to find them); defining the software maintenance; activities to be followed in a specific software maintenance, and also the resources necessary to perform those activities. These and other situations induced us to organize the knowledge around five different aspects (Fig. 5.1 illustrates how the sub-ontologies combine in the general ontology): knowledge about the Software System itself; knowledge about the Maintainer's Skills; knowledge about the Maintenance Process; knowledge about the Organizational Structure; and knowledge about the Application Domain. Each of these aspects was described in a sub-ontology. For each one of the sub-ontologies we defined competency questions, captured the necessary concepts to answer these questions, established relationships among the concepts, described the concepts in a glossary, and validated them with experts.

To express the constraints over the concepts and relations, we defined 53 axioms in first-order logic. These do not include axioms formalizing the specialization and composition relationships (i.e., axioms for the "is_a" and "has_a" relations). Some examples of axioms will be presented in the description of each sub-ontology.Building such an ontology is a significant task. Our first difficulty was to define clearly what was to be the focus of the ontology. This was solved by defining scenarios for the use of the knowledge. A second difficulty was to review the relevant literature in search of definitions and validation of the concepts. In this phase, we deemed it important to base each and every concept on independent sources from the literature. This literature review is summarized in the concept glossary, which will not be presented here for lack of space.

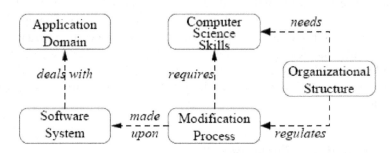

Fig. 5.1. Ontology overview

In the following subsections, we present each sub-ontology and its concepts and relations. To ease the understanding of the explanations, ontology CONCEPTS are written in capitals and <u>relations</u> are underlined.

5.3.2 The System Sub-ontology

Intuitively, knowledge about the system is fundamental to software maintenance. The sub-ontology is depicted in Fig. 5.2.

The competency questions for the System sub-ontology are: What are the artifacts of a software system? How do they relate to each other? Which technologies are used by a software system? Where is the system installed? Who are the software system users? Which functionalities from the application domain are considered by the software system?

Answering these questions led to a decomposition of the software system into ARTIFACTS, a taxonomy of those artifacts and the identification of the HARDWARE where the SYSTEM is <u>installed on,</u> its USERS and the TECHNOLOGIES that were <u>used</u> in its development.

The ARTIFACTS of a SYSTEM can generally be decomposed into DOCUMENTATION and software COMPONENTS. Briand et al.[4] consider three kinds of documentation: PRODUCT related, describing the system itself (i.e., SOFTWARE REQUIREMENT SPECIFICATION, SOFTWARE DESIGN SPECIFICATION, and SOFTWARE PRODUCT SPECIFICATION); PROCESS related, used to conduct software development and maintenance (i.e., SOFTWARE DEVELOPMENT PLAN,

QUALITY ASSURANCE PLAN, TEST PLAN, and CONFIGURATION MANAGEMENT PLAN); and SUPPORT related, helping to operate the system (i.e., USER MANUAL, OPERATOR MANUAL, SOFTWARE MAINTENANCE MANUAL, FIRMWARE SUPPORT MANUAL). Considering that the SOFTWARE DESIGN SPECIFICATION proposed by Briand et al. should represent the behavior and structure of the system and that we can have different abstraction models, we refined the SOFTWARE DESIGN SPECIFICATION into LOGICAL MODEL and PHYSICAL MODEL.

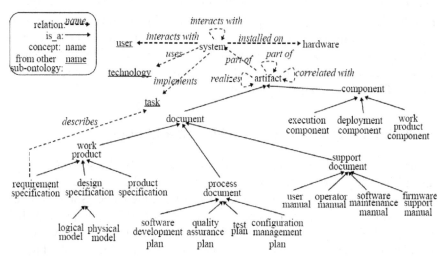

Fig. 5.2. System sub-ontology

Software COMPONENTS represent all the coded artifacts that compose the software program itself. Booch et al. [3] classify them into: EXECUTION COMPONENTS, generated for the software execution; DEPLOYMENT COMPONENTS, composing the executable program; and WORK PRODUCT COMPONENTS, which are the source code, the data, and anything from which the DEPLOYMENT COMPONENTS are generated.

All those ARTIFACTS are, in some way, interrelated. For example, a REQUIREMENT SPECIFICATION is related to DESIGN SPECIFICATIONS, which are related to DEPLOYMENT COMPONENTS. We call this first kind of relation realization, relating two artifacts of different abstraction levels. Another relation between artifacts is a correlation between artifacts at the same abstraction level. And finally, artifacts may be composed of other artifacts (e.g., one document may be composed of several parts).

Other relations in this sub-ontology are: the software SYSTEM is in-stalled on some HARDWARE, it may interact with other SYSTEMS and with USERS, it implements some domain TASKS to be automated (the functionalities of the system), and, finally, the SOFTWARE REQUIREMENT SPECIFICATIONS describe these domain TASKS. To express the constraints over the relations (e.g., realization or correlation) we defined axioms like $(\forall a1, a2)(correlation(a1,a2) \wedge requirement\text{-}spec(a1) \rightarrow requirementspec(a2))$ and $(\forall a1, a2)(realization(a1,a2) \wedge requirementspec(a1) \rightarrow \neg requirementspec(a2))$. The fist one speci-fies that if $a1$ is a REQUIREMENT SPECIFICATION and $a1$ is correlated to $a2$, then $a2$ must also be a REQUIREMENT SPECIFICATION (i.e., the correlation relation stands between ARTIFACTS of the same type). Simi-larly, the second axiom specifies that realization may only stand between two ARTIFACTS of a different kind.

5.3.3 The Computer Science Skills Sub-ontology

Figure 5.3 shows the sub-ontology on the skills needed by software main-tainers in computer science. A scenario of use would be to be able to se-lect the best participants for a given type of maintenance. Some compe-tency questions we identified are: What kinds of CASE (Computer-Aided Software Engineering) tools does the software maintainer know? What kinds of procedures (methods, techniques and norms) does he/she know? What programming and modeling languages does he/she know?

There are several things a MAINTAINER must know or understand to perform his/her task adequately: he/she must know (be trained in) the spe-cific MAINTENANCE ACTIVITY he/she will have to perform (e.g., team management, problem analysis and code modification), the HARDWARE the system runs on, and various COMPUTER SCIENCE TECHNOLOGIES (detailed below). Apart from that, the MAINTAINER must also understand the CONCEPTS of the application domain and the TASKS performed in it. To express those relations, we defined axioms like: $(\forall m)(ma\text{int}ainer(m) \rightarrow (\exists t)(techno\log y(t) \wedge knowCCT(m,t)))$ and $(\forall m)(ma\text{int}ainer(m) \rightarrow (\exists a)ma\text{int}ainerActivity(a) \wedge knows\text{-}Activity(m,a))$ (any MAINTAINER knows at least one TECHNOLOGY and one ACTIVITY).

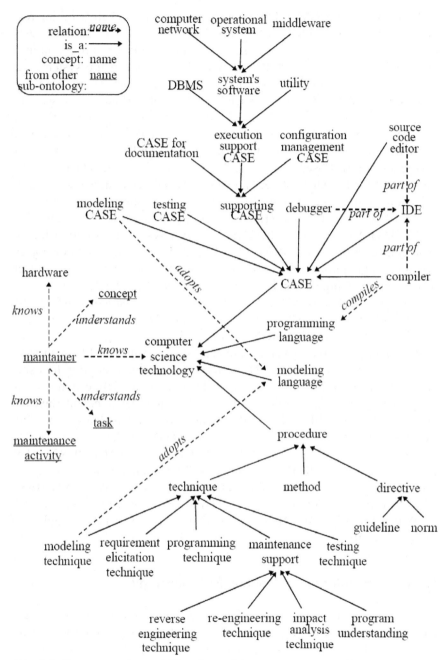

Fig. 5.3. Computer science skills sub-ontology

There are four COMPUTER SCIENCE TECHNOLOGIES of interest: possible PROCEDURES to be followed, MODELING LANGUAGE used (e.g., the UML), CASE TOOLS used (e.g., for modeling or programming), and finally the PROGRAMMING LANGUAGE used in the system. According to [16], PROCEDURES are all structured descriptions used in a software development activity such as METHODS (kinds of systematic procedures with semantic and syntactic definitions to be followed), TECHNIQUES (systematic procedures less formal and rigorous than a method), and DIRECTIVES (standards like GUIDELINES or NORMS in an organization). Based on [5, 17, 23], we classified the TECHNIQUES into: (a) REQUIREMENT ELICITATION, procedures to assist in the identification of the requirements (e.g., interviews, brainstorming, etc.); (b) MODELING PROCEDURES, adopting specific MODELING LANGUAGES, to assist in the definition of a systematic solution for the problem; (c) PROGRAMMING PROCEDURES (e.g., structured or object-oriented programming); (d) TESTING PROCEDURES (e.g., white or black box testing techniques); and (e) MAINTENANCE SUPPORT, procedures to assist in the MAINTENANCE of a program (classified in REVERSE ENGINEERING, RE-ENGINEERING, IMPACT ANALYSIS and PROGRAM COMPREHENSION techniques [22]).

Pressman [23] gives a very complete list of CASE TOOLS, with tools for MODELING, used for the design model definition according to a specific MODELING LANGUAGE; TESTING, used to define and control tests for a system; developing the IDE (Integrated Development Environment – with COMPILER, DEBUGGER and EDITOR, which are also CASE TOOLS on their own), and SUPPORTING the EXECUTION, DOCUMENTATION or CONFIGURATION MANAGEMENT. The EXECUTION SUPPORTING CASE TOOLS represent any tool that can be used in some way during the system's execution, like DATABASE MANAGEMENT SYSTEMS, UTILITIES and SYSTEM SOFTWARE (COMPUTER NETWORK, OPERATIONAL SYSTEM and all MIDDLEWARE).

5.3.4 The Maintenance Process Sub-ontology

Fig 5.4 shows the concepts of the Maintenance Process sub-ontology. Here, we are interested in organizing concepts from the modification request (and its causes) to the maintenance activities. Possible competency questions are: What are the types of modification requests? Who can submit them? What are their possible sources? What are the activities performed during maintenance? What does one need to perform them? Who performs them? What do they produce?

According to [22], a MAINTENANCE PROJECT <u>originates</u> from a MODIFICATION REQUEST <u>submitted</u> by a CLIENT (Fig. 5.4). The REQUESTS are classified as either PROBLEM REPORT, describing the problem detected by the USER, or ENHANCEMENT REQUEST, describing a new requirement. Pigoski also lists the different origins of a MODIFICATION REQUEST (where the problem was detected or the new requirement originates): ON-LINE DOCUMENTATION (like help and tool tips), EXECUTION (features about the execution of the system itself, like performance or instability), ARCHITECTURAL DESIGN (like dynamic library reuse), REQUIREMENT (change in a requirement or a specification of a new one), SECURITY (like access not allowed), INTEROPERABILITY (features related to the communication with other systems) and DATA STRUCTURE (like structure of data files or databases). One or more MODIFICATION REQUESTS GENERATE a MAINTENANCE PROJECT that will ADOPT a specific PROCESS <u>composed</u> of different software MAINTENANCE ACTIVITIES.

Based on [4, 16, 22] we classified the MAINTENANCE ACTIVITIES into the following types: (a) INVESTIGATION ACTIVITY, assessing the impact of undertaking a modification; (b) MANAGEMENT ACTIVITY, relating to the management of the maintenance process or to the configuration control of the products; (c) QUALITY ASSURANCE ACTIVITY, aiming at ensuring that the modification does not damage the integrity of the product; and (d) MODIFICATION ACTIVITY, which may be CORRECTIVE MAINTENANCE or ENHANCEMENT MAINTENANCE (ADAPTATIVE, PREVENTIVE or PERFECTIVE MAINTENANCE). A MAINTENANCE ACTIVITY <u>uses</u> one or more input ARTIFACTS and affects one or more output ARTIFACTS, it <u>precedes</u> some other ACTIVITY (in the PROCESS it is <u>part of</u>), it addresses some MAINTENANCE ORIGIN (already detailed), <u>uses</u> HARDWARE RESOURCES, and <u>uses</u> some COMPUTER SCIENCE TECHNOLOGIES.

Axioms are used, for example, to specify that the MAINTENANCE ACTIVITIES are ordered: $(\forall a1, a2)(preactivity(a1, a2) \rightarrow \neg preactivity(a2, a1))$ and $(\forall a1, a2, a3)(preactivity(a1, a2) \wedge preactivity(a2, a3) \rightarrow preactivity(a1, a3))$ (expressing the asymmetry and transitivity of the ordering of activities).

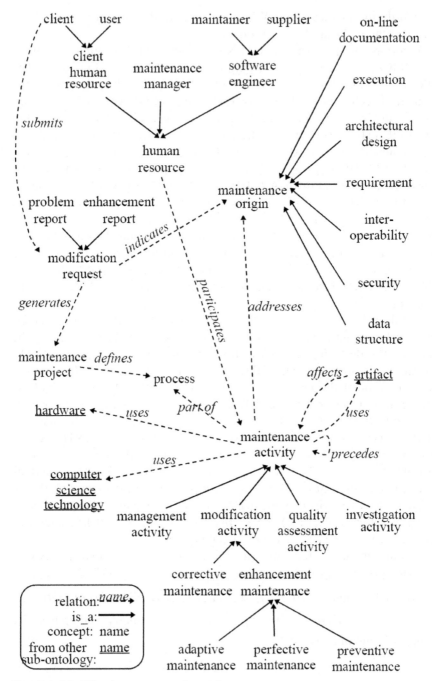

Fig. 5.4. Modification process sub-ontology

Finally, different people (HUMAN RESOURCE) can <u>participate</u> in these ACTIVITIES (from [4, 14, 16, 22]): SOFTWARE ENGINEERS (SUPPLIER or MAINTAINER, respectively, who developed and maintain the system), MAINTENANCE MANAGER and CLIENT'S HUMAN RESOURCES (CLIENT who pays for the modification, and USER who uses the system).

5.3.5 The Organizational Structure Sub-ontology

The fourth sub-ontology, on the organizational structure, is depicted in Fig. 5.5. We considered a definition of an organization (see for example [9]) composed of units where different functions are performed by human resources. We also included the fact that an organization defines directives to be followed in the execution of the tasks. Our goal here was not to define all possible aspects of an organization, but only to define that the maintenance is an activity performed by people in some organizational unit that composes the whole organization with its own rules.

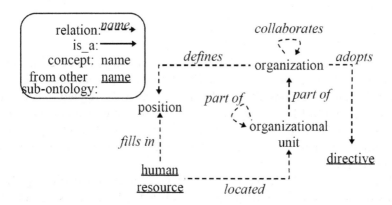

Fig. 5.5. Organizational structure sub-ontology

In order to define the scope of this sub-ontology we set the following competency questions: What organizational units compose the organization? What positions exist and who occupies each position? What directives does the organization adopt? How do the organizations relate to one another?

Based on [9, 26] we defined that any ORGANIZATION <u>adopts</u> its own DIRECTIVES and defines the POSITIONS to be <u>filled in</u> by a HUMAN RESOURCE. Also, ORGANIZATIONS can <u>collaborate</u> with each other and each one is <u>composed</u> of ORGANIZATIONAL UNITS. Those

ORGANIZATIONAL UNITS are organized in a hierarchical structure where one unit is <u>composed of</u> other units.

5.3.6 The Application Domain Sub-ontology

Finally, the last sub-ontology (Fig. 5.6) organizes the concepts of the application domain. The competency questions are: What concepts and tasks compose an application domain? What are the properties of each concept? How do the concepts relate to one another? What concepts are used in each task? What restrictions apply to the application domain?

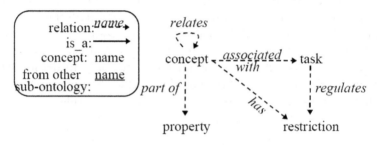

Fig. 5.6. Application domain sub-ontology

Instead of an actual application domain, which depends on each specific software system maintained, we had to define a meta-ontology specifying that a domain is composed of DOMAIN CONCEPTS, <u>related</u> to each other and <u>having</u> PROPERTIES and RESTRICTIONS. We also considered that the CONCEPTS in an application domain are <u>associated with</u> the TASKS performed in that domain and those TASKS are <u>regulated</u> by some RESTRICTIONS.

This meta-ontology should be instantiated for each specific application domain with a domain ontology as exemplified in [7] (see also Chap. 10).

5.4. Validating the Ontology

After the ontology conceptualization (see Sect. 5.3), the next step is to validate it. We did this in two ways: validation of the quality of the ontology itself (how clear it is, how complete, concise, etc.), and validation of the usefulness of the concepts for maintenance (which was the ontology's purpose). This validation will be presented here and in Sect. 5.5.

5.4.1 Quality Validation

To validate the quality of the ontology we considered the following six desirable criteria (see for example [10, 12]): (a) consistency, referring to the absence (or not) of contradictory information in the ontology; (b) completeness, referring to how well the ontology covers the real world (software maintenance for us); (c) conciseness, referring to the presence (or not) of needless information or details; (d) clarity, referring to how effectively the intended meaning is communicated; (e) generality, referring to the possibility of using the ontology for various purposes inside the fixed domain (software maintenance); and (f) robustness, referring to the ability of the ontology to support changes.

To evaluate these criteria, we asked four experts to study the ontology and fill out a quality assessment report composed of several questions for each criterion. These people were chosen for their extensive experience in software maintenance or for their academic background in ontology definition. The evaluations were good; on a scale of 0 to 4, no sub-ontology received a mark below 3 for any criterion.

This evaluation was useful in pointing out specific problems. For example, we had not included a relation to specify that software systems may interact amongst each other, the CASE taxonomy (skills sub-ontology) did not contemplate utility tools for execution, some definitions were not clear (this was the cause of a generally lower score of the maintenance process sub-ontology), and some restrictions were not expressed.

Besides the expert assessments experiment, we also validated the ontology by instantiating its concepts for real software systems. One instantiation was performed, for pure validation purposes, on the existing documentation of a system. It resulted in the instantiation of 73 concepts out of 98. Another validation was performed when we used the ontology in a knowledge management experiment (with another system in another organization). This second experiment instantiated 39 concepts out of 62 (the computer science skill sub-ontology was not considered in this example).

Not all concepts were instantiated for either of the two systems because of the particularities of these systems or the organizations that were maintaining them:

- Some skills may not be mastered by all software organizations (e.g., reverse engineering technique).
- Not all software organizations use a well-defined maintenance process with clear activities.
- Not all CASE tools are used by all organizations (e.g., testing tool).

- Specific examples of concepts may not have appeared when we performed the validation (e.g., possible causes for a maintenance operation as security, or on-line documentation, etc.).
- Documentation is, in many cases, a missing item in the maintenance of legacy software systems (e.g., configuration plan, quality plans, etc.).

5.4.2 Relevance Validation

The purpose of the ontology is (Sect. 5.3) to describe the knowledge relevant to the practice of software maintenance. Therefore, we also needed to validate the relevance of the concepts for maintenance. To do so, we conducted two types of experiments: observing maintainers while they were maintaining a system, and presenting the instantiated knowledge to the software engineers and asking them what concepts they used.

For the first experiment we used a protocol called think-aloud (see for example [19]) where the maintainers were asked to say everything they did and why they did it. These sessions were recorded and later transcribed on paper to be analyzed. During the analysis, we tried to identify the kind of knowledge that the software engineers were using at each moment based on the defined ontology. Two maintainers participated in this experiment, doing five sessions for a total of 132 minutes (26 minutes per session on average).

In the second experiment, the ontology was presented and explained to the software maintainers and they were asked to fill in, every day, a questionnaire on the concepts they used. This form consisted of all the concepts we had instantiated previously (preceding section) and the list of their instances (as we identified them from the system's documentation in the quality validation). The maintainers were asked to tick the instances they had used during their work (they could not add new instances). The experiment was performed with three maintainers and one manager. They filled in 17 forms on 11 different days over a period of 10 weeks.

The first experiment (think-aloud sessions) instantiated 43 of the 98 concepts. One reason for this low number is the small number of sessions in this experiment which were mostly on short punctual maintenance. The second experiment (tick used instances of a concept) instantiated 67 out of the 73 that we could instantiate for that particular system. Since the maintainers in this experiment had to tick the instances of concepts we had identified from the system's documentation, they could not use more concepts than we had instantiated previously (see previous section).

We feel that these experiments adequately validated the usefulness and quality of the ontology for the particular purpose for which it was designed. In the next section, we will propose a practical example of how this ontology may be used.

5.5 Putting the Maintenance Ontology to Work

We identified in Sect. 5.2 that a significant problem of software maintenance is the lack of knowledge on the systems maintained. To propose a solution to this problem, we decided to use knowledge discovery techniques to try to extract knowledge on the systems after each maintenance and record it. For this, we used a technique, well known in software engineering, called project review, postmortem analysis or project retrospective.

Project review simply consists of "[gather] all the participants from a project that is ongoing or just finished and ask them to identify which aspects of the project worked well and should be repeated, which worked badly and should be avoided, and what was merely 'OK' but leaves room for improvement" [25]. The term postmortem implies that the analysis is done after the end of a project, although, as recognized by Stålhane in the preceding quote, it may also be performed during a project, after a significant mark has been reached.

There are many different ways of performing a project review; for example, [7] differentiate their proposal, a "lightweight postmortem review", from more heavy processes as used in large companies such as Microsoft or Apple Computer. A project review may also be more or less structured, and focused or "catch all". One of the great advantages of the technique is that it may be applied on a small scale with little resources (e.g., a 2 hour meeting with all the members of a small project team, plus 1 hour from the project manager to formalize the results). Depending on the number of persons participating in the project review, it may require different levels of structuring, from a relatively informal meeting where people simply gather and discuss the project, to a more formal process as proposed in [6].

Project review has long been used in software engineering as a successful technique for discovering lessons learned from the execution of a process and thereby improving its next execution. However, in this case, we are mainly interested in discovering new knowledge learned about the system, its application domain, or other issues not specifically related to the maintenance process. To identify what information we could hope to discover in the project reviews, we used the concepts defined in our ontology.

We conducted two types of project reviews:

- We interviewed the members of four short maintenance projects. Each project involved than three maintainers fever.
- We also conducted a brainstorming meeting for two large maintenance projects with more maintainers involved (more than 10 in these cases).

We felt that interviews would be the best tool in the case of the small maintenance projects because the size of the maintenance team allows the interviewer to easily merge the discoveries, whereas individual interviews avoid having to find a time slot when the entire team (however small) can conveniently meet. The interviews where structured according to a questionnaire that would allow us to discover if the maintainers had encountered any new interesting knowledge. Each concept of the ontology was reviewed to discover if the maintainer could instantiate any of them.

The duration of the interviews was about 20 to 25 minutes. It is roughly consistent and does not seem to depend on the duration of the maintenance project (although the number of interviews does depend on the size of the team).

We felt that this way of performing project reviews gave complete satisfaction with results as expected (i.e., knowledge gained on the system as well as lessons learned on the process). The interviews were found to be flexible, easily applied, and at little cost. However, we feel that the method would not scale up well and that larger teams need group meetings to facilitate the convergence of ideas. In this case, the (structured) brainstorming session seemed best fitted because all the team members get a chance to share what they learned. When the team gets bigger, it is important to have this kind of meeting so that all opinions may be expressed and compared. A clear problem with the method is that it is more costly and difficult to organize.

The brainstorming sessions were prepared by the distribution of questionnaires (the same as used in the interviews) intended to revive the important points of the projects in the minds of the participants and focus them on topics of interest. For each project, the project review was divided into two sessions. In the first session, positive and negative points were raised; these were then summarized and organized by the facilitator of the review to prepare the second session where corrective actions were proposed for the negative points. The duration of the review was 6 hours in one case and 8 in the other.

The results were not as satisfying as those for the short maintenance projects, because the points that came out dealt mainly with the maintenance process (one of the sub-ontologies) and not with the system or its application domain (other sub-ontologies). A possible explanation is that because of the difficulty of scheduling the meetings and the urgency of the projects, we could not organize intermediate reviews after specific marks in the maintenance process (e.g., after the initial maintenance request analysis). Instead we only had an after-project review, with a broader scope and where the knowledge gained on the system may already have been lost again (the projects lasted 60 and 90 days respectively). In addition, the organization had recently undergone a redefinition of its processes and therefore the topic was still a "hot" one at the time.

Examples of knowledge gained during a maintenance project and uncovered by the project reviews are:

- Re-engineering opportunity: the re-engineering was not actually performed but was recorded for future analysis.
- Detailed understanding of how a particular module works.
- Description of requirements that were not documented.
- Identification of a requirement that had repeatedly changed.

5.6 Conclusion

Software maintenance is a knowledge-intensive activity. Software maintainers need knowledge of the application domain of legacy software, the problem it solves, the requirements for this problem, the architecture of the system, how it interacts with its environment, etc. All this knowledge may come from diverse sources: experience of the maintainer, from some colleagues, knowledge of the user, documentation, or source code. Studies suggest that 40% to 60% of the cost of maintenance is spent on recreating this knowledge [22, p. 35].

In this chapter, we looked at an ontology of the knowledge used in software maintenance. We detailed the process by which we came to create this ontology, always using references from the literature to guide our efforts. The ontology we presented was divided into five sub-ontologies (system, computer science skills, maintenance process, organization, and application domain). We also briefly discussed its validation according to different criteria (mainly quality and relevance) and concluded that it was adequate for its intended purpose.

This ontology may serve as a structuring framework for other methods trying to deal with the knowledge deficiencies in the maintenance of legacy software systems. It may be seen as a reference, listing all the concepts one needs to worry about; or it may be seen as a classification scheme to categorize pieces of information that one may gather; it could also be used as a common description of maintenance for various tools trying to exchange information. We described an experiment we conducted to extract knowledge on maintained systems using an adaptation of project review.

References

1. Anquetil, N., Characterizing the Knowledge Contained in Documentation Sources. In Proceedings of 8th Working Conference on Reverse Engineering, WCRE 2001, pages 166–175. IEEE, IEEE Computer Society Press, Oct. 2001.
2. Biggerstaff, T.J., Mitbander, B.G., and Webster, D., Program Understanding and the Concept Assignment Problem. Communications of the ACM, 37(5): 72–83, May 1994.
3. Booch, G., Rumbaugh, J., and Jacobson, I., The Unified Modeling Language - User Guide. Addison-Wesley, Reading, MA 1997.
4. Briand, L.C., Basili, V.R., Kim, Y-M., and Squier, D.R., A change analysis process to characterize software maintenance projects. In International Conference on Software Maintenance/ICSM'94, pages 1–12, 1994.
5. Chandra, C., and Ramamoorthy, C.V., An evaluation of knowledge engineering approaches to the maintenance of evolutionary software. In Proceedings of the 8th Software Engineering and Knowledge Engineering Conference, pages 181–188, June 1996.
6. Collier, B., DeMarco, T., and Fearey, P., A defined process for postmortem review. IEEE Software, 13(4): 65–72, July–Aug. 1996.
7. Dingsøyr, T., Moe, N.B., and Øystein, N., Augmenting experience reports with lightweight postmortem reviews. Lecture Notes in Computer Science, 2188:167–181, 2001. PROFES 2001, Sprinter-Verlag, Berlin, Germany.
8. Domingue, J., Tadzebao and Wwebonto: Discussing, browsing, and editing ontologies on the web. In 11th Banff Workshop on Knowledge Acquisition, Modeling, and Management, Banff, Alberta, Canada, 1998.
9. Fox, M.S., Barbuceanu, M., and Grüninger, M., An organization ontology for enterprise modeling: Preliminary concepts for linking structure and behaviour. Computers in Industry, 29:123–134, 1996.
10. Gómez-Pérez, A., Some ideas and examples to evaluate ontologies. In 11th Conference on Artificial Intelligence for Applications, pages 299–305, 1995.
11. Grosso, W.E., Eriksson, H., Fergerson, R.W., Gennari, J.H., Tu, S.W., and Musen, M.A., Knowledge modeling at the millennium (the design and evolution of Protégé-2000). In 12th Banff Workshop on Knowledge Acquisition, Modeling, and Management, Banff, Alberta, Canada, 1999.
12. Gruber, T.R., Toward principles for the design of ontologies used for knowledge sharing. International Journal of Human-Computer Studies, 43(5–6): 907–928, 1995.
13. Grüninger, M., and Fox, M.S.N., Methodology for the design and evaluation of ontologies. In Workshop on Basic Ontological Issues in Knowledge Shar-

ing/IJCAI'95, Aug. 1995. Also available as a Technical Report from the Department of Industrial Engineering, University of Toronto.

14. IEEE Standard for software maintenance. Technical report, Institute of Electrical and Electronics Engineers, May 1998.

15. Jørgensen, M., and Sjøberg, D.I.K., Impact of experience on maintenance skills. Journal of Software Maintenance: Research and Practice, 14(2): 123–146, Mar. 2002.

16. Kitchenham, B.A., Travassos, G.H., von Mayrhauser, A., Niessink, F., Schneidewind, N.F., Singer, J., Takada, S., Vehvilainen, R., and Yang, H., Towards an ontology of software maintenance. Journal of Software Maintenance: Research and Practice, 11:365–389, 1999.

17. Leffingwell, D., and Widrig, D., Managing Software Requirements: A Unified Approach. Addison-Wesley, Reading, MA, 2000.

18. Lehman, M.M., Programs, life cycles and the laws of software evolution. Proceedings of the IEEE, 68(9): 1060–1076, Sept. 1980.

19. Lethbridge, T.C., Sim, S., and Singer, J., Studying Software Engineers: Data Collection Methods for Software Field Studies. Available on the Internet on Sept. 2001:
http://www.site.uottawa.ca/ tcl/papers/ese.html, 1998.

20. Oliveira, K.M., Travassos, G., Menezes, C., and Rocha, A.R., Using domain-knowledge in software development environments. In Software Engineering and Knowledge Engineering, pages 180–187, June 1999.

21. Pfleeger, S.L., What software engineering can learn from soccer. IEEE Software, 19(6): 64–65, Nov. –Dec. 2002.

22. Pigoski, T.M., Practical Software Maintenance: Best Practices for Software Investment. John Wiley & Sons, New York, 1996.

23. Pressman, R.S., Software Engineering: A Practitioner's Approach. McGraw-Hill, New York, 5th edition, 2001.

24. Staab, S., Erdmann, M., Maedche, A., and Decker, S., An extensible approach for modeling ontologies in RDF(s). In ECDL 2000 Workshop on the Semantic Web, 2000.

25. Stålhane, T., Dingsøyr, T., Hanssen, G.K., and Brede Moe, N., Post mortem – an assessment of two approaches. In Proceedings of the European Software Process Improvement 2001 (EuroSPI 2001), 10–12, Oct. 2001.

26. Uschold, M., King, M., Moralee, S., and Zorgios, Y., The enterprise ontology. The Knowledge Engineering Review: Special Issue on Putting Ontologies to Use, 13, 1998. Also available as technical report from AIAI, The University of Edinburgh (AIAI-TR-195).

27. von Mayrhauser, A., and Vans A.M., Dynamic Code Cognition Behaviors For Large Scale Code. In Proceedings of 3rd Workshop on Program Comprehension, WPC'94, pages 74–81. IEEE, IEEE Computer Society Press, Nov. 1994.

6. An Ontology for Software Measurement

Manuel F. Bertoa and Antonio Vallecillo

University of Malaga, Dept. Lenguajes y Ciencias de la Computación, Málaga, Spain,
bertoa@lcc.uma.es, av@lcc.uma.es

Félix García

ALARCOS Research Group. Dept. of Information Technologies and Systems, Escuela Superior de Informática, University of Castilla-La Mancha, Spain,
Felix.Garcia@uclm.es

6.1 Introduction

Software measurement has evolved in such a way that it is no longer a marginal or atypical activity within the software development process and has become a key activity for software project managers. All successful software organizations use measurement as part of their day-to-day management and technical activities. Measurement provides organizations with the objective information they need to make informed decisions that positively impact their business and engineering performance [17]. As a matter of fact, CMMI (Capability Maturity Model Integration) includes software measurement as one of its requisites for reaching higher maturity levels and it helps organizations to institutionalize their measurement and analysis activities, rather than addressing measurement as a secondary function. Other initiatives such as ISO/IEC 15504 [11], SW-CMM (Capability Maturity Model for Software) and the ISO/IEC 90003:2004 standard [12] also consider measurement to be an important element in the management and quality of software. In all these initiatives measurement plays a fundamental role as a means for assessing and institutionalizing software process improvement programs.

However, as with any relatively young discipline, software measurement has some problems. When we approach software measurement and compare diverse proposals or international standards, it becomes apparent that the terminology used is not always the same or the same term may refer to different concepts. Terms such as "metrics", "attribute", or "measure" need to have a single definition accepted by all the researchers and practitioners who work in software measurement. The most serious point is when inconsistencies appear between different measurement proposals or standards.

Standards provide organizations with agreed and well-recognized practices and technologies, which assist them to interoperate and to work using engineering methods, reinforcing software engineering as an "engineering" discipline, instead of a "craft". Furthermore, the Internet is changing how business is done nowadays, promoting cooperation and interoperation among individual organizations, which need to compete in a global market and economy, and share information and resources. Standardization is one of the driving forces to achieve this interoperability, with the provision of agreed domain conventions, terminologies and practices. However, there is no single standard which embraces the whole area of software measurement in its totality, but rather there are diverse standards orientated towards specific areas such as the measurement process or function points. Without an overall reference framework managing these standards, inconsistencies arise in the measurement terminology. This issue has been recognized by ISO/IEC, which has created a work group for the harmonization of systems engineering standards within its Joint Technical Committee 1 (JTC1: "Information Technology", www.jtc1.org), and is trying to explicitly include in its directives the procedures which guarantee consistency and coherency among its standards. Furthermore, there has been an agreement in place since the year 2002 between the IEEE Computer Society and ISOJTC1-SC7 to harmonize their standards, which includes the terminology on measurement.

In spite of these efforts, the problem of terminology harmonization still needs to be resolved in our opinion. The objective of this chapter is to present a coherent software measurement terminology which has been agreed upon by consensus, i.e., without contradictions or disparities in the definitions, and a terminology which is widely accepted. The terminology presented in this chapter has been obtained as a result of an exhaustive analysis of the concepts and terms used in the field of software measurement. First of all, similarities, discrepancies, shortcomings and weaknesses in the terminology used in the main standards and proposals have been identified, including ISO International Vocabulary of Basic and General Terms in Metrology (VIM) [13] in the comparison [5]. The result has been a software measurement ontology that provides a set of coherent concepts, with the relations between these concepts well defined, and which we hope helps to create a unified framework of software measurement terminology.

This chapter is organized as follows. After this introduction, Sect. 6.2 guies a brief analysis of the current situation. Section 6.3 presents the Software Measurement Ontology proposal; the concepts of the ontology and relationships among them are presented in detail grouped according to the sub-ontology to which they belong. A running example based on a real case study is used to illustrate the ontology. Finally, Sect. 6.4 draws some conclusions, proposes some suggestions for harmonization, and identifies future research work.

6.2 Previous Analysis

We selected sources from the existing international standards and research proposals that deal with software measurement concepts and terminology. From IEEE we took IEEE Std. 610.12: "Standard Glossary of Software Engineering Terminology" [7] and IEEE Std. 1061-1998: "IEEE Standard for a Software Quality Metrics Methodology" [8]. From ISO and IEC we selected the ISO/IEC 14598 series "Software engineering – Product evaluation" [9], the ISO VIM: "International Vocabulary of Basic and General Terms in Metrology" [13] and the International Standard ISO/IEC 15939: "Software engineering – Software measurement process" [10]. We also included other relevant research proposals related to software measurement, such as the ones by Lionel Briand et al. [3] and by Barbara Kitchenham et al. [16]. The general enterprise ontology proposed by Henry Kim [15] was also considered in the analysis, since it contains a sub-ontology for measurement concepts and terms. Other proposals that make use of measurement terminology (sometimes adapted to their particular domains) were also analyzed, although they were not included in the comparative study because they were either too specific, or clearly influenced by other major proposals already considered.

Once the sources were identified the next step was to collect from them all the definitions of terms related to software measurement. As a result of this, the first thing we realized was that the different standards and proposals could be basically organized around three main groups, depending on the particular measurement topics they focused on: software measures, measurement processes, and targets-and-goals. The first group of concepts, **software measures**, deals with the main elements involved in the definition of software measures, including terms such as measure, scale, unit of measurement, etc. The second group, **processes**, is related with the actions of measuring software products and processes, including the definition of terms like measurement, measurement result, measurement method, etc. Finally, the third group, **target-and-goals**, gathers the concepts required to establish the scope and objectives of the software measurement process, e.g., quality model, measurable entity, attribute, information need, etc. It is worth noting that no single proposal from the set of analyzed sources covers all three groups. Moreover, the set of concepts covered by each source is not homogeneous, even for those sources focusing on the same group. There is a tendency in the sources, however, to converge around these three topic groups as they evolve over time.

However, once the ontology was created we discovered that it was not fully aligned with the VIM and with the new harmonization efforts taking place at ISO. Therefore, it was decided to adapt it in order to make it converge with these efforts, and the ontology presented here was subsequently created. The resulting software measurement ontology is therefore based mainly on the ISO VIM and ISO/IEC 15939 standards. It also includes some terms which are missing from these two documents (e.g., "quality model") that we think are essential in software measurement, and presents some discrepancies with ISO/IEC 15939, e.g., the treatment of indicators.

6.3 A Running Example

To illustrate the ontology, let us use an example based on a real case of software measurement which uses all of the concepts and terms of the ontology. It occurs in the context of a component-based development process of an industrial application, which needs to select a set of commercial off-the-shelf (COTS) software components to be integrated into the system.

More precisely, the software architect has decided not to develop a software component to provide the "print and preview" facilities of the application, but to obtain it from an external source, i.e., go to a software component repository (e.g., ComponentSource) and buy or license a commercial product. There seem to be some candidate components in the repository that provide similar functionality, from different vendors, and that could be used. Of course, the software architect wants to select the "best" component, i.e., the one that best suits the requirements and preferences. Therefore, he/she needs to evaluate the candidate components, i.e., measure them in order to rank them according to such requirements. To simplify the example, let us suppose that the software architect is only interested in evaluating the **Usability** of the candidate components.

In this example we will also suppose that the organization counts on a set of analysis tools to facilitate the selection of COTS software. The major problem encountered when COTS software is assessed is the lack of source code. COTS components are developed and licensed by a third company, so their evaluation must be done without access to their code and internals. The organization has developed some tools to asses the component from two standpoints: its documentation (manuals, demos, marketing information, etc.), and its design. For the first, the organization uses an analysis tool for manuals in electronic format (as they are commonly provided). The software design is assessed by a tool that uses reflection techniques to interrogate and evaluate the COTS software. Thus, the tool can load a Java .jar file and then count the number of classes, methods, arguments, fields, etc., and also get their names and types.

This is the setting that we will use to illustrate the concepts of the ontology presented here.

6.4 The Proposal of Software Measurement Ontology

In this section we present the Software Measurement Ontology (SMO) proposal which we have developed to facilitate harmonization efforts in software measurement terminology. This ontology is based on an initial proposal [4], which had been created to address the lack of consensus on Spanish software measurement terms, based on the most representative measurement standards and proposals. Once the Spanish ontology was defined, it was translated into English. Finding the correct translation of each Spanish term became a rather difficult task and was done by comparing the different proposals again, and selecting the most appropriate terms in each case.

6.4.1 The SMO

With our comparison analysis we pursued the following goals: to locate and identify synonyms, homonyms, gaps and conflicts; to generalize the different approaches to measuring attributes; and to provide a smooth integration of the concepts from the three groups, so that measurement processes can be built using clearly defined measures, while quality models identify the targets and goals of the measurement processes.

A natural approach to achieving these goals was to use a common software measurement ontology, able to identify all concepts, provide precise definitions for all the terms, and clarify the relationships between them. Such an ontology also served as the basis for comparing the different standards and proposals, thus helping to achieve the required harmonization and convergence process for all of them. Another important requirement for the SMO was that its terms should try to conform to general terminology accepted in other fields, including measurement—which is a quite mature field with a very rich set of terms.

The SMO was developed with these goals in mind. The main features and characteristics of the SMO (shown in Fig. 6.1) are the following:

- It uses the term "measure" instead of "metric". This issue is one of the most controversial ones amongst software measurement experts nowadays. Although the term metric is widely used and accepted by many practitioners and researchers, this term has many detractors who argue the following reasons against its use. First, formally speaking a metric is a function that measures the distance between two entities—and therefore it is defined with the precise mathematical properties of a distance. Secondly, the definition of metric provided by both general and technical dictionaries does not reflect the meaning with which it is informally used in software measurement. Furthermore, metric is a term that is not present in the measurement terminology of any other engineering disciplines, at least with the meaning commonly used in software measurement. Therefore, the use of the term "software metric" seem to be imprecise, while the term "software measure" seems to be more appropriate to represent this concept. As a matter of fact, all new harmonization efforts at ISO/IEC and IEEE are trying to avoid the use of the term metric in order to fall into line with the other measurement disciplines, which normally use the vocabulary defined in metrology. In our proposal we finally decided to avoid the use of the term metric, using the term "measure" instead.

- It differentiates between "measure", "measurement" and "measurement result". These terms are used with different meanings in the different proposals (one of the reasons is that "measure" can be used as both a noun and a verb, and therefore it can be used to name both an action (to measure) and the result of the action). In our proposal the action is called "measurement"; the result is called "measurement result"; while the term "measure" defines the measurement approach that needs to be used to perform the measurement, and the scale in which the result is expressed.

- It distinguishes between base measures, derived measures and indicators, but considers them all as measures, generalizing their respective measurement approaches (measurement method, measurement function and analysis model).
- It integrates the software measures with the quality model that defines the information needs that drive the measurement process.

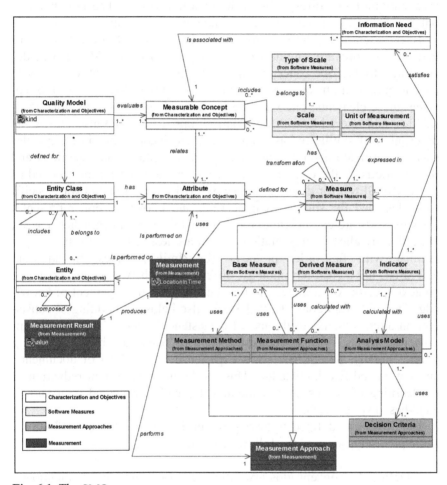

Fig. 6.1. The SMO

Figure 6.1 shows the terms of the SMO and their relationships, using the UML (Unified Modeling Language) notation. As can seen, the SMO has been organized around four main sub-ontologies: **Software Measurement Characterization and Objectives**, to establish the context and goals of the measurement; **Software Measures**, to clarify the terminology involved in the measures definition; **Measurement Approaches**, to describe the different ways of obtaining the measurement results for the measures; and **Measurement**, which includes the concepts related to performing the measurement process. These four sub-ontologies are closely related to the three main groups of concepts identified above. Thus, the first sub-ontology corresponds to the target-and-goals group. The software measures sub-ontology corresponds to the measures group. The last two sub-ontologies together cover the measurement process group.

To represent the SMO we have chosen REFSENO (Representation Formalism for Software Engineering Ontologies) [18]. REFSENO provides constructs to describe concepts (each concept represents a class of experience items), their attributes and relationships. Three tables are used to represent these elements: one with the glossary of concepts, one table of attributes, and one table with the relationships. REFSENO also allows the description of similarity-based retrievals, and incorporates integrity rules such as cardinalities and value ranges for attributes, and assertions and preconditions on the elements' instances. Several main reasons moved us to use REFSENO for defining our ontology. First, REFSENO was specifically designed for software engineering, and allows several representations for software engineering knowledge whilst other approaches, e.g. [6, 19, 20], only allow representations which are less intuitive for people not familiar with first-order predicate (or similar) logics. In addition, REFSENO has a clear terminology, differentiating between conceptual and context-specific knowledge, and thus enabling the management of knowledge from different contexts. REFSENO also helps the building of consistent ontologies thanks to the use of consistency criteria. Unlike other approaches, REFSENO uses constructs known from case-based reasoning (CBR). Finally, REFSENO stores experience in the form of documents, and not as codified knowledge. This results in an important reduction of the learning effort required, something typically associated with knowledge-based systems [1].

The SMO was defined following the process suggested by REFSENO. More precisely, we used the following steps:

1. Define the concept glossary from the knowledge sources mentioned above.
2. Define the semantic relationships among the concepts by representing them in the UML notation, and create the relationship class tables.
3. Analyze the concepts which have some kind of relationship in order to identify the commonalities among two or more concepts. Then, we need to decide whether these commonalities are concepts (inserted

for modeling reasons) and, if so, to include them in the glossary of concepts.
4. Identify the terminal attributes of all the concepts and include them in the UML diagrams. Each time a new attribute type is identified, it must be included in the table of types.
5. Complete the attributes concept tables by including the non-terminal attributes.
6. Check the completeness of all the attribute tables.

The REFSENO representation of the SMO is presented in the following subsections. For simplicity, we describe only the terms and relationships for each sub-ontology.

6.4.1.1 "Software Measurement Characterization and Objectives" Subontology

The "Software Measurement Characterization and Objectives" sub-ontology includes the concepts required to establish the scope and objectives of the software measurement process. The main goal of a software measurement process is to satisfy certain information needs by identifying the entities (which belong to entity classes) and the attributes of these entities (which are the focus of the measurement process). Attributes and information needs are related through measurable concepts (which belong to a quality model). Figure 6.2 shows the concepts and relationships of the sub-ontology "Software Measurement Characterization and Objectives" expressed in a UML diagram. The terms of this sub-ontology are given in Table 6.1. The first two columns show the term being described and its super-concept in the ontology, respectively. The third column contains the definition of the term in the SMO. The final column shows the source (standard or proposal) where the term has been adopted from. Possible values in the fifth column can be:

- a reference to a source (e.g., 15939, VIM, 14598), meaning that the term and its definition have been adopted from that source without any changes;
- "Adapted from (source)", if the term has been borrowed from a source, but its definition has been slightly changed for completeness or consistency reasons;
- "Adapted from (source) (other term)", if the definition of the term has been borrowed from a source, but that term is known differently in the source; or

- *new*, if the term has been coined for the SMO, or has a new meaning in this proposal.

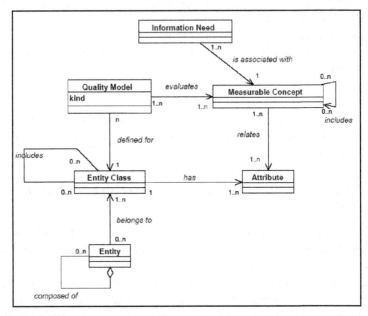

Fig. 6.2. "Software Measurement Characterization and Objectives" Sub-Ontology

Table 6.1. Concepts table of the sub-ontology characterization and objectives

Term	Super-concept	Definition	Source
Information Need	Concept	Insight necessary to manage objectives, goals, risks and problems	15939
Measurable Concept	Concept	Abstract relationship between attributes of entities and information needs	15939
Entity	Concept	Object that is to be characterized by measuring its attributes	15939
Entity Class	Concept	The collection of all entities that satisfy a given predicate	New
Attribute	Concept	A measurable physical or abstract property of an entity that is shared by all the entities of an entity class	Adapted from 14598
Quality Model	Concept	The set of measurable concepts and the relationships between them which provide the basis for specifying quality requirements and evaluating the quality of the entities of a given entity class	Adapted from 14598

Table 6.2 describes the relationships defined in the sub-ontology.

Table 6.2. Relationships table of the sub-ontology characterization and objectives

Name	Concepts	Description
Includes	Entity Class –Entity Class	An entity class may **include** several other entity classes An entity class may be included in several other entity classes
Defined for	Quality Model– Entity Class	A quality model is **defined for** a certain entity class. An entity class may have several quality models associated
Evaluates	Quality Model– Measurable Concept	A quality model **evaluates** one or more measurable concepts. A measurable concept is evaluated by one or more quality models
Belongs to	Entity–Entity Class	An entity belongs to one or more entity classes. An entity class may characterize several entities
Relates	Measurable Concept–Attribute	A measurable concept **relates** one or more attributes
Is associated with	Measurable Concept– Information Need	A measurable concept **is associated with** one or more information needs. An information need is related to one measurable concept
Includes	Measurable Concept– Measurable Concept	A measurable concept may **include** several measurable concepts. A measurable concept may be included in several other measurable concepts
Composed of	Entity–Entity	An entity may be **composed** of several other entities
Has	Entity Class– Attribute	An entity class **has** one or more attributes. An attribute can only belong to one entity class

6.4.1.2 Examples

In our example, the *Entity Class* is the "COTS components which provide services of print and preview", and an *Entity* is the component "C005 ElegantJ Printer V1.1 developed by Elegant MicroWeb". We use a *Quality Model* which is the one proposed in the norm ISO/IEC 9126 or we can adapt this generic model to the DSBC context and use our own quality model (for instance, we could use one specific quality model defined for software components, such as the COTS-QM quality model [2]).

Quality software is a complex and broad topic so we focus on only one quality characteristic, the **Usability**. We will try to assess COTS Usability measuring three sub-characteristics: Understandability, Learnability and Operability. Our goal will be to look for indicators for them.

Therefore, our *Information Need* is "to evaluate the Usability of a set of 'print and preview' COTS components that are candidates to be integrated into a software application, in order to select the best among them". These sub-characteristics which we wish to measure are related, to a greater or lesser degree, to two *Measurable Concepts*: "Quality of Documentation" and "Complexity of Design".

Each measurable concept is related to one or more *Attributes*, so the Quality of Documentation is related to the attribute "Manual Size" and the Complexity of the Design is related to the "Customizability" among other attributes

6.4.1.3 "Software Measures" Sub-ontology

This sub-ontology aims at establishing and clarifying the key elements in the definition of a software measure. A measure relates a defined measurement approach and a measurement scale (which belongs to a type of scale). Most measures may or may not be expressed in a unit of measurement (e.g., nominal measures cannot be expressed in units of measurement), and can be defined for more than one attribute. Three kinds of measures are distinguished: base measures, derived measures and indicators. Figure 6.3 shows the concepts and relationships of the "Software Measures" sub-ontology.

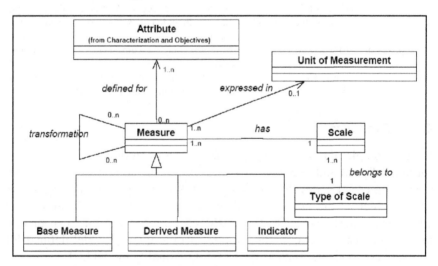

Fig. 6.3. "Software Measures" sub-ontology

Tables 6.3 and 6.4 show the terms and relationships of this sub-ontology, respectively.

Table 6.3. Concepts table of the sub-ontology software measures

Term	Super-concept	Definition	Source
Measure	Concept	The defined measurement approach and the measurement scale. (A measurement approach is a measurement method, a measurement function or an analysis model)	Adapted from 14598 "metric"
Scale	Concept	A set of values with defined properties	14598
Type of Scale	Concept	The nature of the relationship between values on the scale	
Unit of Measurement	Concept	Particular quantity, defined and adopted by convention, with which other quantities of the same kind are compared in order to express their magnitude relative to that quantity	VIM
Base Measure	Measure	A measure of an attribute that does not depend upon any other measure, and whose measurement approach is a measurement method	Adapted from 14598 "direct metric"
Derived Measure	Measure	A measure that is derived from other base or derived measures, using a measurement function as measurement approach	Adapted from 14598 "indirect metric"
Indicator	Measure	A measure that is derived from other measures using an analysis model as measurement approach	New

Table 6.4. Relationships table of the sub-ontology software measures

Name	Concepts	Description
Belongs to	Scale–Type of Scale	Every scale **belongs** to a type of scale. A type of scale may characterize several scales
Defined for	Measure–Attribute	A measure is **defined for** one or more attributes. An attribute may have several associated measures
Transformation	Measure–Measure	Two measures can be related by a **transformation** function; the kind of function will depend on the scale types of the scales
Expressed in	Measure–Unit of Measurement	A measure can be **expressed in** one unit of measurement (only for measures whose type is interval or ratio). A unit of measurement is used to express one or more measures of interval or ratio types
Has	Measure–Scale	Every measure **has** a scale. A scale may serve to define more than one measure

6.4.1.4 Examples

Let us define *measures* to measure each attribute. These measures are more complex at each step. The first step is to define a set of *Base Measures*, then *Derived Measures* and, if possible, *Indicators*. Each *Measure*, according to its type, has its corresponding *Measuring Approach* and *Scale*.

Thus, a *Base Measure* could be the "Number of Words of Manuals" (related to quality of documentation) or the "Number of Public Methods" provided by the component (related to complexity of design). For the first measure, its *scale* is "integers between 0 and +∞", its *type of scale* is "Ratio" and its units are "Kilo-words". The *scale* of the second measure is "integers between 1 and +∞", its *type of scale* is "Ratio" and its units are "Methods". Other base measures that we need to use to calculate the indicator presented below are "Number of Classes", "Number of Configurable Parameters" and "Number of Methods without Arguments".

We obtain *derived measures* using one or more base measures. Now, we want to calculate the *Derived Measures* "Ratio of Words per Functional Element". We have designated functional element (FE) to the aggregation of Classes, Methods and Configurable Parameters. Therefore, to calculate this derived measure we must know and calculate the base measures "Number of Words of Manuals", "Number of Classes", "Number of Methods" and "Number of Configurable Parameters". Its *Scale* is "real numbers from 0 to +∞" and its *units* are "Kilo-words/FE" with a ratio *type of scale*.

We wish to calculate the "percentage of methods without arguments" which is another example of a *Derived Measure*. We need to know the "Number of Methods without Arguments" and the "Number of Methods". In this case, the *scale* is "real numbers between 0 and 1" without *units* being a relative value (percentage) and with a "Ratio" *type of scale*.

Now, we could define an Indicator using some derived (or base) measures and defining an analysis model. For instance, we want to asseshs the Understandability inside the proposed quality model. We have an *indicator* named C_UND whose analysis model uses the ratio of words per FE (WpFE) and the percentage of methods without arguments (MwoA), by aggregating these two derived measures. After using its analysis model (i.e., its aggregation function) to calculate the indicator, the result can be given as a numerical value (e.g., 1.5) or a category value (e.g., Acceptable). In this example, the understandability indicator (C_UND) *type of scale* is "Ordinal" and it takes the values Acceptable, Marginal or Unacceptable, where Acceptable is better than Marginal and this is better than Unacceptable.

6.4.1.5 "Measurement Approaches" Sub-ontology

The "Measurement Approaches" sub-ontology introduces the concept of measurement approach to generalize the different "approaches" used by the three kinds of measures for obtaining their respective measurement results. A base measure applies a measurement method. A derived measure uses a measurement function (which rests upon other base and/or derived measures). Finally, an indicator uses an analysis model (based on a decision criterion) to obtain a measurement result that satisfies an information need. Figure 6.4 shows the concepts and relationships of this sub-ontology, and Tables 6.5 and 6.6 show the terms and relationships of this sub-ontology.

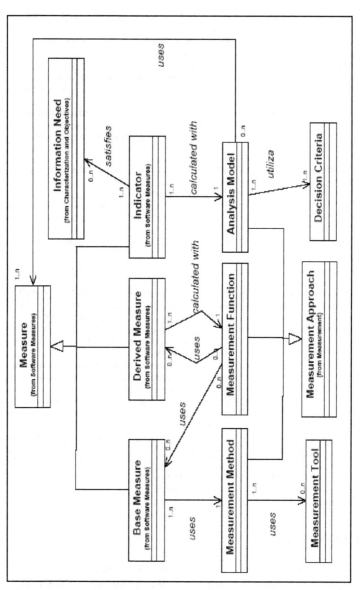

Fig. 6.4. "Measurement Approaches" sub-ontology

Table 6.5. Concepts table of the sub-ontology measurement approaches

Term	Super-concept	Definition	Source
Measurement Method	Measurement Approach	Logical sequence of operations, described generically, used in quantifying an attribute with respect to a specified scale. (A measurement method is the measurement approach that defines a base measure)	Adapted from ISO 15939
Measurement Function	Measurement Approach	An algorithm or calculation performed to combine two or more base or derived measures. (A measurement function is the measurement approach that defines a derived measure)	Adapted from ISO 15939
Analysis Model	Measurement Approach	Algorithm or calculation combining one or more measures with associated decision criteria. (An analysis model is the measurement approach that defines an indicator)	Adapted from ISO 15939
Decision Criteria	Concept	Thresholds, targets or patterns used to determine the need for action or further investigation, or to describe the level of confidence in a given result	15939

Table 6.6. Relationships table of the sub-ontology measurement approaches

Name	Concepts	Description
Uses	Base Measure–Measurement Method	Every base measure **uses** one measurement method. Every measurement method defines one or more base measures
Calculated With	Indicator–Analysis Model	Every indicator is **calculated with** one analysis model. Every analysis model may define one or more indicators
Calculated With	Derived Measure–Measurement Function	Every derived measure is **calculated with** one measurement function. Every measurement function may define one or more derived measures
Satisfies	Indicator–Information Need	An indicator may **satisfy** several information needs. Every information need is satisfied by one or more indicators
Uses	Measurement Function–Base Measure	A measurement function may **use** several base measures. A base measure may be used in several measurement functions
Uses	Measurement Function–Derived Measure	A measurement function may **use** several derived measures. A derived measure may be used in several measurement functions
Uses	Analysis Model–Measure	An analysis model **uses** one or more measures. A measure may be used in several analysis models
Uses	Analysis Model–Decision Criteria	An analysis model **uses** one or more decision criteria. Every decision criterion is used in one or more analysis models

6.4.1.6 Examples

Let us look at some examples of measurement approaches for the measures proposed in previous sections. We have base measures, derived measures and indicators. All of them have their own measurement approach but, depending on the type of measure, they have a measurement method, measurement function or analysis model, respectively.

"Number of Words of Manuals" is a base measure and, therefore, its measurement approach is a *Measurement Method*. In this case, it is composed of the following steps:

1. Run the software application for automatic evaluation of electronic manuals.
2. Load the executable component files (e.g., C005.jar).
3. Load the files of the component manuals
   a. If it is a HTML manual, indicating the path of the index file (index.htm).
   b. If it is a ".chm" file, selecting the file or files which compose the manual.
4. Select the function which counts words from the manual (e.g., select the "manual" drop-down flap and click on the "manual info" button).
5. Finally, read the obtained result from the screen or save it in a text file for later use.

The rest of the base measures have a similar measurement method describing the steps for calculating them using other options or different software tools if available.

The derived measure "Ratio of words per FE (WpFE)" has a measurement approach which is a *Measurement Function*. This *Measurement Function* uses some (previously calculated) base measure and its formula is the following:

$$\frac{NumberOfWords/1000}{NumberOfClasses + NumberOfMethods + NumberOfConfigParam}$$

The other derived measure "Percentage of Methods without Arguments (MwoA)" has the following *Measurement Function*:

$$\frac{NumberOfMethodsWithoutArguments}{NumberOfMethods} * 100$$

We use these two derived measures to evaluate the understandability indicator C_UND. We have a small *Analysis Model* that gives us a numerical value using a formula. Using this numerical value, we have *Deci-*

sion Criteria to obtain a final result. Therefore, its *Analysis Model* includes the following formula:

$$C\_UND = 0.2 \cdot WpFE - 1.4 \cdot MwoA + 1.6$$

Subsequently, we analyze the resulting values using the following *Decision Criteria*:

If $C\_UND > 1.2$ then the component is ACCEPTABLE;

If $C\_UND < 0.8$ then the component is UNACCEPTABLE;

Otherwise, the component is MARGINAL

6.4.1.7 Sub-ontology "Measurement"

This sub-ontology establishes the terminology related to the act of measuring software. A measurement (which is an action) is a set of operations having the object of determining the value of a measurement result, for a given attribute of an entity, using a measurement approach. Measurement results are obtained as the result of performing measurements (actions). Figure 6.5 shows the concepts and relationships of the sub-ontology.

Tables 6.7 and 6.8 show the terms and relationships of this sub-ontology.

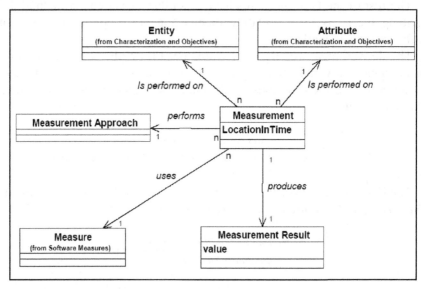

Fig. 6.5. "Measurement" sub-ontology

Table 6.7. Concepts table of the sub-ontology measurement

Term	Super-concept.	Definition	Source
Measurement Approach	Concept	Sequence of operations aimed at determining the value of a measurement result. (A measurement approach is a measurement method, a measurement function or an analysis model)	New
Measurement	Concept	A set of operations having the object of determining the value of a measurement result, for a given attribute of an entity, using a measurement approach	Adapted from VIM
Measurement Result	Concept	The number or category assigned to an attribute of an entity by making a measurement	Adapted from ISO 14598 "Measure"

Table 6.8. Relationships table of the sub-ontology measurement

Name	Concepts	Description
Performs	Measurement– Measurement Approach	A measurement is the action of **performing** a measurement approach (the kind of measurement approach will be dictated by the kind of measure used for performing the measurement). A measurement approach may be used for performing several measurements
Produces	Measurement– Measurement Result	Every measurement **produces** one measurement result. Every measurement result is the result of one measurement
Is Performed on	Measurement– Attribute	Every measurement **is performed** on one attribute of an entity (the attribute should be defined for the entity class of the entity)
Is Performed on	Measurement–Entity	Every measurement **is performed** on an entity, through one of its attributes (the attribute should be defined for the entity class of the entity)
Uses	Measurement– Measure	Every measurement **uses** one measure. One measure may be used in several measurements

6.4.1.8 Examples

A *Measurement* of the component understandability incorporates all the operations mentioned in previous points, using software tools and calculating base and derived measures and indicators. In the end, we obtain as a *Measurement Result* that the understandability of the component is "Acceptable" since its C_UND value is 1.5. Another *Measurement* for the component C012 could give us "Unacceptable" as a measurement result because C_UND has a value of 0.6.

Examples of *Measurement Results* are the following: "135,423 words", "243 methods", "34 classes", "22 Configurable Parameters", "0.41 kilowords/FE", "73%", or "Acceptable".

6.5 Conclusions

In the current (and not mature enough) software measurement field, the lack of a common terminology and inconsistencies between the different standards may seriously jeopardize the usefulness and potential benefits of these standardization efforts. Measurement terms have often been defined in unique and inconsistent ways from organization to organization. This has led to confusion and difficulty in widespread measurement implementation. In many cases, decision makers were unsure of what the measurement results actually represented [14].

In this chapter, a software measurement ontology has been presented, which aims to contribute to the harmonization of the different software measurement proposals and standards, by providing a coherent set of common concepts used in software measurement. The ontology is aligned with the most representative standards and proposals in the references and also with the metrology vocabulary used in other more mature measurement engineering disciplines. The common vocabulary provided by this common ontology has been used to resolve the problems of completeness and consistency identified in several international standards and research proposals and the ontology has been used as the basis for a comparative analysis of the terminology related to measurement [5].

The definition of the measurement terms to an adequate level of detail provides everyone with a common understanding of what is being measured, and how this relates to the measurement goals or information needs. Most of the problems in collecting data on a measurement process are mainly due to a poor definition of the software measures being applied. Therefore, it is important not only to gather the values pertaining to the measurement process, but also to appropriately represent the metadata associated to this data [16]. In this sense, the ontology provides the companies with the necessary conceptual basis for carrying out the measurement process and storing their results in an integrated and consistent way based on a rigorously defined set of measurement concepts and their relationships. Based on the ontology, companies can develop metamodels and languages to define their models for process and product measurement in a homogeneous and consistent way which can facilitate the integration and communication of their measurement process-related data and metadata. Consequently, a consistent software measurement terminology may also provide an important communication vehicle to companies when interoperating with others.

On the other hand, the proposed ontology can serve as a basis for discussion from where the software measurement community can start paving the way to future agreements. Without these agreements, all the standardization and research efforts may be wasted, and the potential benefits that they may bring to all users (software developers, ICT suppliers, tools vendors, etc.) may never materialize.

As a result, this proposal tries to address the needs of two main audiences: first, software measurement practitioners, who may be confused by the terminology differences and conflicts in the existing standards and proposals; and, second, software measurement researchers and standards developers (e.g., international standardization bodies and committees), who do not currently have at their disposal a cohesive core set of concepts and terms over which their existing standards could be integrated, or new ones built.

Our future plans include the extension of the ontology to account for most of the concepts in the forthcoming version of the VIM, in order to provide a complete ontology for software measurement, and fully aligned with the VIM beyond the core concepts contemplated in this proposal.

References

1. Althoff, K., Birk, A., Hartkopf, S. and Müller, W. (1999). Managing software engineering experience for comprehensive reuse. In Procedings of ICSE'99, Kaiserslautern, Germany,
2. Bertoa, M.F. and Vallecillo, A.(2002). Quality Attributes for COTS Components. I+D Computación, 1(2):128–144.
3. Briand, L., Morasca, S. and Basili, V. (2002). An operational process for goal-driven definition of measures. IEEE Transactions on Software Engineering, 28(12):1106–1125.
4. García, F., Ruiz, F., Bertoa, M., Calero, C., Genero, M., Olsina, L.A., Martín, M.A., Quer, C., Condori, N., Abrahao, S., Vallecillo, A. and Piattini M. (2004). An ontology for software measurement. Technical Report UCLM DIAB-04-02-2, Computer Science Department, University of Castilla-La Mancha, Spain, (in Spanish)
   http://www.info-ab.uclm.es/descargas/thecnicalreports/DIAB-04-02-2/UCLMDIAB-04-02-2.pdf
5. García, F., Bertoa, M., Calero, C., Vallecillo, A., Ruiz, F., Piattini, M. and Genero, M. (2006). Towards a consistent terminology for software measurement. Information and Software Technology, 48(8),. Elsevier 631–644.
6. Gómez-Pérez, A. (1998). Knowledge Sharing and Reuse. CRC Press, Boca Raton, FL.
7. IEEE (1990). STD 610.12-1990. Standard Glossary of Software Engineering Terminology.
   http://standars.ieee.org/reading/ieee/std_public/description/se/610.12-1990_desc.html

8. IEEE (1998). IEEE Std 1061-1998 IEEE Standard for a Software Quality Metrics Methodology – Description. http://standards.ieee.org/reading/ieee/std_public/description/se/1061-1998_desc.html
9. ISO/IEC (1999). ISO 14598: 1999-2001. Information Technology – Software Product Evaluation – Parts 1–6.
10. ISO/IEC (2002). ISO 15939: Software Engineering – Software Measurement Process.
11. ISO/IEC (2004a). ISO/IEC 15504-1:2003, Information technology – Process assessment – Part 1: Concepts and vocabulary.
12. ISO/IEC (2004b). ISO/IEC 90003, Software and Systems Engineering – Guidelines for the Application of ISO/IEC 9001:2000 to Computer Software.
13. ISO (1993). International Vocabulary of Basic and General Terms in Metrology (ISO VIM). International Organization for Standardization, Geneva, Switzerland, 2nd edition.
14. Jones, C. (2003). Making Measurement Work. CROSSTALK The Journal of Defense Software Engineering, pp. 15-19.
15. Kim, H. (1999). Representing and Reasoning about Quality using Enterprise Models. PhD thesis, Dept. Mechanical and Industrial Engineering, University of Toronto, Canada.
16. Kitchenham, B., Hughes, R. and Linkman, S. (2001). Modeling software measurement data. IEEE Transactions on Software Engineering, 27(9):788–804.
17. McGarry, J., Card, D., Jones, C., Layman, B., Clark, E., Dean, J. and Hall, F. (2002). Practical Software Measurement. Objective Information for Decision Makers. Addison-Wesley, Reading, MA.
18. Tautz, C. and Von Wangenheim, C. (1998). REFSENO: A representation formalism for software engineering ontologies. Technical Report No. 015.98/E, version 1.1, Fraunhofer IESE, October.
19. Staab, S., Schnurr, H. and Sure, Y. (2001). Knowledge processes and ontologies. IEEE Intelligent Systems, 16(1):26–34.
20. Uschold, M. and Gruninger, M. (1996). Ontologies: Principles, methods, and applications. The Knowledge Engineering Review, 11(2):93–196.

7. An Ontological Approach to SQL:2003

Coral Calero and Mario Piattini

ALARCOS Research Group. Dept. of Information Technologies and Systems, Escuela Superior de Informática, University of Castilla-La Mancha, Spain,
{Coral.Calero, Mario.Piattini}@uclm.es

7.1 Introduction

Databases nowadays are a crucial component of most information systems, playing a strategic role in the support of organizational decisions. Among the different query languages present in the earliest database management systems (DBMSs), SQL has imposed itself as both a *de jure* and *de facto* standard. It has been the focus of an intense process of standardization over the years [4–10], where the most important stakeholders, such as DBMS manufacturers, have been actively involved. SQL support can be found today in the vast majority of DBMSs, sometimes with some slight variations.

Although the merit of standards is unquestionable, sometimes their relevance may fade away an audience beyond their creators, due either to the lack of understandability, or to the presence of inconsistencies.

This last aspect is especially crucial regarding voluminous standards of thousands of pages, for example, the SQL:2003 standard. In a standard like the SQL:2003, there are a considerable number of interweaved concepts, where the semantics of the interrelationships are often very rich.

When this happens, an ontology is the best option to complement the standard. An ontology representation language should have rich and formal abstractions for specifying the meaning of terms. UML class diagrams, enriched with OCL (Object Constraint Language) [13], fulfill this purpose. So, an ontology for complementing a standard should represent its relevant concepts and its interrelationships.

In this chapter, we will present the ontology we have defined for the last version of the SQL standard, the SQL:2003.The next section will show the historical evolution of the standard, and Sect. 7.3 will present the ontology. After that, we will present an example of ontology instantiation through an object-relational schema defined by means of the standard. Conclusions will appear in the last section.

7.2 SQL Evolution

The relational model resulted from E. Codd's research at IBM during the 1960's. SQL, originally named SEQUEL (Structured English QUEry Language), was implemented into an IBM prototype (SEQUEL-XRM), during 1974–1975. Some years later, a subset of this language was implemented into IBM's System-R.

In 1979, ORACLE appeared as the first commercial DBMS based on SQL, followed by several other products (SQL/DS, DB2, DG/SQL, SYBASE, INTERBASE, INFORMIX, UNIFY, etc.). Even other products that had not originally implemented SQL as the base query language offered SQL interfaces (INGRES, ADABAS, SUPRA, IDMS/R). So, SQL became a *de facto* standard, although with various dialects.

In 1982, the database committee X3H2 of ANSI presented a "Standard Relational Language" based on SQL, and in 1986 this standardization body approved the SQL/ANSI standard. This standard was also approved by the ISO the following year [4].

In 1989, the first version of the SQL standard was revised and an addendum [5], which improved mainly referential integrity issues, was published. Meanwhile, ANSI published a standard for embedded SQL [1].

Several commercial proposals based on SQL standards, such as Apple's DAL (Database Access Language), IBM's DRDA (Distributed Relational Database Access), Microsoft's ODBC (Open Database Connectivity), Borland's IDAPI (Integrated Database Application Programming Interface), were disclosed during the following years.

In 1992, a new version was published, known as SQL2 or SQL-92 [6]. Both the semantic capabilities of the language and error management were then considerably improved. That standard was complemented a few years later with the approval of SQL/CLI (Call-Level Interface) [7] and SQL/PSM (Persistent Stored Modules) [8]. With the latter SQL a complete computational language was created, with provisions such as control structure and exception handling.

During the last half of the 1990's, very difficult work for extending SQL with object-oriented capabilities was undertaken. The resulting standard was voluminous and, as such, was divided into several parts. This version, early on known as SQL3 and finally named SQL:1999, includes new features such as new basic data types (e.g., very large objects), user-defined data types, triggers, query recursive operators, sensitive cursors, generalization of tables and user roles.

Recently, another version of the standard has been published, SQL:2003 [10], which makes revisions to all parts of SQL:1999. This last version includes, among other things, SQL/XML (XML-related specifications) and additional features such as new basic data types (e.g., bigint, multiset and XML), enhancements to SQL-invoked routines, extensions to the CREATE TABLE statement, a new MERGE statement, a new schema object (the sequence generator) and two new sorts of columns (identity and generated). Table 7.1 summarizes the evolution of SQL.

Table 7.1. Evolution of SQL

1970s	Relational Model DBMS prototypes (SEQUEL XRM) First relational DBMS
1980s	ANSI SQL-86 Standard ISO SQL-87 Standard SQL-89 Addendum ANSI Embedded SQL
1990s	SQL 92 SQL/CLI SQL/PSM SQL: 1999
2003	SQL: 2003

As represented in Table 7.2, SQL:2003, like its predecessor SQL:1999 (SQL3), has a multipart structure composed of nine parts, which are briefly reviewed in the table. As we can see, the enumeration of the parts is not contiguous. This is due to historical reasons: some parts have disappeared (for instance, all content of SQL:1999's part 5 – SQL/Bindings – has been included in part 2) and other parts are new, either because a previous part has been split (this is the case of part 11 which was previously included in SQL:1999's part 2) or because a fully new part has been created in order to fulfill new requirements (part 14 regarding handling of XML data).

Table 7.2. Structure and summary of the SQL:2003 standard

Part	Name	Description
1	Framework (SQL/Framework)	Overview of the standard. It describes the conceptual framework used in other parts of the standard to specify the grammar of SQL and the result of processing statements in that language by an SQL-implementation. It also defines terms and notation used in the other parts
2	Foundation (SQL/Foundation)	This part defines the data structures and basic operations on SQL-data. It provides functional capabilities for creating, accessing, maintaining, controlling, and protecting SQL-data. This part also specifies the syntax and semantics of a database language and it provides a vehicle for portability of data definitions and compilation units between SQL-implementations and a vehicle for interconnection of SQL-implementations
3	Call-Level Interface (SQL/CLI)	This defines the structures and procedures that may be used to execute SQL statements from within an application written in a standard programming language, such that procedures used are independent of the SQL statements to be executed
4	Persistent Stored Modules (SQL/PSM)	This part specifies the syntax and semantics of a database language for declaring and maintaining persistent database language routines in SQL-server modules
9	Management of External Data (SQL/MED)	Here extensions to Database Language SQL in order to support management of external data through the use of foreign-data wrappers and datalink types are defined
10	Object Language Bindings (SQL/OLB)	This defines extensions to support embedding of SQL statements into programs written in the Java programming language, commonly known as "SQLJ". This part specifies the syntax and semantics of SQLJ, as well as mechanisms to ensure binary portability of resulting SQLJ applications. In addition, it specifies a number of Java packages and their classes
11	Information and Definition Schema (SQL/Schemata)	This part specifies an Information Schema and a Definition Schema that describe the SQL object identifier, the structure and integrity constraints of SQL-data, the security and authorization specifications relating to SQL-data, the features, sub-features and packages of this standard, and the support that each of these has in an SQL implementation. It also includes SQL-implementation information and sizing items
13	Routines and Types Using the Java Programming Language (SQL/JRT)	This specifies the ability to invoke static methods written in the Java programming language as SQL-invoked routines and to use classes defined in the Java programming language as SQL structured user-defined types
14	XML-Related Specifications (SQL/XML)	This last part defines ways in which Database Language SQL can be used in conjunction with XML

7.3 The Ontology for SQL:2003

On the one hand, we developed the ontology using the information of part 1 (Framework) but basically that of part 2 (Foundation) of the standard. On the other hand, we also reengineered Part 11 (Information and Definition Schema) considering those schemata as metamodels of SQL:2003 which implement into their tables all the concepts of the language. Also, in order to clarify some concepts, trying to decide the elements of the ontology and the associations between them, we have used, when possible, the books by Melton [11] and Melton and Simon [12]. Complete information about the construction of the ontology can be found in [3].

The ontology only considers the object-relational aspects of the standard. Due to legibility restrictions, we decided to split the ontology into two sub-ontologies: the data types sub-ontology and the schema object sub-ontology.

The first one contains the aspects related to data types and the other includes information about the SQL schema objects (which has also been split into three views). The sub-ontologies have been represented as ontological diagrams (using UML class diagrams) where a class represents a concept (with its properties represented as class attributes) and relationships among classes represent the existing links between the corresponding concepts (the semantic relationship c is established by the UML relationship type, generalization, aggregation, association, etc.).

The graphical abstractions of UML class diagrams do not allow us to convey several types of restrictions that occur in the modeled domain, such as well-formedness rules for the ontological concepts. Those rules have been expressed as OCL invariants (constraints which must be satisfied at all times), and can be found in [3].

Now, we present the sub-ontologies. For each one, we will present two kinds of information:

- The UML diagram representing the elements with their relationships.
- A set of tables constructed following the methodology REFSENO (Representation Formalism for Software Engineering Ontologies) [14] for presenting the information. REFSENO provides us with constructs to describe concepts (each concept represents a class of experience items), their attributes and relationships. So, for each sub-ontology two tables are used to represent these elements: one with the glossary of concepts and another with the relationships. The table with the attributes has not been included but the definitions of each one can be found in the SQL:2003 standard. The definitions included in the attributes and relationship tables have been extracted from the standard.

7.3.1 The Data Types Sub-ontology

Within the data types sub-ontology, all elements related to SQL:2003 data types are included. In Fig. 7.1, the sub-ontology is shown. The tinted classes (in this figure and in the rest of them) represent abstract classes. Looking at this figure we can see that there are three different kinds of data types: Predefined, Constructed Types and UDTs. The Constructed types can be Composite Types or Reference Types.

The Composite Types can be either *Collection Types* (*Arrays* or *Multiset*, a new type of the SQL:2003 standard) composed of elements, or *Row Types* composed of *Fields*.

Each field has a *Data Type*. The *UDTs* can be either *Distinct Types* (which are defined over a predefined data type) or *Structured Types*. These *Structured Types* are composed of one or more *Attributes* and optionally *Methods*. Each attribute has one data type.

There is a direct inheritance between two structured types, two row types or two reference types.

In Tables 7.3 and 7.4, the attributes and relationships for this sub-ontology are described.

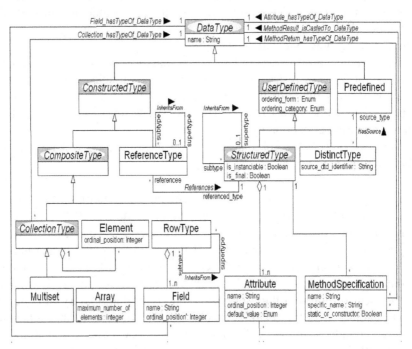

Fig. 7.1. Data types sub-ontology

Table 7.3. Attributes of the data types sub-ontology

Term	Super-concept	Description
DataType	Concept	A data type is a set of representable values. Every representable value belongs to at least one data type and some belong to several data types
Constructed Type	DataType	A constructed type is specified using one of SQL's data type constructors, ARRAY, MULTISET, REF and ROW
UserDefined Type	DataType	A user-defined type is a schema object, identified by a user-defined type name. The definition of a user-defined type specifies a representation for values of that type
Predefined	DataType	SQL defines predefined data types named by the following keywords: CHARACTER, CHARACTER VARYING, CHARACTER LARGE OBJECT, BINARY LARGE OBJECT, NUMERIC, DECIMAL, SMALLINT, INTEGER, BIGINT, FLOAT, REAL, DOUBLE PRECISION, BOOLEAN, DATE, TIME, TIMESTAMP and INTERVAL. Every predefined data type is a subtype of itself and of no other data types. It follows that every predefined data type is a supertype of itself and of no other data types
Composite Type	Constructed Type	A composite type is a data type each of whose values is composed of zero or more values, each of a declared data type
Reference Type	Constructed Type	A *reference type* is a constructed data type, a value of which references (or points to) some site holding a value of the referenced type. The only sites that may be so referenced are the rows of typed tables. It follows that every referenced type is a structured type
Structured Type	UserDefined Type	A *structured type* is a named, user-defined data type. A value of a structured type comprises a number of *attribute values*. Each attribute of a structured type has a data type, specified by an *attribute type* that is included in the descriptor of the structured type
Distinct Type	UserDefined Type	A *distinct type* is a user-defined data type that is based on some predefined type. The values of a distinct type are represented by the values of the type on which it is based
Collection Type	Composite	A *collection* comprises zero or more elements of a specified data type known as the *element type*
Element	Concept	This is part of a collection type and has a type
RowType	Composite	A row type is a sequence of one or more (field name, data type) pairs, known as fields. A value of a row type consists of one value for each of its fields
Multiset	Collection	A multiset is an unordered collection of not necessarily distinct values. A multiset type is specified by a multiset type constructor
Array	Collection	An *array* is an ordered collection of not necessarily distinct values, whose elements are referenced by their ordinal position in the array. An array type is specified by an array type constructor
Field	Concept	A field is a (field name, data type) pair. A value of a field is a value of its data type.
Attribute	Concept	An *attribute* is a named component of a structured type. It has a data type and a default value
Method Specification	Concept	A method specification includes all the information about the method (method name, SQL parameter declaration list, returns data type, etc.)

Table 7.4. Relationships of the data type sub-ontology

Concepts	Description
ReferenceType–ReferenceType	A reference type can inherit from another reference type
StructuredType–StructuredType	A structured type can inherit from another structured type
ReferenceType–StructuredType	A reference type references a structured type
Distinct–Predefined	A distinct type has as a source a predefined type
Collection Type–Element	A collection type is composed of one or more elements. An element belongs to a collection type
RowType–Field	A row type is composed of one or more fields. A field belongs to a row type
RowType–RowType	A row type can inherit from one or more row types
StructuredType–Attribute	A structured type is composed of one or more attributes. An attribute belongs to a structured type
StructuredType–Method Specification	A structured type can have method specifications. A method specification belongs to a structured type
DataType–Method Specification	A method specification result is cast to a data type
DataType–Method Specification	A method specification return has a type of data type
DataType–Attribute	An attribute has a type of data type
DataType–Field	A field has a type of data type
DataType–CollectionType	A collection type has a type of data type

7.3.2 The Schema Objects Sub-ontology

For the sake of simplicity, this sub-ontology (Fig. 7.2), has been split into three views: tables view (Fig. 7.3), constraints view (Fig. 7.4) and columns view (Fig. 7.5). In Fig. 7.2 we can note that, regarding object-relational aspects, there are four different SQL schema objects: *Constraints*, *Domains*, *UDTs* and *Tables*. Each *Domain* is defined in one *Data Type*. *Tables* are composed of *Columns* which are defined in one *Domain* or one *Data Type*.

In Tables 7.5 and 7.6, the attributes and relationships for the general view of this sub-ontology are described.

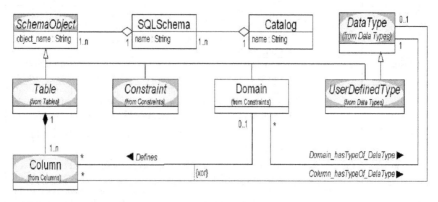

Fig. 7.2. Schema objects sub-ontology (general view)

Table 7.5. Attributes of the schema objects ontology (general view)

Term	Super-concept	Description
Catalog	Concept	A *catalog* is a named collection of SQL schemas, foreign server descriptors, and foreign data wrapper descriptors in an SQL environment
SQLSchema	Concept	An *SQL schema*, often referred to simply as a *schema*, is a persistent, named collection of descriptors.
SchemaObject	Concept	Any object whose descriptor is in some SQL schema is known as an *SQL-schema object*. Every schema object has a name that is unique within the schema among objects of the name class to which it belongs.
Table	SchemaObject	A *table* has an ordered collection of one or more columns and an unordered collection of zero or more rows
Constraint	SchemaObject	A constraint defines the valid states of SQL data by constraining the values in the base tables. A constraint is described by a constraint descriptor. A constraint is a table constraint, a domain constraint, or an assertion and is described by, respectively, a table constraint descriptor, a domain constraint descriptor, or an assertion descriptor
Domain	SchemaObject	A *domain* is a named user-defined object that can be specified as an alternative to a data type in certain places where a data type can be specified. A domain consists of a data type, possibly a default option, and zero or more (domain) constraints
UserDefined Type	SchemaObject	A user-defined type is a schema object, identified by a user-defined type name. The definition of a user-defined type specifies a representation for values of that type
DataType	Concept	A data type is a set of representable values. Every representable value belongs to at least one data type and some belong to several data types
Column	Concept	A *column* is a named component of a table. It has a data type, a default and a nullability characteristic

Table 7.6. Relationships of the schema object sub-ontology (general view)

Concepts	Description
Catalog–SQLSchema	A catalog has one or more SQL schemas. A SQL schema belongs to a catalog
SQLSchema–SQLObject	A SQL schema has one or more SQL objects. A SQL object belongs to a SQL schema
Table–Column	A table is composed of one or more columns. A column belongs to a table
Column–Domain	A column is defined over a domain.
DataType–Column	A column has a type of data type
DataType–Domain	A domain has a type of data type

As can be seen in Fig. 7.3 there are three kinds of tables: Derived (including Views), Transient and Base.

A Typed Table is a Base Table or a View whose rows are instances of one associated Structured Type.

All Typed Tables have a Self-Referencing Column which is the way to implement the object identify characteristic typical of object-oriented environments. Base Tables can be part of an inheritance hierarchy playing supertable and/or subtable roles.

In Tables 7.7 and 7.8, the attributes and relationships for the tables view of this sub-ontology are described.

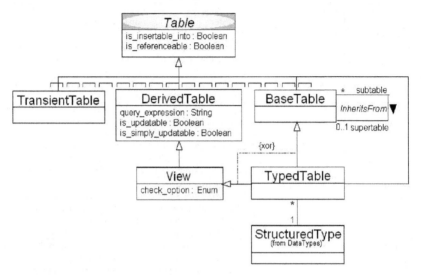

Fig. 7.3. Schema objects sub-ontology (tables view)

Table 7.7. Attributes of the schema objects sub-ontology (tables view)

Term	Super-concept	Description
Table	Concept	A *table* has an ordered collection of one or more columns and an unordered collection of zero or more rows
TransientTable	Table	A transient table is a named table that may come into existence implicitly during the evaluation of a query expression or the execution of a trigger
DerivedTable	Table	The result of a query is called a *derived table*
BaseTable	Table	SQL data consists entirely of table variables, called *base tables*.
View	Derived-Table	A *view* (strictly, a view *definition*) is a named query, that may for many purposes be used in the same way as a base table. Its value is the result of evaluating the query
TypedTable	View	A table that is declared to be based on some structured type is called a "typed table"; its columns correspond in name and declared type to the attributes of the structured type. Typed tables have one additional column, called the "self-referencing column" whose type is a reference type associated with the structured type of the table
Structured-Type	Concept	A *structured type* is a named, user-defined data type. A value of a structured type comprises a number of *attribute values*. Each attribute of a structured type has a data type, specified by an *attribute type* that is included in the descriptor of the structured type

Table 7.8. Relationships of the schema object sub-ontology (tables view)

Concepts	Description
BaseTable–BaseTable	A base table can inherit from another base table
TypedTable–StructuredType	A typed table uses a structured type

On the other hand, *Constraints* can be *Assertions*, *Table Constraints* or *Domain Constraints* (see Fig. 7.4). A *Table Constraint* affects one *Base Table* and there are three kinds of table constraints: *Unique Constraints* (including here *Primary Keys)*, *Table Check Constraints* and *Referential Constraints* (for representing foreign keys). A *Unique Constraint* is defined in a set of *Columns* while a *Referential Constraint* refers to one *Unique Constraint* and has two associated sets of columns: the referencing columns and the referenced columns which are the corresponding columns for the *Unique Constraint*. A *Domain Constraint* affects one *Domain*. Lastly, a *Base Table* has one or more *Candidate Keys* and each one of those corresponds to a *Unique Constraint*.

In Tables 7.9 and 7.10, the attributes and relationships for the constraint view of this sub-ontology are described.

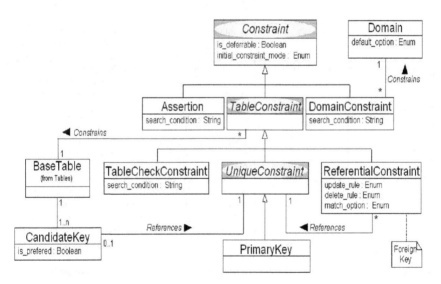

Fig. 7.4. Schema objects sub-ontology (constraints view)

Table 7.9. Attributes of the schema objects sub-ontology (constraints view)

Term	Super-concept	Description
Constraint	Concept	There are three kinds of schema object that describe constraints: assertions and table constraints, and domain constraints, and they are checked in the same way
Assertion	Constraint	An *assertion* is a check constraint. The constraint is violated if the result of the search condition is false (but not if it is unknown)
TableConstraint	Constraint	A *table constraint* is an integrity constraint associated with a single base table.
Domain Constraint	Constraint	A *domain constraint* applies to every column that is based on that domain, by operating as a table constraint for each such column. Domain constraints apply only to columns based on the associated domain
Domain	Concept	A *domain* is a named user-defined object that can be specified as an alternative to a data type in certain places where a data type can be specified. A domain consists of a data type, possibly a default option, and zero or more (domain) constraints
BaseTable	Concept	SQL data consists entirely of table variables, called *base tables*
TableCheck Constraint	TableConstraint	A table check constraint specifies a *search condition*. The constraint is violated if the result of the search condition is false for any row of the table (but not if it is unknown)
Unique Constraint	TableConstraint	A unique constraint is satisfied if and only if no two rows in a table have the same non-null values in the unique columns
Referential Constraint	TableConstraint	A referential constraint specifies one or more columns as *referencing columns* and corresponding *referenced columns* in some (not necessarily distinct) base table, referred to as the *referenced table*
Candidate Key	Concept	A candidate key constraint is a unique constraint that is satisfied if and only if no two rows in a table have the same non-null values in the unique columns and none of the values in the specified column or columns are the null value.
PrimaryKey	UniqueConstraint	A primary key constraint is a unique constraint that specifies PRIMARY KEY. A primary key constraint is satisfied if and only if no two rows in a table have the same non-null values in the unique columns and none of the values in the specified column or columns are the null value

Table 7.10. Relationships of the schema objects sub-ontology (constraints view)

Concepts	Description
Domain–DomainConstraint	A domain constraint constrains a domain
BaseTable–TableConstraint	A table constraint constrains a base table
BaseTable–CandidateKey	A base table has one or more candidate keys
CandidateKey–UniqueConstraint	A candidate key references a unique constraint
ReferentialConstraint–UniqueConstraint	A referential constraint references a unique constraint

Details regarding *Columns* are showed in Fig. 7.5. Three special kinds of *Columns* are identified:

1. *Unique Column* if it is included in any *Unique Constraint*.
2. *Identify Column* if it is used for implementing the object identifying characteristic.
3. *Generated Column* if its values are derived from other columns.

In Tables 7.11 and 7.12, the attributes and relationships for the columns view are described.

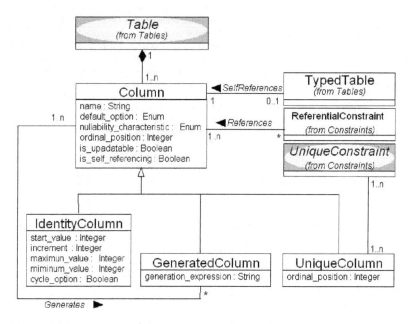

Fig. 7.5. Schema objects sub-ontology (columns view)

7.4 Example

In this section, we will present an example of a database schema defined using the SQL:2003 standard. The example includes all the elements that have been considered in the ontology.

The SQL code is shown in Table 7.13 and the representation of the schema using the elements of the ontology can be found in Fig. 7.6.

Table 7.11. Attributes of the schema objects sub-ontology (columns view)

Term	Super-concept	Description
Table	Concept	A *table* has an ordered collection of one or more columns and an unordered collection of zero or more rows
Column	Concept	A *column* is a named component of a table. It has a data type, a default and a nullability characteristic
TypedTable	Concept	A table that is declared to be based on some structured type is called a "typed table"; its columns correspond in name and declared type to the attributes of the structured type
ReferentialConstraint	Concept	A referential constraint specifies one or more columns as *referencing columns* and corresponding *referenced columns* in some (not necessarily distinct) base table, referred to as the *referenced table*
UniqueConstraint	Concept	A unique constraint specifies one or more columns of the table as *unique columns*. A unique constraint is satisfied if and only if no two rows in a table have the same non-null values in the unique columns
IdentityColumn	Column	An identity column has a *start value*, an *increment*, a *maximum value*, a *minimum value* and a *cycle option*. An identity column is associated with an internal sequence generator
GeneratedColumn	Column	A generated column is one whose values are determined by evaluation of a *generation expression*, a value expression whose declared type is by implication that of the column.
UniqueColumn	Column	A unique constraint specifies one or more columns of the table as *unique columns*

Table 7.12. Relationships of the schema objects sub-ontology (columns view)

Concepts	Description
Table–Column	A table has one or more columns
TypedTable–Column	A typed table self-references one column
ReferentialConstraint–Column	A referential constraint references one or more columns
UniqueColumn–UniqueConstraint	A unique constraint specifies one or more unique columns
Column–GeneratedColumn	A column can generate a generated column. A generated column is generated by one or more columns

Table 7.13. An SQL:2003 example

```
CREATE SCHEMA video_and_music
AUTHORIZATION m_s_enterprises
DEFAULT CHARACTER SET "Latin_1"

CREATE DOMAIN price DECIMAL (7,2)
CHECK (VALUE IS NOT 0);

CREATE DISTINCT TYPE money AS
DECIMAL (9,2);

CREATE TYPE movie AS(
movie_id INTEGER,
title      CHARACTER VARYING (100),
languages MULTISET ['English', 'French',
'Spanish', 'Portuguese', 'Italian'],
genre CHARACTER VARYING (20) ARRAY
[10],
run_time INTEGER
)
INSTANTIABLE
NOT FINAL
METHOD length_interval ()
RETURNS INTERVAL HOUR (2) TO MINUTE

CREATE       INSTANCE       METHOD
length_interval ()
RETURNS INTERVAL HOUR (2) TO MINUTE
FOR MOVIE
RETURN CAST (CAST (SELF.run_time AS
INTERVAL (4) )
AS INTERVAL HOUR (2) TO MINUTE );

CREATE TABLE movies (
stock_number         CHARACTER(10)
CONSTRAINT                       mov-
ies_stock_number_not_null NOT NULL,
movie                          movie,
our_tape_cost                  price,
tapes_in_stock      INTEGER
CONSTRAINT              movies_primary_key
PRIMARY KEY (stock_number)
);


CREATE TABLE movies_stars (
movie_title CHARACTER (30)
   CONSTRAINTmov-
ies_stars_movie_title_not_null NOT NULL,
movie_year_released DATE,
movie_number CHARACTER (10),
actor_last_name CHARACTER (35)
   CONSTRAINT                    mov-
ies_stars_actor_last_name_not  _null   NOT
NULL,
actor_first_name CHARACTER (25)
   CONSTRAINT                    mov-
ies_stars_actor_first_name_not  _null   NOT
NULL,
```

```
CREATE TABLE music_distributors OF mu-
sic_distributors (
REF IS dist_ref SYSTEM GENERATED,
distributor_id WITH OPTIONS
CONSTRAINT                       mu-
sic_distributors_distributor_id_not_null
NOT NULL,
distributor_name WITH OPTIONS
CONSTRAINT                       mu-
sic_distributors_distributor_name_not_null
NOT NULL,
);

CREATE TYPE address AS(
street     CHARACTER VARYING (35),
city   CHARACTER VARYING (40),
country character (3)
);

CREATE  TYPE  US_address  UNDER  ad-
dress AS(
state       CHARACTER (2),
zip         ROW (
            Basic      INTEGER,
            Plus4      SMALLINT)
)
METHOD zipcode ()
RETURNS CHARACTER VARYING (10);

CREATE INSTANCE METHOD zipcode ()
RETURNS CHARACTER VARYING (10)
FOR US_address
BEGIN
IF SELF.zip.plus4 IS NULL
THEN RETURN CAST (SELF.zip.basic AS
   CHARACTER VARYING (5));
       ELSE RETURN CAST (SELF.zip.basic
AS
       CHARACTER VARYING (5))
|| '-' || CAST (SELF.zip.basic AS
   CHARACTER VARYING (4))
ENDIF;
END;


CREATE TABLE customers(
nr_of_customer   INTEGER   GENERATED
ALWAYS AS IDENTITY (START WITH 1
INCREMENTED BY 1MINVALUE 1),
cust_last_name CHARACTER (35)
CONSTRAINT                       custom-
ers_cust_last_name_not_null
NOT NULL,
cust_first_name CHARACTER (35)
CONSTRAINT                       custom-
ers_cust_first_name_not_null
NOT NULL,
cust_complete_name          GENERATED
ALWAYS   AS   (cust_first_name     ||
```

```
actor_middle_name CHARACTER (25),              cust_last_name),
   CONSTRAINT movies_stars_unique           cust_address US_address,
      UNIQUE (movie_title, actor_last_name, ac-   cust_current_charges money,
tor_first_name, actor_middle_name)              number_of_problems SMALLINT );
      NOT DEFERRABLE,
   CONSTRAINT movies_stars_fk_movie          CREATE VIEW problem_customers ( last,
      FOREIGN KEY (movie_number)            first)
         REFERENCES movies (stock_number)   AS
         ON DELETE CASCADE                      SELECT cust_last_name, cust_first_name
         ON UPDATE CASCADE                      FROM  customers
);                                              WHERE number_of_problems >
                                                   0.8           *           (SELECT
                                                MAX(number_of_problems)
                                                   FROM customers);
CREATE TYPE music_distributors AS (
distributor_id               CHARACTER       CREATE                       ASSERTION
(15),                                        limit_total_movie_stock_value
distributor_name    CHARACTER (25)              CHECK (( SELECT COUNT(*)
);                                                     FROM customers
                                                       WHERE number_of_problems > 5
                                                          AND    cust_current_charges   >
                                                150,00
                                                          AND    cust_current_charges   <
                                                1000,00)
                                                   <10 );
```

7.5 Conclusions

In this chapter we have presented the ontology developed for the object-relational aspects of the SQL:2003 standard. With this ontology we have the aim of increasing the understandability of the standard.

The ontology also helped us detect some inconsistencies, such as the following:

- The definition of distinct and structured types as specializations of user-defined types (UDTs) is proposed but not strictly followed in all parts of the standard.
- There is an inconsistency in the definition of inheritance among data types. The suggestion that all data types can be specialized is contradicted by the fact that predefined types cannot be specialized. Our interpretation was that inheritance is only possible in structured types, reference types or row types but it does not make any sense in others, such as distinct and collection types (see Fig. 7.1).
- Similar problems appeared regarding inheritance among tables, since not all of them can be specialized. Our interpretation was to limit inheritance to the base tables (see Fig. 7.3).

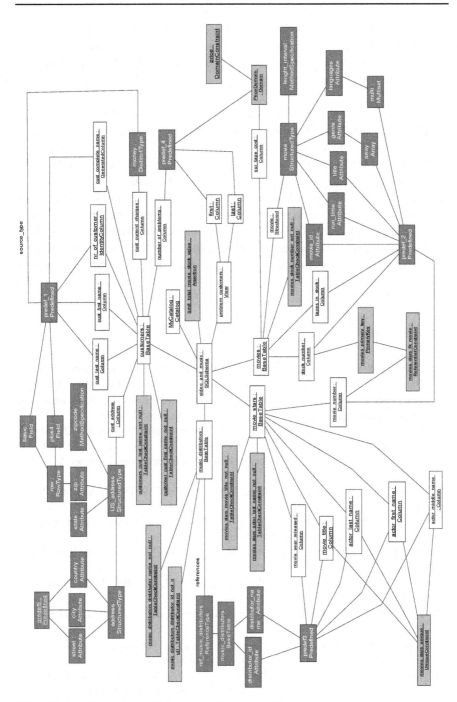

Fig. 7.6. Ontology instantiation example

- Another example which is ill-explained in some parts of the standard is that the concept of a method specification should be associated with a UDT. In our opinion it is better to link the method specification to a structured type (see Fig. 7.1).

For carrying out the ontology we have used the SQL:2003 Schemata (part 11 of the standard) in a mapping exercise against the proposed ontology, as a means for validating and refining it.

The full coverage of the standard is now being made. As a result of this work we will have the ontology of the complete standard

The final goal of the definition of the SQL:2003 ontology is to use it, for example, in the formalization of metrics for object-relational database schemas defined with SQL:2003. In that case, metrics can be formalized using OCL and calculated over a schema represented using the UML representation for the ontology. These metrics can be used, for example, for the reengineering of the databases [2].

References

1. ANSI (1989). "Database Language Embedded SQL". ANSI.X3.168.
2. Baroni, A., Brito e Abreu, F. and Calero, C. (2005). Finding where to apply object-relational database schema refactorings: an ontology-guided approach. Jornadas de Ingeniería del Software y Bases de Datos, 99–106.
3. Calero, C., Ruiz, F., Baroni, A., Brito e Abreu, F. and Piattini, M (2005). An ontological approach to describe the SQL: 2003 object-relational features. Computer Standards & Interfaces. Elsevier. ScienceDirect. In press Available online 2 December 2005.
4. ISO (1987). "Database Language SQL". ISO/IEC 9075 International Standard.
5. ISO (1989). "Database Language SQL with Integrity Enhancement". ISO/IEC 9075 International Standard.
6. ISO (1992). "Database Language SQL". ISO/IEC 9075 International Standard.
7. ISO (1995). "SQL/CLI – Call Level Interface". ISO/IEC 9075-3: International Standard.
8. ISO (1996). "SQL/PSM – Persistent Storage Module". ISO/IEC 9075-4: International Standard.
9. ISO (1999). "Information Technology – Database languages – SQL". Parts 1 to 5. ISO/IEC 9075-1 to 9075-5 International Standards.
10. ISO (2003). "Information Technology – Database languages – SQL". Parts 1 to 4 and 9 to 14. ISO/IEC 9075-1 to 9075-14 International Standards.
11. Melton, J. (2003). SQL:1999. Understanding Object-Relational and Other Advanced Features. Morgan Kaufmann, San Francisco.

12. Melton, J. and Simon, A.R. (2002). SQL: 1999. Understanding Relational Language Components. Morgan Kaufmann, San Francisco.
13. OMG (2003). "UML 2.0 OCL Specification". Final Adopted Specification. October.
14. Tautz, C. and Von Wangenheim, C.G. (1998). REFSENO: A Representation Formalism for Software Engineering Ontologies. Fraunhofer IESE Report No. 015.98/E, version 1.1, October 20.

8. The Object Management Group Ontology Definition Metamodel

Robert Colomb

School of Information Technology and Electrical Engineering, The University of Queensland, QLD 4072 Australia
colomb@itee.uq.edu.au

Kerry Raymond

DSTC Pty Ltd,
k.raymond@qut.edu.au

Lewis Hart and Patrick Emery

AT&T Government Solutions, Inc.,
lewis.hart@appliedminds.com, patemery@att.com

Chris Welty

IBM Watson Research Center,
welty@us.ibm.com

Guo Tong Xie

IBM China Research Lab,
xieguot@cn.ibm.com

Elisa Kendall

Sandpiper Software, Inc.,
ekendall@sandsoft.com

8.1 Introduction

The Object Management Group (OMG) is a consortium which develops standards for various aspects of software engineering which are widely used in industry, including UML (Unified Modeling Language). With the advent of the Semantic Web movement [1] and the consequent development of ontology modeling languages like OWL by the World-Wide Web Consortium (W3C), the development of ontologies has become mainstream. Consequently, in 2003 the OMG issued a Request for Proposal for an Ontology Development Metamodel, for a Meta-Object Facility (MOF-2) metamodel intended to support:

- Development of ontologies using UML modeling tools.
- Implementation of ontologies in the W3C Web Ontology language OWL.
- Forward and reverse engineering for ontologies.

The four organizations which the authors represent (DSTC, Gentleware/AT&T, IBM, Sandpiper Software) made preliminary submissions in August, 2003. They have since joined together to develop a Final Submission, presently scheduled for completion in mid-2006. A preliminary distribution of work in progress was made in August, 2004 [7]. Several revisions have been published within the OMG community since, and comments solicited not only from the OMG but from the W3C and ISO communities as well. The latest revision of the specification is available at http://www.omg.org/cgi-bin/doc?ad/05-09-08.

This chapter first argues for a MOF-based metamodel, and why UML is not a universally suitable metamodel for ontology development. It then describes the main features of the ODM, which supports several different ontology representation systems: RDFS/OWL, Common Logic, Topic Maps, as well as UML. These different metamodels are tied together by UML profiles and mapping, some aspects of which are described. Finally, there are many more specific requirements for ontology modeling facilities for particular broad classes of application. The MOF has a modular structure which makes it a straightforward process for third parties to develop and publish plugins which extend and enhance the standard. A few examples illustrate the possibilities.

8.2 Why a MOF Ontology Metamodel?

There are actually three questions packed into this one:

- Why have a metamodel at all?
- Why have a MOF metamodel?
- Why a MOF metamodel other than UML?

8.2.1 Why a Metamodel?

In order for an ontology to be used in a computing application, it must be represented as some sort of computer-readable data structure. In OMG terminology an ontology is an example of a data model. The syntactic rules for representing this data structure are called a metamodel. So in order to develop an ontology at all, there needs to be a metamodel for it.

A programming language is a sort of metamodel. In the early days of programming languages, each programming language was developed in idiosyncratic fashion (eg FORTRAN and COBOL), but it soon became clear that it was better to develop programming languages with uniform types of formation rules. Backus–Naur Form (BNF) was developed for this purpose, and most programming languages today are developed in BNF or one of its derivatives. BNF is an example of a metametamodel, that is a metamodel for developing metamodels.

An important distinction in this space is that between abstract and concrete syntax. Originally, metamodels were used to specify the syntax of programming languages. A BNF specification of Pascal could be used to develop a compiler which could be used to parse all and only Pascal programs. However, it turns out to be useful for some languages to have several quite different but formally equivalent representations, sometimes called syntactic sugar. SQL is a good example, with formally equivalent relational algebra, tuple relational calculus, QBE, structured natural language and embedded syntaxes. So it has become common for a language designer to choose one representation for publication of the language specification, but to recognize that an implementation might have a very different representation. The formal structure is called *abstract syntax* and the representations *concrete syntaxes*.

Standard metametamodels are an advantage because every metamodel exists in a software environment tailored to fit it. A programming language needs a compiler, for example. If the programming language (metamodel) is expressed in a standard metametamodel, much of the effort needed to develop the software environment can be reused. If a programming language is represented in BNF, a compiler can be created easily using a compiler–compiler like YACC.

So a computer realization of an ontology requires a metamodel, and if the metamodel is expressed in a widely–used metametamodel there is scope for its supporting software to be created by configuring a standard set of tools based on that metametamodel.

Note, by the way, that a metametamodel is itself a metamodel (for expressing metamodels). So it is quite common for the formation rules of the metametamodel to be expressed in itself. The formation rules for BNF are themselves expressed in BNF. There is typically not an infinite regress of meta…models.

8.2.2 Why MOF?

The OMG has developed many metamodels for various purposes, including CORBA for interoperating systems and the UML for the design of computer systems. All OMG metamodels are developed in the metametamodel MOF, which is a subset of the UML class metamodel. MOF is expressed in itself. A fragment of the MOF is shown in the MOF diagram of Fig. 8.1. The diagram has five instances of the MOF class *Class* (*Class*, *association*, *type*, *classifier* and *property*), five instances of the MOF class *Association* (*ownedAttribute*, *type*, *memberEnd*, *ownedEnd* and *generalization*), and three instances of the MOF association *generalization* (*Type* is a generalization of *Classifier*, *Classifier* is a generalization of *Class* and *Association*), and so on.

MOF is a metametamodel with roughly the expressive power of BNF. More expressive constraints can be expressed with the textual constraint language Object Constraint Language (OCL, which is itself modeled in the MOF) [13]. There are many software tools based on the MOF, including Rational Rose, a tool for editing and visualizing models in UML and hence MOF; an XML serialization called XML Metadata Interchange (XMI); and a variety of tools based on the integrated development environment *Eclipse*,[31] including facilities to generate Java application program interfaces.

What differentiates MOF from other metametamodels, though, is the visual syntax used as a concrete syntax in representing the abstract syntax of the system to be modeled. Part of the specification of the MOF is a set of rendering conventions, so that instances of the MOF class *Class* are rendered as rectangles, instances of the MOF class *Association* are ren-

---

[31] eclipse.org

dered as lines connecting the *ownedEnd* and *memberEnd,* and instances of the MOF association *generalization* are rendered with arrows, all as shown in Fig. 8.1.

So a MOF-based metamodel has not only the advantages of a metamodel based on any standard metametamodeling system with a well-developed suite of software tools, but also the advantage of a standard visualization. The visualization is a concrete syntax used to edit and render the abstract structure of the system modeled, while the software tools use a different concrete syntax, namely the repository schemas. Models are interchanged as XML serializations using a different concrete syntax, namely XMI. And an implementer is free to represent the syntax in any way they like, so long as the resulting concrete syntax is formally equivalent to the abstract syntax. In other words, any concrete syntax must be formally equivalent to the concrete syntax in which the system is specified.

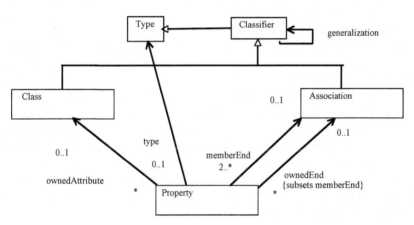

Abstracted from UML Infrastructure [UML2I] Figure 73, Section 11.3 page 111
Note that the MOF does not support n-ary associations (upper multiplicity of
memberEnd is limited to 2, rather than 2..*)

Fig. 8.1. Fragment of the MOF (and UML) expressed in the MOF

8.2.3 Why Not UML?

An ontology is a kind of data model. The UML Class Diagram is a rich representation system, widely used, and well supported with software tools. Why not use UML for representing ontologies?

One reason is that a UML Class Diagram is a specification for a system. It shows schemas, but does not necessarily fully specify instances. Even if instances are fully specified, it is not common to represent a large population of concrete instances. We know that the shared worlds modeled with ontologies contain instances as well as schemas, for example the periodic table of the elements includes classes like rare earths and noble gases, but also individuals like hydrogen and helium. UML is intended to be used with some sort of implementation, like an SQL database manager, which completes the specification of the instances, and represents and stores the concrete populations.

Further, a UML Class Diagram is generally used by the software engineers building a system as part of the design specification. It can be a component of a computer-aided software engineering tool which can automatically generate implementations. But class diagrams are not intended for public use, to be combined as components in larger ontologies, or to be used at run-time. It is of course possible to adapt UML to these purposes, but they are not part of its design.

Finally, and perhaps most importantly, an ontology by definition is intended to be reused, or to have multiple implementations across applications. While reuse is also an important aspect of the OMG's Model-Driven Architecture methodology, in the case of an ontology, the ability to unambiguously interpret the definitions and axioms expressed is essential to enabling automated reasoning. There must be some way of verifying that two implementations committed to a single ontology are logically consistent with one another. Common Logic and OWL enable this by having a formal semantics expressed as a model theory. Two implementations which generate the same objects by definition agree. UML does not at present have a published model theory or proof theory that would enable such automated validation or reasoning processes.

So this is why the OMG called for development of an ontology development metamodel distinct from UML.

8.3 The Ontology Development Metamodel

A trigger for the call for development of an ODM was the development by the World-Wide Web Consortium of the Web Ontology Language OWL. OWL has a number of features which emphasize weaknesses in UML for ontology development, including:

- The ability to fully specify individuals apart from classes, and for individuals to have properties independently of any class they might be an instance of.
- The OWL property is much more flexible than the UML association. In particular it can be used to model complex mereotopological relationships and hence complex objects. (Mereotopological relationships are whole-part relationships, including those involving spatial parts and their geometric and topological relationships.)
- OWL Full allows classes to have instances which are themselves classes.

But there are other language development efforts in the ontology space, including in particular the International Organization for Standardization (ISO) projects Topic Maps and Common Logic (CL). Topic Maps is a metalanguage designed to express the "aboutness" of an information structure with key model elements *topic* and *association*. Common Logic is a syntax for the first-order predicate calculus, seen as a successor to KIF (Knowledge Interchange Format).

Furthermore, organizations developing ontologies will often build on legacy data models represented in UML or one of the dialects of Entity–Relationship (ER) Modeling, even if the development is carried on in one of the newer metamodels.

Since there are so many metamodels which a developer might need to take into account in an ontology project, the ODM Group decided that it would not be sufficient to develop a metamodel for OWL only, but instead to develop a suite of MOF metamodels, for RDFS/OWL, Topic Maps and CL. UML of course already has a MOF metamodel.

The different metamodels express a concept quite differently. To show this difference, we will use a simple running example, illustrated in Fig. 8.2 as a UML model, of a simple model which might be a fragment of a university teaching ontology, namely that students enroll in courses.

Fig. 8.2. Fragment of a university teaching ontology, expressed in UML

One of the advantages of UML, and hence the MOF, is that there is a well-established relationship between UML Class Diagrams and database schemas, implemented by many more or less automatic tools. This relationship allows a first cut at a repository for any of the metamodels in the ODM. We will use the example in Fig. 8.2 represented as repository table populations to show how the various metamodels work.

A class in UML is a set of instances. The set of instances associated at a particular time with a class is called the class's *extent*. An instance consists of a set of slots each of which contains a value drawn from the type of the property of the slot. A type is a computer-representable set which is the value set for an attribute function (*ownedAttribute*). The instance is associated with one or more classifiers. Sample instances of the classes and associations (classifiers) of Fig. 8.2 are shown in Table 8.1. The properties in the model are *code*, *title* and *NumEnrolled* owned by *Course* and *ID*, *name* owned by *Student*.

Table 8.1. Sample instances of classifiers of Fig. 8.2

a. Course

Classifier	code	Title	NumEnrolled
Course	INFS3101	Ontology and the Semantic Web	0

b. Student

Classifier	ID	Name
Student	02468135	Robert Colomb

c. Enrolled

Classifier	ID	code
enrolled	02468135	INFS3101

But the implementation of a classifier is not fully constrained. For example, an equally valid instance of *Course* would be the name *INFS3101*, if it were decided that that name would identify an instance of the class. The remainder of the slots could be filled dynamically from other properties of the class.

8.3.1 RDF/OWL Metamodel

OWL is developed by the W3C as a specialization of RDFS, which is an extension to RDF. The OWL metamodel therefore includes concepts from RDFS and RDF. A fragment of the OWL metamodel is illustrated in Fig. 8.3. OWL classes are RDFS classes, and OWL properties are RDF properties. The subclass and subproperty relationships in OWL are inherited from RDFS.

Note that in Fig. 8.3 *Individual* is shown as a subclass of *RDFSResource*, so that the extent of *Individual* is a set of instances of *RDFSResource*. *OWLClass* is also a subclass of *RDFSResource*. An instance of *OWLClass* is a single class, so classes are also resources. This way of modeling makes it easy for example to distinguish OWL DL from OWL Full by constraining *Individual* to be disjoint from *Property* and *OWLClass*. Note also that the two kinds of property are modeled by subclassing, and that *EnumeratedClass* and *OWLRestriction* are subclasses of *OWLClass*. There are of course other restrictions in OWL besides the cardinality restriction shown, and other kinds of classes.

Comparing the fragment of RDFS/OWL in Fig. 8.3 with Fig. 8.1 interpreted as a fragment of UML, we see that each has an element *Class*. The two model very similar concepts. But in OWL, the subclass and subproperty associations are defined separately (in the W3C standard, they are in fact defined identically but separately), whereas in UML, both subclass and subassociation are inherited from the *generalization* meta-association with their common meta-superclass *Classifier*.

The comparison also shows that OWL has one relationship between classes, namely *Property*, while UML has two, namely *Association* and *ownedAttribute*. (In Fig. 8.1, a *Class* is a *Type*, and a *Property* is a representation associated with a *Type* via the meta-association *type*. So an *Association* is a relationship between two instances of *Type*, and *ownedAttribute* is a relationship between an instance of *Class*, hence one instance of *Type*, and another.) Note that the concept of *Property* in UML is not at all the same as the concept of *Property* in OWL.

This shows an advantage of MOF metamodels – the MOF visualization provides a dense notation which leverages the common metametamodel (ie MOF) and makes moderate scale comparisons easier.

Our university teaching ontology fragment of Fig. 8.2 is represented in tables from the default repository for OWL in Table 8.2.

Note that unlike UML, OWL does not distinguish between a class and its representation, so what are classes in OWL are properties in UML, not directly classes. (Recall that a property in UML is a computer-representable type, the target of *ownedAttribute*, *ownedEnd* and *memberEnd* meta-associations, a very different kind of thing from an OWL property. See Fig. 8.1.) All the instances in the ontology are shown in Table 8.2 as the domain of a property or the range of an *objectProperty*.

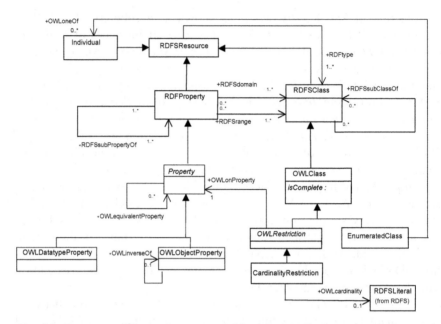

Fig. 8.3. Fragment of the MOF metamodel for RDFS and OWL: class and property

Table 8.2. OWL repository representation of university teaching ontology

Classes: CourseCode, Title, StudentID, Name
Datatype: integer

Properties:

PropertyName	Type	Domain	Domain Instance	Range	Range Instance
hasTitle	Object	CourseCode	INFS3101	Title	Ontology and the Semantic Web
numEnrolled	Data	CourseID	INFS3101	integer	0
name	Object	StudentID	02468135	Student Names	Robert Colomb
enrolled	Object	StudentID	02468135	CourseCode	INFS3101

There is a significant impedance mismatch between the MOF and RDFS/OWL. For example, the diagram in Fig. 8.3 does not show that the metaclass *Individual* is itself an instance of *OWLClass* (called owl:Thing), and further that every instance of *OWLClass* participates in the *RDFSsub-*

classOf association with the instance owl:Thing. In the MOF there is a strict separation of metalevels, so that the MOF Class model shows only the metaclasses and meta-associations, but no instances. RDFS is its own metamodel and the metamodel for OWL, so the metalevels are mixed.

For example, RDFS includes built-in resources rdfs:Class and rdf:Property, together with a built-in property rdf:type. The characteristics of *Individual* are specified using the following RDF triples:

owl:Thing	rdf:type	rdfs:Class	(1)
rdfs:subClassOf	rdf:type	rdf:Property	(2)
rdfs:domain	rdf:type	rdf:Property	(3)
rdfs:range	rdf:type	rdf:Property	(4)
rdfs:subClassOf	rdfs:domain	rdfs:Class	(5)
rdfs:subClassOf	rdfs:range	rdfs:Class	(6)

That owl:Thing is a universal superclass is specified by applying a restriction class owl:hasValue owl:Thing on property rdfs:subClassOf. Even a restriction class has its structure represented as a collection of RDF triples:

owl:Restriction	rdfs:subClassOf	rdfs:Class	(7)
owl:hasValue	rdfs:subClassOf	owl:Restriction	(8)
owl:onProperty	rdf:type	rdf:Property	(9)
owl:value	rdf:type	rdf:Property	(10)

And the restriction class in question by:

res	rdf:type	owl:hasValue	(11)
res	owl:onProperty	rdfs:subClassOf	(12)
res	value	owl:Thing	(13)
RestrictedClass	rdfs:subClassOf	res	(14)

Of course the semantics of the built-in resources of RDF, RDFS and OWL are defined. But they are defined outside RDF, by textual means in [11]. The textual means in many cases includes a formal model theory defined using the predicate calculus.

The impedance mismatch problem can be overcome to a large degree by adding to the MOF Class model constraints expressed in the UML constraint language OCL asserting the existence of particular instances of particular metaclasses along with their structural constraints.

The MOF metamodel expressed in Class models with constraints goes much of the way towards specifying the detailed structure of RDFS and OWL, but is incomplete in a key way. In the MOF there is no way to formally state that for example the instance "RDFS:Resource" is the same thing as the metaclass *RDFSResource*. These are specified in the text accompanying the formal metamodels.

8.3.2 Topic Maps

Topic Maps are under development as an ISO standard designed to express the "aboutness" of information resources. It is conceptually based on the metaphor of the index in the back of a book. Fragments of the ODM MOF metamodel for Topic Maps are shown in Figs. 8.4 and 8.5. At present, the ODM Topic Maps metamodel follows closely the UML diagrams in the ISO Topic Maps Data Model (TMDM) [12].

The central concept in Topic Maps is the *Topic*, which is a textual statement of what some subject is about, analogous to an index entry in a book. The subject can be a computer-accessible thing, accessed by a *Locator* (a URI), or something outside the computing environment, like "Australia" or "the idea of topic maps". Topics can be linked together in *n*-ary *Associations* via *AssociationRoles*. An occurrence of a topic is some resource which that topic is about, either the resource itself or a URI. A Google search on the topic "Australia" generates 63,500,000 references, most of which are occurrences of the topic (taking into account limited precision in search engine results).

Name, Variant, occurrence and *association roles* are subordinate constructs. Larger scale organization is given by the grouping of *Topic* and *Association* into a *Topic Map*. Any construct other than *Topic* can itself be the subject of a topic (*reification*).

Associations, association roles and occurrences are all individual-level constructs. They are organized into something like OWL properties by the requirement that each of them be associated with a topic as its *type* (Fig. 8.5). A structure analogous to a database view is given by the concept of *scope*, also named by a topic.

But topics themselves are not necessarily organized into class/instance relationships, even to the loose extent of OWL, where owl: Thing is a class whose extent is all individuals. There is a mechanism for representing class/instance relationships using a specific instance of *Association*, as shown in the MOF instances diagram of Fig. 8.6, where some topics can be regarded as types having other topics as instances. There is another specific instance of *Association* specifying a subtype/supertype relationship, as shown in Fig. 8.7.

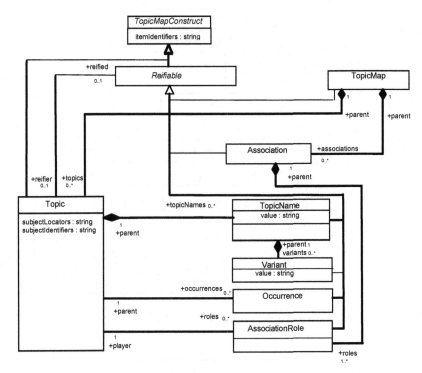

Fig. 8.4. Main model elements of Topic Maps

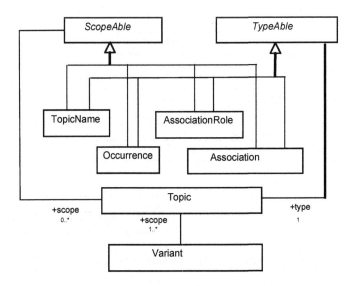

Fig. 8.5. Intermediate structural mechanisms of Topic Maps

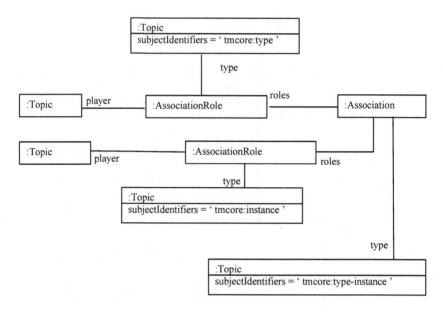

Fig. 8.6. The type-instance relationship in the TMDM

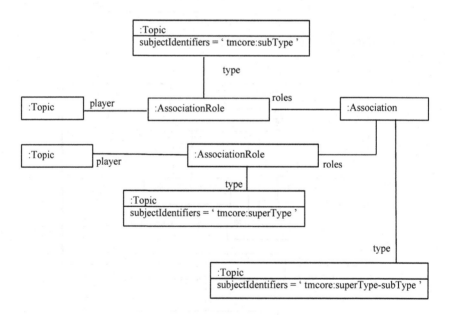

Fig. 8.7. The subtype–supertype relationship in the TMDM

Figure 8.4 illustrates a feature of the MOF, that it can model a complex object with parts, shown by associations with a solid lozenge at the whole end of a whole–part relationship. So a *Topic Map* consists of a set of topics and associations, an *Association* consists of a set of roles, and a *Topic* consists of *TopicNames*.

Compared with OWL, Topic Maps have a much richer structure of classes and a correspondingly poorer structure of properties. A model expressed as a Topic Map would have instances of *Topic*, the various kinds of subordinate constructs, and *Association*, all of which would be most naturally expressed in OWL as instances of *Class*. But a *Class* in OWL is a simple construct, while a *Topic* is a complex construct with parts (see Fig. 8.4). So the meta-associations in the Topic Maps metamodel would be represented in OWL as properties.

Our university teaching ontology fragment of Fig. 8.2 would be represented in a default repository for Topic Maps as in Table 8.3. Topic and association instances are identified by OIDs. Notice that the structure of the ontology is given almost entirely by links among topics. Notice also that *Association Role* and *Parent* in the *Topics* table do not contain enough information to know which student is enrolled on which course. The *Associations* table is needed for that purpose.

8.3.3 Common Logic

Common Logic (CL) is a syntax for the first-order predicate calculus. A fragment of a MOF metamodel for CL is shown in Fig. 8.8. The native metamodel for CL is EBNF, so the representation in the MOF is fairly straightforward.

The basic construct in CL is a *term*. *Terms* can be *AtomicSentences* which have a *predicate* and zero or more *arguments*, *FunctionalTerms*, also with *arguments*, or *LogicalNames*. A term can be commented.

On a macro scale, an instance of a CL model is a *Text*, which consists of a collection of *Phrases*. A *Phrase* is generally a *Sentence* (there are comments and imports not shown on the fragment). A sentence is built from *Atoms* according to structural principles similar to those shown, involving connectors and quantifiers.

CL is a very rich system. A model instance represented in one of the other metamodels can also be represented in CL (including all the nominally second-order facilities of OWL Full). But the metamodel constructs are different. A class in UML or OWL is represented as a (unary) *AtomicSentence* in CL, a property in OWL also by a (binary) *AtomicSentence*.

The class constructors of OWL are represented in CL as logical connectors in a predicate definition.

Table 8.3. Topic Map repository population for University teaching ontology fragment

a. Repository of Topics

Topic	Name	Type	Ass.Role Type	Parent Type
1	02468135	StudentID	student	enrolled
2	Robert Colomb	Student Name		
3	INFS3101	Course Code	course	enrolled
4	Ontology and the Semantic Web	Course Name		
5	StudentID			
6	Student Name			
7	Course Code			
8	Course Name			
9	student			
10	course			
11	enrolled			

b. Repository of Associations

Association	Type	roles	roles Type	player
1	Enrolled	1	student	1
1	Enrolled	2	course	3

Our university teaching ontology fragment is represented in the default repository for CL in Table 8.4. Notice that there is only one metamodel construct, the *AtomicSentence*. The representation does not show the unary type predicates, which would in practice often be omitted.

Sentences of course can have more than one atom, together with quantifications, negation and so on. The repository for more complex sentences would look very similar to Table 8.4, with additional columns for sentence ID and so on. Atoms would be identified relatively within a sentence rather than absolutely as in Table 8.4. But atomic sentences are very common, so there is a case for implementing them specially.

The subclass relationship in UML or OWL would be represented in CL as a two-atom sentence with a connector *implication*. But not all binary

implications, even if both atoms have the same arity, represent subclass relationships

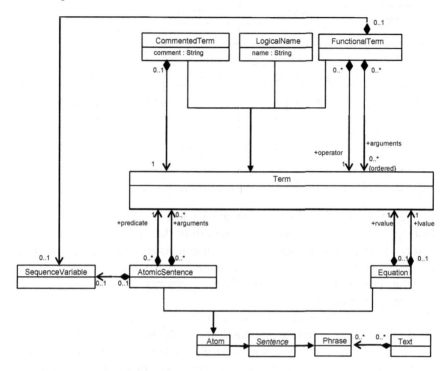

Fig. 8.8. Fragment of MOF metamodel for CL

8.3.4 General Structure of Metamodels

We have looked at the detailed structure of the metamodels, but have not
discussed their larger scale structure. If we think about a model instance
stored in a repository, the metamodel must do two things: supply identifiers to distinguish instances of the various metaclasses, and collect the
various parts of a model instance into a single whole.

MOF metamodels often supply an identifier from a single (or possibly a
few) most general classes. For example, the diagram in Fig. 8.4 has a most
general class *TopicMapConstruct*, which supplies an identifier which can
be used in a repository to distinguish the various objects in a Topic Map
instance. The OWL metamodel has a similar construct. In Fig. 8.3, the
most general class is *RDFSResource*, which supplies the identifier URI.

234 Robert Colom et al.

Table 8.4. Representation of university teaching ontology fragment in CL

Atomic Sentence	Predicate	Arguments	Value
1	Student.name	1	02468135
1	Student.name	2	Robert Colomb
2	Course.description	1	INFS3101
2	Course.description	2	Ontology and the Semantic Web
2	NumEnrolled	1	INFS3101
	NumEnrolled	2	0
3	enrolled	1	02468135
3	enrolled	2	INFS3101

In contrast, UML and CL do not specify identifiers in their metamodels. Instead, they get their object identifiers from the MOF, which specifies an object identifier for instances of MOF metaclasses. An instance of one of the ODM metamodels gets its object identifiers from the metaclasses in the MOF instances model. To show these structures takes us too far afield from the present chapter.

The ODM metamodels all collect the parts of a model instance into a single whole using similar mechanisms. UML has a construct *Package*, which has a one-to-many association with a general metaclass *PackageableElement*. All the metaclasses are subclasses of *PackageableElement*, so inherit the link to an instance of *Package*. Topic Maps have a similar system, as shown in Fig. 8.4. The packaging construct is *TopicMap*, having a one-to-many association with both *Topic* and *Association*. The other Topic Map constructs are all linked to either a topic or association by a many-to-one association, so a link to the packaging construct can be derived. CL also has a similar structure, *Module* in Fig. 8.8.

In OWL, the packaging construct is the metaclass *OWLOntology*. Although the metaclass *OWLOntology* supports the OWL ontology properties like owl:imports, it is not limited to the semantics of owl:Ontology, but is the packaging construct "Ontology" as described in [8].

If the packaging worked like the other metamodels, there would be a meta-association *includes* from *OWLOntology* to *RDFSResource*, so that one could navigate from an ontology instance to the objects contained in it, and from an object to the ontology containing it. This is not possible in the OWL metamodel, since the objects metaclass *RDFSResource* is interpreted as being things in the world that an ontology could represent. So although it would be possible to navigate from *OWLOntology* to *RDFSRe-*

source, the opposite is not navigable. Given an instance of *RDFSResource*, it is in principle not possible to link to the instances of *Ontology* that might include it. This is in much the same spirit that a web site knows which sites it links to but not the sites linking to it.

This is actually an artifact of modeling OWL as a specialization of RDFS. Even though a resource is not attached to an ontology, an instance of one of the OWL metaclasses is. A resource can be an instance of *Individual* in one ontology, *OWLClass* in another and *Property* in a third. In OWL DL, these three metaclasses are pairwise disjoint. OWL metaclass is not an essential property of a resource, but depends on the ontology referring to it.

So taking advantage of the fact that in OWL Full, *OWLClass* and *Property* are subclasses of *Individual*, we can introduce an abstract superclass *Universe* and a meta-association *UniverseForOntology* with *Ontology* which is navigable in both directions. This structure functions like *Package* in UML.

8.4 Profiles and Mappings

8.4.1 The Need for Translation

The various metamodels in the ODM are all treated equally, in that they all have free-standing metamodels. It is not necessary to know about any of the others to understand any one.

However, in an ontology development project it might be necessary to use several of the metamodels, and to represent a given fragment of the ontology in more than one. For example, consider a large e-commerce exchange project. The developers might choose to represent the ontology specifying the shared world governing the exchange in OWL. But the exchange might have evolved from a single large company's electronic procurement system (as was the case for example with the General Electric Global Exchange Service [9]). The original procurement system might have been designed using UML, so that it would be a significant saving in development cost to be able to translate the UML specification to OWL as a base for development of the ontology.

Once the exchange is operating, it will have possibly thousands of members, each of which will have its own information system performing a variety of tasks in addition to interoperating through the exchange. These systems are all autonomous, and the exchange has no interest in how they generate and interpret the messages they use to interoperate so long as they commit to the ontology. Let us assume that the various members have systems with data models in UML or dialects of the ER model.

A given member will need to subscribe to at least a fragment of the ontology and make sure its internal data model conforms to the fragment. It would therefore be an advantage to be able to translate a fragment of the ontology to UML or ER to facilitate the member making any changes to its internal operations necessary for it to commit to the ontology.

The ODM therefore needs to provide facilities for translating data model instances from one of the metamodels to another. There are two ways to do this: UML profiles and mappings.

8.4.2 UML Profiles

UML has a facility called *profile* which does not translate from UML to another metamodel, but allows at least some of the features of the target metamodel to be represented as specializations, called *stereotypes*, of UML constructs. We can think of a profile as a sort of view. The main use of profiles is to allow a MOF metamodel of a system other than UML to make use of UML visualization conventions, and of the software used to visualize UML models.

OWL is similar to UML in that both are based largely on the mathematical theory of sets and relations, so that the metaclass *OWLClass* and its subclasses *OWLRestriction* etc. as shown in the OWL metamodel of Fig. 8.3 are semantically similar to the metaclass *Class* in the UML metamodel of Fig. 8.1. The profile mechanism allows the OWL metamodel class-like constructs to be treated as specializations of *Class*. Further, the metaclasses *OWLObjectProperty* and *OWLDatatypeProperty* of Fig. 8.3 are semantically similar respectively to the metaclasses *Association* and *Property* of Fig. 8.1.

For example, suppose we have an OWL model of a fragment of an airline ontology, including the classes *Flight* and *City*. *Flight* and *City* are the domains respectively of the datatype properties *flightID* and *cityName*, both of which are of type xsd:string, and *Flight* is the domain of a datatype property *departs*, of type xsd:time. There are two object properties *from* and *to*, both with domain *Flight* and range *City*. We can use the UML profile for OWL to visualize our fragment using UML conventions, as shown in Fig. 8.9. The stereotypes are represented as the OWL metaclass names enclosed in <<...>>.

Fig. 8.9. UML profile of OWL ontology

However, the UML profile mechanism applies only to UML model elements which are represented as instances of the MOF model element *class* (called metaclasses). If we see Fig. 8.1 as a MOF model of UML, the metaclasses are *Class, Property, Association, Classifier* and *Type*. Only these UML model elements can be profiled. The model elements *ownedAttribute* and *generalization* are modeled as instances of the MOF Class *Association*, hence are meta-associations, hence cannot be stereotyped.

OWL and UML are semantically similar, so there are not too many constructs that cannot be adequately profiled. But Topic Maps are quite different. In particular, the metaclass *Topic* of Fig. 8.5 has some instances which are interpreted as sets, others which are interpreted as members of sets, and still others which are neither, depending on whether or not they participate in the associations of Figs. 8.6 and 8.7. Only those instances of *Topic* which are linked to instances of *AssociationRole* of *type* a *Topic* with *name* "tmcore:type", "tmcore:subtype" or "tmcore:supertype" have the semantics of UML Class. Therefore, in the ODM UML profile of Topic Maps, the stereotype <<*Topic*>> of *Class* can be used to model only a subset of instances of *Topic*.

More radically, the metaclass *Association* in Topic Maps has as instances atomic objects. Relationships among topics are modeled not by instances of *Association* alone, but by complexes of instances of *Association* and instances of *AssociationRole*. So it does not make sense to model *Association* in the UML profile for Topic Maps by stereotyping the UML construct *Association*. Rather, every instance of the Topic Map construct *Association* is linked to an instance of *Topic* which is its *type*. So the ODM UML profile of Topic Maps includes a stereotype <<*Association*>> of *Class* which models instances of *Topic* which are types of instances of *Association* in Topic Maps.

Instances of *AssociationRole* are similarly instance-level constructs, linking an instance of *Topic* with an instance of *Association*. But every instance of *AssociationRole* is linked to an instance of *Topic* which is its *type*. So the ODM UML profile of Topic Maps includes a stereotype <<*AssociationRole*>> of the UML construct *Association*, which models instances of *Topic* which are types of instances of *AssociationRole*.

In this way a model instance of Topic Map can be represented more or less adequately by a population of the UML profile for Topic Maps, but the structure of the profiled model is quite different from that of the Topic Map original. In particular, if a Topic Map model instance is created to represent something like a book index, where the topics do not have a type/instance structure, a UML profile may not be a suitable representation.

Besides UML visualization tools like Rational Rose [10], other tools producing XML serializations or Java APIs support profiles, so can be made use of.

8.4.3 Mappings

Working with multiple metamodels will often require a model element by model element translation of model instances from one metamodel to another. We have seen that UML profiling is not exactly a mapping, although one could map aspects of, say, an OWL model to a UML profile for OWL.

Mappings are of much broader interest in the OMG than just the ODM, so much so that there is a parallel RFP in the OMG called QVT (Query/View/Transform) which promises to provide a standardized MOF-based platform for mapping instances of MOF metamodels from one metamodel to another [6]. The mappings in the ODM will be specified in QVT.

The ODM RFP calls for normative mappings (if a mapping is normative, then any implementation to be compliant must follow these mappings). However, in developing the mappings for the various ODM languages, our team concluded that the mappings we specify cannot in practice be normative.

For example, there are two different ways to map N-ary associations from UML to OWL, depending on whether we take OWL Full or OWL DL as target. OWL has a mandatory universal superclass (owl:Thing) which can map to a universal superclass in UML, but this is contrary to normal practice in UML modeling. A particular project might analyze the uses of universal properties in the OWL source model and choose to declare a number of more general but not universal superclasses in the UML target.

In the W3C Semantic Web Best Practices working report on Topic Map mappings [14], the point is made several times that there are different ways to map particular structures, and that each way has its advantages and disadvantages. In any particular project, design decisions will be taken in favor of advantages and against disadvantages so different projects will map in different ways.

There are several kinds of problems. One we can call *structure confla-tion*, where two constructs in one system map to a single construct in the other. In this case, a general-purpose mapping does not round trip. UML binary associations and class-valued attributes map to OWL properties, for example. In topic maps, three different kinds of identifier map to one kind in OWL.

But there is nothing to stop a particular project from specifying naming conventions so there is a record in the target of what construct the source was, and from maintaining that convention in subsequent development.

A second kind of problem we will call *structure loss*. Here a complex construct is mapped to a collection of simpler constructs. There is insuffi-cient information in the target metamodel for a general mapping to map collections of simple constructs to complex constructs in the source meta-model. Examples here are UML *N*-ary associations and association classes, which get mapped to a class and a collection of properties in OWL DL. In Topic Maps, the *Association* construct is typed itself and has *N* typed roles. The association maps to a class and the typed roles to proper-ties. It is in general impossible to reliably map the reverse.

But again, there is nothing to stop a particular project from using nam-ing conventions or annotations to retain a memory of the structure, and maintaining those conventions in subsequent development so as to be able to reverse-map.

Alternatively, a Topic Map project could decide to limit itself to binary associations, making possible mapping associations directly to properties in that particular case.

The third kind of problem we will call *trapdoor mappings*, where a kind of construct in the source is mapped to a very specific arrangement of a general structure in the target. The analogy is with cryptography, where the encryption function takes any plaintext into an encrypted text, but al-most no encrypted texts map back to plaintexts.

In Topic Maps, this occurs with the mapping of scope and variant names to specific properties in OWL identified with Topic Map URIs. OWL properties map to Topic Map associations with specific roles named with OWL URIs. Unless the source for a reverse mapping happened to maintain these conventions, it would be impossible to reverse in a sensible way.

A fourth kind of problem stems from what we will call *feature lack*, that is the target metamodel lacks a feature present in the source. In this case there is no apparent general way to map the feature from the source. But in a particular project the feature may for example be used in a particular way leading to a mapping to target features particularized by naming conventions. OWL restriction classes relative to UML or Topic Map (TM) are of this kind.

The fifth kind of problem is what we will call *incompatible structural principles*. The different metamodels are organized very differently. UML is organized around classes, with instances as subordinate objects. OWL has both classes and individuals typed only by a universal superclass. In TM, a Topic instance can be either typed or not. But a particular project might use a particular discipline in its use of these structures leading to mappings not otherwise feasible.

In practice, the mappings provided in the ODM can be useful, though. First, they show feasibility of one set of design choices for the mappings, providing a baseline from which a particular project can vary. Second, they bring clearly to the fore the detailed relationships among the metamodels. These relationships can help those who understand one of the target languages to come to an understanding of the others. UML, RDFS/OWL and TM are quite different from each other, while CL has far greater functionality than any of the others.

So although normative mappings are not feasible, we argue that the mappings presented have strong informative value.

The mapping strategy in the ODM is illustrated in Fig. 8.10. Note that there will be mappings from each metamodel to and from OWL Full, except for CL for which there is only a mapping from OWL Full.

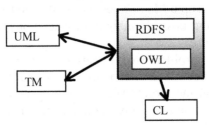

Fig. 8.10. Mapping relationships in the ODM

8.4.4 Mapping CL

CL is much more expressive than the other metamodels. It is therefore much more difficult to map a model instance from CL into one of the other metamodels. The ODM intends CL to be used to implement predicates which cannot be expressed in the other less expressive metamodels. It is intended that a predicate be specified in a primary metamodel, in particular OWL, and implemented in CL.

One way to do this is for the relevant elements of the model instance expressed in the primary metamodel to be mapped into CL. So only a uni-directional mapping from OWL to CL will be included. It is possible to specify a subclass of *property* in OWL which is a predicate (a functional property whose range is the enumerated set {true, false}, for example). Instances of *predicate* can be implemented in CL.

When an instance of *predicate* is encountered by an OWL reasoner, the reasoner could execute the associated OWL to CL mapping, then call a CL engine to evaluate the predicate. This would be a fairly straightforward way to extend the functionality of OWL using the ODM.

8.4.5 Interaction of Profiles and Mappings

Profiles and mappings are related. Consider these cases:

- We use a MOF tool to develop an OWL ontology, which is then serialized using the XML markup XMI defined for the MOF. In this case we use the ODM OWL MOF model alone, and do not need mapping or profile.
- We have a native UML model which we want to serialize as OWL XMI (using OWL-derived markups). In this case we use both the MOF UML and MOF OWL metamodels, together with the UML -> OWL mapping, but no profile.
- We have an OWL-profiled UML model to be serialized as OWL XMI. Here we use the ODM OWL MOF model and the UML2 MOF model with the UML2 -> OWL mapping and information from the ODM OWL profile for UML.

These three are all useful and plausible scenarios. The third would be a more complete OWL model using UML notation than the second, while the first does not care about UML at all.

Further, if profiles are being used the modeler might want to use UML notation to create and visualize an ontology (say in OWL). This implies that two MOF models are required, one for UML and the other for OWL. The mapping UML -> OWL is required, because without application of a mapping the final result would be UML XMI rather than OWL XMI.

8.5 Extendibility

There is an enormous variety of kinds of application for ontologies. An analysis was made in an early phase of the ODM project, which has been published in detail elsewhere [5]. They can be used at design time only or at both design and run-time. They can be schemas only or involve both schemas and instances. Their structure can be imposed from outside their domain or can emerge from the activities of interoperating parties. And so on.

Many of these kinds of application have special requirements which are common to many application instances but which are not at all universal. The ODM project has limited its efforts to the most general structural issues.

However, in practice one can envisage particular extensions to the general structures which support significant numbers of application instances, which would be published by third parties outside the OMG ODM process but which would be consistent with the ODM, in much the same way as the *Dublin Core* metadata standard is published as an RDFS namespace.

MOF models have a structural unit called a package which is used to divide them into modules so that one model can import packages from others, then perhaps specialize them. Figure 8.1 is an example of this, showing a fragment of a package from the UML2.0 Infrastructure which is imported into the MOF2.0 metamodel and then specialized. So anyone wishing to develop specific facilities for specific applications can publish them as packages which reuse model elements from the ODM, but provide additional elements.

We will illustrate this facility with three examples, all of which use model elements from OWL packages so are seen as extending OWL. The examples are respectively of metaclass taxonomies, semantic domain instance models, and *n*-ary associations.

8.5.1 Metaclass Taxonomy

The first example, shown in Fig. 8.11, that of a *metaclass taxonomy*, extends OWLClass with the distinction between countable and bulk classes as advocated by Guarino and Welty [3]. A *countable* class has an extent consisting of identifiable individuals while a *bulk* class is a sort of amorphous mass like length measured in meters or value measured in euros. In a model instance, classes would be instances of one of the specialized subclasses rather than of the more general *OWLClass*.

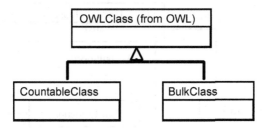

Fig. 8.11. Countable/bulk package extending OWL

This same approach can be used with other taxonomies of metaclasses, for example the taxonomy of endurants and perdurants proposed in the DOLCE system [2].

It is possible to develop these packages as extensions to one of the metamodels, in this case OWL, then use the ODM mapping facilities to migrate it to any of the other metamodels. Note that all of the metamodels supported by the ODM permit multiple inheritance, so that several such extensions can be used simultaneously.

8.5.2 Semantic Domain Models

A feature of OWL is that properties are by default defined globally, with range and domain both *Thing*. This makes it possible to represent mereological relationships as instances of property. Instances of meta-classes can be modeled using semantic domain models, a facility of MOF 2.0. For example, Fig. 8.12 defines a version of *isPartOf* which is transitive, every part belongs to at least one whole (and by transitivity to all the wholes up the chain), and a part cannot exist without its corresponding whole. This kind of part-of relation could be suitable for modeling say the Olympic family. An athlete is part of an event (if a competitor), an event is part of a sporting program, a sporting program is part of the Olympics of a given Olympiad, and anyone who competes in any event in any program in any Olympics is a part of the Olympic family. But an Olympics cannot exist without at least one program, a program must have at least one event, and an event at least one competitor.

There are a large number of varieties of mereotopological relationships [15]. They could be catalogued and published as a package, perhaps with specialized software.

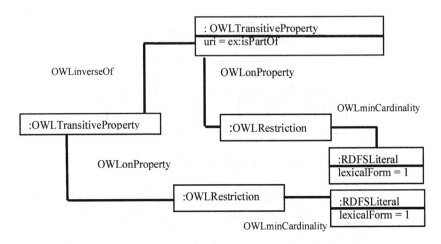

Fig. 8.12. Semantic domain model for kind of isPartOf property

8.5.3 *n*-ary associations

A key aspect of the OntoClean methodology [4] is the concept of a metaproperty. For example, a property has the metaproperty *essential* with respect to a class if being an instance of that class determines the value of the property. Besides *essential*, the metaproperties include *rigid*, *identity* and *unity*. A property with respect to a class can *necessarily*, *necessarily not* or *not necessarily* have a given metaproperty. A natural way to model metaproperties is as quaternary associations.

Most of the metamodels in the ODM permit *n*-ary associations, except RDFS/OWL. But an *n*-ary association can be represented as a class with *n* binary properties. To be consistent with the previous examples, a possible package to model metaproperties in Fig. 8.13 extends the OWL meta-model. Note that the metaproperty is modeled as a subclass of OWLClass. This can facilitate mapping from OWL to an *n*-ary association or equivalent in another metamodel. Note also the enumerations, which are instances of the MOF element *type*.

8.6 Discussion

In this chapter we have argued for a MOF-based metamodel for ontology developments, but that not one but several different systems needed to be included: RDFS/OWL, Topic Maps, Common Logic, as well as UML.

These metamodels are tied together with UML profiles and metamodel-to-metamodel mappings. Finally, the package structure of the MOF makes it simple for third parties to publish extensions to the ODM for specialized purposes.

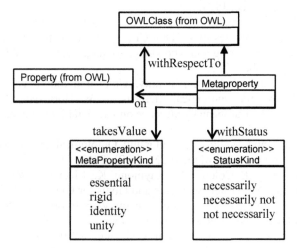

Fig. 8.13. Metaproperty package for OWL

Lessons learned from the exercise include:
- Representation of multiple models in the same metalanguage makes detailed comparisons easier.
- The different systems modeled are not formally equivalent. In fact, in some cases they are quite incompatible, making normative mappings not practical.
- UML profiles can be used to give a more or less adequate representation of the other systems, so can leverage the UML toolset for the other languages.

8.7 Acknowledgments

The work reported in this chapter has been funded in part by the Co-operative Centre for Enterprise Distributed Systems Technology (DSTC) through the Australian Federal Government's CRC Programme (Department of Education, Science and Training), and funded in part through the United States Government Defense Advanced Research Program Office's DAML program.

References

1. Berners-Lee, T., and Fischetti, M., Weaving the Web: the original design and ultimate destiny of the World Wide Web by its inventor, San Francisco: HarperSanFrancisco, 1999.
2. Gangemi, A., Guarino, N., Masolo, C., Oltramari, A., and Schneider, L., Sweetening Ontologies with DOLCE, 13th International Conference on Knowledge Engineering and Knowledge Management (EKAW02), Sigüenza, Spain, 1–4 October 2002.
3. Guarino, N., and Welty, C., Identity, Unity and Individuality: Towards a Formal Toolkit for Ontological Analysis, in: W. Horn (ed.) Proceedings of ECAI-2000: The European Conference on Artificial Intelligence, Amsterdam: IOS Press 2000.
4. Guarino, N., and Welty, C., Evaluating Ontological Decisions with Onto-Clean, Communications of the ACM, 45(2) (2002) 61–65.
5. Hart, L., Emery, P, Colomb, R., Raymond, K., Chang, D., Ye, Y., Kendall, E., and Dutra, M., Usage Scenarios and Goals for Ontology Definition Meta-model, Fifth International Conference on Web Information Systems Engineering (WISE2004), Berlin: Springer, 2004.
6. MOF Query/Views/Transformations OMG ad/2002-04-10, omg.org
7. Ontology Definition MetaModel Preliminary Revised Submission to OMG RFP ad/2003-03-40, http://codip.grci.com/odm/draft/
8. OWL Web Ontology Language Semantics and Abstract Syntax. W3C Recommendation 10 February 2004, Peter F. Patel-Schneider, Patrick Hayes, Ian Horrocks (eds.) Latest version is available at http://www.w3.org/TR/owl-semantics/
9. Paul, J., Withanachchi, S., Mockler, R., Gartenfeld, M., Bistline, W., and Dologite, D., Enabling B2B Marketplaces: the case of GE Global Exchange Services, in Annals of cases on information technology, Hershey, PA: Idea Group, 2003.
10. Rational Rose, http://www-306.ibm.com/software/info/developer/rsduc/index.jsp
11. RDF Semantics. Patrick Hayes (ed.), W3C Recommendation, 10 February 2004. Latest version available at http://www.w3.org/TR/rdf-mt/
12. [TMDM] ISO/IEC FCD 13250-2: Topic Maps – Data Model, 2005-12-16. Latest version is available at http://www.isotopicmaps.org/sam/sam-model/
13. UML 2.0 OCL Final Adopted Specification, ptc/03-10-14, omg.org
14. W3C A survey of RDF/Topic Maps Interoperability Proposals W3C Working Draft 29 March, 2005. Latest version is available at http://www.w3.org/TR/2005/WD-rdftm-survey-20050329

15. Winston, W., Chaffin, R., and Herrmann, D., A taxonomy of part-whole relations, Cognitive Science, 11 (1987) 417–444.

9. Ontologies, Meta-models, and the Model-Driven Paradigm

Uwe Aßmann and Steffen Zschaler

Technische Universität Dresden, Institut für Software- und Multimedi-atechnik, Lehrstuhl für Softwaretechnologie, 01062 Dresden
uwe.assmann@tu-dresden.de, steffen.zschaler@tu-dresden.de

Gerd Wagner

Brandenburgisch-Technische Universität Cottbus, Institute of Informatics, Lehrstuhl Internet-Technologie, Postfach 101344, 03013 Cottbus
g.wagner@tu-cottbus.de

> In memory of Emma Larsdotter-Nilsson who, while working on a thesis in bio-logical modelling [26], died unexpectedly in October 2005

9.1 Introduction

Refinement-based software development centres around the production of several models, going from abstract to concrete (Fig. 9.1), cumulating in the implementation as the most refined model [45]. Step by step, con-structs in abstract models are *refined* to more concrete model elements. Roughly speaking, development can be divided into two phases. The *analysis phase* constructs a requirement specification describing all fea-tures the user would like to have, building on a domain model, a business model, and a context model. Later on, the *design phase* produces an archi-tectural design specification and a detailed design specification. In a last phase, the *implementation phase*, the design specifications are filled out to an implementation of the software system.

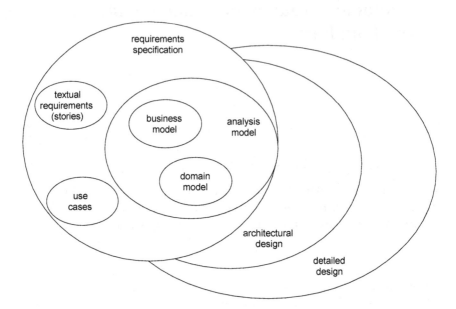

Fig. 9.1. Models in a typical object-oriented software development process

Model-driven engineering (MDE) is a variant of this refinement-based software development in which models are no longer loosely coupled, but connected in a systematic way [9, 10]. On the one hand, MDE improves on the software refinement method of the 1970s in the sense that more concrete phases are distinguished. On the other hand, every phase derives a more concrete model not only by manual refinement, but also by semi-automatic or automatic transformation. To this end, models must be connected; that is, model elements must be traceable from a more abstract model to a more concrete model and vice versa. This is achieved through meta-modelling: *meta-models* define sets of valid models, facilitating their transformation, serialization, and exchange.

In recent years, model-driven engineering has been popularized by a specific incarnation, *model-driven architecture (MDA)*. In this process, one specific type of model information, the *platform information*, plays an important role. In MDA, models differ in how much platform information they contain (Fig. 9.2). For instance, one platform can be the programming language of the system, another can be the employed libraries or frameworks, a third can be the binary component model. The designer begins with a high-level model that abstracts from all kinds of platform issues, and iteratively transforms the model to more concrete models, introducing more and more platform-specific information. Hence, all information that relates to programming language, frameworks, or component model are added to the platform-independent model by platform-specific extensions.

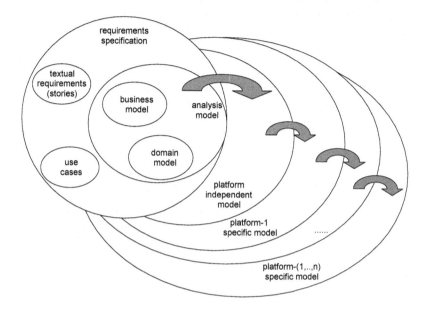

Fig. 9.2. Models in model-driven architecture (MDA)

Essentially, in MDA three types of viewpoints on models are distinguished [30]. The computationally independent (CI) viewpoint sees the system from the customer's point of view, and manifests it in a computation-independent model (CIM). This model is a typical analysis model, since it is expressed in terms of the problem domain:

> *The computation-independent viewpoint focuses on the environment of the system, and the requirements for the system; the details of the structure and processing of the system are hidden or as yet undetermined.* [30]

The CIM contains a *domain model*, describing the concepts of a domain and their interrelations, a *business model*, describing a company's rules of business, and, finally, the requirements. The platform-independent (PI) viewpoint sees the system from the designer's point of view, abstracts from all platforms a system may run on, and results in a *platform-independent model (PIM)*. Roughly speaking, a PIM contains an architectural model, adorned with sufficient detail of platform-generic implementation issues. Finally, the platform-specific viewpoint adds platform-specific extensions and results in a *platform-specific model (PSM)*. Either this model can be executed directly, or it is used to generate code.

To arrive at a PSM, the PIM must be extended with platform-specific information, for which it is merged with several platform-specific extensions (Fig. 9.3).

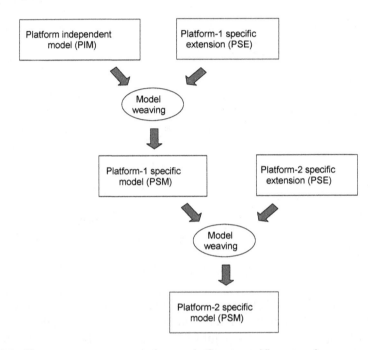

Fig. 9.3. The MDA pattern: weaving a platform-specific extension as an aspect into a PIM as a base

Because the platform-specific extension (PSE) can be regarded as an aspect that cross-cuts the platform-independent information [24], one can speak of *model weaving*. This *MDA pattern*, weaving PSMs from PIMs and PSE, can be repeated over several levels. Often, different kinds of platforms are involved and one would like to vary the system over all combinations of these platform instantiations; for example, by having a system with C# and Java, both on the web and GUI-client platforms. The idea of multi-level MDA is to repeat the model weaving process over several levels (Fig. 9.3), so that on every level, a PSM is reinterpreted as a new PIM for the next platform.

A heretical spectator could remark that MDA (and hence MDE) is not a new technology, but just refinement-based software development. However, since MDA discerns platform-specific information as the main criterion for refinement, the entire process is much more structured than the "free-style" refinement of the 1970s. Also, in MDA, all models are graph-based, while standard refinement worked mainly for syntax trees.

Recently, the Semantic Web has popularized another notion of model: *ontologies*. Ontologies are *formal explicit specifications of a shared conceptualization* [18]. They describe the concepts of a domain, similar to the domain model of a CIM. While they are currently used mainly in the Semantic Web, they could be useful also in general software development [1, 8]. But then, the question arises how ontologies should be integrated into MDE, and more specifically, into the process architecture of MDA. And this is what the rest of the chapter is about. In Sect. 9.2, ontologies are compared to general models, resulting in the insight that ontologies describe reality while models specify artifacts. Section 9.3 investigates these relationships in more detail and explains how the specification relationship instance-of can be used to build up a stack of models, the so-called IRDS meta-pyramid. Section 9.4 extends the meta-pyramid with ontologies, distinguishing a descriptive dimension. A comparison to related work concludes the chapter.

9.2 Models and Ontologies

In this section, we discuss the fundamental terms 'model' and 'ontology' and investigate their primary commonalities and differences. We begin by looking at definitions of 'model' and 'ontology', go on to discuss a fundamental property of models—namely, whether they are descriptive or prescriptive—and finish by showing how this distinction can be applied to distinguish between ontologies and other software models.

9.2.1 What's in a Model?

Models are representations, descriptions, and specifications of things. Pidd defines:

> *A model is a representation of reality intended for some definite purpose.* [34]

Hence, models represent reality (in the following denoted by the is-represented-by relation).

Models have a *causal connection* to the modelled part of reality: they must form *true* or *faithful* representations so that queries of the model give reliable statements about reality, or manipulations of the model result in reliable adaptations of reality. Pidd characterizes this as follows:

> *A model is an external and explicit representation of a part of reality as seen by the people who wish to use that model to understand, change, manage, and control that part of reality.* [34]

Secondly, while models represent reality faithfully, they may *abstract* from irrelevant details. For instance, while models are finite descriptions, they may well describe an infinite language—that is, an infinite set of things or systems. Usually, then, abstractions are involved—for example, about the number of elements in the language.

A model can represent many different kinds of realities, e.g. domains, languages, or, in particular, systems. Hence, we can distinguish *domain models* from *system models*, models that describe or control a set of systems:

> *A model of a system is a description or specification of that system and its environment for some certain purpose.* [31]

where the environment of a system is described by a domain model.

Models can describe structure or behaviour. In the former case, models describe the concepts of a reality and their interrelation, the *static semantics* of a domain, its *context-free* or *context-sensitive structure*. Well-formedness rules (*integrity constraints*) describe valid configurations of reality.

Example 1. UML class diagrams are frequently used together with an *Object Constraint Language* [31]. The OCL integrity constraints describe valid configurations and interrelationships of classes and objects in a UML class model.

Secondly, while a structural model contains abstractions and their interrelationships, a behavioural model also specifies their behaviour, their *dynamic semantics*. In this case, a model may state assertions on the behaviour of things in a domain or of some systems. Models can express such assertions either in a conceptual or in a transitional way. In the former case, dynamic features of a system are expressed as concepts and their interrelationships are explained by constraints. In the latter case, dynamic features and their relationships are expressed in terms of transitions on state spaces [23] or as modifications of a denotational semantics [42].

Sometimes, such transitions or modifications can in turn be expressed in logic. However, as the following example shows, this need not be appropriate. If the state space of the dynamic semantics is continuous, the semantics is better expressed by numerical means—for example, through differential equations.

Example 2. Modelica is a multi-domain modelling language for simulation, visualization, and controlling technical systems. Hence, it is a prescriptive modelling language for the dynamic semantics of technical systems [13].

9.2.2 What's in an Ontology?

Recently, the Semantic Web has popularized another notion of model— *ontologies*. One of the most-cited definitions is:

> Ontologies are *"formal explicit specifications of a shared conceptualization"*. [18]

Since concepts are abstractions and play an important role in models, an ontology is certainly a special kind of model. But what is the exact difference? To answer this question, we have to introduce some other qualities of models.

Following the above definition, an ontology is a model shared by a group of people in a certain domain. This includes ontologies that have been *standardized* by international organizations (such as the Dublin Core ontology [27]), ontologies that are shared by large user groups (such as the gene ontology [3]), and ontologies that are shared between companies and their customers (such as the wine ontology [28]). In general, models need not be shared. For instance, the design model of a product, if it is shared only between the few developers of a small company, should not be regarded as an ontology, but rather as a plain artifact model. Of course, *sharedness* is a relative notion: it is often a matter of taste to consider a user group of a model large enough so that the model can be called an ontology of the user group.

An important property of ontologies is the so-called *open-world assumption* [20]. It states, intuitively, that anything not explicitly expressed by an ontology is unknown. Hence, ontologies use a form of partial description or under-specification as an important means of abstraction. In contrast, most system models underlie the assumption that what has not been specified is either implicitly disallowed or implicitly allowed (*closed-world assumption*), to restrict arbitrary extensions of the system, which could introduce inconsistencies.

It is important to distinguish whether models describe or control reality. If they describe, they monitor reality and form *true*, or *faithful*, abstractions. If they control, they prescribe reality; that is, they specify well-formedness conditions what reality should be like, once it has been constructed. It can also be said that such models are templates or schemas of reality. Hence, a most fundamental feature of a model is that it can be *descriptive* or *prescriptive* [38]. In the former case, the model describes reality, but reality is not constructed from it. In the latter case, the model prescribes the structure or behaviour of reality and reality is constructed according to the model; that is, the model is a *specification* of reality. Favre [11] observes that in a descriptive model truth lies in reality, whereas in a prescriptive model, truth lies in the model itself. Descriptive models are, of course, used in analysis and re-engineering, specifications in design and forward engineering. Since most specifications model systems, a prescriptive system model is also called a *system specification*.

Models are abstractions from reality for some purpose [34]. Ontologies are special models. Most of the models used in software development and design are of a prescriptive nature in that they form the templates from which the system is later implemented. In contrast, because of their open-world assumption, ontologies should be regarded as descriptive models. This is so, because the open-world assumption does not allow for a complete and final description: Anything that has not been said explicitly is unknown. Two very different systems may satisfy an ontology, if they differ in areas not explicitly mentioned in the ontology.

On the other hand, we concede that ontologies can also be—and often are—used in a prescriptive manner. We argue, however, that then they should better not be called ontologies, but specification models. When a model is used as a prescription for systems, it should confine their legal structure, for which the closed-world assumption is required. At least, at a certain point in development, the world must be closed; that is, the additional assumption has to be introduced that everything that has not yet been specified or cannot be derived is wrong. Such a *world closure* is not only hard to comprehend because it changes the semantics of the underlying logic, but may also require the insertion of additional facts in the database or a change in the logic reasoner.

Taking this discussion into account, we define the following:

> An ontology is a *shared, descriptive, structural model, representing reality by a set of concepts, their interrelations, and constraints under the open-world assumption.*

> A specification model is a *prescriptive model, representing a set of artifacts by a set of concepts, their interrelations, and constraints under the closed-world assumption.*

These definitions deserve some elucidating remarks. When comparing hallmark papers, such as [18] and [38], specification models and ontologies look very similar. Both provide vocabulary for a language and define validity rules for the elements of the language. Both specification models and ontologies use integrity constraints to limit the valid instances of the domain.[32]

However, there are also differences. Ontologies are *shared* knowledge; that is, they must be standardized in a certain group of people. Ontologies are not specification models, but descriptive models in Seidewitz's sense. Ontologies do not describe systems, only domains. Hence, in a software engineering process, they should play the role of an analysis model, not of a design or implementation model. With this view we contradict Devedzic, "Generally, an ontology is a meta-model describing how to build models" [8], and Gruber, because he maintains that ontologies are specifications [18]. However, this conceptual distinction creates a natural place for ontologies in model-driven engineering, as will be seen in Sect. 9.4.

To summarize, we will assume the following: Specification models focus on the *specification, control,* and *generation* of *systems,* ontologies on *description* and *conceptualization (structural modelling)* of *things.* Both kinds of models have in common the qualities of *abstraction* and *causal connection.* So, under these circumstances, how can ontologies and specification models cohabit in model-driven engineering?

9.3 Similarity Relations and Meta-modelling

The previous arguments make it possible to distinguish two basic notions of the is-represented-by relation between a model and the corresponding part of reality (Fig. 9.4). In a descriptive model—for example, an ontology—the model describes the world; that is, the world's objects are in relation is-described-by with concepts of the descriptive model. In a specification model, the system's objects are created from the model; that is, an object is an instance-of a model element. Both relationships are representation relations: one is descriptive, the other is prescriptive. Their generalization is-represented-by is a similarity relation, in which a causal connec-

---

[32] Both are structural models in the sense that while they can contain concepts that model behaviour, they usually do not model dynamic semantics.

tion—delivering true and faithful statements—is defined between the represented things and the representing model. Beyond that, more similarity relations can be defined; for example, two things may share features (often expressed as is-a, i.e., structural or behavioural inheritance), or they may be included in a hierarchy of sets (set inclusion, subset-of). In Fig. 9.4, is-a is defined as a sub-relationship of subset-of, because inheritance usually has a set-based semantics; namely, that all objects in a subclass are also members of the superclass. Additionally, is-a is a sub-relationship of is-described-by, because a superclass also describes all objects in a subclass. In contrast, is-a cannot be a sub-relationship of instance-of, because a superclass cannot necessarily be regarded as a template, schema, or specification for a subclass.

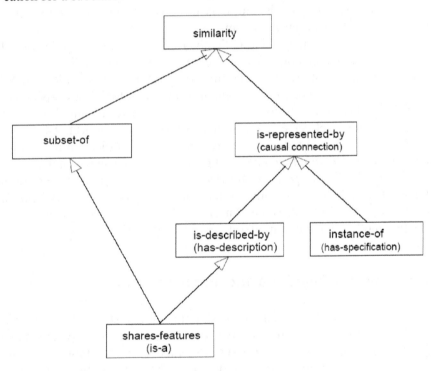

Fig. 9.4. A classification of similarity relations

9.3.1 Meta-models

In MDE, the specification relationship instance-of plays a special role. When the specification principle is applied repeatedly, models are regarded as the reality or system under study, so that models specifying models can be defined: namely, meta-models. Meta-models represent and specify models; that is, they describe about what are the valid ingredients of a model. More precisely:

A meta-model makes statements about what can be expressed in the valid models of a certain modelling language. [38]

Hence, a meta-model is a prescriptive model of a modelling language [38]. In general, meta-models are language specifications, not only of modelling, but also of arbitrary languages. In the current stage of MDE, they are mainly concerned with the static semantics—that is, with context-sensitive syntax of models, integrity, and well-formedness constraints. However, modelling languages for dynamic semantics could also be applied to construct meta-models [42].

A language concept or construct in a meta-model is captured by a *meta-class*. While its structure and embedding describe the static semantics of the language constructs, its methods describe the dynamic behaviour of the language construct. Usually, meta-classes are assembled in a behavioural meta-model, the *meta-object protocol (MOP)* [25], a reflective meta-model that describes an interpreter for the language.

A big incentive for meta-modelling has been the need of CASE (Computer-Aided Software Engineering) tool vendors to exchange models [32]. Since a meta-model describes, rather specifies, valid instances of a modelling language—models—it enables control over the structure and validity of models. If two CASE tools agree on the same meta-model, they impose the same structure on their models, so that they can easily exchange them.

A language, described by a meta-model, can have a specific purpose or domain in which it is applied. Such purposes or modelling domains are called the *subject areas* of meta-models [12].

Example 3. For instance, the common warehouse meta-model (CWM) [29] defines a data specification language, a meta-model for data and information system applications. Work-flow systems are another special subject area whose data, functions, and tasks can also be described with meta-models [36]. Software processes, being specific work flows, can be meta-modelled [14] and used to construct software environments [5].

Subject areas can be organized in hierarchies or partial orders. Then, meta-models in a certain subject area can build on others from lower-level subject areas, so that complex languages can reuse simpler languages [12].

Example 4. The CASE Data Interchange Format (CDIF) has structured its meta-model into several subject areas (Fig. 9.5). The Foundation module contains information about names and relations; the Common module defines name aliasing for objects; and the Data module describes access paths to data and roles of objects. Based on these, data flow can be defined (Data Flow module). Another module specifies facilities for the presentation of objects. Finally, the full integrated meta-model uses all other modules and provides their concepts in an integrated way to the users.

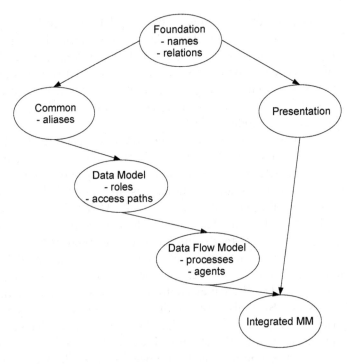

Fig. 9.5. The subject areas of CDIF and their meta-models in a use relationship

9.3.2 Metameta-models

The specification principle can be applied repeatedly. Metameta-models *represent* and *specify* meta-models; that is, they describe what are the valid ingredients of a meta-model. They specify languages, and are thus a form of *language specification languages (meta-languages)*.

In order to model anything useful, such a minimal meta-language should contain the following concepts [12]:

- classes (concepts);
- attributes (or properties) of classes, contained in the classes;
- binary relations between classes.

Thus, the Entity–Relationship Diagram (ERD) language [6] can be used as a very simple meta-language. It defines modelling concepts, their attributes, and their relationships. Other meta-languages exist that describe other forms of languages, or describe specific aspects:

1. Grammar specification languages—for example, EBNF—specify the concrete or abstract syntax of a text-based language [17].
2. Attribute grammars describe context-sensitive syntax in the form of attribution rules of syntax trees [7].
3. Natural semantics can be employed for type systems, but are also able to specify dynamic semantics of systems [23].
4. In SGML [16], mark up languages can be defined. XML [44] is a variant of SGML, allowing for defining context-free mark up languages.
5. EXPRESS [37], a modelling language in the spirit of UML, is frequently used in mechanical engineering.

9.3.3 The Meta-pyramid, the Modelling Architecture of MDE

Based on the meta-principle, a so-called meta-pyramid can be defined, which displays systematically the mentioned stack of models and meta-models [22]. In essence, a meta-pyramid is a specification hierarchy linked by the instance-of relation, in which upper-level meta-models in some way specify other sets of lower-level models. Since sets of models can be regarded as languages, the meta-pyramid is a hierarchy of language specifications.

In this chapter, we focus on the standard meta-pyramid of OMG, originally presented in the ISO Information Resource Dictionary System (IRDS) standard [22] (Fig. 9.6), which contains four levels: M0 level (objects), M1 level (models), M2 level (meta-model or language level), M3 level (metameta-model or language description level). There are alternatives and a debate is going on whether the IRDS meta-pyramid is precise enough, because it is one-dimensional, while multi-dimensional model pyramids exist [2]. However, at the moment, this is the mainstream meta-pyramid of MDE.

On level M3, the IRDS/OMG meta-pyramid employs the *meta-object facility (MOF)* as metameta-model. Essentially, its concepts are similar to those of the ERD. The stereotypical models of MDA, CIM, PIM, and PSM live on level M1. All of them are specified on level M2 by meta-models (CIM-MM, PIM-MM, PSM-MM), dialects of UML, enriching the UML core by *profiles* containing markup for model elements (stereotypes and tagged values).

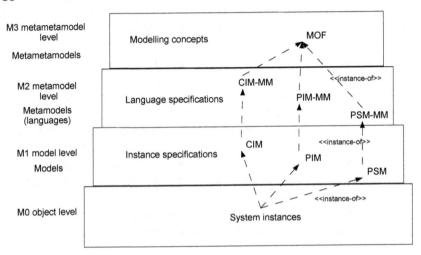

Fig. 9.6. The meta-pyramid with the MDA-related model types CIM, PIM, PSM

Each of these meta-models covers different subject areas of a PSM: the CIM-MM covers the requirements, the PIM-MM covers the platform-independent concepts, while the PSM-MM adds the platform issues. While all of these models are prescriptive—that is, using the `instance-of` relationship—the question remains how ontologies, being models relying on `described-by`, can be integrated into the meta-pyramid. This is the topic of the next section.

9.4 MDE and Ontologies

This section discusses the role of descriptive and structural models, in particular ontologies, in the model-driven process. First, the different role of domain and upper-level ontologies is discussed. We postulate that upper-level ontologies can also be used as language descriptions. Secondly, we propose an embedding of parts of the CIM as ontologies into the MDA meta-pyramid (ontology-aware meta-pyramid). In fact, this delivers a first ontology-aware mega-model of MDE [10], and we discuss its conceptual advantages. On the one hand, the mega-model suggests an extended, ontology-aware software process. On the other hand, the technologies for tool construction in the MDA and MOF world can be transferred to the ontology world.

9.4.1 Domain and Upper-Level Ontologies

The basic idea of the ontology-aware meta-pyramid is that most models in MDE are specifications, but can integrate ontologies on different meta-levels as descriptive analysis models. Since ontologies differ from specifications due to their descriptive nature, the standard M0–M3 meta-pyramid can be refined from using pure specification models to also using ontologies.

Depending on the meta-level, an ontology may serve different purposes. In fact, there are different qualities of ontologies in the literature. First of all, the word *ontology* stems from philosophy, where it characterizes *Existence*:

Ontology is a systematic account of Existence. [18]

We call such a systematic account of existence a *World ontology*, a conceptualization of the world, that is all existing concepts. Usually, a World ontology is split into an *upper-level ontology (concept ontology, frame ontology)*, providing basic concepts for classification and description, and several lower-level ontologies, *domain ontologies* describing domains of the world [19, 41]. Sowa characterizes domain ontologies as follows:

> *The subject of ontology is the study of the categories of things that exist or may exist in some domain. The product of such a study, called an ontology, is a catalogue of the types of things that are assumed to exist in a domain of interest D from the perspective of a person who uses a language L for the purpose of talking about D. The types in the ontology represent the predicates, word senses, or concept and relation types of the language L when used to discuss topics in the domain D.* [40]

In contrast, upper-level ontologies can be defined as follows:

> *An upper ontology is limited to concepts that are meta, ge-*
> *neric, abstract and philosophical, and therefore are general*
> *enough to address (at a high level) a broad range of domain*
> *areas. Concepts specific to given domains will not be in-*
> *cluded; however, this standard will provide a structure and a*
> *set of general concepts upon which domain ontologies (e.g.,*
> *medical, financial, engineering, etc.) could be constructed.*
> [21]

Usually, concepts of the domain ontology *inherit* from concepts in the upper-level ontology. For better interoperability and understanding, some researchers try to create a normalized upper-level ontology, from which all possible domain ontologies may inherit [33]. If a standardized upper-level ontology with modelling concepts existed, all domain ontologies could rely on a standardized concept vocabulary.

9.4.2 Relationship of Ontologies and System Models on Different Meta-levels

With this terminological distinction, we can relate the different forms of ontologies to meta-levels in the meta-pyramid. Domain ontologies live on level M1; they correspond to models. An upper-level ontology, also a standardized one, should live on level M2, because it provides a language for ontologies. Figure 9.7 summarizes this insight, showing both dimensions and descriptive and prescriptive models, on different meta-layers.

Interestingly, on the ontology side, inheritance is used as the connecting relation of M1 and M2, and not `instance-of`. We believe that this historic choice, which might have been made unconsciously, has a deep semantic reason in the difference between descriptiveness and prescriptiveness. A concept in a domain ontology on M1 needs to express its `similarity` to a modelling concept of an upper-level ontology (on M2). For this, the `is-a` relationship is sufficiently precise (cf. Fig. 9.4), and therefore it has been selected in the ontology world to connect the meta-levels. A concept in a specification model, however, has to express *that it has been made from* a specification model, which is clearly a more specific relationship than `is-a`. And this is the reason why in the IRDS world the `instance-of` relationship has been employed.

We argue that on level M3 of the descriptive side of the ontology-aware meta-pyramid, also a specification meta-language should be employed (Fig. 9.7). The language that describes or specifies an ontology language cannot be descriptive, because ontology languages are not something given, but artificial languages. Hence, a model to represent them should be prescriptive. We argue that the same meta-language can be used on the ontology as well as on the system model side.

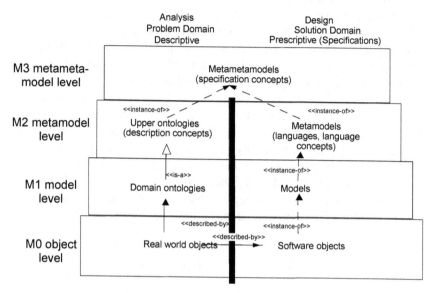

Fig. 9.7. The ontology-aware meta-pyramid

In fact, inheritance is not required in Fig. 9.7. While, usually, concepts in a domain ontology *inherit* from a concept in an upper-level frame ontology, we suggest that to distinguish them better from concepts in specification models, ontology modelling should causally connect ontological concepts by the described-by relationship. This would introduce a parallelism to using instance-of on the specification side and retain the basic ontological modelling principle of descriptiveness. Because of the parallel structure to the specification dimension, the advantage of such a meta-pyramid is that connections from ontologies to specifications can easily be made. In particular, this holds for the application of the meta-pyramid in the MDE.

9.4.3 Employing Domain Ontologies in the MDA

This version of an ontology-aware meta-pyramid permits us to group the MDA-based models around ontologies. In particular, the CIM plays a special role.

A CIM contains information about the system from the perspective of the system user. It is an *analysis model*. As such, it may contain a domain model, a business model, and requirements (Fig. 9.1) [30]. The gap between descriptive and prescriptive models concerns the CIM in particular. The domain model of a CIM can be selected to be a domain ontology (CIM-DO in Fig. 9.8). A business model, capturing business rules for a company that should prevail in all software products, can also be regarded as a domain ontology, namely that of the rules of the company (i.e. a domain ontology for a company, CIM-BO in Fig. 9.8). However, the parts of the CIM that deal with requirements cannot be grasped by ontologies, because they *specify* requirements of a system to-be-made. Hence, this specification is grouped in CIM-RM in Fig. 9.8 as a specification model. This difference is also the reason why only for CIM-RM, the specification part of the CIM, is a meta-model needed. Concepts of CIM-DO or CIM-BO *describe* existing things, and may inherit from concepts on the language or concept ontological level. Concepts in CIM-RM, on the other hand, are instances of a CIM meta-model, because they specify parts of functions of a system.

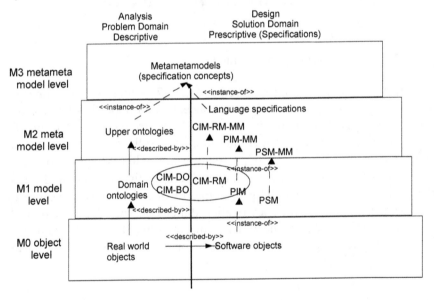

Fig. 9.8. A proposal for the role of ontologies in meta-pyramid of MDE and the MDA

Usually, a CIM is extended towards a PIM by hand, by enriching it with operational model elements. Hence, at least CIM-DO and CIM-BO play the role of standardized analysis models, whose elements can be traced back from the PIM [1]:

> *In an MDA specification of a system, CIM requirements should be traceable to the PIM and PSM constructs that implement them, and vice versa.* [30]

Hence, surprisingly, the MDA can benefit from ontologies, because via the standardized domain and business ontologies, once parts of a CIM, connection to PIM specifications can be made in a clear and systematic way.

9.4.4 Conceptual Benefits of an Ontology-Aware Meta-pyramid

The ontology-aware meta-pyramid offers several other benefits. First of all, it suggests a more concrete model-driven software development process. The designer starts from standardized analysis models, ontologies, which may have been defined long before project start. These domain and business models are refined towards design models. First, the requirements are added to yield a complete CIM. This is refined to a PIM and, then, conventionally, via several PSMs towards an implementation. Employing ontologies as analysis models should increase the reliability of software products, because these models are well engineered, often used, and hence trustworthy. This avoids the risks of a self-made domain analysis.

Secondly, ontologies as analysis models offer a more common vocabulary for the software architect, customer, and domain expert. This should improve the understanding of the parties that order and construct software. Then, the standardization of the ontologies improves the interoperability of applications, because applications that use the ontology contain a common core of common vocabulary. Finally, domain and business ontologies can be reused in many software products. In particular, they may form the core of a software product line [1], around which many products are grouped, and from which they reuse domain terminology. Overall, this improves reuse in the software process.

It is also beneficial to make an explicit distinction between descriptive and prescriptive models in the MDA. Modelling becomes easier, because designers and domain experts can always answer the question: where does the truth lie? In the model or in reality? Specification models have to confine themselves to the modelling of *artificial things*, things that are made, while ontologies can focus on the description of *real things*, things that exist. (In particular, this can be seen from the example of the CIM, which in fact contains descriptive and prescriptive models.)

Finally, the ontology-aware meta-pyramid distinguishes conceptual from behavioural models. It seems to be convenient to centre software modelling around the concepts of a domain, or structure of a domain, while adding behaviour to it step by step. In essence, this supports one of the central ideas of MDA: refinement.

9.4.5 Tools Based on an Ontology-Aware Meta-pyramid

Ontology-aware meta-pyramids not only deliver a conceptual integration of the Semantic Web and MDE, but also enable us to compare engineering practices of both paradigms to derive common tools.

In MDE, type systems are mediated by an *interface definition language (IDL)* [39]. Based on the meta-models for two type systems (on level M2), automatic conversion code (on level M1) between objects typed in type system 1 and objects typed in type system 2 can be generated. This is the task of an IDL compiler and facilitates *interoperability* between components and services, because data can easily be serialized and de-serialized in appropriate forms. At the moment, interoperability between ontology-based applications is an unsolved problem, but it might be possible to transfer the IDL tools to ontology languages.

The division of M1 models into platform-aware subject areas (CIM, PIM, PSM) is a structuring principle that can be applied to the ontology world. Because the principle has been invented for the reuse of models in product families (CIM and PIM are reused in many PIMs and PSMs, respectively), it could enable reuse of abstract ontologies in *ontology families*. Domains are not always disjoint, but often overlap. This suggests that *abstract ontologies* should be developed that can be shared between domains and are refined towards *concrete ontologies* by adding the differences of domains. Whether the notion of *platform* is the right criterion for abstraction remains to be seen; however, MDE tools, such as MDE code generators, could easily be transferred to such ontology families.

The success of ontologies and ontology languages suggests the use of logic in specification models. This is often the reason why, in practice, ontologies are abused in a prescriptive way. However, it would be more beneficial to reflect the role of open- and closed-world assumptions in ontology and specification languages. For a given modelling language, when is it possible to change the assumption? And how far can tools be reused if the assumption is orthogonal to the modelling language?

In the MDE world, the exchange of meta-data has been simplified by the XMI standard [32]. Essentially, XMI defines meta-model mappings on level M2 between the UML meta-model, XML schema definitions, and a programming language—for example, Java. Based on these mappings, serialization of graph-like UML models to tree-shaped XML models can be automated. Also, Java class models, which use a restricted form of inheritance, can be generated automatically. XMI lays the foundation for meta-data repositories such as MDR [43] or Eclipse-MDR [15], which seem to be the basis for future CASE tools and integrated software–development environments. Based on the ontology-aware meta-pyramid, the XMI technology could be transferred to ontology repositories.

Figure 9.8 suggests a common meta-language for the ontology and specification world. It should be clear by now that such a meta-language should be based on an expressive logic. If this logic is decidable (as in the case of OWL-DL), decidable tool technology can be built. If the logic is undecidable, it is more expressive, which might be more useful. Perhaps it is possible to define a hierarchy of compatible logic languages that combines expressive power with flexibility of use. Such a language hierarchy would certainly be of great help to build tools in both the descriptive ontology as well as the prescriptive specification world.

9.4.6 The mega-Model of Ontology-Aware MDE

The above-presented ontology-aware meta-pyramid can be called a mega-model of ontology-aware MDE:

A mega-model is a model that describes a meta-pyramid. [11]

A mega-model stands outside of the meta-pyramid and describes all its levels. It has a global influence on all levels of the meta-pyramid. As such, the presented mega-model sheds new light on the relation of ontologies and meta-models in MDE. Systematically, ontologies can be related to specification models and meta-models in the meta-pyramid. It is important to distinguish the representation relations is-described-by and instance-of, because then ontologies can be differentiated from specification models on all levels. As a whole, we propose that:

1. An ontology-aware MDA should employ domain and business ontologies as parts of the CIM.
2. An ontology-aware MDE should additionally incorporate a second dimension of ontologies as descriptive models in the meta-

pyramid, and maintain interrelations between the descriptive and prescriptive models on all levels.

9.5 Related Work

One of the works integrating meta-models and ontologies is [35], which extends software process and measurement ontologies to meta-models from which software can be built. The work demonstrates the usefulness of ontologies in a meta-modelling scenario.

The standard aforementioned meta-pyramid is not undebated in the literature. Other pyramids can be described, in particular if some design principles for meta-pyramids found in the literature are varied. A central role is played by the similarity relations: since different notions can be defined, different model hierarchies result.

Favre dissects the `instanceOf` relation into `representationOf` and `member-of` [9]. A model *represents* a language, and a system is an element of that language. This leads to a *relative* model hierarchy which is not restricted to four levels, but in which certain composite patterns denote more complex similarity relations, such as `instance-of` or `described-by`.

If every element on level $n+1$ is an instance of exactly *one* element on level n, a meta-pyramid is called *strict* [2]. With strict similarity, meta-pyramids must be lists or trees and are essentially one-dimensional. Based on this distinction, [2] defines a non-strict meta-pyramid consisting of two dimensions arranged in a matrix. One dimension of the matrix is characterized by physical (technical, *linguistic*) instantiation. The linguistic similarity describes the *specification language aspect* of modelling: which language construct is an instance of which language concept. Linguistic similarity is distinguished from logical *(ontological)* similarity, which spans the other dimension, the matrix-like meta-pyramid. Ontological similarity describes the similarity of real-world concepts, e.g. that a dog is a mammal, and Fido is a dog. Clearly, this dimension corresponds to our descriptive, ontological dimension. However, [2] does not distinguish prescriptive vs. descriptive models, nor further different forms of similarity relations. Future work will combine both approaches; at this time, it seems unclear whether a two-dimensional matrix-like approach or the presented approach of parallel descriptive and prescriptive dimensions will prevail.

9.6 Conclusions

Ontologies are no silver bullet. They can be employed in the software process as descriptive standardized domain models, domain-specific languages, and modelling (description) languages. However, they should not be mingled with specifications of software systems. In MDE, both forms of models are needed and complement each other. It is time to develop appropriate mega-models that clarify the role of ontologies in MDE. This chapter has presented one approach; however, this can be only an intermediate step, because we restricted ourselves to the standard IRDS meta-pyramid. Other, more sophisticated meta-pyramids exist and must be extended to be ontology-aware.

9.7 Acknowledgments

Work partially supported by the European Community under the IST programme, contract IST-2003-506779-REWERSE [4].

References

1. Aßmann, U., Reuse in semantic applications. In Norbert Eisinger and Jan Małuszynski, editors, Reasoning Web, First International Summer School 2005. Lecture Notes in Computer Science 3564, Springer, Berlin, July 2005.
2. Atkinson, C., and Kühne, T., Model-driven development: A metamodeling foundation. IEEE Software, 20(5):36–41, 2003.
3. Smith B., Williams, J., and Schulze-Kremer, S., The ontology of the Gene Ontology. In AMIA 2003 – Annual Symposium of the American Medical Informatics Association, 2003.
   http://www.gene-ontology.org
4. Bry, F. et al. Rules in a Semantic Web Environment (REWERSE). EU Project 6th framework. IST-2004-506779.
   http://www.rewerse.net
5. Canfora, G., García, F., Piattini, M., Ruiz, F., and Visaggio, C.A., Applying a framework for the improvement of software process maturity. Software - Practice and Experience, 36(3): 283–304, March 2005, Wiley, New York.
6. Chen, P.P.-S., The entity-relationship model - towards a unified view of data. Transactions on Database Systems, 1(1):9–36, 1976.
7. Deransart, P., Jourdan, M., and Lorho, B., Attribute grammars - definitions, systems and bibliography. Lecture Notes in Computer Science 323, Springer, Berlin, 1988.

8. Devedzic, V.,   Understanding ontological engineering. Communications of the ACM, 45(4):136–144, 2002.
9. Favre, J.-M., Foundations of model (driven) (reverse) engineering: Models. Technical Report, vol. 1–3ADELE Team, Laboratoire LSR-IMAG, Université Joseph Fourier, Grenoble, France, 2004.
10. Favre, J.-M., Megamodeling and etymology - a story of words: From MED to MDE via MODEL in five milleniums. In Dagstuhl Seminar on Transformation Techniques in Software Engineering, no. 05161 in DROPS 04101. IFBI, 2005.
11. Favre, J.-M., and Nguyen, T., Towards a megamodel to model software evolution through transformations. Electronic Notes in Theoretical. Computer Science 127(3):59–74, 2005.
12. Flatscher, R., Metamodeling in EIA/CDIF - meta-metamodel and metamodels. ACM Transactions on Modeling and Computer Simulation, 12(4):322–342, 2002.
13. Fritzson, P, and Engelson, V., Modelica—A unified object-oriented language for system modeling and simulation. In Eric Jul, editor, ECOOP '98 – Object-Oriented Programming, Lecture Notes in Computer Science 1445 pages 67–90. Springer, Berlin, 1998.
14. García, F., Ruiz, F., Piattini, M., and Polo, M., Conceptual architecture for the assessment and improvement of software maintenance. In Mario Piattini and Joaquim Filipe, editors, Enterprise Information Systems IV (ICEIS), pages 219–226. Kluwer Academic Publishers, Dordrecht, 2002.
15. Geer, D., Eclipse becomes the dominant Java IDE. IEEE Computer, 38(7):16–18, 2005.
16. Goldfarb, S.F., The SGML Handbook. OUP, Oxford, 1990.
17. Goos, G., and Waite, W.M., Compiler Construction. Springer, Berlin, 1984.
18. Gruber, T.R., A translation approach to portable ontology specifications. Knowledge Acquisition, 5(2):199–220, 1993.
19. Guizzardi, G., Herre, H., and Wagner, G., On the general ontological foundations of conceptual modeling. In S. Spaccapietra, S.T. March, and Y. Kambayashi, editors, 21st International Conference on Conceptual Modeling (ER 2002), Lecture Notes in Computer Science 2503, pages 65–78, Springer, Berlin, 2002.
20. Horrocks, I., Patel-Schneider, P., and van Harmelen, F., From SHIQ and RDF to OWL: The making of a web ontology language. Journal of Web Semantics, 1(1):7–26, 2003.
21. IEEE. Standard upper ontology knowledge interchange format. Technical Report, 2003.
    http://suo.ieee.org/suo-kif.html
22. ISO and IEC. Information technology – information resource dictionary system (IRDS). International Standard ISO/IEC 10027, 1990.
23. Kahn, G., Natural semantics. Report no. 601, INRIA, February 1987.
24. Kiczales, G., Aspect-oriented programming. ACM Computing Surveys, 28(4), December 1996.

25. Kiczales, G., des Rivières, J., and Bobrow, D.G., The Art of the Metaobject Protocol. MIT Press, Cambridge, MA, 1991.
26. Larsdotter-Nilsson, E., and Fritzson, P.,. Using Modelica for modeling of discrete, continuous and hybrid biological and biochemical systems. In the 3rd Conference on Modeling and Simulation in Biology, Medicine and Biomedical Engineering. The University of Balamand, May 2003.
27. Needleman, M.H., Dublin core metadata element set. Serials Review, 24(3–4):131–135, Elsevier, 1998.
28. Fridman, N., and Musen, M.A., Ontology versioning in an ontology management framework. IEEE Intelligent Systems, 19(4):6–13, 2004.
29. Object Management Group (OMG). Common warehouse metamodel (CWM), February10, 2000.
30. OMG. MDA Guide, June 2003.
   http://www.omg.org/mda
31. OMG. UML 2.0 Object Constraint Language (OCL) specification, 2003.
   http://www.omg.org/docs/ptc/03-10-14.pdf
32. OMG. XML Metadata Interchange (XMI), January 2002.
   http://www.omg.org/technology/documents/format/xmi.htm
33. Pease, A., Niles, I., and Teknowledge Corporation. Towards a standard upper ontology. In FOIS, Ogunquit, Maine, ACM, October 2001.
34. Pidd., M., Tools for Thinking - Modeling in Management Science. Wiley, New York, 2000.
35. Ruiz, F., Vizcaíno, A., Piattini, M., and García, F., An ontology for the management of software maintenance projects. International Journal of Software Engineering and Knowledge Engineering, 14(3):323–349, 2004.
36. Scheer, A.-W., ARIS - Business Process Frameworks. Springer, Berlin, 1998.
37. Schenck, D., The express language reference manual. Technical Report ISO TC184/SC4/WG1 N466 Working Document, ISO, March 1990.
38. Seidewitz, E., What models mean. IEEE Software, 20:26–32, September 2003.
39. Siegel, J., OMG overview: CORBA and the OMA in enterprise computing. Communications of the ACM, 41(10):37–43, October 1998.
40. Sowa, J.F., Ontologies Website.
   http://www.jfsowa.com/ontology/index.htm
41. Sowa, J.F., Knowledge Representation: Logical, Philosophical, and Computational Foundations. Brooks Cole Publishing, Belmont, 2000.
42. Stoy, J.E.,, Denotational Sematics: The Scott-Strachey Approach to Programming Language Theory. MIT Press, Cambridge, MA, 1977.
43. Surveyer, J., Sun adds to opensource Java IDE roster: A review of NetBeans Java IDE. Application Development Trends, 11(9):48–48, 2004.
44. W3C. Extensible markup language (XML) 1.0. Technical Report REC-xml-19980210, February 1998.
45. Wirth, N., Program development by stepwise refinement. Communications of the ACM, 14(4): 221–227, 1971.

10. Use of Ontologies in Software Development Environments

Káthia M. de Oliveira

Catholic University of Brasília, Brazil,
kathia@ucb.br

Karina Villela

University of Salvador, Brazil,
kvillela@unifacs.br

Ana Regina Rocha and Guilherme Horta Travassos

Federal University of Rio de Janeiro, Graduate School of Engineering –
COPPE, Brazil,
{darocha, ght}@cos.ufrj.br

10.1 Introduction

Software development is a knowledge-intensive business. Different kinds of knowledge are important for software practitioners to support their activities in software organizations, such as that knowledge about the domain for which software is being developed, new technologies, local practices and policies, who knows what in the organization, guidelines, best practices, and previous experiences with techniques, methods and the software process [43].

We have observed this while developing software within different organizations for different domains such as cardiology [32, 33], acoustic propagation [31] and telecommunications [25]. These experiences had shown that a risky situation for the software systems development was the lack of domain knowledge by the software developers. Users usually consider the process of knowledge acquisition and requirements elicitation to be boring and stressful because they need to explain the same basic domain concepts to the computer science personnel for each new software project development. When a software developer starts to work on a software project under development, s-he must understand not only the software products already built, but also, and prior to this, the domain itself. While learning about the domain, the software developers usually have to understand the tasks or activities that are implicitly associated with the concepts of that domain. Those tasks are directly related to the problem that the software system being developed intends to solve. It can get worse when there is a high turnover of software developers in the software project.

This basic development scenario, which describes a concrete reality concerned with the building of software projects lacking domain and task knowledge, motivated the investigation of feasible approaches to support the use of such knowledge throughout the software development process.

A software development environment (SDE) [1, 15] has already been built for each of the software projects previously mentioned. However, these environments, despite the fact that they were supporting the software development activities by providing integrated case tools, guidance to the software process and common repositories to the development teams, had not provided any kind of knowledge regarding the domain and related tasks. To address this problem we decided to extend this traditional notion of the SDE by introducing into it domain and task knowledge to guide the software developers through the several software development phases [33], which gave rise to the concept of: the Domain – Oriented Software Development Environment (DOSDE).

After the definition, building and use of DOSDEs within different domains [31, 35, 34, 32] it become possible to observe that besides domain and task knowledge, other kinds of knowledge are also necessary and can be useful during a software project. They include knowledge about the organization itself, and data and experience obtained on previous software development projects within the organization. Another aspect observed was the importance of identifying key personnel in the organization who have the specific knowledge for an activity to be carried out during a software project, as latter highlighted by [43]. Using the DOSDE perspective, having an organizational model, looking at its structure, its processes, and the distribution of knowledge and skills throughout this structure and these processes, could help support such issues. Then, going one step further, the idea of DOSDE was broadened to include an Enterprise-Oriented Software Development Environment (EOSDE).

Ontologies represent one of the basic building blocks for DOSDE's and EOSDE's infrastructure. To support the definition and to build the environment's infrastructure, different kinds of ontologies have been used. Although there are different definitions for ontology, that being used in this context is the traditional one proposed by Gruber [19]: "ontology is an explicit specification of a conceptualization". Basically, ontology consists of concepts and relations, their definitions, properties and constraints expressed by axioms [7].

This chapter describes our experience of building SDEs supported by the use of ontologies. So far, the information presented in this chapter intends to build a concise compilation of some research results that have been individually presented in [33, 31, 35, 34, 32, 60, 44, 53, 52, 54]. The intention is to group all these results to give the whole perspective regarding the use of ontologies in the context of real SDEs, which are currently being used by several software organizations in Brazil to support their software development processes.

In the following sections we first briefly present SDEs and introduce DOSDE as an extension of them (Sect. 10.2). Then, in Sect. 10.3, we present the features of a DOSDE showing examples from DOSDEs developed for cardiology and acoustic propagation domains. In Sect. 10.4, we present the evolution from DOSDE to EOSDE. Sect. 10.5 describes the EOSDE infrastructure. In Sect. 10.6, we briefly describe the implementation of tools in DOSDE and EOSDE built using the defined ontology. Finally, in Sect. 10.7, we present our conclusions and ongoing work.

10.2 From SDE to DOSDE

An SDE is a computational system that provides support for the construction, management and maintenance of a software product [5]. An SDE consists of a repository that stores all the information related to the software project throughout its life cycle, and tools (Computer-Aided Software Engineering tools) that support the technical and managerial activities involved. SDEs differ from one another depending on their database nature, scope of provided tools or adopted technology.

Research in SDEs has explored different aspects concerning the supporting tools: intelligent assistants to support the project planning [48], quality assurance [23] and so on. Other SDEs deal with object-oriented development and reuse [57], cooperation and collaboration [3], software architecture styles [11, 42] and, mainly, software process modeling, with the Process-Centered Software Engineering Environments that support modeling and continued improvement of a software process [1].

All these works were looking for general solutions applicable to any domain. In reaction to this, other researchers emphasized the importance of building solutions for specific domain applications. Some of the most related projects in this context are the Domain-Oriented Design Environment (DODE) [15], Knowledge-Based Software Engineering (KBSE) [17], the Domain-Specific Software Architecture (DSSA) [50], ARPA Knowledge Sharing Initiative [29] and Kactus projects [46].

DODEs [15] support design activities within predefined domains. DODEs have been used for domains such as kitchen, network, voice dialog and user interface designs. Their main aspects are the evolution of knowledge when using the environment together with a human-centered approach. DODE supports problem understanding by offering tools to assist the designers in their activities. These tools offer all the concepts of the domain in a palette and the system assists the designer by giving some design rules (e.g., you cannot put a stove next to a fridge). However, DODEs have been successfully developed for domains whose main feature is the visual design [47]. Further, software is not particularly visual and usually requires specific support.

The KBSE [17] and DSSA [50] projects aim at reusing software requirements and architectures. Both use the description of a domain model. They follow the idea of domain analysis [2] and define a domain model for a family of systems. The idea of using a domain model in the construction of different software applications is very interesting. However, these two projects focused on how to build a solution for a problem in a specific domain by composing artifacts (objects, part of code, and so on) previously defined. They do not strive to help the software engineer understand the application domain and problem, but focus on reuse of design components or architectural styles. KBSE only deals with the design and design models' part reuse. DSSA is centered on the definition and implementation of architectural styles for a specific family of systems, that is, about their implementation details. Some similarities can be found in the works regarding Model-Driven Architecture (MDA), Software Factories and domain-specific languages (DSLs) [18, 36].

Two important efforts in the definition of domain knowledge for software development are the ARPA Knowledge Sharing Initiative [29] and the Kactus project [46]. In these projects, the emphasis is on the knowledge-based organization that can be shared and reused by different knowledge-based systems. They use ontologies to organize this knowledge regardless of the software application that will be developed. The aim is to assist knowledge engineers to develop knowledge-based systems by reusing and composing ontologies from a predefined library.

All of these approaches looked for design and implementation solutions. However, to properly design and implement a software system, one must first understand its application domain. Therefore, to integrate the domain knowledge into an SDE seemed to be a feasible target. Doing so has given rise to the idea of a Domain-Oriented Software Development Environment [35] that would help those developers designing software systems in domains not familiar to them.

10.3 Domain-Oriented Software Development Environment

A DOSDE, like any other SDE, should have a repository storing all the information related to the software project and a set of tools to support the software process activities. On the other hand, this new class of SDE requires two additional features: representation of the domain knowledge and use of this knowledge during software development. These features generate some important questions: What knowledge should be available in the environment? How should this knowledge be organized and represented? When and how can we use this knowledge in the software development?

To define what knowledge should be introduced in an SDE (to make a DOSDE), we must consider the domain in general as it could be used in several applications and not for some specific application. To organize this knowledge we use two kinds of ontologies to describe and organize it, according to Guarino's [20] classification: domain ontologies that describe the vocabulary related to a generic domain (such as medicine, or automobiles); and task ontologies that describe generic tasks or activities (like diagnosis or selling). To use this knowledge we took into account the well-known activities of a software development process. We will now show how both ontologies are used in the DOSDE infrastructure (Sects. 10.3.1 to 10.3.3) and when and how we use these ontologies to support software development activities (Sect. 10.3.4).

10.3.1 Domain Ontology in DOSDE

To help in the software development process, our ontology should cover the main concepts of the domain, it should help understanding of this domain, and it should be useful for software development. Since an applica-

tion domain can be very broad, we need to facilitate the ontology definition. Therefore, we defined that the domain ontology should be divided
into subontologies. Each subontology is a group of domain concepts that
share the same semantic context, i.e., same subject, and relationships
among them. Concepts from one of the subontologies are related to other
concepts from a second subontology. A relationship between two subontologies actually relates two concepts from each one of the subontologies.
All relations can be restricted by axioms that are part of the ontology.

The particular methodology we used for the construction of the domain
ontology is based on [24]. This methodology basically considers the following phases: definition of the purpose of the ontology, conceptualization, formalization (or coding) and, finally, validation. We have already
defined the purpose: to assist software development. The conceptualization is the longest phase and requires the identification of the concepts of
the domain along with a good description of each one. It requires also
identifying the attributes that minimally characterize each concept, possible domain values for these attributes, relationships between the concepts
and constraints on these relationships. This work is performed individually
for each subontology.

For example, in the domain ontology defined for a DOSDE in cardiology [32], we identified five subontologies (partially shown in Fig. 10.1):
(i) heart anatomy (concepts about the heart's structure and physiology),
(ii) findings (concepts that are used in the physician's investigation process), (iii) therapy (general kinds of therapies and their features), (iv) diagnosis (concepts and characteristics that identify syndrome and etiology di-
agnoses); and (v) pathologies (representing different situations of the
heart's components). The domain ontology for cardiology contains 70
concepts with 80 properties. We also formalized the definition, properties
and instance examples of each one of those concepts, as well as a set of
axioms related to those concepts, as exemplified in Table 10.1.

After the definition and validation of the domain ontology, we implemented a knowledge base in Prolog with all the concepts, their relations
and axioms.

10.3.2 Task Ontology in DOSDE

The Artificial Intelligence community has long been interested in describing complex tasks and their resolution (see for example [6, 12, 58]). A task
can be defined as "a sequence of necessary steps for the solution of a problem" [28]. As briefly explained above, task ontology provides us with a
specification of which objects and relationships among these objects are

necessary to perform the task. Mizoguchi et al. [27, 28] state that task ontology is composed of three levels. The first is the lexical level, which lists the syntactic aspects of the problem solving description, using generic nouns (i.e., concepts), generic verbs (i.e., activities) and generic adjectives which modify the objects. The second level is called conceptual and it contains activities, objects and status that correspond to the generic verbs, nouns and adjectives respectively of the lexical level. Finally, the third level, called symbolic, represents concepts and constraints in a formal language.

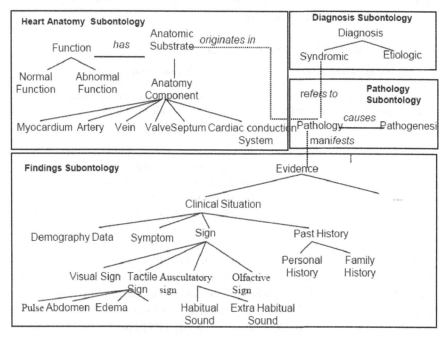

Fig 10.1. Concepts and subontologie for cardiology

A task ontology is thus limited to describing the task conceptually: it does not detail how it can be solved; it does not describe the task's controls. The detailed resolution of a task is described by a Problem Solving Method (PSM). To solve a task, a PSM restricts the size of the problem by decomposing it into smaller parts. A PSM determines how a task can be decomposed into subtasks, how to control the order of execution of these subtasks and what requirements are necessary from the domain knowledge [4]. Each task may have one or more PSMs associated to it. According to its complexity, a task can be considered elementary or composite (decomposed into subtasks). A task is elementary when a PSM describes the necessary inferences to perform it. A task is composite when a PSM decomposes it into subtasks and describes the order in which the subtasks should be performed and how they interact [49]. A given task may be solved directly through inferences by one PSM, and decomposed into subtasks by another. The method that will be applied to each of these subtasks is what defines whether they will be solved directly or decomposed further. The choice of decomposing a task or not is a subjective one, the only rule being that the developer of the PSM must strive to describe it as clearly as possible. The subtasks resulting from the decomposition are also tasks, and therefore have PSMs associated to them. This decomposition offers better potential for (sub)task reuse.

Table 10.1. Axiom examples for cardiology

Axiom description	Axiom formalization
If there is a pathology then we can define the syndromic diagnosis	$(\forall p)$ pathology(p) $\rightarrow$ ($\exists d$) syndromic_diag(d) $\wedge$ identify(d, p)
All pulses are arrhyth-mic, rhythmic or bisfe-rious	$(\forall p)$ pulse(p) $\rightarrow$ (type(p, arrhythmic) $\wedge \neg$ type(p, rhythmic) $\wedge \neg$ type (p, bisferious)) $\vee$ ($\neg$type (p, arrhythmic) $\wedge$ type (p, rhythmic) $\wedge \neg$ type (p, bisferious)) $\vee$ ($\neg$type (p, arrhythmic) $\wedge \neg$ type (p, rhythmic) $\wedge$ type (p, bisferious))

As already mentioned in DOSDE, our objective is to organize the task descriptions so that they can support software engineers in understanding the domain from an understanding of the tasks it contains. Therefore, to describe a task in a DOSDE we combine task ontology and PSMs in a single model that we call the Problem Solving Theory (PST) [60]. The PST follows the structure of the task ontology description in the three levels proposed by Mizoguchi et al. [28] as described in the following sections. To exemplify the PST we will use the Configuration task solved by the Propose & Revise PSM (P&R).

10.3.2.1 Lexical Level: Verbal Description

This is a first view on what the task is. This description needs to be made with a view on the actions to perform, which means that we must be able to identify, from the description, the necessary actions to solve the problem. Initially, the textual description is written in natural language, as can be seen in Fig. 10.2. Then, we apply the chosen PSM to the task being described to decompose the task into simpler subtasks and describe the order in which the subtasks must be performed and how they interact. To solve the Configuration task, we selected, for example, the Propose and Revise method (P&R) [26, 9]. This decomposition includes four subtasks:

- Selection chooses, from all the parameters of a system, one which does not yet have a value, but for which all the parameters it depends on have already been given a value.
- Proposition assigns a value to the parameter computed from a formula that is part of the task ontology. The computation of this value is based on the values of the parameters it depends on.
- Verification analyzes whether a constraint was violated after the value of the parameter has been computed.
- Review repairs the violated constraint and recomputes a new value for the parameter.

```
The Configuration task aims at determining how the parameters
of a system should be organized to satisfy some constraints
applying to them. The parameters' constraints have the
objective of limiting the space of solutions for the task,
once they restrict the number of possible valid
configurations. The Configuration task provides values to
parameters of a system always verifying whether the
constraints are being satisfied, and if a parameter violates
one of its constraints, it establishes a new value for it, so
that the violated constraints can be satisfied. The task ends
when all the values of all the parameters are computed.
```

Fig. 10.2. Textual description of the PST for the Configuration task [35]

According to the P&R method, the first step to solve the Configuration task is to give an initial value to one parameter of the system. The subtask Selection chooses a parameter to compute its value. Then, the subtask Proposition suggests an initial value for this parameter. This is only an attempt and can be changed if a constraint is violated. The subtask Verification is responsible for testing if the value satisfies the constraints of the system. If there are violated constraints, they need to be analyzed so that a new value can be generated for the parameter. This operation is performed by the subtask Review, which repairs the value of the parameters in order to satisfy all the constraints. These steps are repeated until all the parameters have a value and no constraint is violated.

Note that the P&R method decomposes the solution of the Configuration task into four subtasks. Therefore, PSMs for each of these subtasks should be included in the PST. If the PSM considers a task elementary, it will simply describe its solution with inference rules showing how we can solve the task from the interaction among its concepts. If the PSM does not consider a task elementary, it will decompose it into subtasks and will show how they should be called. For the Configuration task, the P&R method decomposed it into the subtasks Selection, Proposition, Revision and Verification as described above. The first three will be solved as elementary tasks by their respective PSMs. For the fourth subtask (Verification), a decomposition method will be applied to aid its resolution; it will be decomposed into two new subtasks: Examination, which identifies whether the parameters involved in the constraint have values; and Validation, which evaluates whether the constraint is being violated. The Verification task is then described, considering a control flow that first performs the Examination task and then Validation. Thus, the subtasks Examination and Validation are solved as elementary tasks. Figure 10.3 illustrates the complete resolution of the Configuration task by application of a decomposing PSM.

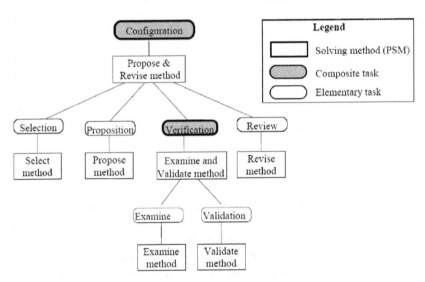

Fig. 10.3. Task and method structure [35]

10.3.2.2 Conceptual Level: Conceptual Description

The conceptual level of the PST is an intermediary level to pass from the natural language description of the verbal level to the formal description of the formal level. While the verbal level allows a series of ambiguities because it does not have a well-defined structure, the descriptions in the formal level will demand a detailed, logical description. The intermediary conceptual description possesses enough structure to avoid many interpretation errors and, at the same time, it is informal enough to be easily understood. A conceptual description is composed of (i) a list of the concepts involved in the problem and their relations, and (ii) an algorithm to represent the necessary control to solve the task.

The task's concepts (item (i)) are, in fact, the roles that will be filled by domain concepts when we apply the task in a specific application. Identifying these concepts is nothing more than identifying the objects defined in the lexical description of the task. As a task is characterized by its input and output concepts, it is important that, when defining the concepts involved in the problem, we identify their respective roles. For the Configuration task, we can identify a concept with an input role: the Parameter, which represents all the parameters of the system. As a parameter's value may depend on other parameters, we identify two other concepts: Parameter Association, defining the dependence relationships among the parameters; and Parameter Formula, specifying the formula to compute the value of a parameter. We also have as input concepts the Constraint, which specifies how to test the value of the related parameters, and the Dependence Constraint, which defines the parameters involved in a constraint. When a constraint is violated, the parameters' values are repaired so as to satisfy the constraints again. This introduces two new input concepts: Repair, which determines how the parameter values can be altered to repair the constraint; and Dependence Repair, which defines the necessary parameters to repair a constraint. Finally, the last concept, Valued Parameter, represents any parameter of the system with a given value. This last concept has both the roles of input and output of the task, since for some parameters, the value is already provided even before the task is performed (input concepts), while for others, the value has yet to be computed (output concepts).

The second part (item (ii)) of the conceptual description is the algorithm controlling the task execution. To allow this control to be easily formalized and at the same time easily understood by software engineers, irrespective of their knowledge of the formal language used, we decided to use structured natural language. Fig. 10.4 presents the control for the Configuration task.

```
While there exists a parameter without computed value
or a constraint is violated do
        Select a parameter
        Propose a value for  the parameter
        For each constraint do
                Verify constraint
        End-For-Each
        For each violated constraint do
                Revise constraint
        End-For-Each
End-While
```

Fig.10.4. Control (algoritm) for the Configuration task [35]

10.3.2.3 Symbolic Level: Formal Description

The symbolic level of the PST does not introduce any new knowledge that has not yet been described in the conceptual description. Its responsibility is only to further formalize the conceptual description, that is, to formalize the defined concepts and relations and the necessary inferences to solve the task. We opted to formalize this knowledge with first-order logic, using the Prolog language, which describes knowledge through facts and rules.

As we are working with task ontologies, it is necessary that the concepts and their constraints be expressed through axioms that formally define their meaning. For example, we show the Parameter Association concept, which represents the dependence relation among Parameters. This dependence is formalized in first order logic by the following axiom:

$(\forall p1,p2)(parameter\_association(p1,p2) \rightarrow parameter(p1) \wedge parameter(p2))$

coded in Prolog as:

parameter(P1):- association-parameter(P1,_).
parameter(P2):- association-parameter(_,P2).

All the dependencies among the concepts are formalized similarly. These axioms are used to represent the relationships among the concepts of the Configuration task. The inferences to solve the problem also need to be described formally. This can be done by translating into Prolog the algorithm in structured natural language of the conceptual level.

10.3.3 Mapping Domain and Task

The task ontology and the PSMs describe the tasks using domain-independent concepts that may be filled by concepts from the application domain (concepts which are listed in the domain ontology). However, it would be extremely difficult to identify all possible mappings between the task concepts and the domain concepts. There are many possible applications of a given task in a given domain. Therefore, we considered that, while learning about the concepts of a domain, it would be useful to know in which tasks those concepts can be used. Also, while understanding a specific problem for developing a software system, it is important to know which concepts from the domain we should learn about. Consequently, we decided to map the domain ontology and the PSTs at a more abstract level than the concepts: we map the subontologies of the domain ontology to the tasks of the PST. The mapping indicates those concepts more closely related to the task and to which the software developers should pay particular attention. We called the final result (i.e., the domain ontology mapped to the PST) a domain theory.

It can be difficult to identify all possible tasks of a domain, but we consider it important to identify, at least, the most typical ones. Each identified task is mapped with the subontologies that contain important concepts related to that task. Furthermore, it is easier to understand the concepts knowing in which tasks they can be used and how they can be used.

In our example for cardiology we identified the following task: diagnosis, planning (e.g., therapeutic planning), simulation and monitoring. We mapped the Diagnosis task with the Findings, Pathology and Diagnosis subontologies, since to do a diagnosis one needs to know about findings, kinds of pathologies and kinds of diagnosis. Similarly, for Therapeutic Planning, the important subontologies are Therapy and Pathology; for the Monitoring task, the subontologies are Heart Anatomy and Findings; and for the Simulation task, only the Heart Anatomy subontology. If we needed to develop a system for diagnosis in cardiology, we would know that it is important to study first the kinds of pathology we can diagnose, their diagnosis and the associated findings. In the same way, when studying signs (concept from Findings) we can see in which tasks or activities they are used (in this case they are used for Diagnosis and Monitoring).

10.3.4 Using Knowledge Throughout the Software Development

To develop software according to the best practices of software engineering we should use a software process establishing a sequence of development activities [21]. In general, the basic activities in software development are system definition (or context modeling), planning, software requirements analysis, design, coding and testing. We will now analyze how we are using the domain and task knowledge to support these activities.

In one way or another, all the software development activities depend on domain knowledge. This can be observed in the system definition activity, when one needs to understand the domain and the tasks to be automated; to undertake the software development planning, one needs to analyze the domain complexity; and for software system coding and testing, one uses the domain knowledge again to help understanding of the concepts and modeling their information. However, we observe a stronger influence of domain knowledge for those activities closer to the application domain, such as software requirements analysis and design of the software system, rather than those closer to the solution domain, such as coding or even testing. The next sections describe how one can use the domain knowledge in those activities.

10.3.4.1 Assisting Domain Understanding in Requirements Elicitation

In the software requirements analysis, domain orientation is very important. The main subactivity in the software requirements analysis is requirements elicitation (or knowledge acquisition for knowledge-based systems). During this subactivity, the domain theory works as a starting point for the software developers. They can identify what knowledge is relevant to the future application. The domain theory by itself represents knowledge for any possible software application in this domain. By exploring the mapping between the tasks and subontologies (see Sect. 10.3.3) or just identifying some data used for those tasks (e.g., collecting documents used for a task in the client organization) developers can find out what concepts of the domain theory they need to study and understand. These concepts represent a source of information (features and descriptions) supporting the understanding of the entire domain of the future application, the elicitation of requirements. To assist in this process, we built a tool allowing the software developers to browse the domain theory (see Sect. 10.6.1).

10.3.4.2 Assisting in Requirement Documentation

When the software developers understand the domain and the requirements elicitation with the users is complete, they should describe those requirements. This can be done, for example, with use cases [37]. Use cases
describe the operations that the system needs to perform; they are developing into a standard for describing requirements. One use case needs to be
defined for each of the functionalities that the system must carry out. In
summary, a use case is composed of: (i) a name and description, which
states the functionality of the system; (ii) actors, who are users, other systems, or any external agent that interacts with the system; (iii) a flow of
events, which defines the sequence of steps that the use case must perform; and (iv) when a use case refers to another use case, the latter is said
to be included in the former, or to extend the former.

We experimented using a task description to help defining a use case
with a DOSDE for the acoustic propagation domain [31] that involves
concepts about sonar, its types and components; emitted and received
sound; all the surrounding liquid, like the ocean layers, zones, ducts, and
so on; boundaries, in the ocean surface, etc. In this domain, one of the
problems to be automated is the configuration of the sonar. The objective
of a sonar is to detect distant targets. Sonar configuration is a difficult
task: among its numerous parameters (e.g., sensitivity, acoustic axis, direction index, terminal voltage, acoustic intensity, frequency) some already
have a predetermined value (direction index = 30 dB, frequency = 10 Hz),
while others need to be computed from the value of the rest (e.g., sensitivity = 20 log(terminal voltage) − 10 log(acoustic intensity)). After being
computed, the parameters of the sonar may affect some of its constraints,
related to another parameter or to its own minimum/maximum limits (e.g.,
0 dB ≤ sensitivity ≤ 200 dB). If this happens, the values of the parameters
are readjusted so that the constraint can be repaired.

Consulting the PST for the Configuration task (defined in Sect. 10.3.2)
helps the developer understand the task (see Fig. 10.2 and Fig. 10.4) and,
from the information obtained, identify the concepts needed to perform
this task (input and output concepts). These concepts must be searched in
the domain theory itself (they can be represented as concepts or sometimes
as concept properties) or identified at the moment of requirements elicitation.

Besides supporting the understanding of the problem and what should
be taken into consideration, the PST may also help in documenting the use

cases. With the exception of the participating actor(s), we can use the PST to help in the description of the use case,[33] as presented below:

- Name and description: The use case can be defined using a description of the problem in natural language (verbal level of the PST). The software developers can always modify the proposed description to better adapt it to the system functionality. The name of the use case must be related to the functionality of the system being described, but it should also be based on the name of the task. Figure 10.5 gives a possible description for the use case Sonar Configuration (compare the textual description of the Configuration task in Fig. 10.2).

```
The Sonar Configuration must provide values to the
attributes of a sonar, always verifying if the constraints
are satisfied. If some attribute of the sonar violates one
of its constraints, it is necessary to assign a new value
to it, so that the violated constraint can be satisfied.
The function ends when all the values of all the attributes
are computed.
```

Fig. 10.5. Description of the use case Sonar Configuration [35]

- Main flow of events: The flow of events of a use case can be obtained from the order in which the subtasks are called, in the task control. Among the three levels of the PST, the best one to help with the definition of the flow of events is the conceptual level, since it presents a well-defined structure and is, at the same time, independent of any formal language. Clearly, the software engineers can always alter any information obtained through the task control, or even add events that were not given by the PST, and reject others that have been presented. After all, the PST aims at supporting the software engineers in the software development, not to substitute them. Figure 10.6 shows the main flow of events for the use case Sonar Configuration, defined from the control of Configuration (Fig. 10.4).
- Included use cases: The software engineer may identify included use cases, using the subtask identification defined in the PST. The software engineer identifies, among the specified subtasks, the ones for which s-he needs to model a use case. For example, to configure a sonar, it would be interesting for the sonar technician to be able to call, at any moment, the functionality that verifies whether the values of the sonar attributes are satisfying all the existing constraints or not. This would mean defining a use case for this functionality. The definition of this

---

[33] We present the use case here according to the structure defined by [45].

use case, which we will call Verify Sonar, can be helped by the Verification PST in the same way that the Configuration task helped in defining the Sonar Configuration use case. To identify that Verify Sonar is a use case included in the use case Sonar Configuration, the software engineer can use a textual description of subtasks at the verbal level of the PST. We could find no general rule indicating if a subtask should yield an included use case or not. This must be decided by the software engineer.

```
1. Sonar technician asks for the beginning of the sonar
configuration.
2. While there is an attribute of the sonar without a computed
value, or a constraint that has been violated:
    2.1-The system selects an attribute of the sonar.
    2.2-The system proposes a value for the attribute.
    2.3-For each constraint of the sonar:
          The system verifies if the constraint has been
violated.
        End-for-each
    2.4-For each  violated constraint of the   sonar:
          The system revises the constraint
        End-for-each
  End-while
3. The system informs the values of the attributes and the use
case ends.
```

Fig. 10.6. Flow of events for the use case Configuration Sonar [35]

Figure 10.7 shows the use case diagram for the configure sonar task. This function, however, is part of a group of other functions in the sound propagation system.

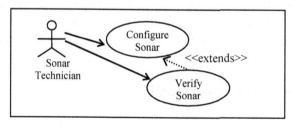

Fig. 10.7. Use case Diagram

Note that this method for deducing use cases from the PST has a potential problem in that the software engineer will be tempted to follow the particular PSM documented in the PST. However, we saw that every task may have different PSMs (Sect. 10.3.2). It may be that, for a particular application, the PSM documented in the PST is not the best one to apply. We found no easy way out of this difficulty and can only suggest that, when possible, more than one PST be created for a given task, each one making use of a different PSM.

It may be possible to further use the ontology to help realize use cases in the analysis activity [22]. It might also be possible to relate the PST with structured analysis since this is another approach for requirement documentation. However, we did not explore these research paths [59].

10.3.4.3 Assisting in Design

DOSDEs may also assist during the design activity, particularly in data modeling. Software developers can use the organization of the domain ontology as a suggestion for the first draft of the design. Considering the work from [55, 56, 38] that highlights the links between ontological structures and data entity relationship and object-oriented design, we investigated how we could generate a first draft of a conceptual data model based on the domain ontology. To do this, we defined a mapping between ontological constructs and entity–relationship constructs (see Table 10.2). With this mapping, and all the information presented in the domain ontology, we can support the software developers in the conceptual data modeling. After the conceptual data modeling we can still use the domain ontology to define the integrity rules of the data design, based on the axioms defined. The most common integrity rules are [10]: primary key integrity, referential key integrity, and domain integrity for attributes and semantic integrity. The first two are usually guaranteed by the database management system (DBMS) when one defines the key attributes. The other two can be defined using the axioms of the domain theory. We can consider, for example, the second axiom listed in Table 10.1, as information to define domain integrity for the attribute "type of pulse". The semantic integrity represents some domain restrictions for the entity instances.

10.4 From DOSDE to EOSDE

In developing DOSDE for different domains we were able to see the importance of the knowledge in an organization supporting their activities. Further we were able to verify that as well as domain knowledge, other kinds of knowledge are of interest to increase software productivity and quality. This includes knowledge about the organization itself, specialized knowledge about software development and maintenance obtained on previous software projects within the organization, and also knowledge about its clients. To deal with these different kinds of knowledge, there is a complete discipline named knowledge management.

Table 10.2. Mapping between ontological constructs and entity – relationship constructs [35]

Ontological constructs	Entity–relationship constructs
Simple and composed concept (object)	Entity
Intrinsic property	Attribute of entity
Mutual property	Binary or *n*-ary relationship
Composition	Part-of relationship
Relation between instances (roles)	Roles
Specialization	Specialization
Cardinality	Cardinality

Knowledge management can be defined as a systematic and active management of organizational knowledge assets, using appropriate technology and aiming at generating strategic benefits to the organization. This can involve promoting satisfactory communication and sharing knowledge among individuals, obtaining relevant knowledge from internal and/or external sources, making available and distributing the obtained knowledge appropriately to satisfy the user's needs, generating new knowledge and eliminating outdated knowledge.

Generally, there are two types of software developing companies: software companies, in which the business activity consists of the development of software solutions for several clients; and non-software companies, in which the software development activity aims at supporting business activities. The introduction of knowledge management in the practice of software development is critical to both types of companies, since, for the first type, knowledge about software development accumulated throughout time is the basis for creativity and innovation in terms of software products and services, and, for the second type, software applications are on the critical path of almost all organizational activities.

In knowledge management systems, ontologies can be used to [30]:

- define the scope of discussion groups, making it possible to distinguish what different groups discuss;
- supply keywords or concepts that capture the nature of the desired knowledge to provide filtering capabilities;
- categorize all artifacts in knowledge bases to facilitate their reusability;

- provide an appropriate level of precision in search mechanisms to unambiguously determine which topic can be found in each knowledge base; and
- support contact between experts and people in search of their expertise, assisting in the choice of collaborative partners and preventing confusion in collaboration.

Knowledge management could, therefore, be incorporated in SDEs in order to develop and capture organizational knowledge relevant to the software engineering activity and to improve the flow of knowledge among software developers and project managers.

Taking into account this potentiality, we have decided to extend DOSDE to incorporate not only the knowledge of domain and task, but also organizational knowledge. Moreover, the resulting environments should support knowledge identification, organization, storage, usage and evolution, that is, support knowledge management. Therefore, we have defined Enterprise-Oriented Software Development Environments [52, 53, 54] to support the activity of software engineering, making it possible to manage knowledge that can be useful to software engineers when accomplishing an organization's software projects.

10.5 Enterprise-Oriented Software Development Environments

EOSDEs have the following goals: (i) to provide software developers with all relevant knowledge for software development held by the company, and (ii) to support organizational learning about software development. EOSDEs are strongly based on ontologies.

Figure 10.8 gives an overview of the components of an EOSDE. The Knowledge Management Infrastructure is composed of the Organizational Memory and the Knowledge Management Services/Tools. Knowledge Management Services/Tools support the storage of data, knowledge and experiences in the Organizational Memory, promoting the dissemination and evolution of its contents. Software Engineering Services/Tools support the activities of software development and maintenance as well as the management of these activities. These services/tools must be able to provide software engineers with all the knowledge held by the organization which is relevant for the activity being carried out, using the Knowledge Management Infrastructure. A project repository stores all data related to the software project. The organizational memory is composed of the following components:

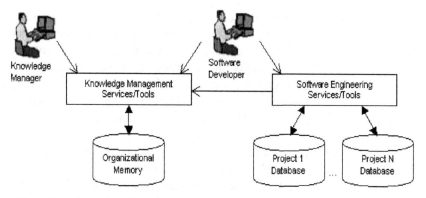

Fig. 10.8. Overview of the EOSDE components [53]

- The *Domain Theory* and *Description of Tasks* components that organize, respectively, the domain theory and PST knowledge as defined in previous sections.
- The *Software Engineering (SE) Theory* component that guides the registration and dissemination of organizational knowledge about software engineering, such as historical data, lessons learned and best practices.
- The *Enterprise Description* component that contains a description of the organization, identifying the generic tasks that are performed and the software engineering knowledge necessary in the context of the organizational structure and processes. If the organization develops and maintains software for its own use (non-software company), this component also sets which domain knowledge is required throughout the organizational structure and processes. The organizational process models allow the specification of the context in which a knowledge item was created and the application context for it. The organization's knowledge map is also part of this component and defines the competencies each employee has and to which degree these competencies are held.
- The *Description of Clients* component that is specific to EOSDE created for software companies, which develop and/or maintain software for clients. It is similar to the *Enterprise Description* component, but it describes the client organizations. Possessing knowledge, even if only limited, about clients and their domains can give a strategic advantage to holders of this knowledge in competition for new projects. In this

context, an *Enterprise Ontology* is fundamental to define a common vocabulary to guide the description of any organization.

The Knowledge/Databases component stores the knowledge and data relevant to the organization, acquired and updated over the course of many software projects. Each knowledge item stored in the environment is associated to one or more concepts and instances of these concepts obtained from the EOSDE ontologies. This enables subsequent retrieval of different types of knowledge items based on the selection of concepts and instances, regardless of the specific tools used to record and read the knowledge items.

From this description of the EOSDE components, it can be seen that the use of ontologies is critical to make both the retrieval of knowledge stored in the environment as well as communication among multiple users and tools more straightforward. When retrieving knowledge items, the purpose of ontologies is to supply vocabulary whose terms are used as indexes to access the knowledge items and also as links among multiple knowledge/database contents. Furthermore, when defining synonyms and acronyms for concepts, ontologies provide linguistic equivalents that may occur in text documents and can be used to access knowledge. As regards communication, the defined ontologies have the purpose of reducing terminological and conceptual mismatches by providing shared vocabularies. A common class model can be created based on an ontology and used by various tools, and matches among classes from different models can be made through their association to the ontology terms.

10.5.1 Enterprise Ontology

As mentioned previously, the Enterprise Ontology aims at supplying a common vocabulary that can be used to represent useful knowledge on the organizations involved in a software project for the software developers. It can be useful for:

- supplying a structure to organize knowledge and guide knowledge acquisition in one or more organizations;
- allowing the development of generic tools based on its structure;
- promoting the integration among tools that manipulate knowledge related to the ontology;
- facilitating the development of systems that manipulate knowledge on the organization (e.g., a system that supports an organizational process); and

- assisting the identification of professionals with the appropriate competencies for discussing ideas about a subject, for guiding the execution of a task or for putting together a team to suit the characteristics of the project.

Figure 10.9 shows the subontologies of the Enterprise Ontology, which were defined to answer the questions on: how the organization is perceived in its environment; how the organization is structured and how the distribution of authority and responsibility is accomplished; who works in the organization and how the desired and possessed competencies have been distributed within it; how the organization behaves and the objectives it has.

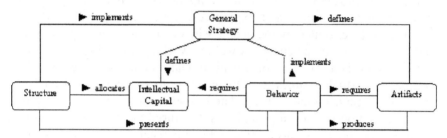

Fig. 10.9. Subontologies of the Enterprise Ontology [44]

The Enterprise Ontology was developed by combining new concepts with others defined by Fox et al. [16] and the TOVE project (TOronto Virtual Enterprise) [51].

The *Intellectual Capital* subontology deals with aspects such as: taxonomy of competence, interaction between experience and knowledge, availability of competencies and breakdown of knowledge domain. People are the basic components of an organization, executing the necessary activities for the fulfillment of the organization's mission. The competencies existing among the organization's professionals are of great importance to both them and the organization because these competencies are used to establish their role and value inside the organization, while for the organization they represent its intellectual capital. Competencies are characteristics that make people capable of carrying out activities that involve some degree of difficulty. They can be classified according to their nature into knowledge, skill and experience. Knowledge is the understanding of a subject obtained by thinking, using definitions, perception, analysis, comprehension or other ways of understanding. Skills are personal characteristics or acquired abilities not associated with specific activities or knowledge domains: for example, the ability to negotiate and leadership.

Experiences are acquired through practice; in other words, the carrying out of activities. Examples are experience in defining client–server architectures and airport administration. Experiences usually involve the use of knowledge in practice. Finally, a knowledge domain organizes knowledge items according to content similarity.

The *Structure* subontology deals with the organization of organizations, distribution of authority and responsibilities among organizational units, how they are broken down into organizational units, distribution of authority and responsibilities among positions, specification of functions and positions, staff allocation, definition of teams and definition of objectives. An Organization can be defined as an organized group of people working together for the fulfillment of a mission. There are several ways to break down an organization, but the main components normally used are functions, organizational units and committees. A Function specifies the set of activities to be executed by the people who occupy it, their responsibilities and the required competencies as well as working conditions. An Organizational Unit is a grouping of organizational components (e.g., activities and people) which enables the Organization to be economical and efficient. An Organizational Unit is related to other ones through cooperation or subordination relationships and it is structured in positions. A Position specifies activities, responsibilities and competencies in line with the purpose of the specific Organizational Unit and also determines the location of a person in the organizational structure. Each position relates to other positions through subordination relationships. An Agent represents a profile that allows the Organization to accomplish its mission throughout the execution of activities and it can represent a function or position. Staff allocation involves selecting people for positions, taking into consideration people's functions and competencies and the functions and competencies required by the positions. People also take part in committees inside the organization. A Committee is a group of people with a specific goal that usually work together for a period of time until that specific goal is achieved: for example, a committee for planning a new product or a committee for guaranteeing security at work. Finally, Objectives are statements about the results to be reached in a fixed period of time and may be applied to the organization, organizational units or positions.

The *Artifacts* subontology groups the concepts and relationships that define artifacts in terms of their nature and composition. An Artifact is anything produced by humans and not by natural causes that is able to exert different roles in an organization, such as the product of an activity. Artifacts can be composed by other artifacts and are classified according to their nature into goods, documents and components. Goods can be classified into goods for use and goods for production. Goods for production can in turn be classified into hardware, software and device. A component can be a hardware component, a software component or a spare part.

The aspects covered by the *Behavior* subontology include: activity as an action of transformation, taxonomy of activity, process and activity break-down, adoption of procedures, taxonomy of procedures, method as systematic procedure, automation of procedures, organizational processes and related norms as well as organizational projects. An Activity is the action of transforming raw material and/or input artifacts into output artifacts, which may require competencies and the use of goods for production. An Activity can be classified as an operational activity, managerial activity or quality control activity according to its nature and into a main activity or a support activity according to its role in the fulfillment of the organization's mission. An Activity can also be made up of a set of other activities. A Process is a set of structured activities which produce artifacts or services of value to the organization itself, for a client or for a business market. Procedures are instructions for executing activities and are classified into methods, techniques and guidelines. Methods as well as techniques can be classified according to the type of activities they can support. Guidelines are further classified into templates and norms. A procedure may be supported by software tools. An organization has its behavior defined by the set of processes executed within it and they may comply with norms. Projects are undertakings initiated by the organization which entail processes to guide their activities and have project teams allocated to them.

The *General Strategy* subontology establishes the vocabulary to describe how the organization interacts with its environment: that is, its domain of performance, the artifacts/services it offers and the relationships with client organizations. An organization works in a knowledge domain, which means it possesses intellectual capital related to the domain and executes activities which require knowledge from this domain. A Service is an abstract notion, an intangible product offered by an organization to satisfy the need or desire of a client or market, as opposed to an *Artifact* which is a tangible product. Artifacts and services are negotiated among organizations which assume the roles of either supplier or client.

We also implemented the axioms defined for the Enterprise Ontology in Prolog.

10.6 Tools in DOSDE and EOSDE

To build a DOSDE and EOSDE, we use the framework provided by a meta-environment (named TABA) that aims at creating SDEs in different application domains [40] according to the specific requirements of each application domain and the technology chosen. Creating an SDE involves defining a software development process, and selecting CASE tools to be provided in the SDE. The resulting SDE may then be used by software developers in the development of specific software products. TABA has several components addressing the various aspects of building SDEs and CASE tools [14]. One of these components, the knowledge component, is responsible for the integration of knowledge in the generated SDEs [13]. It provides a convenient interface, accessible from the generated SDEs, to populate and use knowledge bases in the form of Prolog facts and rules. A more detailed description of TABA and its components falls outside of the scope of this chapter.

To generate an SDE with TABA the user must define a software process to be used in the environment and select the CASE tools. To generate a DOSDE the user needs also to include the domain theory for the specific domain and the software process defined should have subactivities named domain investigation, specifically targeted to take advantage of the available knowledge. Domain investigation is the study of the domain concepts or tasks for some purpose during the execution of a specific software process activity.

TABA has two editors to allow inclusion of the domain theory and the PST to be used in the defined environments [35]. The domain theory editor allows into define domain concept, property, relationship, etc., and also allows as to enter axioms in Prolog that specify the constraints among the domain concepts. When TABA generates a DOSDE, each concept (such as "symptom") becomes a class in the DOSDE. The PST editor allows as to create a task, entering its verbal description, its control including the task concepts definition, and the formalization description (in Prolog). To support the domain investigation in a DOSDE we defined a Domain Theory Browser briefly presented in Sect. 10.6.1.

Using the Enterprise Ontology, three tools were developed to support software development activities: (i) a tool to allow the description and visualization of processes executed by an organization, (ii) a "yellow pages" software tool, and (iii) a software tool to support the planning of human resources for software projects based on organizational knowledge. In the first tool, the organization's process models are able to provide the context in which certain knowledge is used, making it easier to understand both the activity and the knowledge required to implement it. Sections 10.6.2 and 10.6.3 briefly present the other two tools.

10.6.1 Domain Theory Browser

The Domain Theory Browser [35] allows the software developers to browse the domain theory, looking for the definition of concepts, related concepts, their properties, any other application in which they were used, possible synonyms, and some suggestions for literature where more details may be found.

Figure 10.10 (background window) shows the main screen of a DOSDE where the left side lists all the software development activities and the right side the tools that support each one of those activities. This process was defined to make it possible for the TABA to generate the DOSDE. In the software process we can see the domain investigation as a subactivity of the *Initial Requirements Definition* activity.

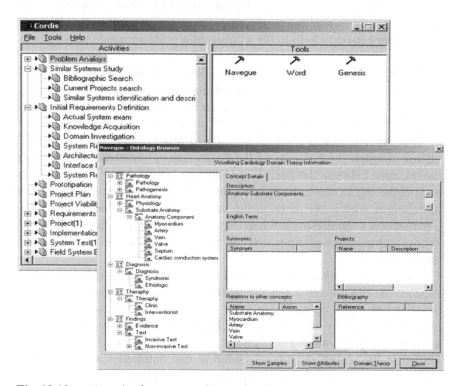

Fig. 10.10. DOSDE (main screen and Domain Theory Browser)

The foreground window shows the main screen of this Domain Theory browser. On the left side we can see all the concepts from the subontologies organized in a tree view. On the right side we can see information on the selected concept: its description, attributes, related tasks, references to project where the concept was used, and so on.

10.6.2 Sapiens: A Yellow Page's Software Tool

Sapiens [44] is a software tool for the representation of the organizational structure along with the competencies required. Besides supporting staff allocation, including the competencies of each professional, it also contains search and navigation mechanisms. This way, it is possible to create a culture of identification, acquisition and dissemination of the existing knowledge that can be used by the organization to know itself better and take greater advantage of its potential. Sapiens is based on the infrastructure defined for EOSDE, making use of the Enterprise Ontology to describe the organizations that develop and maintain software for other companies or for their own use. Software developers can use it to find the most appropriate person to help in the solution of a problem inside the organization.

The organizational structure can be viewed through an organizational chart that shows the subordination relationships between Organizational Units and allows the visualization of each item's details. A hyperbolic tree structure [39] (as shown in Fig. 10.11), which indicates the visualization of large amounts of organized data into a hierarchical form, is used to browse through the contents of the organizational database by exploring the relations between the items that comprise this database. The initial root node is the organization itself. From this point of view the user can browse its relations with other items in the database. It is possible to search the organization's database for things like: Who has a specific competence? Who occupies a specific position? In which positions is a certain competence required?

The Enterprise Ontology described in Sect. 10.5.1 provides the knowledge on the structure of a generic organization. The concepts and relations described by the ontology have been used during the construction of the class model used by all tool modules. Each class of this class model keeps a reference to the ontological concepts that originated it. This fact is exploited in the search module, considering that ontologies are particularly useful for recovering and accessing knowledge [30]. When carrying out a search the original relations described in the ontology become important and allow the identification of the related concepts to the class of the class model.

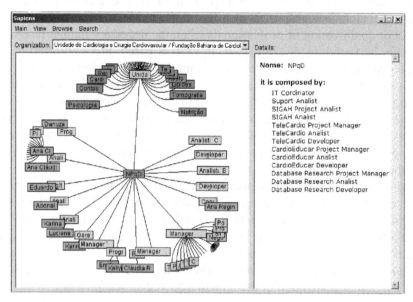

Fig. 10.11. Visualization of the organizational structure through the hyperbolic tree [44]

The Sapiens search form shows some previously defined consults created on the basis of the existing relations between the concepts that comprise the Enterprise Ontology; thus the user is able to carry out searches even without knowing the ontology structure or posing a very specific question. Each predefined search contains a description, an item to be looked for (generally an ontology concept) and a related item to this (possibly another ontology concept related to the first one). In case the user does not wish to carry out one of the listed searches, the existing concepts in the Enterprise Ontology are shown. So, when the user chooses one of these concepts, the relations involving it are listed.

When the knowledge map is being recorded or updated, the knowledge about software engineering that a certain employee possesses is defined based on the concepts of the Software Engineering Ontology. The software engineering knowledge stored in the environment is also associated to the Software Engineering Ontology concepts. Each knowledge item is associated to one or more concepts, which enables subsequent retrieval of different types of knowledge items based on the Software Engineering Ontology concepts.

10.6.3 RHPlan: A Software Tool for Human Resource Planning

The goal of RHPlan [44] is to help human resource allocation in a software development project. It also has mechanisms to help with the contract or qualification of professionals when the necessary human resources cannot be found inside the organization. It is based on a definition of the necessary competence profiles for accomplishing of project activities, and a posterior search for the organization's professionals who possess similar profiles to the desired one. The project manager can search for the knowledge on the existing competence inside the organization and find who possesses it for well as being able to use the lessons learned. The database of the professional's capabilities is provided by the Sapiens tool, as described in the previous section.

Figure 10.12 presents a screenshot of the RHPlan tool, showing an example of human resource allocation in project activities. On the right it is possible to see all the activities for creating the staff allocation plan: the definition of profiles needed in the execution of each process activity, selection of professionals, request for hiring or training other professionals when the available professionals in the organization do not fit the desired profile, and visualization of the human resource allocation plan.

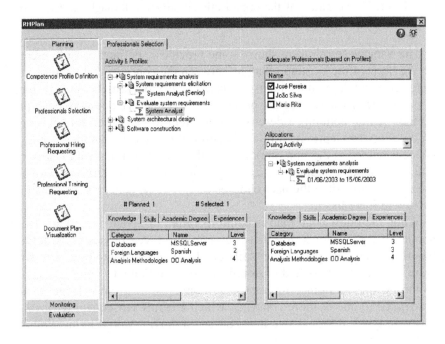

Fig. 10.12. Professionals selection in the RHPlan tool [44]

During the project its manager can monitor the human resource allocation by checking the development of activities and carrying out the allocation or reallocation of each selected professional who participates in the project.

As well as Sapiens, RHPlan uses the Enterprise Ontology for its class model definition. However, although in Sapiens classes are related to staff allocation in the organizational structure, in RHPlan the allocation is carried out through specific software development process activities. Both of these manipulate the same database of the organization's members' competencies; thus they also benefit from the same mapping infrastructure of ontology concepts to physical model classes. RHPlan also uses the concepts defined in the subontology of Behavior to describe projects, software processes, activities, resources and distribution of the necessary competencies to accomplish the activities.

10.7 Conclusion

Software engineering is a knowledge-intensive activity and knowledge is thought to be the most important asset in an organization. This chapter presented our efforts in defining ontologies and implementing ontology-based supporting tools for software development environments.

We began by exploring domain and task knowledge with Domain-Oriented Software Development Environments (DOSDEs), and then moved on to the definition of organizational knowledge and support for knowledge management activities with Enterprise-Oriented Software Development Environment (EOSDEs). These families of environments are based strongly on the ontologies described in this chapter.

Since the end of 2003, the EOSDE and its tools have been used in Brazilian software companies. An experimental study was planned and executed in 2004 to evaluate the use of the EOSDE and the processes deployed in it [41]. More than 90% of the participants in this study recognized that the EOSDE reduced the effort required to execute most of the process activities. The participants also stated that the EOSDE facilitated the dissemination of best practices and supported decision making. The initial results are promising: three companies obtained ISO 9000:2000 certification and three other companies have just achieved CMMI (Capability Maturity Model Integration) level 2 [8].

References

1. Ambriola V, Conradi R, Fuggetta A (1997) Assessing Process-Centered Software Engineering Environments. ACM Transactions on Software Engineering and Methodology, v. 6, n. 3 (July): 283–328.
2. Arango G, Prieto-Díaz R (eds.) (1991) Part 1: Introduction and Overview - Domain Analysis Concepts and Research Directions. In: Domain Analysis and Software Systems Modeling. IEEE Computer Society Press: Los Alamitos, CA, 1991., chapter 1: 9–32.
3. Bandinelli S, Di Nitto E, Fuggetta A (1996) Supporting Cooperation in the SPADE-1 Environment. IEEE Transactions on Software Engineering, v. 22, n. 12 (Dec): 841–865.
4. Breuker J, Van Der Velde W (1994) CommonKADS Library for Expertise Modeling. Reusable Problem Solving Components. IOS Press, Amsterdam.
5. Brown A, Earl A, Mcdermid J (1992) Software Engineering Environments: Automated Support for Software Engineering. McGraw-Hill, New York.
6. Chandrasekaran B, Josephson JR, Benjamins V (1998) The Ontology of Tasks and Methods. Proceedings of KAW'98 - 11th Workshop on Knowledge Acquisition, Modeling and Management, Apr.
7. Chandrasekaran B, Josephson JR, Benjamins VR, (1999) What Are Ontologies, and Why Do We Need Them? IEEE Intelligent Systemss, v. 14, n. 1 (Jan/Feb): 20–26.
8. Chrissis MB, Konrad M, Shrum S (2003) CMMI – Guidelines for Process Integration and Product Improvement. Addison Wesley, Reading, MA.
9. Coelho E, Lapalme G (1996) Describing Reusable Problem Solving Methods with a Method Ontology. In Gaines B R and Musen M A (eds.) Proceedings of the 10th Banff Knowledge Acquisition for Knowledge-Based Systems Workshop, SRDG Publications, Calgary:: 3.1–3.20.
10. Date CJ (1999) An Introduction to Database Systems, 7th edition. Addison-Wesley, Reading, MA.
11. Davis MJ, Wilians RB (1997) Software Architecture Characterization. Proceedings of Symposium on Software Reuse: 30–38.
12. Eriksson H et al. (1995) Task Modeling with Reusable Problem-Solving Methods. Artificial Intelligence, v. 79: 293–326.
13. Falbo RA, Menezes CS, Rocha AR (1999) Using Knowledge Servers to Promote Knowledge Integration in Software Engineering Environment. Proceedings of the 11th International Conference on Software Engineering and Knowledge Engineering: 170–174.
14. Falbo, RA, Travassos GH (1997) Improving Tools' Integration on Software Engineering Environments using Objects and Knowledge. Proceedings of SCI'97/ISAS, Caracas, Venezuela, July.
15. Fischer G (1996) Seeding, Evolutionary and Reseeding: Capturing and evolving knowledge in domain-oriented design environments. In: Sutcliffe A, Benyon B van Assche (eds.) IFIP 8. 1/13. Joint Working Conference on Domain-Knowledge for Interactive System Design: 11–16.

16. Fox M, Barbuceanu M, Gruninger M (1996) An Organization Ontology for Enterprise Modeling: Preliminary Concepts for Linking Structure and Behaviour. Computers in Industry, v. 29: 123–134.
17. Gomma H et al. (1996) A Knowledge-Based Software Engineering Environment for Reusable Software Requirements and Architectures. Automated Software Engineering. The International Journal of Automated Reasoning and Artificial Intelligence in Software Engineering, v. 3, n. 3–4 (Aug): 285–307.
18. Greenfield J, Short K, Cook S, Kent S (2004) Software Factories. Wiley, New York.
19. Gruber TR (1995) Toward Principles for the Design of Ontologies used for Knowledge Sharing, International Journal of Human-Computer Studies, n. 43: 907–928.
20. Guarino N (1998) Formal Ontology and Information System. In: Guarino N (ed.) Formal Ontology in Information System, IOS Press, Amsterdam: 3–15.
21. ISO/IEC 12207 (1995) International Standard – Information Technology Software Process Life Cycle.
22. Jacobson I, Booch G, Rumbaugh J (1999) The Unified Software Development Process, 1st edition. Addison-Wesley, Reading, MA.
23. Liu XF (1998) A quantitative approach for assessing the priorities of software quality requirements. The Journal of Systems and Software, n. 42: 105–113.
24. López MF et al. (1999) Building a Chemical Ontology Using Methontology and the Ontology Design Environment, IEEE Intelligent Systems, v. 14, n. 1 (Jan/Feb): 37–44.
25. Maidantchick C, Oliveira K, Teixeira HV, Masiero ML, Rocha AR, (2000). Applying Management Model and Ontology on a Telecommunication. Company. Proceedings of 13th International Conference on Software & Systems Engineering and their Applications, v. 2.
26. Marcus S (1988) SALT: A Knowledge-Acquisition Tool for Propose-and-Revise Systems. In Marcus S, Automating Knowledge Acquisition for Expert Systems, Kluwer Academic Publishers, Dordrecht: 81–123.
27. Mizoguchi R, Ikeda M, Sinitsa K (1997) Roles of Shared Ontology in AI-ED Research. In de Boulay B and Mizoguchi R (eds.) Artificial Intelligence in Education AI-ED 97. IOS Press, Amsterdam: 537–544.
28. Mizoguchi R, Vanwelkenhuysen J, Ikeda M (1995) Task Ontology for Reuse of Problem Solving Knowledge. IOS Press, Amsterdam.
29. Nectches R (1994) Knowledge Sharing in Iterated User Support Environments: Applications, Framework and Infrastructure. In: Fuchi K, Tokoi T (eds.) Knowledge Building and Knowledge Sharing, IOS Press, Amsterdam: 165–174.
30. O'Leary DE (1998) Using AI in Knowledge Management: Knowledge Bases and Ontologies. IEEE Intelligent Systems, v. 13, n. 3 (May/June): 34–39.
31. Oliveira KM, Galotta C, Rocha AR, Travassos GH, Menezes C (1999) Defining and Building Domain-Oriented Software Development Environments. Proceedings of 12th International Conference on Software & Systems Engineering and their Applications.

32. Oliveira KM, Rocha AR, Travassos GH (1999) A Domain-Oriented Software Development Environment for Cardiology. Journal of the American Medical Informatics Association: 1113–1113.
33. Oliveira KM, Rocha AR, Travassos GH, Menezes C (1999) Using Domain-Knowledge in Software Development Environments. Proceedings of the 11th International Conference on Software Engineering and Knowledge Engineering: 180–187.
34. Oliveira KM, Ximenes A, Matwin S, Travassos G, Rocha AR (2000) A Generic Architecture for Knowledge Acquisition Tools in Cardiology. 5th Intelligent Data Analysis in Medicine and Pharmacology Workshop at the 14th European Conference on Artificial Intelligence (Aug): 43–45.
35. Oliveira KM et al. (2004) Domain-oriented software development environment. Journal of Systems and Software, v. 72, n. 2: 145–161.
36. OMG – Object Management Group (2003) Model Driven Architecture. http://www.omg.org/mda/ (last accessed February 11, 2006).
37. OMG – Object Management Group (2004) UML 2.0. Unified Modeling Language. htpp://www.uml.org (last accessed February 11, 2006).
38. Parsons J, Wand Y (1997) Using Objects for Systems Analysis. Communications of the ACM, v. 40, n. 12: 104–110.
39. Pirolli P, Card SK, Wege MMVD (2000) The effect of information scent on searching information visualizations of large tree structures. Proceedings of the Working Conference on Advanced Visual Interfaces: 161–172.
40. Rocha AR, Aguiar TC, Souza JM (1990) Taba: A Heuristic Workstation for Software development. COMPEURO 90, Tel Aviv, Israel, May.
41. Rocha AR et al. (2005) Reference Model for Software Process Improvement: a Brazilian Experience. Lecture Notes in Computer Science 3792. Software Process Improvement, 12th European Conference: 130–141.
42. Rossak W, Kirova V, Jololian L, Lawson H, Zemel T (1997) A Generic Model for Software Architecture, IEEE Software, Jul/Aug: 84–92.
43. Rus I, Lindvall M (2002) Knowledge Management in Software Engineering. IEEE Software, v. 19, n. 3, May/June: 26–38.
44. Santos G, Villela K, Schnaider L, Rocha AR, Travassos GH (2004) Building ontology based tools for a software development environment. Learning Software Organization: 19–30.
45. Schneider G, Winters J (1998) Applying Use Cases: A Practical Guide. Addison-Wesley, Reading, MA.
46. Schreiber G, Wielinga B, Jansweijer W (1995) The Kactus View on the 'O' Word. Workshop on Basic Ontological Issues in Knowledge Sharing/IJCAI95, Montreal, Canada, Aug.
47. Selfridge PG (1994) Commentary on 'Domain-Oriented Design Environments' by Gerhard Fischer. Automated Software Engineering. The International Journal of Automated Reasoning and Artificial Intelligence in Software Engineering, v. 1, n. 2 (June): 219–222.

48. Shepperd M, Schofield C (2000) Estimating Software Project Effort Using Analogies. IEEE Transactions on Software Engineering, v. 23, n. 12 (Nov): 736–743.
49. Tautz C, Althoff H (2000) A Case Study on Engineering Ontologies and Related Processes for Sharing Software Engineering Experience. Proceedings of 12th International Conference on Software Engineering and Knowledge Engenineering: 318–327.
50. Taylor RN, Tracz W, Coglianese L (1995) Software Development Using Domain-Specific Software Architectures. Software Engineering Notes, v. 20, n. 5 (Dec): 27–37.
51. Uschold M et al. (1998) The Enterprise Ontology. The Knowledge Engineering Review, Special Issue on Putting Ontologies to Use (eds. Mike Uschold and Austin Tate) v. 13, n. 1: 31–39.
52. Villela K et al. (2003) Cordis-FBC: an Enterprise Oriented Software Development Environment. In: Workshop on Learning Software Organization, Lucerne, Switzerland.
53. Villela K, Santos G, Schnaider L, Rocha AR, Travassos GH (2005) The Use of Ontologies to Support Knowledge Management in Software Development Environments. Journal of Brazilian Computer Science, v. 11, n. 2: 45–60.
54. Villela K, Zlot F, Santos G, Bomfim C, Salvador B, Oliveira KM, Travassos GH, Rocha AR (2001) Knowledge Management in Software development Environments. 14th International Conference on Software & Systems Engineering and their Applications: 1–8.
55. Wand Y (1996) Ontology as a foundation for meta modeling and method engineering, Information and Software Technology, n. 38: 281–287.
56. Wand Y, Storey VC, Weber R (1999) An Ontological Analysis of the Relationship Construct in Conceptual Modeling. ACM Transactions on Database Systems, v. 24, n. 4 (Dec): 494–528.
57. Werner CML et al. (1997) Memphis: A Reuse Based O. O. Software Development Environment. Proceedings of TOOLS, Beijing, China, Sept.
58. Wielinga BJ et al. (1998) A Competence Theory Approach to Problem Solving Method Construction. International Journal of Human and Computer Studies, v. 49, n. 4 (Oct): 315–338.
59. Yourdon E (1989) Modern Structured Analysis. Prentice Hall, Englemood Cliffs, NJ.
60. Zlot F, Oliveira KM, Rocha AR (2002) Modeling Task Knowledge to Support Software Development. Proceedings of the 14th International Conference on Software Engineering and Knowledge Engineering, July: 35–42.

11. Semantic Upgrade and Publication of Legacy Data

Jesús Barrasa Rodríguez

Ontology Engineering Group, Departamento de Inteligencia Artificial, Facultad de Informática, Universidad Politécnica de Madrid, Spain, jbarrasa@eui.upm.es

11.1 Introduction and Motivation

Nowadays an enormous quantity of data can be found on web pages generated from relational databases. This information is often referred to as the Deep Web [7] as opposed to the surface web comprising static web pages. The same can be said about almost every organization's legacy data which usually hides behind all kinds of applications, and publishing systems like intranets, web portals, blogs, etc.

For these large amounts of data the challenge is no longer to head for better performances, i.e., to store more and more information in less space and to answer queries faster; the database community has realized that now it is all about the provision of "smart information", information which can easily be interchanged, combined, integrated among systems and processes or automatically reasoned about. In other words, we face the challenge of "upgrading" this large amount of existing content into Semantic Web content. But this challenge clashes with a huge problem: that of the absence of explicit data semantics. These two ideas are summarized in the following quotation appearing in [10]:

> *The three most important research problems in Databases used to be 'Performance', 'Performance' and 'Performance'; in years to come, the three most important and challenging problems will be 'Semantics', 'Semantics' and 'Semantics'.*

If we face this problem from the perspective of the Semantic Web, we see that one of its biggest barriers is the generation of semantic content [6] out of the existing one. The question of how to add semantics to the large amount of existing content on legacy databases and the Deep Web has been answered in several ways: annotation of web pages, migration of content stored in different sources, translation, etc. [10]. In every case, this task takes as input existing content, either structured, semi-structured or unstructured, and provides as output instances of ontologies. The semantics is contained in the ontologies and that is why such content can be seen as the "smart" version of the existing one, by describing it in terms of these ontologies. The key point in this task is how to link the existing content to ontologies to profit from the knowledge they contain. This is described further in this chapter.

Semantic content generation can be performed in many different ways, ranging from completely manual to fully automatic. In our particular case, the existing content is stored in relational databases, which can be considered a high level of structure. Our approach is based on the processing of a mapping specification where correspondences between the elements of the database and those of the ontology are defined formally and declaratively.

Let's set the following scenario: we have a legacy database and we want to generate Semantic Web content from it. Until now, the following approaches have been reported in the literature: The first approach, described in [21, 20], is based on the semi-automatic generation of an ontology from the database's relational model by applying reverse engineering techniques supervised by the designer. Then mappings are defined between the database and the generated ontology. Because the level of similarity between both models is very high, mappings will be quite direct and complex mapping situations do not usually appear. A second approach, described in [16], proposes the manual annotation of dynamic web pages which publish database content, with information about the underlying database and about how each content item in a page is extracted from the database. This approach does not deal with complex mapping situations and assumes we want to make our database schema public, which is not always the case. A third approach, the one described in [9] and extended in [4], proposes a language to define correspondences between ontology concepts and database schema views with a processor that takes such descriptions and extracts massively the content of the database to generate a set of ontology instances out of it. This last approach is richer than the preceding ones but its expressiveness is limited to the definition of mappings between database views and ontology concepts and direct mappings between attributes/relations of the ontology and attributes of the database views.

Conditions and transformations which are often needed to describe complex mapping situations cannot be defined with this language.

From a more general point of view, related approaches to this work can also be found in the intelligent information integration area, in which data from existing heterogeneous databases is extracted and integrated according to ontologies. The main difference between such approaches and ours is that in information integration systems the ontologies used as global schemas (mediator views) are generally created by integrating and/or merging the schemas of each of the data source,s which leads again to simple mapping situations. Another difference is the fact that mappings are described with views (normally SQL) but not with specific purpose languages for the definition of mappings. Examples of such systems are Observer [19], MOMIS [8] and Picsel [15], among others.

Our proposal tries to be more generic in the sense that it will map existing and independently developed and maintained databases and ontologies. One important aspect of our approach is that we will use the database and the ontology "as they are" and we will just define a declarative specification of the mappings between their modeling components. That is why the R_2O (Relational to Ontology) language, which is the base of our approach, has been conceived as expressive enough to cope with complex mapping situations arising from low similarity between the ontology and the database model (one of them is richer, more generic or specific, better structured, etc., than the other).

From the point of view of the expressive power, the approach presented in this chapter is intended to extend and enhance the mapping description capabilities of the ones described previously.

This chapter is organized as follows. Section 11.2 describes the global approach to database-to-ontology mapping proposed by our framework. Section 11.3 enumerates a set of significant mapping situations covered by the R_2O language. Section 11.4 provides an informal description of R_2O, its BNF grammar, and some representative examples of mappings expressed in this language. Section 11.5 describes the ODEMapster processor in charge of exploiting the mapping definitions in R_2O. Section 11.6 gives an outline of the fund finder application where the ideas presented in this chapter have been implemented. Finally, Sect. 11.7 draws some conclusions and gives a glimpse of future trends.

11.2 Global Approach to Database-to-Ontology Mapping

Any modeling scenario contains three main components according to [10]:

- A set of queries Q_S about a specific domain S that we want to be answered by a model
- The model itself, M, a data source capable of answering certain queries Q_M described in terms of its elements.
- A correspondence enabling the transformation of Q_S queries into Q_M queries and an inverse correspondence enabling the translation of the answers provided by M into answers of S.

Figure 11.1 shows a high-level description of this situation following the R$_2$O approach. An ontology and a database schema with some semantic overlap in the domains they cover are to be related. Thus, the database schema can be queried in terms of the ontology elements in a transparent way.

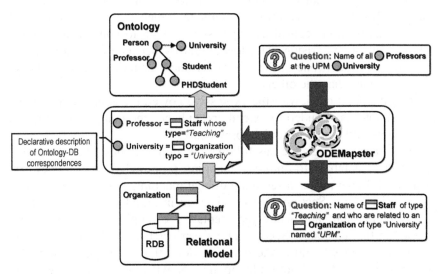

Fig. 11.1. Global description of the database-to-ontology mapping approach

As can be seen in Fig. 11.1, an ontology (S in the description above) defines terms in a particular domain (*Professor, University, PHDStudent,* etc.) and a database (M in the description above) does the same in another (*Organization, Person*). The level of overlap of these two domains allows the definition of correspondences between the terms of one and the other even if these terms model the intersection domain differently from a semantic point of view.[34]

A query Q_S like the one described in Fig. 11.1, "Give me the names of all professors in UPM university", would have its corresponding Q_M (probably SQL) over the database and, similarly, the tuples returned by the database would have their equivalent in a set of instances of the ontology answering the initial question.

In this chapter we propose the definition of these correspondences using a declarative and formal mapping description language (R_2O) which will be described further below. These mapping definitions will allow a processor (ODEMapster) to translate (on demand or as a batch process) queries defined in terms of the ontology concepts into other queries defined in terms of specific database concepts.

11.3 Mapping Situations between Databases and Ontologies

Because the domains covered by the ontology and the database do not always coincide and because the design modeling criteria used for building the database are different from those used for ontology creation, the correspondences between their elements will be sometimes straightforward, sometimes tricky. This section presents different mapping situations arising from database-to-ontology mapping scenarios which are intended to be covered by the R_2O language which will be described in Sect. 11.4.

If we have a look at how components of the database schema map ontology concepts, we can distinguish, as shown graphically in Fig. 11.2, the following cases:

- Case 1. One database table or view maps to one concept in the ontology. In this case the columns of the table map the attributes and/or relations of the concept, and with each database table record we generate an instance of the concept. With the data of the record we fill in the attribute values of the instance.

---

[34] Different authors have categorized the dissimilarities (heterogeneity) between models at different levels by generally grouping them in two main categories: non-semantic and semantic dissimilarities. The first contains all differences relative to the language and representation formalism used and the second contains all terminological and conceptual mismatches (granularity, perspective, etc.). For a deeper description see [19], [13] and [14].

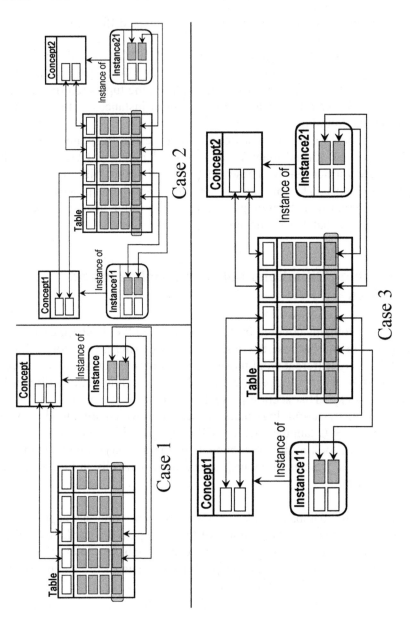

Fig. 11.2. Mapping cases classification for concepts

- Case 2. One database table or view is used to instantiate more than one concept in the ontology, but only one instance per concept. In this case each column of the table maps to the attributes and/or relations of the same or different concepts, and with each database table record we generate an instance of each concept. With the data of the record we fill in the attribute values in each instance.

- Case 3. One database table or view is used to instantiate more than one concept in the ontology, but multiple instances of the ontology can be generated. In this case each column of the table maps to the attributes and/or relations of the same or different concepts, and with each database table record we generate one or more instances of each concept. With the data of the record we fill in the attribute values of the instances.

It is important to mention that sometimes all the columns in a table map properties of the concepts, though sometimes only a few of them are needed. The same happens for records. In both cases, before generating ontology instances, some standard relational algebra operations (projection, selection, etc.) should be executed. We distinguish the cases presented in Fig. 11.3.

- Direct Mapping. A database table directly maps to a concept in the ontology. Every record of the table will correspond to an instance of an ontology concept.
- Join/Union. A set of database tables maps to a concept in the ontology when the tables are joined. Every join record of the joined tables corresponds to an instance of an ontology concept.
- Projection. This appears when a subset of the columns of a database table is needed to map a concept in the ontology.
- Selection. A subset of the rows of a database table maps to a concept in the ontology.
- Any combination of them is also possible.

The values of the attributes and relations can be filled in directly from the values of the fields in a database record or after applying a transformation function. The function can affect more than one data field. Figure 11.4 shows these ideas.

Although SQL relational algebra operations cover many cases, there are situations in which some additional transformations might be needed. Some examples of these situations are more complex operations, such as natural language processing techniques over text data fields, regular expression matching for dates, URL or email extractions, etc. The R_2O language provides the means for specifying declaratively such selections and transformations.

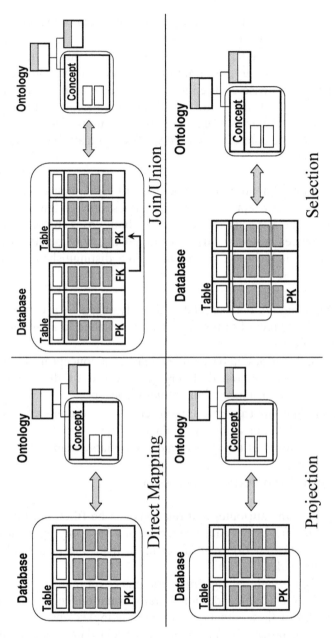

Fig. 11.3. Mapping cases for concepts

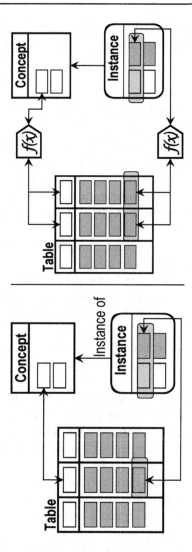

Fig. 11.4. Mapping cases for attributes and relations

11.4. The R₂O Language

R$_2$O is an extensible and fully declarative language to describe mappings between relational database schemas and ontologies. R$_2$O is intended to be expressive enough to describe the semantics of these mappings and not just a degree of similarity between entities. R$_2$O is proposed as a database management system (DBMS) independent high-level language that can work with any DBMS implementing the SQL standard. R_2O's main features are:

1. A R_2O mapping defines how to create instances in the ontology in terms of the data stored in the database. A R_2O mapping definition can be used either to automatically populate an ontology with instances extracted from the database (as a batch process of massive instance extraction) or to answer (on demand) queries defined in terms of an ontology with data from a relational database. The intended flow of data is from the database to the ontology and the approach followed in the definition of mappings is Global As View (GAV) [18].
2. R_2O can be used to express mappings generated by automatic mapping discovery tools.
3. R_2O mapping definitions can be verified against the ontology. Due to its fully declarative nature, inconsistencies and ambiguities in the definition of a mapping can be automatically detected.
4. A R_2O mapping definition might also be used to verify the integrity of parts of a database according to the ontology by applying the ontology's axioms to the database's elements.

This section gives an informal description of the R_2O language. To improve readability we use a compact pseudo XML syntax where opening tags are indicated with bold characters, grouping of sub-content is indicated by indentation and closing tags are omitted. A mapping description in R_2O is a structure made up of several components, some of which may themselves be structures, some are optional, and some may be repeated. We will write **component?** if it is an optional component, **component+** if it is a component that may be repeated one or more times (i.e., that must occur at least once), and **component*** if it is a component that may appear zero or n times (i.e., that may be completely omitted). We also provide the BNF grammar of the language with examples of usage (Table 11.1).

11.4.1 A Mapping Description Specified in R_2O

A mapping description in R_2O consists of the following components: a set of URI instances to be added to the instance set extracted from the data base (**import?**), a description of the database schema (**dbschema-description***), one or more URI ontologies for which instances will be generated when executing the R_2O mapping (**ontology+**), and the list of mapping definitions (**conceptmapping-definition+**) between the components of the database schema and the ontology.

Table 11.1. BNF and examples of usage of a R_2O mapping description

BNF for R_2O mapping descriptions	Example of mapping description
r2o::= import? dschema-description+ conceptmapping-definition+ ontology+	**import** http://www.instancesets.net/instance1
	import http://www.instancesets.net/instance2
	dbschema-desc *<dbschema-description>*
import::= **import** literal	**dbschema-desc** *<dbschema-description>*
ontology::= **ontology** literal	**ontology** http://www.ontologies.net/onto1#
literal::= '<string literal>'	**ontology** http://www.ontologies.net/onto2#

11.4.2 Description of Database Schemas

A database schema description (**dbschema-desc**) provides a copy of the main structural elements in the SQL schema of the database. It will generally be extracted automatically from the source database. The database schema definition is a "sort of internal" representation of a database and will be needed to restrict the domain and range of the components of a mapping definition as will be seen later. Some technical information about the database (url, port, user/pwd, etc.) necessary for implementation is omitted for the sake of clarity. Table 11.2 presents the BNF and an example of how a database (DB) schema description is used.

A **dbschema-desc** consists of the name of the database (**name**), a natural language description of the schema (**documentation?**), and one or more table descriptions (**hasTable+**) where each database table is described by means of (**table-desc**).

A table description (**table-desc**) provides a description of a database table. A **table-desc** consists of a name of the table (**name**), the type of the table (**tableType**) – which can be either a system table, a user table or a view –, its natural language description (**documentation?**), and a set of column descriptions (**column-description+**).

A column description (**column-description**) can be a key column (**key-col-desc**), a foreign key column (**forkeycol-desc**), or a non-key column (**nonkeycol-desc**). Any of them consists of a name for the column (**name**), a type for the data it contains (**ColumnType**), its natural language description (**documentation?**), and the key column referred (**refers-to?**) if it is a foreign key **forkeycol-desc**. These language elements can be used to make explicit referential integrity constraints that exist and are verified by the data but are not declared explicitly as such in the database schema. The database schema definition elements in the R_2O language also provide a workaround for badly designed database schemas.

Table 11.2. BNF and an example of usage of a DB schema description

BNF for R₂O DB schema descriptions	Example of a DB schema description
dschema-description::= **dbschema-desc** name documentation? (**has-table** table-desc)+	**dbschema-desc** **name** FISUB **has-table**
name::= **name** literal	**name** FundingOpps
documentation::= **documentation** literal	**documentation** "Stores funding info"
table-desc::= name tabletype documentation? (column-description)+	**keycol-desc** **name** FundingOpps.FundId
tabletype::= **tableType** literal	**columnType** integer
column-description::= (**keycol-desc** | **forkeycol-desc** | **nonkeycol-desc**) name columnType documentation? col-reference? implicit-col-reference?	**documentation** "Identifies a f.o." **nonkeycol-desc** **name** FundingOpps.FundTitle
columnType::= **columnType** datatype	**columnType** string
col-reference::= **refers-to** literal	**forkeycol-desc** **name** FundingOpps.FundSector
implicit-col-reference ::= **implicitlyrefers-to** literal	**columnType** integer **refers-to** Sector.Id
datatype::= **string** | **boolean** | **decimal** | **float** | **double** | **date** | **integer** ... (XML Schema Datatypes)	**documentation** "Points at Sector" **has-table** **name** Sector **documentation** "Productive sectors." **keycol-desc** **name** Sector. Id **columnType** integer

11.4.3 Definition of Concept Mappings

This section shows how to define the concepts of the ontology in terms of the database elements using R₂O. A concept mapping definition (**conceptmap-def**) is equivalent to a *basic mapping expression* as defined in [19]. A concept mapping definition associates the name of a class in the ontology with a description of how to obtain it from the database. A **conceptmap-def**, as presented in Table 11.3, consists of the following components:

• The identifier of a concept (URI of the class) in the target ontology (**name**).
• Natural language description of the rationale behind the concept mapping (**documentation?**).
• One or more column names that identify (**unique-att+**) the instance (tuple) uniquely in the database. Each column is described with the **column-desc** element previously defined.

- A pattern expressed in terms of transformations (see **transformation** elements in Sect. 11.4.5) describing how URIs (**uri-as+**) will be generated for the new instances extracted from the database. URIs will normally be obtained from the key columns after applying some transformations. The absence of this element will generate anonymous instances.
- A concept in the ontology is described (**described-by***) by a set of attributes and relations. As we will see in Sect. 11.4.6, a property mapping definition (**propertymap-def**) associates the name of an attribute and/or relation in the ontology with a description of how to obtain them from the database columns with the transformations (**transformation**) needed. The URI extraction described in the preceding point is actually a particular case of this.
- A mapping will only be applied under certain conditions. The element **applies-if?** contains a conditional expression (see **cond-expr** in Sect. 11.4.4) describing these conditions. In other words, it specifies the subset of values from the database that will be transformed to populate this concept.
- Sometimes more than one table will be implied in the definition of a concept mapping, and join operations will be needed. The optional (**joins-via?**) element describes how these tables are joined. The content of such element will have the structure of a condition which will be described in the next section.

Table 11.3. BNF and an example of usage of a concept mapping definition. The concept mapping is identified by a single database column (transformation and cond-expr are described later)

BNF for concept mapping definitions in R_2O	Example of concept mapping definition
conceptmapping-definition::= **conceptmap-def** name documentation? unique-atts+ (**uri-as** transformation)? (**described-by** propertymap-def)* (**applies-if** cond-expr)? (**joins-via** join-list)?	**conceptmap-def**
	name Customer
	unique-atts Users.userID
	uri-as
	<transformation>
unique-atts::= **unique-atts** literal	**applies-if**
join-list::= documentation? (**join** joindesc)+ (**overwrites** literal)?	*<cond-expr>*
	documentation Select all rows from
joindesc::= (**hasCol** literal)2	table Users...

11.4.4 Describing Conditions and Conditional Expressions

As described above not all the records in a table generate instances of the concepts in the ontology, so we will need to describe under which conditions the mapping takes place. A conditional expression **(cond-expr)** can be either a single condition **(condition)**, or a boolean combination of multiple ones using the operators **AND, OR** and **NOT** as presented in Table 11.4.

Table 11.4. BNF and an example of usage of a condition expression. The condition is true if the value of column period is "Modern" or if the date is after "01/01/1999"

BNF for condition expressions in R_2O	R_2O condition expression example
cond-expr::= orcond-expr | **AND** andcond-expr orcond-expr	**OR**
orcond-expr::= notcond-expr | **OR** orcond-expr notcond-expr	equals
notcond-expr::= condition | **NOT** condition	**arg-restriction**
condition::= primitive-condition (**arg-restriction** arg-restriction)*	**on-param** value1
primitive-condition::= **lo_than | loorequal_than |**	**has-column** Paintings.period
lo_than_str | loorequal_than_str | hi_than | hio-	**arg-restriction**
requal_than | hi_than_str | hiorequal_than_str |	**on-param** value2
equals | equals_str | in_keyword | in_set |	**has-value string** "Modern"
in_set_str | between | between_str | date_before	date-after
| date_after | date_equal	**arg-restriction**
arg-restriction::= parameter-selector restriction	**on-param** date1
parameter-selector::= **on-param** literal	**has-column** Paintings.date
restriction::= **has-value** constant-value | **has-column** literal | **has-transform** transformation	**arg-restriction**
constant-value::= datatype literal	**on-param** date2
	has-value date "01/01/1999"

A condition **(condition)** describes an invocation to a single conditional operation defined with the primitives **(primitive-condition)** provided by R_2O and assigns argument values **(arg-restriction*)** to each of the parameters required by the particular conditional operation. The core list of R_2O primitive conditional functions is: numerical and string equality **(equals, equals_str)**, numerically and alphanumerically lower than **(lo_than, lo_than_str)**, numerically and alphanumerically higher than **(hi_than, hi_than_str)**, the keyword is contained in the string **(in_keyword)**, numerically and alphanumerically contained in a range **(between, between_str)**, a date precedes, succeeds or is equal to another one **(date_before, date_after, date_equal)**. For each condition, R_2O defines: its parameters and their domain types indicating whether they are needed or optional and two descriptions of their use. The complete list of primitive conditional functions is available at the web site http://www.esperonto.net/r2o. An excerpt of this information appears in Table 11.5.

Table 11.5. Excerpt of the R_2O condition set

Condition	Params	Domain	Needed	Condition description
Lo_than	value1	float U decimal U double	Yes	Compares two values
	value2	float U decimal U double	default=0	numerically. Returns value1<value2

As we mentioned earlier, **arg-restriction*** is used for assigning values and their types to arguments. Values can be taken typically from a database table column, issued by a transformation, or, in the simplest case, they can be constant. So, an **arg-restriction** element is defined by means of a parameter name (**on-param**) and the type of argument we want to assign to the parameter. R_2O distinguishes the following types: constants (**has-value?**), a database table column (**has-column?**), and a transformation (**has-transform?**). So **has-value?** contains a constant value for the parameter, whose type are XML Schema Datatypes; **has-column?** contains a column (previously described as **column-desc**) indicating that values for this formal parameter will be taken dynamically for each row from this database table column; **has-transform?** contains a **transformation** (see Sect. 11.4.5) to allow composing transformations and using their results as an input to **conditions**.

11.4.5 Describing Transformations

As mentioned in Sect. 11.3, the mapping between database field values and ontology properties and relations is not always straightforward. So we will need to specify the necessary transformations to be applied to them. A transformation (**transformation**) describes an invocation to a single primitive transformation defined with the primitive (**primitive-transformation**) provided by R_2O and assigns argument values (**arg-restriction***) to each of the parameters required by the particular transformation. Table 11.6 presents the BNF grammar and an example of usage of a transformation. Note that the **arg-restriction*** element is already defined in the previous section.

The core list of the R_2O primitive transformation (**primitive-transformation**) is: get character at position n (**get_nth_char**), get the string delimited by a particular character (**get_delimited**), get the substring between an upper and a lower limit (**get_substring**), concatenate strings (**concat**), add, subtract, multiply or divide numbers (**add,subtract,multiply,divide**), a constant value (**constant**). In Table 11.7 we define a list of parameters and their domain types for a R$_2$O transformation by giving the type returned, indicating whether the parameters are needed or optional, as well as a description of their use. A complete list can be found at http://www.esperonto.net/r2o.

Arbitrarily complex expressions can be formed through the composition of multiple transformations. This is done by using the transformations as arguments inside other transformations. For instance, the expression **concat(get_delimited('#',t1.c1), concat(' -> ', get_nth_word('3',t2.c3)))** gets for each row of table t1 the substring delimited by '#' and '#' in column c1, then it gets the third word in column c3 of the same table and then links both results through the string ' -> '.

Table 11.6. BNF and example of usage of a transformation. The transformation concatenates a constant string with the content of two columns (name and IATA)

BNF for transformations in R$_2$O	R$_2$O transformation example
transformation::= primitive-transformation (**arg-restriction** arg-restriction)* primitive-transformation::= **get_nth_char** | **get _delimited** | **get_substring** | **concat** | **add_type** | **Subtract_type** | **Multiply_type** | **divide_type** | **constant**	**concat** **arg-restriction** **on-param** string1 **has-value string** "Coordinates of airport " **arg-restriction** **on-param** string2 **has-transform** **concat** **arg-restriction** **on-param** string1 **has-column** Airports.name **arg-restriction** **on-param** string2 **has-column** Airports.IATA

Table 11.7. Excerpt of the R$_2$O transformation set

Transf.	Return	Params	Domain	Needed	Condition description
get_substring	string	Str	string	Yes	Extracts the substring be-
		lo_limit	string	At least	tween upper and lower
		hi_limit	string	one	limits

11.4.6 Attribute and Relation Mappings

A property mapping description (understanding properties as attributes and relations) associates an attribute or a relation belonging to a concept in the target ontology with an expression describing how to obtain such an attribute or relation from the database. Depending on the type of property we deal with and on how we get its values from the database, these types of mappings can be described either with **attributemap-def**, with **relfro-matt-def** or with **relationmap-def** (Table 11.8). The first one describes attribute mappings, the others describe relation mappings.

We will also add a new level of complexity by adding conditions at the property level. With this, we allow properties to have multiple values and we enhance the language expressivity. This idea is shown in Fig. 11.5 and will be explained in detail later.

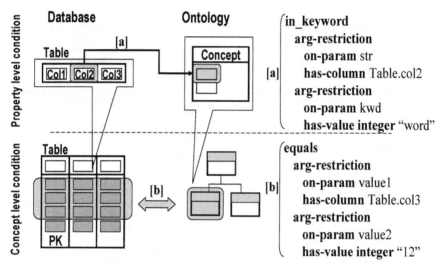

Fig. 11.5. Mapping cases classification for concepts

An **attributemap-def** contains an identifier (**name**) of the property in the target ontology (its URI). To generate its value, we will use zero or more database columns (previously described with a **column-desc** element), so we declare them with a **use-dbcol?** element. After that, a set of "rule" elements are listed *([condition1 → action1; condition2 →action2...])*. Depending on what condition applies, different transformations are performed. This idea is represented by a **Selector?** element which will contain zero or more **applies-if** - **aftertransform** pairs (condition-action).

Table 11.8. BNF and an example of usage of a property (attribute and relation) mappings

BNF for property mappings in R2O	Using dbrelationmap-def
propertymap-def::= attributemap-def | relfromatt-def | relationmap-def attributemap-def::= **attributemap-def** name use-dbcol* selector* documentation relfromatt-def::= **relfromatt-def** name use-dbcol* selector* newobj-type? documentation? Relationmap-def::= **relationmap-def** name db-rel-def use-dbcol::= **use-dbcol** literal selector::= **selector** (**applies-if** cond-expr)? (**aftertransform** transformation)? newobj-type::= **newobject-type** literal db-rel-def::= schema-defined-rel | direct-rel | defined-rel schema-defined-rel::= **schema-defined** name direct-rel::= **direct** defined-rel::= **defined** join-list	**dbrelationmap-def** **name** hasSector **db-defined** sector-fk **dbrelationmap-def** **name** hasAddress **direct** **dbrelationmap-def** **name** hasRelFunding **joins-via** **equals** **arg-restriction** **on-param** value1 **has-column** t1.c1 **arg-restriction** **on-param** value2 **has-column** t2.c2

Example of usage of **attributemap-def**	Example of usage of **relfromatt-def**

attributemap-def
  name paperRating
  selector
    applies-if
      AND
        in_keyword
          arg-restriction
            on-param string
            has-column Papers.keywords
          arg-restriction
            on-param keyword
            has-value string "ontologies"
        in_keyword
          arg-restriction
            on-param string
            has-column Papers.keywords
          arg-restriction
            on-param keyword
            has-value string "DB"
    aftertransform
      constant
        arg-restriction
          on-param const_val
          has-value string "Interesting"
	relfromatt-def
	  name officiallyAnnounced
	  newobject-type OfficialPublication
	  selector
	    aftertransform
	      concat
	        arg-restriction
	          on-param string1
	          has-value string
	          "http://officialPubs.com/num-"
	        arg-restriction
	          on-param string2
	        has-transform
	          get-delimited
	            arg-restriction
	               on-param string
	               has-column
	               FundingOpportunity.legalRef
	            arg-restriction
	               on-param start-delim
	               has-value string "["
	            arg-restriction
	               on-param end-delim
	               has-value string "]"

If the **applies-if** element is missing, it will be considered as true and the transformation will be performed. If the **aftertransform** element is missing, a direct mapping will be applied. This situation and some other notational particularities of R_2O are explained in detail in the web site http://www.esperonto.net/r2o. In the **applies-if?**, a **cond-expr** element describes under which conditions the attribute mapping is applicable or, in other words, which is the subset of values from the database schema that will be mapped according to the concept matching being defined. Note that the columns appearing in this **cond-expr** can belong to different tables from those stated in the **unique-atts** element of the concept mapping definition to which this property definition belongs. In this case two situations may arise:

1. If no extra information is provided and the tables containing the columns that are used to describe the condition are reachable without ambiguities from those tables specified in the **unique-atts** of the concept mapping description, the join is made automatically. This means that there is a single foreign key from one table to the other.
2. If a table restriction is provided, it will be considered local to a property mapping definition as opposed to the restrictions defined inside a concept mapping definition which are global.

The **aftertransform+** element contains the **(transformation)** on the database columns that participate in obtaining the value of the property being defined. The structure of a **transformation** is that described in the previous section.

The cases in which a data field after applying a transformation generates a resource would lead to the creation of a relation rather than of an attribute. These cases are represented with the **relfromatt-def** element, the structure of which is identical to that of the **attributemap-def** element, and the extra element **newObject-type?** containing the type of the new resource generated with the transformation (if any).

A relation mapping definition (**dbrelationmap-def**) describes how to obtain the target resource of a relation from its corresponding implementation in the database. A **dbrelationmap-def** then consists of an identifier (**name**) of the relation in the target ontology (its URI) and a conditional element (**condition**) describing how the join is to be performed between the source and target concepts.

The following examples show a property mapping of each type. The first example uses the **dbrelationmap-def** to define a relation mapping that links a funding opportunity to its productive sector. A link between table *FundingOpps* and Sectors exists because a foreign key has been defined in column *FundingOpps.sector* pointing at the *sectorId* primary key in column *Sectors*. The second example uses the **attributemap-def** element to rate a chapter as "Interesting" if it is about ontologies and databases. This condition is based on a keyword search on the values of rows of the *Papers* table in *keywords* field. The last example uses the **relfromatt-def** to create instances of relation *officiallyAnnounced*. This relation links a funding opportunity with the official publication where it appears.

An official publication instance is created for each property instance and its URI is obtained from the *legalRef* column in table *FundingOpportunity* after a simple transformation.

11.5 The ODEMapster Processor

Once mappings are defined in a R_2O mapping document, they are processed automatically by the ODEMapster mapping processor to generate a semantic repository of data (populate an ontology) or to answer queries defined in terms of the ontology. The first one is a batch process that carries out a complete dump of the mapped database content and the second one extracts "on the fly" just the necessary information to answer the queries asked by the user. The two diagrams in Fig. 11.6 show the two different modes of operation of the ODEMapster processor.

Both (batch and on-demand) processes are based on three main steps: (1) **R_2O processing**, (2) **query unfolding** and **execution,** and (3) **ontology instance generation**:

1. R_2O document parsing to check lexical and syntactical correction and basic integrity validations on the document like data type verification, rule compatibility checking, etc.
2. SQL expression generation from the R_2O document (based on query unfolding) and execution on source DBMS.
3. Generation of Semantic Web individuals (ontology instances) out of the content retrieved from the database in a quite straightforward way: one record generates one instance.

11.6 Experimentation: The Fund Finder Application

There are several portals containing information related to funding in the European Union, such as the Community Research and Development Information Service search page (CORDIS, http://ica.cordis.lu/search/) or the EU's Grants and Loans site (http://europa.eu.int/grants/index_en.htm).

In Spain, the Centre for Innovation and Business Development (CIDEM, www.cidem.com) is an organization based in the region of Catalonia whose objective is to improve the region's industrial community and increase its competitiveness. One of the services it provides is the update and maintenance of a section in its public web site [3] with information about European funding opportunities gathered from different sources.

These funding opportunities are compiled manually from several official publications by the CIDEM staff on a daily basis and stored in a database.

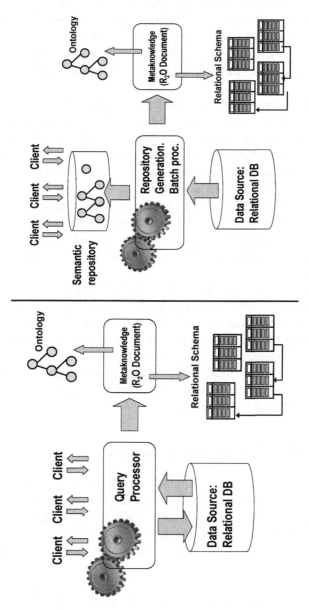

Fig. 11.6. Two modes of operation of the ODEMapster processor

Access to this content is provided by standard form-based web pages; these pages allow users to set some basic search criteria such as the productive sector (Agriculture, Industry, Services, Tourism, Non-profit Organizations, etc.) to which the funding applies, the funding objective (Technical and Financial Consultancy, Business cooperation, Culture, Energy, Tax incentives, Environment, R&D, Training, etc.), the date of last update (to get the latest funding opportunities) and a traditional full text search engine.

These kinds of search interfaces can be helpful for basic information retrieval "*Give me all the funding opportunities in the agriculture sector*" or "*Give me all the funding opportunities containing the words* 'sustainable development'", but when complex queries involving relations between concepts appear, those techniques fall short. For instance, it would be hard for a form and keyword-based search engine to answer a question like: "*Give me all the fundings that can provide a supplement to those aiming at company creation*" or "*Give me all the fundings that are incompatible with funding 651*" because the key point for answering this question lies in understanding the meaning of relations "*provide-a-supplement*" and "*be-incompatible-with*".

In this section we describe the construction of the Fund Finder application (http://www.esperonto.net/fundfinder) whose objectives are to allow semantic access to the content available in the backbone database of the portal of the CIDEM and to integrate this content with others from different sources. We understand "semantics" in this context as meaning related to the domain of Funding. In other words, we wanted to upgrade the portal of the CIDEM to the Semantic Web. This work has been developed in the context of the ESPERONTO[35] project.

11.6.1 Ontologies in the Funding Domain

The ontologies used by the Fund Finder application have been structured in a two-level architecture. The higher level contains general-purpose ontologies (Person, Location, Organization, Official Publication), while the lower level contains specific ontologies related to funding (Funding Opportunity, Funding Body, Applicant). Figure 11.7 contains an interontology relation diagram.

Each of the seven ontologies in Fig. 11.7 is fully described in [3, 5] by the intermediate representations proposed in the METHONTOLOGY

---

[35] Esperonto Project IST-2001-34373. http://www.esperonto.net

methodology [14]. The knowledge modeled by each of them and some statistics about their content are briefly described in Table 11.9.

All ontologies have been implemented with the help of experts in the domain of funding in the European Union, using the WebODE [2] workbench for ontological engineering, and have been evaluated using ODEval [12]. The ontologies are available at http://webode.dia.fi.upm.es/.

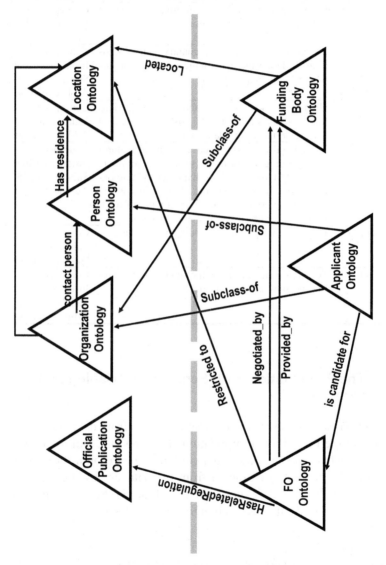

Fig. 11.7. Interontology relationships between the different Fund Finder ontologies

Table 11.9. Brief description of the ontologies used by the Fund Finder application

Ontology	Description	Statistics
Official Publication	European, national and regional regulations and their corresponding official publications such as the *European Official Journal*, The Spanish *Boletín Oficial del Estado*, and others	Concepts: 9 Instance attributes: 6 Subclass-of: 7 Ad-hoc relations: 1
Person	General-purpose personal information, mainly focused on postal information	Concepts: 5 Instance attributes: 9 Ad-hoc relations: 4
Location	Locations, countries and country subdivisions used to define the geographical scope of a particular funding opportunity	Concepts: 4 Instance attributes: 2 Subclass-of: 3 Ad-hoc relations: 3
Organization	High-level knowledge about organizations (name, set up year, web site, postal address, etc.) used to define a candidate's profile	Concepts: 6 Instance attributes: 10 Ad-hoc relations: 6
Funding Opportunity	The central ontology. It covers general features of a funding opportunity such as description, deadlines, types, relations and other funding opportunities, restrictions, etc. The main concept splits into a taxonomy of different types of fundings (i.e., credits, discounts, awards, etc.)	Concepts: 32 Instance attributes: 12 Subclass-of: 25 Ad-hoc relations: 8
Funding Body	Organizations providing funding opportunities	Concepts: 7 Subclass-of: 5 Ad-hoc relations: 2
Applicant	Potential beneficiaries of the funding opportunities: persons and organizations	Concepts: 22 Instance attributes: 4 Subclass-of: 18 Ad-hoc relations: 4

11.6.2 The Presentation Part: Semantic Publishing and Navigation

Two approaches to present the content extracted from databases have been tested with the Fund Finder application. The first one, mainly intended for massive batch semantic content generation, is based on a three-step process: First, the content is extracted from the database by the ODEMapster processor. Such content is represented in RDF(S). Second, this semantic content is imported into the WebODE[36] environment using WebODE im-

---

[36] WebODE [7] is a workbench for ontological engineering that allows the collaborative editing of ontologies at the knowledge level. One of its main functionalities is the import/export service from/to different ontology languages.

port services. Finally, the content is presented to the user using the ODE-SeW[37] portal.

The second approach, focused more on semantic query processing, is intended to process on-demand queries and provides a lightweight presentation layer on top of a simple semantic query engine.

The Semantic Query Engine that has been developed for the Fund Finder application intends to provide "smart" access to database-stored legacy data. A semantic query engine returns instances of an ontology that constitute answers to queries instead of documents containing keywords, as traditional keyword-based engines would. Semantic query engines profit from the meaning of the terms in the query. The meaning of these terms is defined in the corresponding ontology.

A user can ask for a list of instances of a selected concept by setting constraints on its attribute values. For example, if the user wants to know all awards for the current month, he or she would type *"December 2004"*. Traditional engines would return all documents containing that very string, including those having it as date of last update, deadline, or even date of official publication of the funding in the relevant official journal, and those occurrences written differently *"dec.2004"*, or *"12/04"*, would not be retrieved. A semantic query engine will return instead all instances of the concept *"Award"* (which is a subconcept of *"Funding opportunity"*) whose deadline occurs after December 2004. The user can also make a compound query by nesting concepts via their attributes: for example, *"Give me all subventions incompatible with funding opportunity number 11"*.

The interface for the search engine is based on forms representing domain concepts and existing relations. The user chooses a concept and constructs a complex query by putting values for attributes and/or nesting more concepts through relations.

11.7 Conclusions and Future Work

In this chapter we have presented R$_2$O, a database-to-ontology mapping language, whose strength lies in its expressivity, its declarative nature and

---

Currently, available services exist in WebODE for the exportation and importation of OWL, RDFS, DAML+OIL, among others.

[37] ODESeW [8] is an ontology-based application (designed on top of WebODE) that automatically generates and manages a knowledge portal for intranets and extranets. Figure 11.8 shows the look and feel of the portals generated with the two approaches.

its DBMS and ontology language independence. With R$_2$O we facilitate the "upgrade" of database content into instances of an ontology under the assumption that database and ontology models are different and that both are already existing and have not been created specifically for this purpose. The ODEMapster processor presented in [1] has been enhanced to process R$_2$O documents.

Fig. 11.8. Two screenshots of the semantic portals. On the left, the one generated by ODESeW and, on the right, the web interfaces that use the semantic query engine

R$_2$O and ODEMapster have been used in the context of the ESPERONTO project, in particular for the Fund Finder application (http://www.esperonto.net/fundfinder) as described in Sect. 11.6 but also to upgrade the ONTOROADMAP[38] database.

---

[38] http://webode.dia.fi.upm.es/ontoweb/wp1/OntoRoadMap/index.html

Regarding the future trends of our work, the extension of the framework to include a semi-automatic mapping discovery tool is under development. In addition, intensive testing with other databases as well as the development of tools, middleware, APIs, etc., to generate and exploit R_2O mapping descriptions are carried out. A graphical user interface for both visualizing and writing R_2O mapping documents has recently been developed.

11.8 Acknowledgements

Part of this work has been funded both by the European Commission in the context of the project Esperonto Services IST-2001-34373 and by the Spanish government in the context of the project Servicios Semánticos TIN 2004 – 02660.

I would like to thank Asunción Gómez-Pérez for her supervision and highly interesting comments and contributions to this work.

I would like to thank as well Raúl Blanco and Carles Gómara from CIDEM for providing the database and all information needed, Angel Lopez Cima for the development of ODESeW and Rosario Plaza for the revision of the English writing of this chapter.

References

1. Aguado G, Barrasa J, Corcho O, Gómez-Pérez A, Suárez M, Blanco R, Gómara C. Accompanying document to D8.3 Test Case application development. Fund Finder. Esperonto project deliverable. October 2003
2. Azpírez JC, Corcho O, Fernández-López M, Gómez-Pérez, A. WebODE in a nutshell. AI Magazine 24(3):37–48, 2003
3. Barrasa J, Corcho O, Blanco R et al. Esperonto Project (IST-2001-34373) Deliverable 8.1. Test Case System Specification. Fund Finder. Subject: Ontology Integration & Mapping June 2003
   www.esperonto.net
4. Barrasa J, Corcho O, Gómez-Pérez A. FundFinder – A case study of Database-to-ontology mapping. Semantic Integration Workshop, ISWC 2003, Sanibel Island, Florida, Sept. 2003
5 Barrasa J, Suarez de Figueroa MC, Blanco R et al. Esperonto Project (IST-2001-34373) Deliverable 8.2. Test Case Ontology Specification. Fund Finder. Subject: Ontology Integration & Mapping August 2003
   www.esperonto.net
6. Benjamins VR, Fensel D, Decker S, Gomez-Perez A. (KA)2: Building ontologies for the internet: a mid term report. International Journal of Human-Computer Studies 51(3):687–712, 1999

7. Bergman MK. The Deep Web: Surfacing hidden value. White paper. Sept. 2001
8. Bergamaschi S, Castano S, Vincini M. Semantic integration of semistructured and structured data sources. SIGMOD Record 28(1):54–59, 1999
9. Bizer C. D2R MAP – A DB to RDF Mapping Language. 12th International World Wide Web Conference, Budapest, May 2003
10. Borgida A, Mylopoulos J. Data semantics revisited. In Semantic Web and Databases, 2nd International Workshop, SWDB 2004, Toronto, Canada. Springer-Verlag, Berlin. August 2004
11. Bouquet P, Euzenat J, Franconi E, Serafín L, Stamou G, Tessaris S. Specification of a common framework for characterizing alignment. Knowledge Web: deliverable 2.2.1, 2004
12. Corcho O, Gómez-Pérez A, González-Cabero R, Suárez-Figueroa MC. ODEval: a Tool for evaluating RDF(S), DAML+OIL, and OWL Concept Taxonomies. IFIP WG12.6 – First IFIP Conference on Artificial Intelligence Applications and Innovations (AIAI2004), Toulouse, France, August 2004
13. Corcho O, Gómez-Pérez A, López-Cima A, López-García V, Suárez-Figueroa MC. ODESeW. Automatic Generation of Knowledge Portals for Intranets and Extranets. Lecture Notes in Computer Science Vol 2870. The Semantic Web - ISWC 2003. Springer-Verlag, Berlin. pp. 802–817. October 2003
14. Fernández-López M, Gómez-Pérez A, Pazos-Sierra A, Pazos-Sierra J. Building a Chemical Ontology Using METHONTOLOGY and the Ontology Design Environment Vol 14(1). IEEE Intelligent Systems, January/February: 37–46, 1999
15. Goasdoué F, Lattes V, Rousset M. The Use of CARIN Language and Algorithms for Information Integration: The PICSEL Project. International Journal of Cooperative Information Systems (IJCIS) 9(4):383–401, 2000
16. Handschuh S, Staab S, Volz R. On deep annotation. 12th International World Wide Web Conference, Budapest. May 2003
17. Klein M. Combining and relating ontologies: An analysis of problems and solutions. In Asuncion Gomez-Perez, Michael Gruninger, Heiner Stuckenschmidt, and Michael Uschold, editors, Workshop on Ontologies and Information Sharing, IJCAI'01, Seattle, USA, August 4–5, 2001
18. Lenzerini M, Data integration: A theoretical perspective In ACM Proceedings of the Twenty-First ACM SIGMOD-SIGACT-SIGART Symposium on Principles of Database Systems: PODS 2002, Madison, Wisconsin, June 3–5, 2002. ACM Press, New York. pp. 233–246
19. Mena E, Illarramendi A, Kashyap V, Sheth AP. OBSERVER: An Approach for Query Processing in Global Information Systems based on Interoperation across Pre-existing Ontologies. International Journal on Distributed and Parallel DBs 8(2):223–271, 2000.
20. Stojanovic N, Stojanovic L, Volz R. A Reverse Engineering Approach for Migrating Data-intensive Web. Sites to the Semantic Web. Intelligent Information Processing, Montreal, August 2002

21. Stojanovic L, Stojanovic N, Volz R. Migrating data-intensive Web Sites into the Semantic Web. Symposium on Applied Computing. Madrid, Spain, March 2002

22. Visser PRS, Jones DM, Bench-Capon TJM, Shave MJR. An analysis of ontological mismatches: Heterogeneity versus interoperability. In AAAI 1997 Spring Symposium on Ontological Engineering, Stanford, USA, 1997